DEREK PRINCE
ON
EXPERIENCING
GOD'S
POWER

DEREK PRINCE
ON
EXPERIENCING
GOD'S
POWER

DEREK PRINCE

Whitaker House

Scripture quotations marked (KJV) are taken from the *King James Version* of the Bible.

Scripture quotations marked (NKJV) are taken from the *New King James Version*, © 1979, 1980, 1982 by Thomas Nelson, Inc. Used by permission. All rights reserved.

Scripture quotations marked (NAS) are from the *New American Standard Bible*, © 1960, 1962, 1968, 1971, 1973, 1975, 1977 by The Lockman Foundation. Used by permission.

Scripture quotations marked (NIV) are from the Holy Bible, *New International Version*, © 1973, 1978, 1984 by the International Bible Society. Used by permission.

Scripture quotations marked (TLB) are from *The Living Bible*, © 1971 by Tyndale House Publishers, Wheaton, Illinois. Used by permission.

Scripture quotations marked (AMP) are from the *Amplified New Testament*, ©1954, 1958, 1987 by the Lockman Foundation, and are used by permission; or are from the *Amplified Bible, Old Testament*, © 1962, 1964 by Zondervan Publishing House, and used by permission.

Scripture quotations marked (PHILLIPS) are from *The New Testament in Modern English*, ©1958, 1959, 1960, 1972 by J. B. Phillips, and ©1947, 1952, 1955, 1957 by The Macmillan Company.

Scripture quotations marked (RSV) are from the *Revised Standard Version Common Bible* © 1973 by the Division of Christian Education of the National Council of Churches of Christ in the U.S.A. Used by permission.

Scripture quotations marked (NEB) are from *The New English Bible*, © 1961, 1970 by The Delegates of the Oxford University Press and The Syndics of the Cambridge University Press. Reprinted by permission.

Excerpts from *Of Plymouth Plantation* by William Bradford, edited by Samuel Eliot Morison, © 1952 by Random House, Inc. Used by permission.

Excerpts from *A Christian History of the Constitution* by Verna M. Hall, © 1960 by the American Constitution Press, San Francisco, California.

DEREK PRINCE ON EXPERIENCING GOD'S POWER

ISBN: 0-88368-551-5
Printed in the United States of America
Copyright © 1998 by Whitaker House

Whitaker House
30 Hunt Valley Circle
New Kensington, PA 15068

Library of Congress Cataloging-in-Publication Data

Prince, Derek.
    Derek Prince on experiencing God's power / Derek Prince.
        p.   cm.
    Includes bibliographical references.
    ISBN 0-88368-551-5 (alk. paper)
    1. Christian life. 2. Prince, Derek. I. Title.
BV4501.2.P743 1998
248.4—dc21   98-40533

1 2 3 4 5 6 7 8 9 10 11 12 / 06 05 04 03 02 01 00 99 98

Contents

About the Author

Derek Prince was born in India, of British parents. He was educated as a scholar of Greek and Latin at two of Britain's most famous educational institutions: Eton College and Cambridge University. From 1940 to 1949, he held a Fellowship (equivalent to a resident professorship) in Ancient and Modern Philosophy at King's College, Cambridge. He also studied Hebrew and Aramaic, both at Cambridge University and at the Hebrew University in Jerusalem. In addition, he speaks a number of other modern languages.

In the early years of World War II, while serving as a hospital attendant with the British Army, Derek Prince experienced a life-changing encounter with Jesus Christ, concerning which he wrote the following:

> Out of this encounter, I formed two conclusions which I have never since had reason to change: first, that Jesus Christ is alive; second, that the Bible is a true, relevant, up-to-date book. These two conclusions radically and permanently altered the whole course of my life.

At the end of World War II, he remained where the British Army had placed him—in Jerusalem. Through his marriage to his first wife, Lydia, he became father to the eight adopted girls in Lydia's children's home there. Together the family saw the rebirth of the State of Israel in 1948. While serving as educator in Kenya, Derek and Lydia Prince adopted their ninth child, an African baby girl.

After Lydia died in 1975, Derek Prince married his second wife, Ruth, in 1978. Ruth's three children bring Derek Prince's immediate family to a total of twelve, with many grandchildren and great-grandchildren.

Derek Prince's nondenominational, nonsectarian approach has opened doors for his teaching to people from many different racial and religious backgrounds. He is internationally recognized as one of the leading Bible expositors of our time. His daily radio broadcast, *Today with Derek Prince*, reaches more than half the globe, including translations into Arabic, five Chinese languages (Mandarin, Amoy, Cantonese, Shanghaiese, and Swatow), Mongolian, Spanish, Russian, and Tongan. He has published more than thirty books, which have been translated into over fifty foreign languages.

Through the Global Outreach Leaders Program of Derek Prince Ministries, his books and audio cassettes are sent free of charge to hundreds of national Christian leaders in countries in the Third World, Eastern Europe, and the Commonwealth of Independent States.

Now past the age of seventy-five, Derek Prince still travels the world—imparting God's revealed truth, praying for the sick and afflicted, and sharing his prophetic insights into world events in the light of Scripture.

The international base of Derek Prince Ministries is located in Charlotte, North Carolina, with branch offices in Australia, Canada, Germany, Holland, New Zealand, South Africa, and the United Kingdom.

THE HOLY SPIRIT
IN YOU

CONTENTS

CHAPTER ONE

BEFORE PENTECOST

Through the Scriptures we receive knowledge we could receive in no other way. One of the supremely important revelations of the Bible is the nature of God. The Bible unfolds a mystery that we could know through no other source. The mystery is that God is both one and yet more than one; three persons, yet one God. The three persons revealed in Scripture are the Father, the Son, and the Holy Spirit. This book will deal with the Holy Spirit.

One of the most profound and distinctive revelations of the whole Bible is that of the person and the work of the Holy Spirit. The first thing we must understand is that the Holy Spirit is Himself a person, just as much as the Father and the Son. Because of human parallels, it is comparatively easy for us to realize that God the Father is a person and God the Son is a person, but it is not as easy to realize that the Holy Spirit is a person.

Through the Holy Spirit, God knows everything; there is nothing hidden from God; and through the Holy Spirit, God is present everywhere at the same time. These two characteristics are represented by the theological terms *omniscient* and *omnipresent*, respectively. These traits are unfolded in various passages of Scripture. For instance, in Jeremiah 23:23–24, the Lord said,

> *"Am I only a God nearby," declares the LORD, "and not a God far away? Can anyone hide in secret places so that I cannot see him?" declares the LORD. "Do not I fill heaven and earth?" declares the LORD.* (NIV)

13

God fills heaven and earth. There is no place where God is not. There is no place where things happen and God does not know about them. This is very beautifully unfolded in the opening verses of Psalm 139:

O LORD, you have searched me and you know me. You know when I sit and when I rise; you perceive my thoughts from afar. You discern my going out and my lying down; you are familiar with all my ways. Before a word is on my tongue you know it completely, O LORD. You hem me in— behind and before; you have laid your hand upon me. Such knowledge is too wonderful for me, too lofty for me to attain. Where can I go from your Spirit? Where can I flee from your presence? If I go up to the heavens, you are there; if I make my bed in the depths, you are there. If I rise on the wings of the dawn, if I settle on the far side of the sea, even there your hand will guide me, your right hand will hold me fast. If I say, "Surely the darkness will hide me and the light become night around me," even the darkness will not be dark to you; the night will shine like the day, for darkness is as light to you.   (vv. 1–12 NIV)

What beautiful language! What a wonderful unfolding of the greatness of the wisdom of God. God's presence permeates the entire universe. There is nowhere that you can go and be hidden from God. No distance can separate you from Him. No darkness can hide you from Him. God is everywhere, throughout the entire universe. He knows all that is happening in every place.

The key that unlocks the secret is in the seventh verse, where the psalm says: *"Where can I go from your Spirit? Where can I flee from your presence?"* This is a typical example of Hebrew poetry, where the two halves of the verse say essentially the same thing. God's presence throughout the universe is His Holy Spirit. Through the Holy Spirit, God is present everywhere, and through the Holy Spirit, God knows all that is going on in the universe at any time.

The Holy Spirit has been active in the universe from Creation onwards. The psalmist told us about the actual process of Creation:

> *By the word of the LORD the heavens were made, And by*
> *the breath of His mouth all their host.*   *(Ps. 33:6 NAS)*

Where the English translation says *"breath,"* the Hebrew says, literally, "spirit." That would change the reading to: *"By the word of the LORD the heavens were made, and by the* [spirit] *of His mouth all their host."* In other words, the two great agents of Creation that brought the whole universe into being were the Word of the Lord and the Spirit of the Lord, or the Holy Spirit. If we turn back to the verses at the beginning of the Bible that describe Creation, we see this unfolded in greater detail. Genesis 1:2–3 reads,

> *Now the earth was formless and empty, darkness was over*
> *the surface of the deep, and the Spirit of God was hovering*
> *over the waters. And God said, "Let there be light," and*
> *there was light.*   *(NIV)*

The presence of the Spirit of God was there in the formless darkness, in the void, in the waste. The word *"hovering"* suggests a bird. Many times in Scripture, the Holy Spirit is identified as being the heavenly Dove. Here we have heaven's Dove, the Holy Spirit, hovering over the dark, formless waste of waters.

Verse 3 says, *"And God said, 'Let there be light,' and there was light."* Here again are the two agents of Creation: the Spirit of God and the Word of God. When they are united, Creation takes place. When the Spirit of God and the Word of God are there, then a new thing—in this case, light—is created. Light comes into being, formed by the Spirit and by the Word of God. You can see that the Holy Spirit has been at work in the universe from Creation onwards and has always been present everywhere in the universe. In a sense, the Holy Spirit is the active, effective agent of the Godhead.

The Holy Spirit inspired and empowered all the men of God in the Old Testament. The list is too long to give all the names, but we will consider several examples.

The first one is Bezalel, the man who designed and created the ark of the covenant and all the furniture for the tabernacle of Moses. The Lord is speaking in Exodus 31:2–3:

See, I have chosen Bezalel son of Uri, the son of Hur, of the tribe of Judah, and I have filled him with the Spirit of God, with skill, ability and knowledge in all kinds of crafts. (NIV)

It was the Spirit of God filling Bezalel that gave him the ability to produce such outstanding creative workmanship. It always impresses me that he is the first man in Scripture of whom it was said that he was filled with the Spirit of God. The result, in his case, was craftsmanship. That gives a very high value to craftsmanship.

In Deuteronomy 34:9, we read about Joshua:

Now Joshua son of Nun was filled with the spirit of wisdom [that's another way of saying the Spirit of God] *because Moses had laid his hands on him. So the Israelites listened to* [Joshua] *and did what the LORD had commanded Moses.* (NIV)

Joshua was the great military leader who conquered the Promised Land, and he did it because he was filled with the Spirit of God.

In Judges 6:34, we read about Gideon:

Then the Spirit of the LORD came upon Gideon, and he blew a trumpet, summoning the Abiezrites to follow him.
(NIV)

The Spirit of the Lord came upon Gideon and made him the mighty leader that he was. Before that, he was a timid young man, cowering at the winepress, unable to do anything effective. But he was changed by the Spirit of God coming upon him.

Then we read about David, the great king and psalmist, in 2 Samuel 23:1–2. This is what David said:

Now these are the last words of David. David the son of Jesse declares, And the man who was raised on high declares, The anointed of the God of Jacob, And the sweet psalmist of Israel, "The Spirit of the LORD spoke by me, And His word was on my tongue." (NAS)

David gave us those beautiful psalms because, *"The Spirit of the LORD spoke by me...His word was on my tongue."* Notice again, it is the Spirit of God and the Word of God.

In 2 Peter 1:21, Peter summed up the ministry of all the Old Testament prophets when he said:

> *For prophecy never had its origin in the will of man, but men spoke from God as they were carried along by the Holy Spirit.*　　　　　　　　　　　　　　　　　　*(NIV)*

Every prophet who brought a true message from God never spoke out of his own initiative or from his own thinking, reasoning, or understanding, but he was inspired (prompted or *"carried along"*) by the Holy Spirit. That made his message more than human; it became a message from God Himself.

As we look at the examples of these and many other men, we come to the conclusion that all the Old Testament men who served God acceptably and effectively did so solely through the power and inspiration of the Holy Spirit. Surely, this is a lesson for us. If they were unable to serve God effectively without the Holy Spirit, neither can we.

CHAPTER TWO

THE HOLY SPIRIT IN THE LIFE OF JESUS

We will now look at the Holy Spirit in the ministry and teaching of Jesus Himself. First, we need to see that John the Baptist, who came specifically to introduce Jesus and prepare the way for His ministry, introduced Him under one particular title, "the Baptizer in the Holy Spirit."

> *I baptize you with water for repentance. But after me will come one who is more powerful than I, whose sandals I am not fit to carry. He will baptize you with the Holy Spirit and with fire.* (Matt. 3:11 NIV)

Notice the distinction between Jesus and all the men that had come before Him: *"He will baptize you with the Holy Spirit and with fire."* This ministry of Jesus as Baptizer in the Holy Spirit is mentioned in all four Gospels. The Bible attaches particular importance to it.

We find, too, that the Holy Spirit was the sole source of power for the entire ministry of Jesus. Until the Holy Spirit came upon Jesus at the Jordan River after John's baptism, He never preached or performed a miracle. He waited for the Holy Spirit to come upon Him.

In Acts 10:38, Peter, speaking to the crowd of people gathered in the house of Cornelius, described the ministry of Jesus:

> *God anointed Jesus of Nazareth with the Holy Spirit and power, and...he went around doing good and healing all*

who were under the power of the devil, because God was
with him.   (NIV)

The source and power of the ministry of Jesus on earth was
the Holy Spirit. We have pointed out already that God is revealed as a triune God—three persons in one God—Father, Son,
and Spirit. In this one verse, all three persons are identified.
God the Father anointed Jesus the Son with the Holy Spirit.
The result of the triune God in action on the level of humanity
was healing: *"He went around doing good and healing all who*
were under the power of the devil." This was the secret and the
source of the ministry of Jesus.

Even after the Resurrection, Jesus still depended on the
Holy Spirit. This is a remarkable fact. In Acts 1:1–2, Luke
started with these words:

In my former book [the gospel of Luke], *Theophilus, I wrote*
about all that Jesus began to do and to teach until the day
he was taken up to heaven, after giving instructions through
the Holy Spirit to the apostles he had chosen.   (NIV)

Luke was speaking about the ministry of Jesus during the
forty days between His resurrection and ascension. It says that
Jesus gave instructions to His apostles through the Holy Spirit.
Jesus is our pattern of total dependence upon the Holy Spirit. He
relied on the Spirit for the power for His miracles and for His
teaching; He did nothing apart from the Holy Spirit. The challenge of the ministry of Jesus is a challenge to us to depend on the
Holy Spirit just as He did. Jesus not only moved in the power of
the Holy Spirit throughout His ministry, He also promised that
His disciples would receive the same Holy Spirit that had empowered and inspired Him. In John 7:37–39, we read the following:

On the last and greatest day of the Feast, Jesus stood and
said in a loud voice, "If anyone is thirsty, let him come to
me and drink. Whoever believes in me, as the Scripture has
said, streams of living water will flow from within him."
By this he meant the Spirit, whom those who believed in
him were later to receive. Up to that time the Spirit had not
been given, since Jesus had not yet been glorified.   (NIV)

19

Here is a tremendously dramatic contrast. We are first presented with a thirsty man: *"If anyone is thirsty."* Then, through the incoming and indwelling of the Holy Spirit, this same man who had been thirsty and without sufficiency for himself becomes a channel for *"streams of living water."* He is no longer in need, but a source of supply through the Holy Spirit. For every believer, the Holy Spirit is to be a limitless resource.

The writer of the gospel then went on to make it clear that though the promise was given during the earthly ministry of Jesus, it was not fulfilled until after Jesus had been glorified. He said, *"Up to that time the Spirit had not been given, since Jesus had not yet been glorified."*

In John 14:15–18, Jesus said to His disciples,

If you love me, you will obey what I command. And I will ask the Father, and he will give you another Counselor to be with you forever—the Spirit of truth [this is one of the titles of the Holy Spirit]. *The world cannot accept him, because it neither sees him nor knows him. But you know him, for he lives with you and will be in you. I will not leave you as orphans; I will come to you.* (NIV)

There are some important points we need to notice here. First, Jesus said, *"The Father...will give you another Counselor."* What is the meaning of the word *"another"* in that context? It means that Jesus, as a person, had been with His disciples for three-and-a-half years. He said, in effect, "Now, as a person, I'm going to leave you. But when I go, another person, the Holy Spirit, will come in my place."

Second, He used a particular word to describe the Holy Spirit that is translated *"Counselor"* in the New International Version. The Greek word is *parakletos,* and the Catholic versions translate it *"Paraclete."* A *paraclete* is "somebody called in alongside to help." Other translations are *"Comforter"* (KJV) and *"Helper"* (NKJV, NAS). Here we have the three related concepts: counselor, comforter, and helper.

Third, Jesus went on to point out that the Holy Spirit will remain with the disciples forever. Again, there is a contrast with His own relationship to the disciples. He was basically saying,

"I've been with you a brief three-and-a-half years. I'm leaving now, and your hearts are broken. You feel you're going to be left without help. But I'm going to send you another Helper, the Holy Spirit, and when He comes, He'll never leave you. He'll be with you forever." Then Jesus said, "I will not leave you as orphans, but I'll come to you." The implication there is that without the Holy Spirit, they would have been left as orphans with no one to care for them, help them, or instruct them. But through the Holy Spirit, full provision had been made for them.

A little further on in the same discourse, Jesus returned to this theme:

> But I tell you the truth: It is for your good that I am going away. Unless I go away, the Counselor will not come to you; but if I go, I will send him to you. *(John 16:7 NIV)*

Jesus was going, but another person was coming in His place. In John 16:12–15, Jesus returned once more to this vital message:

> I have much more to say to you, more than you can now bear. But when he, the Spirit of truth, comes, he will guide you into all truth [Jesus emphasized the personality of the Holy Spirit by using the personal pronoun *"he."*]. He will not speak on his own; he will speak only what he hears, and he will tell you what is yet to come. He will bring glory to me by taking from what is mine and making it known to you. All that belongs to the Father is mine. That is why I said the Spirit will take from what is mine and make it known to you. *(NIV)*

Since that promise was fulfilled, the Holy Spirit is now the personal, resident representative of the Godhead on earth. He is the interpreter, the revelator, and the administrator for the Father and the Son. Jesus said, "He will take from what is Mine and impart it to you." But He added, *"All that belongs to the Father is mine."* The Holy Spirit, then, is the interpreter, the revelator, and the administrator of all that the Father and the Son have—all is revealed, interpreted, and administrated by the Holy Spirit.

21

CHAPTER THREE

WHAT HAPPENED AT PENTECOST

R ecall that John the Baptist introduced Jesus as the Baptizer in the Holy Spirit. It was His distinctive introduction to Israel. Second, the Holy Spirit was the source of power for the whole ministry and teaching of Jesus; Jesus depended totally on the Holy Spirit. Third, Jesus promised His disciples that when He Himself went back to heaven, He would send the Holy Spirit in His place as His personal representative to be their Paraclete—Counselor, Comforter, or Helper—"the one called in alongside to help them."

We now want to consider the fulfillment of this promise that Jesus made. In particular, we will examine the wonderful new thing that happened when the Holy Spirit descended on the Day of Pentecost. As with many of the promises of the Bible, this promise of the Holy Spirit was not completely realized in a single event; rather, it was fulfilled in phases. The first phase took place on what we call Easter Sunday, which was the day of Jesus' resurrection. In John 20:19–22, we find the following:

> *On the evening of that first day of the week, when the disciples were together, with the doors locked for fear of the Jews, Jesus came and stood among them and said, "Peace be with you!" After he said this, he showed them his hands and side* [He demonstrated He was the same one they had seen crucified]. *The disciples were overjoyed when they saw the Lord. Again Jesus said, "Peace be with you! As the Father has sent me, I am sending you." And with that he breathed on them and said, "Receive the Holy Spirit." (NIV)*

The twenty-second verse makes an important statement. The Greek word for Spirit, *pneuma,* also means "breath" or "wind." This act of breathing on them was related to the words Jesus spoke: *"He **breathed** on them and said, **'Receive the Holy** [**breath**: Holy Spirit, the breath of God]'"* (author's emphasis).

I believe this was one of the most critical and decisive phases in the entire working out of God's purpose of redemption. What happened at this dramatic moment? First, at that moment, those first disciples entered into what I would call New Testament salvation. In Romans 10:9, Paul laid down the basic requirements for salvation:

> *That if you confess with your mouth Jesus as Lord, and believe in your heart that God raised Him from the dead, you shall be saved.* (NAS)

John 20:19–22 was the first moment at which the disciples really believed God raised Jesus from the dead. Up to that time, they could not enter into salvation as it is presented in the New Testament. At that moment, when they confessed Jesus as their Lord and believed that God had raised Him from the dead, they were saved with New Testament salvation.

The second thing that took place was that the disciples were regenerated, or born again. They became new creations—each passed out of the old creation into the new creation (2 Cor. 5:17) through the inbreathed breath of God. To understand this, we must look back at the description of the original creation of man in Genesis 2:7:

> *The LORD God formed the man from the dust of the ground and breathed into his nostrils the breath of life, and the man became a living being* [or a living soul]. (NIV)

The first creation of man took place as God breathed the Spirit of Life (the Breath of Life or the Holy Spirit) into that figure of clay that was on the ground. The inbreathed breath of God, the Holy Spirit, transformed that figure of clay into a living soul. The passage in John, however, speaks of the new creation described by Paul in 2 Corinthians 5:17: *"If anyone is in*

Christ, he is a new creation" (NIV). There is a direct parallel between the first creation and the new creation.

In the new creation, Jesus is the resurrected Lord and Savior who has conquered sin, death, hell, and Satan. Having done this, He appeared to His disciples and breathed into them the breath of resurrection life. This was a new kind of life, one that had triumphed over all the forces of evil, death, and sin. Through that experience, the disciples passed out of the old order and entered into New Testament salvation, into the new creation in Christ, through the resurrection breath of life received from Jesus.

However, it is important to understand that even after this Easter Sunday experience, the total fulfillment of the promise of the Holy Spirit had not yet come. After the Resurrection, Jesus said the following to the disciples in Luke 24:49:

> *Behold, I am sending forth the promise of My Father upon you; but you are to stay in the city* [Jerusalem] *until you are clothed with power from on high.* (NAS)

Even more explicitly, shortly before His ascension into heaven and nearly forty days after Resurrection Sunday, Jesus said to them,

> *For John baptized with water, but in a few days you will be baptized with the Holy Spirit.* (Acts 1:5 NIV)

By this we see that Resurrection Sunday was not the total fulfillment of the promise. Almost all theologians and commentators on Scripture agree that the final, complete fulfillment took place on the Day of Pentecost, which is described in Acts 2:1–4:

> *When the day of Pentecost came, they were all together in one place. Suddenly a sound like the blowing of a violent wind came from heaven and filled the whole house where they were sitting. They saw what seemed to be tongues of fire that separated and came to rest on each of them. All of them were filled with the Holy Spirit and began to speak in other tongues as the Spirit enabled them.* (NIV)

Pentecost was the actual manifestation and fulfillment of the promise. The Holy Spirit descended from heaven, in person, in the form of a mighty wind, filled each one of them individually, and gave each one a new and supernatural utterance in a language they had never learned.

At the end of this second chapter of Acts, Peter gave a theological explanation of what had taken place:

God has raised this Jesus to life, and we are all witnesses of the fact. Exalted to the right hand of God, he has received from the Father the promised Holy Spirit and has poured out what you now see and hear. (Acts 2:32–33 NIV)

Again, all three persons of the Godhead are in this verse. Jesus the Son received the Holy Spirit from the Father and poured out the Holy Spirit on the waiting disciples in the Upper Room in Jerusalem. At that point, the final fulfillment of the promise of the coming of the Holy Spirit took place. The Holy Spirit Himself was released from heaven by the Father and the Son together and descended upon the waiting disciples in the Upper Room in Jerusalem.

Notice that at this point, Jesus was not merely resurrected, but He was also exalted and glorified. Remember, too, that in John 7:39, the writer of the gospel had pointed out that the promise of the Holy Spirit could not be fulfilled until Jesus had been glorified.

We are confronted with two dramatic, wonderful Sundays. The first is Easter Sunday, where we have the resurrected Christ and the inbreathed Spirit. The second is Pentecost Sunday, where we have the glorified Christ and the outpoured Spirit. Remember, each are patterns for all believers, even today.

Easter Sunday	The Resurrected Christ	The Inbreathed Spirit
Pentecost Sunday	The Glorified Christ	The Outpoured Spirit

We will now summarize the permanent significance of the events we have just examined. On the Day of Pentecost, the Holy Spirit came down to earth as a person. He is now the resident, personal representative of the Godhead on earth. It seems to be a law, which I cannot explain, that only one person of the Godhead can be resident on earth at any one given time. For some years, it was Jesus the Son. But when Jesus was leaving to return to heaven, He promised that another person would come in His place who would stay with us forever, not just for a few brief years. That promise was fulfilled on the Day of Pentecost. Jesus the Son, as a person, had gone back to the Father in heaven. Then, from the Father and the Son together, the Holy Spirit came to take the place of Jesus.

Where does the Holy Spirit now live? There are two answers. First, He lives in the church, the corporate body of Christ. Paul asked the Corinthian believers the following:

> *Don't you know that you yourselves are God's temple and that God's Spirit lives in you?*   *(1 Cor. 3:16 NIV)*

Paul was talking here about the corporate temple of the Holy Spirit.

Second, in 1 Corinthians 6:19, Paul said something even more dramatic. He revealed that not only is the corporate body of Christ the dwelling place of the Holy Spirit, but it is God's purpose that the body of each believer also be the dwelling place of the Holy Spirit:

> *Do you not know that your body is a temple of the Holy Spirit, who is in you, whom you have received from God?*
>   *(NIV)*

That is one of the most breathtaking statements found anywhere in the Bible! If we are believers in Jesus Christ, our physical bodies are to be the dwelling place of God the Holy Spirit.

CHAPTER FOUR

OUR INDWELLING HELPER

W hat does it mean for us, practically, that the Holy Spirit has come to be our Paraclete? We will begin by looking again at the passage in John 14:16–18 where Jesus gave this specific promise:

And I will ask the Father, and he will give you another Counselor [Paraclete] *to be with you forever—the Spirit of truth. The world cannot accept him, because it neither sees him nor knows him. But you know him, for he lives with you and will be in you.* [You can see that this is a promise only for believers, not for the world.] *I will not leave you as orphans; I will come to you.* (NIV)

The word *paraclete,* derived from a Greek source, was simply transliterated into English. It literally means "someone who is called in alongside to help." A Paraclete is someone who can do something for you that you cannot do for yourself. The same Greek word is used in 1 John 2:1:

My little children, I am writing these things to you that you may not sin. And if anyone sins, we have an Advocate with the Father, Jesus Christ the righteous. (NAS)

The word translated here as *"Advocate"* is the source word for *paraclete.* Our English word *advocate* is derived from Latin: *ad,* "to"; and *vocata,* "called"—"somebody called to or in." In almost all languages derived from Latin, the word *advocate* is the word used to denote a lawyer. It means someone who speaks in our defense. We all know the role of an advocate, attorney, or lawyer in contemporary culture.

Scripture unfolds the beautiful truth that we have two Advocates. On earth, the Holy Spirit pleads our cause. The things we cannot say right, He says for us; the things we do not understand, He interprets for us. In heaven, Jesus is our Advocate with the Father; He pleads our cause. Just think, we have the two greatest Advocates in the universe. We have Jesus Christ, the Son, at the Father's right hand, and we have the Holy Spirit on earth. With two such Advocates or Attorneys, how could we ever lose the case?

Let me go on and amplify what Jesus said about this Advocate, who is our Paraclete—our Attorney, Comforter, Counselor, and Helper. I will comment on some of the things that Jesus said in John 14:16–18, cited earlier.

"The Father...will give you another Counselor" (v. 16). You must understand the importance of that word *"another,"* as it indicates a person. Jesus said, "I'm a person. I'm going away. When I go, another person will come to be your Helper. I've been your Helper while I was here, but now I'm leaving. You're not going to be left without a Helper, though. There'll be another Helper that will come."

He will stay with you forever (v. 16). Jesus said, "I've been with you three-and-a-half years. I'm leaving you, but don't be heartbroken, because there is someone else coming in My place, and He'll never leave you. He'll be with you forever."

"He lives with you and will be in you" (v. 17). There is importance in the phrase *"in you."* This Advocate or Comforter is going to live in us. We will be His resident address.

"I will not leave you as orphans" (v. 18). By implication, if He had gone away and made no provision for them, the disciples would have been left like orphans, without anybody to care for them, help them, or explain things to them.

"I will come to you" (v. 18). This is very important. Christ came back to His disciples in the Holy Spirit. While He was on earth in

His body, Jesus could only be in one place at one time. He could talk to Peter, John, or Mary Magdalene one at a time, but He could not talk to all three of them in different conversations at the same time. He was limited by time and space. Now, when He came back to His people in the Holy Spirit, He was free from the limitations of time and space and is so now. He can be in Australia, talking to a child of God in need there; He can be in the United States, anointing a preacher; He can be somewhere in the deserts or the jungles of Africa, strengthening or healing a missionary. He is not limited. He has come back, but is no longer subject to the limitations of time or space.

I want to dwell just a little longer on this theme of the exchange of persons—one person going, another person coming. In John 16:5–7, Jesus said the following:

> *Now I am going to him who sent me* [the Father], *yet none of you asks me, "Where are you going?" Because I have said these things, you are filled with grief. But I tell you the truth: It is for your good that I am going away. Unless I go away, the Counselor will not come to you* [the Comforter]; *but if I go, I will send him to you.*   *(NIV)*

This is very clear language. "As long as I'm with you, in person, on earth," Jesus said, "the Holy Spirit has to stay in heaven, as a person. But if I go away as a person, then in My place I'll send another person, the Holy Spirit." It is an exchange of divine persons. For a while, the Son, as a person, was on earth; then He went back to heaven with His ministry complete. In His place, the Holy Spirit (another divine person) came to complete the ministry that Jesus had begun.

Jesus said it is for our good that He was going away. The King James Version says, *"It is expedient for you"* (v. 7). This is an amazing statement. We are better off with Jesus in heaven and the Holy Spirit on earth than we would be with Jesus on earth and the Holy Spirit in heaven. Few people realize that. Christians are always saying, "If only I could have lived in the days when Jesus was on earth." But Jesus said to His disciples, "You're better off. When I'm in heaven and the Holy Spirit is on earth, you will have more then than you have now."

Let me interpret this in the light of the experience of the first disciples themselves. Notice what happened immediately after the Holy Spirit came. There were three immediate results:

First, they understood the plan of God and the ministry of Jesus far better than they had ever understood it while Jesus was on earth. It is a remarkable fact they had been very slow and limited in their understanding, but the moment the Holy Spirit came, they had a totally different comprehension of the ministry and the message of Jesus.

Second, they became extremely bold. Even after the Resurrection, they still hid away behind locked doors for fear of the Jews. They were not willing to stand up to preach and proclaim the truth, nor were they equipped. The moment the Holy Spirit came, however, that changed. Peter boldly and straightforwardly told the Jewish people in Jerusalem the whole story of Jesus and laid at their door the guilt of His crucifixion.

Third, they had supernatural confirmations. The moment the Holy Spirit came, miracles began to take place. It was just like Jesus being back with them in person, for Jesus said, "When the Holy Spirit comes, I'll come back in Him. I will be with you. I will not leave you as orphans."

CHAPTER FIVE

REVELATION OF GOD'S WORD

T he Holy Spirit helps us, comforts us, and meets our needs in very specific ways. The first way we will consider is the revelation of God's Word. The Holy Spirit is the revelator and interpreter of the Word of God. In John 14:25–26, Jesus said to His disciples,

> All this I have spoken while still with you. But the Counselor [the Paraclete], the Holy Spirit, whom the Father will send in my name, will teach you all things and will remind you of everything I have said to you.   (NIV)

Two functions of the Holy Spirit that are mentioned in verse 26 are important: He is to remind, and He is to teach. He was to remind the disciples of all that Jesus had already taught them. I understand this to mean that the record of the apostles in the New Testament is not subject to the weaknesses of human memory but is inspired by the Holy Spirit. The disciples might not accurately have recalled some things, but whatever they needed to remember, the Holy Spirit Himself brought to their remembrance.

However, He did not merely take care of the past, He also took care of the future. He taught them everything they needed to learn. That is also true for us today. He is our present teacher here on earth. Jesus was the great teacher while He was on earth, but now He has handed over the task to the Holy Spirit, His personal representative. Whatever we need to know about the Word of God, the Holy Spirit is here to instruct us.

31

This placed the disciples on a level with the Old Testament prophets. Concerning the prophets, Peter wrote in 2 Peter 1:21,

For prophecy never had its origin in the will of man, but men spoke from God as they were carried along by the Holy Spirit.   (NIV)

The accuracy and the authority of the Old Testament prophets was that of the Holy Spirit Himself. He was responsible for what they said as He rested upon them. He inspired them and carried them along. But this is also true of the writings of the New Testament. Jesus made sure that the Holy Spirit would remind the disciples of all that He said and would teach them all that they still needed to know. The Holy Spirit is the true author of all Scripture, both Old and New Testaments. Paul stated this very clearly in 2 Timothy 3:16:

All Scripture is God-breathed and is useful for teaching, rebuking, correcting and training in righteousness.   (NIV)

Other translations use the word *"inspired"* (RSV, NAS), but either *"inspired"* or *"God-breathed"* indicates the activity of the Holy Spirit. The Holy Spirit is the one who breathed all Scripture through the human channels by which Scripture came.

God's perfect provision for us causes my heart to rejoice. The Holy Spirit was the author of Scripture, and He is also our personal teacher of Scripture. Thus, the author Himself becomes the interpreter of the Book. Who could ever interpret a book better for you than the one who wrote it? I have written over twenty books myself. Sometimes I hear other people interpret my books, and often they do a good job, but I always think, "Well, you missed that" or "You didn't get that quite right." In this situation, the Holy Spirit, who is the author of Scripture, is also the interpreter. He misses nothing; He has it all right. If we can listen to Him and receive from Him, we will know what the Scripture really has to say.

The revealing of the Scripture was an immediate result on the Day of Pentecost. When the Holy Spirit fell, the unbelieving crowd said, "They're drunk!" But Peter stood up and said the following:

32

*These men are not drunk, as you suppose. It's only nine in
the morning! No, this is what was spoken by the prophet
Joel."* (Acts 2:15–16 NIV)

Up to that time, Peter had no understanding of the prophecy of Joel. In fact, he had a very limited understanding even of the teaching of Jesus. But the moment the Holy Spirit came, the Bible made sense for him in a totally new way because the author was there to interpret. It was the same with the apostle Paul. He had been persecuting the church and rejecting the claims of Jesus. Acts 9:17 reads as follows:

Then Ananias went to the house [where Paul was] *and entered it. Placing his hands on Saul* [who later became Paul], *he said, "Brother Saul, the Lord—Jesus, who appeared to you on the road as you were coming here—has sent me so that you may see again and be filled with the Holy Spirit."* (Acts 9:17 NIV)

Immediately after that, Paul began to preach in the synagogues that Jesus was the Son of God, the very thing he had been denying. But the moment the Holy Spirit came in, he had a totally different understanding. It was like the transition from darkness to light. It was not something gradual, but almost an instant transformation because the Holy Spirit, the teacher and author of Scripture, was in Paul.

When speaking about the Holy Spirit as the interpreter and the revelator of the Word of God, we need to bear in mind that not only is the Bible the Word of God, but Jesus Himself is called the Word of God. In John 1:1, we read of Jesus,

*In the beginning was the Word, and the Word was with
God, and the Word was God.* (NIV)

Three times in that verse He is called *"the Word."* John 1:14 states the following:

*The Word became flesh and made his dwelling among us.
We have seen his glory, the glory of the One and Only, who
came from the Father, full of grace and truth.* (NIV)

The Bible, the Scripture, is the written Word of God, and Jesus is the personal Word of God. Of course, the marvelous thing is they are in total agreement.

Not only does the Holy Spirit reveal and interpret the written Word of God, but He also reveals and interprets the personal Word of God, Jesus. This is what Jesus said about the Holy Spirit:

> *I have much more to say to you, more than you can now bear. But when he, the Spirit of truth, comes, he will guide you into all truth. He will not speak on his own; he will speak only what he hears, and he will tell you what is yet to come. He will bring glory to me by taking from what is mine and making it known to you. All that belongs to the Father is mine. That is why I said the Spirit will take from what is mine and make it known to you.*
>
> *(John 16:12–15 NIV)*

Verse 12 tells us Jesus did not try to say it all because He trusted the Holy Spirit, and He knew the Holy Spirit was coming. Then He explained what the Holy Spirit would do when He came.

The Holy Spirit takes what belongs to Jesus and makes it known to us. He glorifies Jesus for us. He reveals Jesus in His glory, in His totality. Every aspect of the nature, character, and ministry of Jesus is unfolded to us by the Holy Spirit.

It is very interesting to note that once the Holy Spirit descended on the apostles and the disciples on the Day of Pentecost in Jerusalem, they never had any further doubts where Jesus was. They knew that He had arrived in glory at the Father's right hand. The Holy Spirit had glorified Jesus to the disciples. He had taken the things of Christ—in the Scripture, out of their memories, and out of their contacts with Jesus—and He had revealed them to the disciples.

The Holy Spirit reveals and glorifies Jesus. He also administers the total wealth of the Father and the Son because all that the Father has, is given to the Son and all the Son has, the Holy Spirit administers. In other words, the total wealth of the Godhead is administered by the Holy Spirit. It is no wonder we need not be orphans when He is our administrator and all the wealth of God is at His disposal.

CHAPTER SIX

LIFTED ONTO A SUPERNATURAL PLANE

T he next main result of the coming of the Holy Spirit is that we are lifted onto a supernatural plane of living. Two very interesting verses in Hebrews describe Christians by a New Testament standard:

> *Those who have once been enlightened, who have tasted the heavenly gift, who have shared in the Holy Spirit, who have tasted the goodness of the word of God and the powers of the coming age.* (Heb. 6:4–5 NIV)

Here, five things are listed about the New Testament believers:

1. They have been *"enlightened."*
2. They have *"tasted the heavenly gift"*—which I believe is the gift of eternal life in Jesus.
3. They have *"shared in the Holy Spirit,"* or been made partakers of the Holy Spirit.
4. They have *"tasted the goodness of the word of God"*—that is, God's Word has become living and real to them.
5. They have *"tasted...the powers of the coming age."*

All Christians believe that in the next age we will function in a totally different way. We will be set free of many of the limitations of our physical bodies, because we will have a different kind of body and a totally different lifestyle. But many Christians do not realize that through the Holy Spirit we can taste a little of that lifestyle right now in this life. We can "[taste]...*the powers of the coming age.*" We can only taste them, not appropriate them in their fullness, but we can come to know a little bit of what the next life is going to be like even during this life.

Paul used a very interesting phrase in this connection. In Ephesians 1:13–14, he wrote the following to believers:

> *And you also were included in Christ when you heard the word of truth, the gospel of your salvation. Having believed, you were marked in him with a seal, the promised Holy Spirit, who is a deposit guaranteeing our inheritance until the redemption of those who are God's possession—to the praise of his glory.* (NIV)

The word *"deposit"* is a fascinating word. The Holy Spirit is God's deposit in us, right now, for the next age. I have made a study of the word used here. In Greek, it is *arrabon,* which is really a Hebrew word. Years ago, probably about 1946, when I was living in Jerusalem, I had a very interesting experience that beautifully illustrated for me the meaning of that word *arrabon* or *"deposit."* My first wife and I went to the Old City to buy some material to make drapes for our new home. We saw the material that we wanted, inquired about the price (let us say it was one dollar a yard), and informed the merchant we needed fifty yards. So I told the man, "That's what we want," and he told me the price, fifty dollars. "Well," I said to him, "I don't have fifty dollars with me right now. Here's ten dollars; that's my deposit. Now the material is mine. You put it to one side. You're not free to sell it to anybody else. I'll come back with the rest of the money, and I'll collect the drapes." Well, that is the word *arrabon.*

The Holy Spirit is the Lord's deposit in us. He makes a down payment of the life of the next age in us right now by giving the Holy Spirit. When we receive that down payment, we are like that drapery fabric. We are set aside, not to be sold to anybody else. It is the guarantee that He is coming back with the rest to complete the purchase. That is why Paul speaks about having a deposit *"until the redemption of those who are God's possession."* We already belong to Him but we have only received the down payment—the full payment is yet to come.

The Holy Spirit is the down payment of our life in God in the next age. This supernatural life extends to every area of our experience.

I want to quote a passage from my book *The Spirit-filled Believer's Handbook* that emphasizes this. In this book, I wrote as follows:

> If we study the New Testament with an open mind, we are compelled to acknowledge that the whole life and experience of the early Christians was permeated in every part by the supernatural. Supernatural experiences were not something incidental or additional; they were an integral part of their whole lives as Christians. Their praying was supernatural; their preaching was supernatural; they were supernaturally guided, supernaturally empowered, supernaturally transported, supernaturally protected.
>
> Remove the supernatural from the book of Acts, and you are left with something that has no meaning or coherence. From the descent of the Holy Spirit in Acts 2, and onwards, it is impossible to find a single chapter in which the record of the supernatural does not play an essential part.
>
> In the account of Paul's ministry in Ephesus, in Acts 19:11, we find a most arresting and thought-provoking expression:
>
> > *And God was performing extraordinary miracles by the hands of Paul.*   (NAS)
>
> Consider the implications of that phrase *"extraordinary miracles."* The Greek could be translated, somewhat freely, "miracles of a kind that do not happen every day." Miracles were an everyday occurrence in the early church. Normally they would have caused no special surprise or comment. But the miracles granted here in Ephesus through the ministry of Paul were such that even the early church found them worthy of special record.
>
> In how many churches today would we find occasion to use the phrase—"miracles of a kind that do not happen every day"? In how many churches today do miracles ever happen— let alone, happen every day?

One area in which the supernatural was particularly manifested in the lives of the early Christians was in the supernatural

37

direction that they received from the Holy Spirit. In Acts 16, we read about Paul and his companions on his second missionary journey. They were in what we call Asia Minor today, and Scripture says they were *"kept by the Holy Spirit from preaching the word in the province of Asia....They tried to enter Bithynia, but the Spirit of Jesus* [or Jesus, through the Holy Spirit] *would not allow them to* [enter Bithynia]" (Acts 16:6–7 NIV). So they tried to go west, and the Holy Spirit would not let them. Then they tried to go northeast, and the Holy Spirit said, "No." Acts 16:8–10 continues with the following:

> *So they passed by Mysia and went down to Troas* [that was northwest]. *During the night Paul had a vision of a man of Macedonia standing and begging him, "Come over to Macedonia and help us." After Paul had seen the vision, we got ready at once to leave for Macedonia, concluding that God had called us to preach the gospel to them* [in Macedonia]. *(NIV)*

That is a very significant incident, and it is our example of the supernatural intervention and guidance of the Holy Spirit. It would have been natural for them in that geographical situation to go either west into Asia or northeast into Bithynia. It was unnatural to pass those two areas, go northwest, and then cross over into the continent of Europe.

However, if we look back over the subsequent history of the church, we see that the continent of Europe played a unique role—first, in preserving the Gospel through the Dark Ages; and second, in becoming the main continent for many years to send forth the Word of God to other nations. God had a sovereign purpose that included many centuries ahead. Paul and his companions could never have discovered it by natural reasoning, but through the supernatural direction of the Holy Spirit, they walked right into the full purpose of God. All history has been affected by that supernatural guidance of the Holy Spirit in their lives.

That is just a single example out of many of the supernatural interventions of the Holy Spirit in the lives of the early Christians.

CHAPTER SEVEN

HELP IN PRAYER

The third vitally important way in which the Holy Spirit helps us is in our prayers. In Romans 8:14, Paul described our need of the Holy Spirit's guidance to lead the Christian life:

For all who are being led by the Spirit of God, these are sons of God. (NAS)

In order to become a Christian, you must be born of the Spirit of God. But in order to live like a Christian and come to maturity after you have been born again, you must be led continually by the Spirit of God. The form of the verb that Paul used there is the continuing present. *"For all who are being [continually] led by the Spirit of God, these are sons of God."* They are no longer little babies, but mature sons and daughters.

Further on in Romans, Paul applied this principle of being led by the Holy Spirit particularly to our prayer life. He emphasized the necessity of the guidance of the Holy Spirit to pray correctly.

And in the same way the Spirit also helps our weakness; for we do not know how to pray as we should, but the Spirit Himself [the personality of the Holy Spirit is emphasized] intercedes for us with groanings too deep for words; and He who searches the hearts knows what the mind of the Spirit is, because He intercedes for the saints according to the will of God. (Rom. 8:26–27 NAS)

Paul spoke here about a weakness that we all have. It is not a physical weakness, but a weakness of the mind and understanding. We do not know what to pray for, and we do not know how to pray.

I have often challenged congregations by asking people to raise their hands if they always knew what to pray for and how to pray for it. Never once has anybody dared to raise his hand on that challenge. I think we are all honest enough to acknowledge that when we want to pray, we often do not know what to pray for. Sometimes, even if we think we know what to pray for, we do not know how to pray for it. Paul called that *"our weakness."* But he told us that God sends the Holy Spirit to help us in that weakness, to know what to pray for and to know how to pray for it. In a certain sense, Paul's language suggests that the Holy Spirit moves in and does the praying through us.

The key to effective praying is learning how to be so related to the Holy Spirit that we can submit to Him. Then we can let Him guide, direct, inspire, and strengthen, and many times actually pray through us.

The New Testament reveals many ways in which the Holy Spirit can help us, a few of which I will now outline.

The first way is referred to in those verses in Romans 8:26–27. Paul said, *"The Spirit Himself intercedes for us with groanings too deep for words."* I would call that intercession, which is one of the high points of the Christian life. He spoke about *"groanings too deep for words."* Our finite, limited minds do not have the words to pray what needs to be prayed. So one of the ways the Holy Spirit comes to our help is to pray through us with groanings that cannot be expressed in words.

This is a very sacred experience, a spiritual travail that leads to spiritual birth. Isaiah 66:8 refers to this:

As soon as Zion travailed, she also brought forth her sons.

(NAS)

No real spiritual reproduction in the church can occur without spiritual travail in prayer. It is when Zion travails that she brings forth her sons.

Paul confirmed this in Galatians 4:19:

40

My dear children, for whom I am again in the pains of childbirth until Christ is formed in you. (NIV)

Paul had preached to those people, and they had been converted. But for them to become what they needed to be, Paul recognized that it would take more than preaching, it would take intercessory prayer. He described that intercessory prayer as being *"in the pains of childbirth,"* or *"groanings too deep for words."*

A second way in which the Holy Spirit helps us in prayer is that He illuminates our minds. He does not actually pray through us in this way, but He shows us in our minds what we need to pray for and how we need to pray for it. There are two passages from the epistles that speak about the work of the Holy Spirit in our minds. In Romans 12:2, we read the following:

And do not be conformed to this world, but be transformed by the renewing of your mind, that you may prove what the will of God is, that which is good and acceptable and perfect. (NAS)

Only a renewed mind can find out God's will, even in the matter of prayer. Ephesians 4:23 says the following:

That you be renewed in the spirit of your mind.

(NAS)

The renewing of our minds is done by the Holy Spirit. When the Holy Spirit moves in and renews our minds, then we begin to understand the will of God, and we begin to know how to pray according to the will of God. This second way the Holy Spirit helps us is by renewing our minds, illuminating them, and revealing to us how to pray.

The third way in which the Holy Spirit helps us is that He puts the right words in our mouths, often unexpectedly. Whenever I refer to this, I always think of an incident with my first wife. We were in Denmark, which was her native country, at the end of October. We were leaving the next day to spend the whole month of November in Britain. I am British, so I know that November in Britain is a cold, gloomy, misty, foggy month. As we prayed on the day before we were to leave for Britain, I heard Lydia say, "Give us fine weather all the time we're in Britain!" I almost fell out of the bed where we were sitting and praying.

Afterwards, when I asked her if she knew what she had prayed, Lydia replied, "No, I don't remember!" That was sure proof to me it was the Holy Spirit.

"Well," I said, "you prayed for God to give us fine weather all the time we're in Britain, and you know what Britain is like in November." She just shrugged her shoulders. We spent the whole month of November in Britain, and we had not one cold, miserable, wet day! It was like a good spring.

When we left at the end of November, I said to the people who saw us off at the airport, "Look out, because when we leave, the weather's going to change!" Sure enough, it did! That was a prayer that the Holy Spirit put in Lydia's mouth. It was what the Lord wanted her to pray for at that time.

A fourth way the Holy Spirit helps us in prayer is one that is mentioned many times in the New Testament. He gives us a new, unknown language, one that the natural mind does not know. Some people today speak about this as a prayer language. Paul said in 1 Corinthians 14:2,

For anyone who speaks in a tongue [an unknown language] *does not speak to men but to God. Indeed, no one understands him; he utters mysteries with his spirit.* (NIV)

And in verse 4 of that same chapter, Paul said the following:

He who speaks in a tongue edifies himself.

(NIV)

This kind of prayer serves three basic functions:

1. When we pray in an unknown tongue, we are not speaking to men, but to God. To me, that is a tremendous privilege in itself.

2. We are speaking things our minds do not understand. We are speaking mysteries or sharing God's secrets.

3. As we do this, we are edifying ourselves, or building ourselves up.

Further on in 1 Corinthians 14:14, Paul said the following:

For if I pray in a tongue, my spirit prays, but my mind is unfruitful. (NIV)

Here is a situation where the Holy Spirit does not illuminate the mind, but He simply gives us a new language and prays through us in that language. We must not use one form of prayer to the exclusion of the other. Paul said very clearly, *"I will pray with my spirit, but I will also pray with my mind"* (v. 15 NIV). Both kinds of prayer are possible.

When we let the Holy Spirit in, yield to Him, and let Him work in us according to Scripture, there is a tremendous richness and variety in our prayer life. This is what God wants for each one of us.

CHAPTER EIGHT

LIFE AND HEALTH FOR OUR BODIES

T
he fourth function of the Holy Spirit as Paraclete is His impartation of supernatural life and health to our physical bodies. Jesus came to give us life, as He declared in John 10:10:

The thief comes only to steal and kill and destroy; I have come that they may have life, and have it to the full. (NIV)

Two persons are set before us here, and we need to distinguish very clearly between them: the Life-giver, Jesus, and the life-taker, Satan. The Devil only comes into our lives to take life. He comes to steal the blessings and the provisions of God; he comes to kill us physically and destroy us eternally. Every one of us needs to realize that if we permit the Devil to have any place in our lives, that is what he is going to do—steal, kill, and destroy to the extent we permit him to do so.

On the other hand, Jesus came to do the exact opposite: He came that we may have life and that we may have it to the full. It is important for us to realize that this life Jesus came to give us is administered by the Holy Spirit. We only have His life in the proportion that we allow the Holy Spirit to do His work in us. If we resist or refuse the work of the Holy Spirit, then we cannot experience the fullness of divine life that Jesus came to bring us. We need to understand that it was the Holy Spirit who raised the dead body of Jesus from the tomb. Paul said the following about Jesus in Romans 1:4:

[Jesus] *through the Spirit of holiness was declared with power to be the Son of God by his resurrection from the dead.* (NIV)

"The Spirit of holiness" is a Greek translation of the Hebrew phrase for the Holy Spirit. Though Paul was writing in Greek, he was thinking in Hebrew. So when Paul said, *"through the Spirit of holiness,"* it is the same as saying, "through the Holy Spirit, Jesus was manifested or declared to be the Son of God by the power that raised Him from the dead [that is, the power of the Holy Spirit]."

In previous sections, I pointed out that, in a certain sense, this was the climax of the redemptive process of God in this age: that God Himself, in the person of the Holy Spirit, should indwell our physical bodies and make them His temple or His dwelling place. In Romans 8:10–11, Paul said this:

But if Christ is in you, your body is dead because of sin, yet your spirit is alive because of righteousness. And if the Spirit of him who raised Jesus from the dead is living in you, he who raised Christ from the dead will also give life to your mortal bodies through his Spirit, who lives in you.

(NIV)

The implication of the tenth verse is that when Christ comes in, when we are converted and regenerated, an old life ends, and a new life begins. The old, carnal life is terminated, and our spirits come alive with the life of God. Then Paul went on to say, in verse 11, what this means for our physical bodies. Very clearly, the same person, the same power, that raised the body of Jesus from the tomb is now dwelling in the body of each yielded believer and is imparting to each mortal body the same kind of life that He imparted to the mortal body of Jesus and the same kind of power that raised Him with an eternal body.

This process of imparting divine life to our bodies will not be consummated until the general resurrection from the dead. It is important to understand that we do not now have resurrection bodies, but what we do have is resurrection life in our mortal bodies. Paul further continued, in several different passages, that resurrection life in our mortal bodies can take care of all the physical needs of our bodies until the time that God separates spirit from body and calls us home.

We must understand how our bodies were formed in the first place because it all relates together. Genesis 2:7 states,

The LORD God formed the man from the dust of the ground and breathed into his nostrils the breath [or the Spirit] of life, and the man became a living being [or a living soul]. (NIV)

What was it that produced man's physical body? It was the inbreathed Spirit of God that transformed a clay form into a living human being with all the miracles and marvels of a functioning human body. The Holy Spirit originally brought the physical body into being. Logically, it follows that He's the one to sustain it. This is so logical, if only Christians can see it. Divine healing and divine health are logical in the light of Scripture.

For instance, if your watch goes wrong, you do not take your watch to the boot maker; you take your watch to the watchmaker. Now, apply that same reasoning: if your body goes wrong, where do you take your body? In my opinion, the logical thing to do is to take it to the body maker, and that is the Holy Spirit.

Here in the United States, we are familiar with the little phrase "Body by Fisher" on the chassis or body of many of our most common cars. When I look at a fellow Christian, I say, "Body by the Holy Spirit." This is who gave him his body, who sustains his body, and who gives power to his body.

Paul's testimony is impressive. In 2 Corinthians 11:23–25, he said the following:

I have worked much harder, been in prison more frequently, been flogged more severely, and been exposed to death again and again. Five times I received from the Jews the forty lashes minus one. Three times I was beaten with rods, once I was stoned, three times I was shipwrecked, I spent a night and a day in the open sea. (NIV)

It is almost incredible that a man could go through all that and be so active, so healthy, and so courageous. What was the power that sustained Paul in all that? The power of the Holy Spirit. This is the account of the stoning of Paul in Lystra:

> *Then some Jews came from Antioch and Iconium and won the crowd over. They stoned Paul and dragged him outside the city, thinking he was dead.* [And it takes a lot of stones to make a man even appear dead.] *But after the disciples had gathered around him, he got up and went back into the city. The next day he and Barnabas left for Derbe.*
>
> (Acts 14:19–20 NIV)

What a man! I have heard some people suggest that Paul was a walking invalid who went around sick most of the time. My comment on that is, "If Paul was an invalid, God give us a lot more invalids like Paul!"

We have looked briefly at the remarkable record of the physical endurance and resilience of the apostle Paul. We will now look at his secret. What does he say about this? In 2 Corinthians 4:7–12, Paul related the following:

> *But we have this treasure in jars of clay* ["this treasure" is the indwelling Spirit of God] *to show that this all-surpassing power is from God and not from us. We are hard pressed on every side, but not crushed; perplexed, but not in despair; persecuted, but not abandoned; struck down, but not destroyed. We always carry around in our body the death of Jesus, so that the life of Jesus may also be revealed in our body. For we who are alive are always being given over to death for Jesus' sake, so that his life may be revealed in our mortal body. So then, death is at work in us, but life is at work in you.*
>
> (NIV)

Verses 7 and 8 tell us we are not different kinds of persons in ourselves, but we have a different kind of power in us. Things that would crush other men need not crush us because we have a power in us that makes us resilient.

We find a beautiful contrast in verse 10. We are to reckon ourselves dead with Jesus. As we do, then His life is manifested

47

in our physical bodies. It is very clear that it is not in the next age, but in this age that the supernatural, indwelling, resurrection life of Jesus in the Holy Spirit is to be manifested in our physical bodies.

The last words of verse 11 are significant: *"So that his life may be revealed in our mortal body."* This is not just a secret, indwelling presence that no one can see; it is a presence that works such results in our physical bodies that it is evident to everybody. The resurrection life of Jesus is revealed in our mortal bodies.

Verse 12 tells us that when we receive the sentence of death in ourselves and come to the end of our own physical strength and abilities, then a new kind of life works through us to others.

Therefore we do not lose heart, but though our outer man is decaying, yet our inner man is being renewed day by day. (v. 16 NAS)

The outward man decays, but there is a life in the inner man that is *"renewed day by day."* The inner, supernatural, miraculous life of God takes care of the needs of the outer man for each of us.

CHAPTER NINE

OUTPOURING OF DIVINE LOVE

The greatest and most wonderful of all the blessings the Holy Spirit offers us is the outpouring of God's divine love in our hearts. Romans 5:1–5 says the following:

Therefore, since we have been justified through faith, we have peace with God through our Lord Jesus Christ, through whom we have gained access by faith into this grace in which we now stand. And we rejoice in the hope of the glory of God. Not only so, but we also rejoice in our sufferings, because we know that suffering produces perseverance; perseverance, character; and character, hope. And hope does not disappoint us, because God has poured out his love into our hearts by the Holy Spirit, whom he has given us. (NIV)

The climax comes in the fifth verse: *"And hope does not disappoint us, because God has poured out his love into our hearts by the Holy Spirit, whom he has given us."*

Paul outlined some stages of spiritual progression in those five verses, which I would like to go through very briefly:

1. We have peace with God.
2. We have access into God's grace through faith.
3. We rejoice in hope of God's glory, the hope of something in the future.
4. We rejoice also in sufferings, because of the results sufferings produce in us when we rightly receive them.

Paul then listed three successive results of suffering, rightly endured: the first, perseverance; the second, proven character; and the third, hope.

Then we come to the climax: God's love is poured out in our hearts by the Holy Spirit. Here, the word for *"love"* is the Greek word *agape,* which in the New Testament is normally, but not invariably, restricted to God's own love. Usually, *agape* love is not humanly achievable except by the Holy Spirit. In most cases, we can never produce *agape* in our natural man.

Further in the fifth chapter, Paul defined the nature of *agape.* He explained how it was manifested in God and in Christ:

> *You see, at just the right time, when we were still power-*
> *less, Christ died for the ungodly. Very rarely will anyone*
> *die for a righteous man, though for a good man someone*
> *might possibly dare to die. But God demonstrates his own*
> *[agape] love for us in this: While we were still sinners,*
> *Christ died for us.* (vv. 6–8 NIV)

When Christ died for us, according to Paul, there were three words that described us: *"powerless," "ungodly,"* and *"sinners."* It is *agape* love that is self-giving and does not lay down any prior conditions. It is not a love that says you must be good, or do this or that. It is freely given out, even to the most unde-serving, the most helpless, and the most unworthy.

Now we will trace in the New Testament the various phases in which *agape* love is produced in us. First, it is the product of the new birth. In 1 Peter 1:22–23, we read the following:

> *Now that you have purified yourselves by obeying the truth*
> *so that you have sincere love for your brothers, love one an-*
> *other deeply, from the heart. For you have been born again,*
> *not of perishable seed, but of imperishable, through the liv-*
> *ing and enduring word of God.* (NIV)

The possibility of loving with *agape* love originates with the new birth—the new birth of the eternal, incorruptible seed of God's Word that produces in us a new kind of life. *Agape* love is the very nature of that new life. First John 4:7–8 says the following:

Dear friends, let us love one another, for love comes from God. Everyone who loves has been born of God and knows God. Whoever does not love does not know God, because God is love.   *(NIV)*

You can see that this kind of love is the mark of the new birth. A person who has been born again has it; a person who has not been born again cannot have it.

Paul described the next phase of this process of imparting divine love to us:

And hope does not disappoint us, because God has poured out his love into our hearts by the Holy Spirit, whom he has given us.   *(Rom. 5:5 NIV)*

After the new birth, in that new nature that is produced by the new birth, the Holy Spirit pours out the totality of God's love into our hearts. We are immersed in love. We are brought in contact with an inexhaustible supply—the total love of God has been poured out into our hearts by the Holy Spirit. I want to emphasize that it is something divine, inexhaustible, and supernatural—something that only the Holy Spirit can do.

Compare what Jesus said in John 7:37–39:

On the last and greatest day of the Feast, Jesus stood and said in a loud voice, "If anyone is thirsty, let him come to me and drink. Whoever believes in me, as the Scripture has said, streams of living water will flow from within him." By this he meant the Spirit, whom those who believed in him were later to receive.   *(NIV)*

You can see the contrast. First, we have a thirsty man who does not have enough for himself. But when the Holy Spirit comes in, that thirsty man becomes a channel for *"streams of living water."* That is the love of God poured out into our hearts. It is not human love; it is not just a portion of God's love. It is the totality of God's love, and we are simply immersed in it. The whole, endless, infinite love of God has a channel to flow through our lives by the Holy Spirit. A thirsty man becomes a channel of streams of living water.

We will now look at the famous Love Chapter written by Paul and found in 1 Corinthians. At the end of chapter 12, he said, *"I show you a still more excellent way"* (v. 31 NAS). That *"still more excellent way"* is unfolded in the opening verses of chapter 13:

If I speak with the tongues of men and of angels, but do not have love [agape], I have become a noisy gong or a clanging cymbal. And if I have the gift of prophecy, and know all mysteries and all knowledge; and if I have all faith, so as to remove mountains, but do not have love, I am nothing. And if I give all my possessions to feed the poor, and if I deliver my body to be burned, but do not have love, it profits me nothing.   *(1 Cor. 13:1–3 NAS)*

It is important to see that all the gifts and manifestations of the Holy Spirit are intended to be channels or instruments of divine love. If we do not use those gifts and make them available to the love of God, we frustrate God's purposes. We may have all the other gifts, but we are simply left like a *"noisy gong"* or a *"clanging cymbal."* We are nothing, and we have nothing without divine love.

In verse 1, Paul said: *"If I speak with the tongues of men and of angels, but do not have love, I have become a noisy gong or a clanging cymbal."* When the Holy Spirit comes in, He comes into a heart that has been purified by faith and is turned toward God. Later on, it is possible to dry up, miss God's purpose, or misuse what God has made available to us. In that case, it happens as Paul said: *"I have become a noisy gong or a clanging cymbal."* In effect, he said, "I wasn't that way when I received, but through missing the purpose, I have become like that, and I frustrated God's purpose."

Compare that with what Paul said in 1 Timothy 1:5–6:

The goal of this command is love, which comes from a pure heart and a good conscience and a sincere faith. Some have wandered away from these.   *(NIV)*

The goal of all Christian ministry is love. The purpose of God for the Christian is the consistent expression of divine love.

I will sum up the three phases in this process of imparting God's love to us:

- The first phase is the new birth. When we are born again, we become capable of that kind of love.

- The second is the outpouring of the totality of God's love into our hearts by the Holy Spirit who is given to us. The inexhaustible resources of God are made available to us.

- Third, the expression of that love is worked out in daily living through discipline and character training. This is when the love that comes from God is made available to our fellow human beings through us.

The first time I saw Niagara Falls, I equated that tremendous quantity of water to the love of God being poured out. Then I thought to myself, "Nevertheless, its real purpose is not fulfilled merely in the outpouring. Only when that power is channeled and used to bring light, heat, and power to the inhabitants of many of the major cities of the North American continent is the purpose achieved."

That is how it is with us. We receive God's love when we are born again; it is poured out over us by the Holy Spirit; but it only becomes available to our fellow human beings as it is channeled through our lives in discipline and training.

CHAPTER TEN

HOW TO OPEN UP TO THE HOLY SPIRIT

How can we open up to the Holy Spirit and receive Him in His fullness, and through Him receive all the blessings promised? We will look at a number of Scriptures that state the conditions we need to satisfy in order to receive the fullness of the Holy Spirit. God does require us to fulfill a number of specific essentials.

REPENT AND BE BAPTIZED

Acts 2:37–38 is the end of Peter's talk on the Day of Pentecost, and it gives the response of the people to his message:

When the people heard this, they were cut to the heart and said to Peter and the other apostles, "Brothers, what shall we do?" [That was a specific question, and God's Word gives a specific answer.] *Peter replied, "Repent and be baptized, every one of you, in the name of Jesus Christ for the forgiveness of your sins. And you will receive the gift of the Holy Spirit."*   *(NIV)*

There we have the promise: *"You will receive the gift of the Holy Spirit."* We also have two conditions clearly stated: *"Repent and be baptized."* To repent means to turn sincerely from all sinfulness and rebellion and submit ourselves without reservation to God and to His requirements. To be baptized is to go through an ordinance or a sacrament by which each of us is personally and visibly identified with Jesus Christ to the world in His death, burial, and resurrection. So there are two basic, primary requirements for receiving the gift of the Holy Spirit: we must repent, and we must be baptized.

ASK GOD

In Luke 11:9–13, Jesus said the following:

So I say to you: Ask and it will be given to you; seek and you will find; knock and the door will be opened to you. For everyone who asks receives; he who seeks finds; and to him who knocks, the door will be opened. Which of you fathers, if your son asks for a fish, will give him a snake instead? Or if he asks for an egg, will give him a scorpion? If you then, though you are evil, know how to give good gifts to your children, how much more will your Father in heaven give the Holy Spirit to those who ask him! (NIV)

Here is a simple condition but a very important one. Jesus said the Father will give the Holy Spirit to His children if we ask Him for the Holy Spirit. I have heard Christians say, "I don't need to ask for the Holy Spirit." I must tell you that is not scriptural. Jesus was speaking to His disciples and He said, "Your Father will give you the Holy Spirit if you ask for it." Elsewhere, Jesus said He would go to the Father and ask the Father to send the Holy Spirit to His disciples. My feeling is that if Jesus had to ask the Father, it will not do us any harm to ask as well. This, then, is the third condition: to ask.

In John 7:37–39, we have three more simple conditions stated:

On the last and greatest day of the Feast, Jesus stood and said in a loud voice, "If anyone is thirsty, let him come to me and drink. Whoever believes in me, as the Scripture has said, streams of living water will flow from within him." By this he meant the Spirit, whom those who believed in him were later to receive. Up to that time the Spirit had not been given, since Jesus had not yet been glorified. (NIV)

The author of the gospel makes it very clear that in this passage, Jesus was talking about believers receiving the Holy

Spirit. With that in mind, let us look at what Jesus said. *"If anyone is thirsty, let him come to me and drink."* These are three simple but practical requirements.

BE THIRSTY

The first is we must be thirsty. God does not force His blessings on people who feel they do not need them. Many people never receive the fullness of the Holy Spirit because they are not really thirsty. If you think you have all you need already, why should God bother you with more? Very probably, you are not making the best use of what you already have. You would be under greater condemnation if God gave you more.

That is an essential condition—to be thirsty. To be thirsty means you have recognized you need more than you already have. As a matter of fact, thirst is one of the strongest desires in the human body. When a person is really thirsty, they do not care about eating or anything else. All they want is a drink. I spent three years in deserts in North Africa, and I have a pretty good picture of what it means to be thirsty. When a man is thirsty, he does not bargain or talk or discuss; he just goes to where the water is. That is what Jesus was saying: you must be thirsty.

COME TO JESUS

Then, if you are thirsty, He said, *"Come to me."* So, the second condition is to come to Jesus. Jesus is the Baptizer in the Holy Spirit. If you want the baptism, you must come to the One who baptizes in the Holy Spirit. No human being baptizes in the Holy Spirit, only Jesus.

DRINK

Then He said you must drink. This is so simple some people leave it out. But drinking is receiving something within you by a decision of your will and a physical response. It is also part of receiving the Holy Spirit. Thirsting, coming to Jesus, and drinking are all essential. Just being totally passive and saying, "Well, if God wants to do it, let Him do it!" is not drinking. Drinking is actively receiving within you.

YIELD

We want to consider two more relevant facts concerning our physical bodies that were touched on in earlier sections. First, our bodies are destined by God to be the temples of the Holy Spirit. First Corinthians 6:19 says the following:

Do you not know that your body is a temple of the Holy Spirit, who is in you, whom you have received from God?
                                                                    (NIV)

Second, we are required to offer or yield to God the parts of our bodies as instruments for His service. This is our responsibility. Romans 6:13 states the following:

Do not offer the parts of your body to sin, as instruments of wickedness, but rather offer yourselves to God, as those who have been brought from death to life; and offer the parts of your body to him [God] *as instruments of righteousness.*
                                                                    (NIV)

We have a responsibility straight from the Scripture to offer, yield, or dedicate the various members of our physical bodies to God for His service. One member particularly needs God's control: the tongue. James said very simply in his epistle:

But no man can tame [or control] *the tongue.*
                                                    (James 3:8 NIV)

We need help from God to control all the members of our bodies, but we need special help with our tongues. When the Holy Spirit comes in His fullness, the first member that He affects, takes control of, and utilizes for God's glory is the tongue. You will find, if you care to check, that every time the New Testament speaks of people being filled with the Holy Spirit or full of the Holy Spirit, the first immediate result is some utterance that comes out of their mouths. They speak, they prophesy, they praise, they sing, they speak in tongues—but the mouth is always engaged. When you come to Jesus and drink, the final result will be an overflow, and it will be out of your mouth. This

57

principle is stated by Jesus very clearly in Matthew 12:34: *"For out of the overflow of the heart the mouth speaks"* (NIV).

When your heart is filled to overflowing, the overflow will take place through your mouth in speech. God wants you not to have just enough, He wants you to have an overflow. Remember, He said, "Out of his inner being will flow rivers of living water." (See John 7:38.) That is the ultimate purpose of God.

GOD'S REQUIREMENTS

The following are the seven conditions that I have found in the Bible for receiving the fullness of the Holy Spirit:

1. Repent.
2. Be baptized.
3. Ask God.
4. Be thirsty.
5. Come to Jesus; He's the baptizer.
6. Drink—receive within yourself.
7. Present your body as a temple for the Holy Spirit and your members as instruments of righteousness.

Perhaps you are left wondering how you can do all this. I want to help you by sharing a pattern prayer that includes the things I have been explaining to you. Read it over, and, if it is your prayer, pray it aloud to the Lord.

> Lord Jesus,
>   I'm thirsty for the fullness of Your Holy Spirit. I present my body to You as a temple and my members as instruments of righteousness, especially my tongue, the member I cannot tame. Fill me, I pray, and let Your Holy Spirit flow through my lips in rivers of praise and worship. Amen.

If you prayed that prayer sincerely, it has been heard, and the results are on the way. You may be quite surprised at the fullness of what you will receive.

GOD'S MEDICINE
BOTTLE

CONTENTS

My son, attend to my words;
incline thine ear unto my sayings.
Let them not depart from thine eyes;
keep them in the midst of thine heart.
For they are life unto those that find them,
and health to all their flesh.
—Proverbs 4:20–22 (KJV)

CHAPTER ONE

TAKE AS DIRECTED

From my own experience, I will share with you how I discovered this wonderful medicine bottle of God. I learned about this great blessing during the early years of World War II.

Because I am British, I served in the British Army as a medical orderly (what the Americans call a hospital attendant) with the British Medical Services for five-and-a-half years during World War II. For the first three years of duty, I was stationed in the deserts of North Africa: first in Egypt, then in Libya, and finally in the Sudan.

In the desert, the two things that we were exposed to more than anything else were sand and sun. I spent nearly one entire year in the desert without ever seeing a paved road. We traveled in sand, we slept in sand, and very often we had the impression that we were eating sand. We were exposed to it day and night. Combined with the sun, it had a very harmful effect on certain people whose skin could not protect them adequately from that kind of exposure. I was one of them. It manifested itself primarily in the condition of my feet and my hands, where the skin broke down. I became incapacitated in many ways.

The officer in command of my particular unit struggled to keep me from being admitted to the hospital because he knew if I were admitted, he would lose me in the unit. Consequently, I spent several months hobbling around trying to do my military duties. However, in the end he had to let me go into the hospital. I went to three or four different military medical facilities, and I was in the hospital for a year. During that time, I met soldiers there who'd been two years in the Middle East and spent eighteen months in the hospital with similar conditions.

The doctors gave many elaborate diagnoses of my problem. Each name tended to be a little longer than the previous one. Eventually, my condition was diagnosed simply as chronic eczema. I received the best medical treatment available, but it really didn't help me.

I saw many other soldiers with similar conditions who also were not helped. Those with really serious problems, burns and so on, were usually shipped to South Africa. However, my condition wasn't considered to be that serious, and my services to the British Army were not so valuable that they were going to waste a passage on a ship to South Africa for me. So I just lay there in bed, day after day, wondering what my future would be. I'll tell you, when you spend an entire year in the hospital, it seems like an eternity!

Shortly before this time, I had come into a real personal relationship with the Lord, had been born again and received the filling of the Holy Spirit. But I was very ignorant about God's Word then, not having had any background in biblical instruction. I had a Bible and really had nowhere else to turn for help but to God and His Word.

In desperation, I began to search the Scriptures to see what they could tell me about my physical condition. I didn't have any theories about healing; I just knew I needed it. I had the Bible and plenty of time to read, since there was very little else to do. So I searched through the Bible for something that would show me if I could really trust God for the healing of my body.

One day I came across some verses in the book of Proverbs that I learned to call "God's Medicine Bottle." I'm quoting from the King James Version, which was the version that I was reading in those days and which is extremely vivid and forceful:

My son, attend to my words; incline thine ear unto my sayings. Let them not depart from thine eyes; keep them in the midst of thine heart. For they are life unto those that find them, and health to all their flesh. (Prov. 4:20–22)

It was that last phrase, *"health to all their flesh,"* that caught my attention. I understood that *"all their flesh"* meant the total physical body, which is the way more modern versions translate it. I reasoned with myself, "Health! If I have health in my whole body, then I have no room anywhere for sickness. That is what God is promising me."

Then I happened to look in the margin of my Bible and saw that the alternative translation for the word *health* was the word *medicine*. That seemed to be even more appropriate for my condition. God was promising me something that would be medicine that would bring health to all my flesh. I thought to myself, "That's precisely what I need." So I went back and read those words over and over again. I saw that, in essence, God's offer was being made to me through His Word.

Verse 20 says, *"Attend to my words; incline thine ear unto my sayings."* Then verse 22 says, *"For they* [that's God's words and God's sayings] *are life unto those that find them, and health to all their flesh."* So somehow life and health are in the words and the sayings of God. I didn't know how that could be, but I knew God was promising it.

When I saw the phrase, *"those that find them,"* I realized this process was more than just reading the Bible. It was reading the Bible in such a way as to find out how to receive what God was offering.

All the medical attention that was available in those conditions had not helped me. So I made a decision, a very naive decision in a way. I decided I was going to take God's Word as my medicine. That was a very crucial point in my life in many ways. When I made that decision, the Lord Himself spoke to me. Not audibly, but nevertheless very clearly, I heard Him say, "When the doctor gives a person medicine, the directions for taking it are on the bottle." Then He instructed, "This is My medicine I'm giving you. The directions are on the bottle. You better study them."

God reminded me that a doctor doesn't promise any benefit from the medicine he recommends unless it is taken according to the directions. Being a medical orderly, I was very aware of that.

I then decided to study the directions on the bottle. Very quickly I saw that there are four specific instructions for taking God's Word as medicine for the physical body. These are His directions:

1. *Attend to my words.*
2. *Incline thine ear unto my sayings.*
3. *Let them not depart from thine eyes.*
4. *Keep them in the midst of thine heart.*

I realized that if I were going to receive the benefits I needed from the medicine, I had to comply with these four guidelines.

I cannot go into detail about all that followed, but I began to bow my head over the Bible three times every day after meals, because that is how people normally take medicine. I said, "God, You have said that these words of Yours will be medicine to all my flesh, and I'm taking them as my medicine now, in the name of Jesus." Within a few months, God's medicine, taken that way, achieved the result God promised. I was totally healthy in every area of my body.

A good many years ago, I recorded this experience on a tape. Just recently, in London, England, I met a young man from Pakistan who told me that he'd become a Christian and that he had suffered for more than twenty years from eczema. One day he heard my tape and decided to do what I had done. In his case, he was completely healed within two or three days. So that is an up-to-date testimony that the medicine still does what it claims to do.

CHAPTER TWO

PAY CLOSE ATTENTION

I now want to share with you the lessons I learned about the directions that are on God's medicine bottle and how to apply them. The first of these four instructions is, *"Attend to my words."* We need to understand that when God speaks to us, He requires our undivided attention. If Almighty God is willing to speak to us at all, surely any sense of propriety would indicate that we need to listen to God with our full and respectful attention. Sadly, that's not really the attitude of many people today.

Because of the tremendous proliferation of the media—radio, television, and so on—and because of various factors in our contemporary culture, we have almost cultivated the practice of listening to two different things at one time. We suffer from a disease that could be called *divided attention*. I'm amazed when I go into a home and see teenagers doing their homework while watching television at the same time. They're not giving full attention to either one or the other.

In many places now, we have what is called background music. We carry on a conversation, but at the same time, with one ear we're listening to the music in the background. I have to say that for me, personally, this is intensely frustrating. I'm the kind of person who desires to concentrate on something without dissipating my attention. I think that's a characteristic God has conditioned in me that I am not willing to relinquish. If I'm having a conversation, I want to listen to the person who is talking. If I'm listening to music, then I want to listen to the music. I love music. When I listen to it, I listen to it with my full attention.

But you see, all through the Bible, the primary key to healing from God is hearing. Let me say that simply: *The key to biblical healing is hearing.* It's what we listen to and how we listen that are so essential. Jesus said to His disciples, *"Take heed what you hear"* (Mark 4:24 NKJV). He also said, *"Take heed how you hear"* (Luke 8:18 NKJV). We have to put the two together. It's what we listen to and how we listen to it.

Another passage that relates to healing is found in the Old Testament and brings out the same emphasis. In Exodus, the Lord told Israel, through Moses,

> *If you diligently heed the voice of the LORD your God and do what is right in His sight, give ear to His commandments and keep all His statutes, I will put none of the diseases on you which I have brought on the Egyptians. For I am the LORD who heals you.* (Exod. 15:26 NKJV)

Notice that final statement. It goes right along with the medicine bottle instructions: "I provide the medicine, and I am your Physician." In modern Hebrew that's exactly how that word would be translated: "I am the Lord, your Doctor." God says to His people, "I'm willing to be your Doctor, the Doctor of your physical body. However, there are conditions." He begins with an *if.*

The first condition, the basic one, is: *"If you diligently heed the voice of the LORD your God."* You see, what we listen to is very important. The Hebrew word that is translated *"diligently heed"* is a repetition of the verb "to listen." It goes something like this: *"If you* [listen listeningly to] *the voice of the LORD your God."* The complete emphasis is on listening.

When I was seeking healing for myself I came across this verse in conjunction with Proverbs 4:20–22. I asked myself, "What does it mean to *listen listeningly?"*

God gave me an answer to my question. He said, "You've got two ears, a right ear and a left one; to *listen listeningly* means to listen to Me with both ears, with your right ear and with your left. Don't listen to Me with your right ear and something else with your left because the result of that will be confusion."

The emphasis is on attending to God, listening for Him, giving God your undivided attention. That is the primary instruction on God's Medicine Bottle. It matters what we hear and how we hear. This is not only the key to being healed, it's also the key to receiving faith. Of course, they go very closely together. It's faith that enables us to receive the healing that God has provided and to benefit from the medicine.

One of my favorite Scriptures, which was also made real to me during this long period in the hospital, is the following:

> *So then faith cometh by hearing, and hearing by the word of God.*   (Rom. 10:17 KJV)

Lying there in that hospital bed, I was continually saying to myself, "I know if I had faith, God would heal me." But then I would say immediately after that, "But then, I don't have any faith." When I repeatedly told myself that I didn't have faith, I found myself in what John Bunyan described in *The Pilgrim's Progress* as the "Slough of Despond," a dark, lonely valley of despair.

One day, as I was reading my Bible, my eyes fell on Romans 10:17: *"So then faith cometh by hearing, and hearing by the word of God."* There were two words that leaped out from the page at me: *"faith cometh."* In other words, you don't need to despair. Maybe you don't have faith, but faith comes. If you don't have it, you can get it.

Of course, I looked to see how faith comes. The Word says, *"Faith comes by hearing, and hearing by the word of God"* (NKJV). Again, just as in Proverbs 4:20–22, I was directed right back to the Word of God. As I began to analyze that verse, I saw that we start with the Word of God. That's the beginning. We listen to the Word of God carefully, and, out of that listening, there comes what the Bible calls *"hearing,"* the ability to hear God. Then out of hearing, faith develops.

It's the Word of God that, when we first attend to it, produces hearing. As we continue hearing, or being focused on God's voice, faith develops out of that hearing.

In a sense, everything depends on how we approach the Word of God. Do we approach it with undivided attention? Do we listen with both ears? Are we focused on the Word of God? Do we get ourselves into a condition, both spiritually and mentally, which the Bible calls hearing, where we are truly able to hear what God is saying to us?

I'm sure many people read the Bible but never hear God. They don't hear God because their minds are occupied with other things. They're wondering how they are going to pay the rent, or what the weather is going to be like, or they're concerned with the political situation. There are other forces at work in their minds. Consequently, they never develop the ability to hear God.

We have to develop hearing, and out of hearing, faith develops. God's Word itself and the right attitude toward God's Word produce hearing. When we are able to hear, then faith comes. We're always directed back to the Word of God and how we are to receive it.

Thus, the first instruction on God's Medicine Bottle is, *"Attend to my words."*

CHAPTER THREE

BEND YOUR EAR

Now I'm going to explain the second of the instructions God has given for taking His medicine: *"Incline thine ear."* The word *incline* is slightly Old English, so we need to make sure that we understand precisely what it means. "To incline" is to bend down, and "an incline" is a hill that slopes. So "inclining your ear" is bending your ear down.

A fact of the human body is that you cannot bend your ear without bending your head down. In inclining your ear, you are actually inclining your head. What does that express? It's an attitude indicating humility and teachableness. I'll illustrate it from experience.

As I was studying the Bible in the hospital, seeking desperately for the answer to my problem, I read many promises of healing, blessing, and prosperity. But my attitude was conditioned by my background, which is probably true of all of us.

My background was in a segment of the Christian church where Christianity was not associated with being happy—in fact, very much the opposite. I had early in life formed the conclusion that if I were going to be a Christian, I would have to be prepared to be miserable. I had also decided pretty early that I wasn't prepared to be miserable and, therefore, I wasn't going to be a Christian. It was only a sovereign intervention of God in my life that changed me, but I still carried a lot of these old concepts with me.

When I found these repeated promises in the Bible of healing, health, strength, long life, prosperity, and abundance, I kept shaking my head—not inclining my head, but shaking my head—and saying, "This couldn't be. That's too good to be true! I can't believe that religion would be like that!" I was reacting this way to one of these statements in the Psalms where it says, "[God] *forgiveth all thine iniquities; [He] healeth all thy diseases...so that thy youth is renewed like the eagle's*" (Ps. 103:3, 5 KJV). I told myself, "You know, that's impossible. God couldn't be like that. I mean, we know we have to anticipate misery being Christians."

As I was responding like that inwardly, God spoke to me so clearly, not audibly, but just as clearly as if someone were actually speaking. He said, "Now tell Me, who is the pupil and who is the teacher?" I thought it over for a moment and replied, "Lord, You're the Teacher, and I'm the pupil." Then He responded, "Well, would you mind letting Me teach you?" I saw then that I wasn't letting God teach me at all. I had my own preconceptions. If He said something different in His Word, I really wasn't capable of hearing it because my mind was blocked by these set ideas. God in essence was saying, "Incline your ear, give up your prejudices, bend that stiff neck of yours, and let Me tell you how good I am and how wonderful is the provision I've made for you. Don't measure Me by human standards because I'm God. I'm almighty and gracious, a faithful and merciful God."

This brings out a very important principle about God's Word. God's Word works in us only insofar as we receive it. If we don't receive it, it doesn't do us any good. In a very powerful passage, James said, when he was speaking about God,

> *Of his own will begat he us with the word of truth* [notice, our becoming Christians is due to the Word: God begat us with the word of truth], *that we should be a kind of firstfruits of his creatures. Wherefore, my beloved brethren, let every man be swift to hear, slow to speak, slow to wrath* [note that: a wise man is swift to hear, but slow to speak]....*Wherefore lay apart all filthiness and superfluity of naughtiness, and receive with meekness the engrafted word, which is able to save your souls.*
>
> *(James 1:18–19, 21 KJV)*

God's Word can save you, it can heal you, and it can bless you in innumerable ways, but only if you receive it with meekness.

One of the things that we have to lay aside is *"naughtiness."* We usually associate naughtiness with children. What is a naughty child? One of the marks of a naughty child is answering back when he's taught or reproved. God says, "Don't answer Me back. When I tell you something, don't argue with Me. Don't tell Me you think it can't be true or that it's impossible or that I couldn't mean that. Let Me teach you." That is the essence of the inclined ear. It means that we come to God and we say, "God, You're the Teacher; I'm the pupil. I'm willing to let You teach me. I bow down my ear and listen."

In this matter of inclining the ear, we have to come face-to-face with the fact that most of us have mental barriers when we begin to read the Bible. They're due, in many cases, to our backgrounds. Many of us have had some kind of denominational affiliation in the past. We may still be active members of some particular denomination. I am not opposed to denominations, but I want to suggest to you that every denomination has its weak points and its strong points. It has areas in which it has been faithful to the truth, and it has areas in which it has not been faithful to the truth. If we measure God from our own de-nominational backgrounds, if we judge the Scriptures by what some church or some denomination teaches, we will exclude from our minds much of the truth that God wants us to receive and that can bless and help us.

For instance, some churches teach that the age of miracles is past. I have never been able to find any basis for that state-ment in Scripture. I can think of dozens of Scriptures that indi-cate the exact opposite. But if you approach the Bible with the attitude that the age of miracles is past, then when God prom-ises you a miracle, you probably can't hear Him or receive it.

Some Christian groups suggest that in order to be holy, you have to be poor. Being anything but poor is considered in some way almost sinful. Well, if it's God's purpose to bless you with material prosperity in order for you to help build His kingdom, as He states many times in Scripture, it can be His purpose. But if you have the attitude that you must be poor, you won't be able to receive the blessing of prosperity that God is offering you on the basis of Scripture. There's a Scripture that I think most of us really need to take to heart:

Beloved, I wish above all things that thou mayest prosper and be in health, even as thy soul prospereth.

(3 John 2 KJV)

I remember when I started to read that verse, it knocked me over. My old prejudices and preconceptions rose up. I thought, "That's impossible. It can't mean what it says." But you see, God said, "Incline your ear. Don't come at Me with your arguments, your prejudices, your preconceptions. Bend that stiff neck of yours and let Me teach you."

That's an essential requirement for receiving healing through the Word of God. By laying down our preconceptions and prejudices, bending our stiff necks, and opening our ears, we become able to listen carefully to what God says and not reject it because it doesn't agree with something we thought God ought to have said.

God is a lot bigger than any denomination. He's a lot bigger than our understandings. He's a lot bigger than all of our prejudices. Don't make God so small that He can't help you. Incline your ear and let Him tell you how much He's willing to do for you.

CHAPTER FOUR

DON'T LET THEM OUT OF YOUR SIGHT

I have dealt with the first two directions on God's Medicine Bottle: *"Attend to my words"* and *"Incline thine ear."* So logically, I'm moving on to the third instruction: *"Let them not depart from thine eyes."* The word *"them"* refers to God's words and God's sayings.

The key thought in this directive could be summed up in the word *focus*. One of the marvelous things about human eyes, which is not true of certain other animals or creatures, is that we have two eyes, but by focusing we can form one image. Of course, that is when our eyesight is healthy and operating the way God intended. Even with good eyesight, incorrect focus can produce blurred vision. I believe that's the problem with many people in the spiritual realm. They haven't yet learned to focus their spiritual eyesight, so their vision of spiritual things is blurred.

I think most people have the impression that the spiritual world is kind of misty, half real, vague, unformed. I know that was my impression of religion before I came to know the Lord in a personal way. I thought of religion as a kind of mist that hung around in old church buildings. I formulated that if I were very good, then perhaps the mist would settle on my head, but it never did. So after a while, I just decided that I wasn't interested in that, and I turned elsewhere to philosophy. But the fact remains that unless we can focus our spiritual eyes, we will always have a blurred vision of spiritual reality. Look at the words of Jesus in dealing with spiritual vision:

The light of the body is the eye: therefore when thine eye is single, thy whole body also is full of light; but when thine eye is evil, thy body also is full of darkness.

(Luke 11:34 KJV)

Here Jesus is speaking about something that affects the whole body. Instantly, it reminds me of the statement in Proverbs 4 about God's words being health to the whole body. But here Jesus is dealing with the way we use our eyes. *"When thine eye is single"*—I think that means, first and foremost, that we form a single image or focus. It means we're not looking in different directions with our two eyes, but they are focused to make one image. Then Jesus says the result will be manifested in the whole body: *"thy whole body also is full of light."*

I believe a body that is full of light does not have room for sickness. I believe light and darkness are mutually exclusive. Sickness is from darkness. Health is from light:

But unto you that fear my name shall the Sun of righteousness arise with healing in his wings. *(Mal. 4:2 KJV)*

The sun, in the natural, is the source of light. The two products of light, when the Sun arises, are righteousness and healing. They are the works of light. The opposite are the works of darkness. The opposite of righteousness is sin; the opposite of healing is sickness. They are works of darkness, but righteousness and healing are works of light. Jesus is saying, "If your eye is singly focused, your whole body will be filled with light, with righteousness, with health." It all depends on having a single eye.

The Greek word that has been translated as *single* is a word that has various meanings, which I rather carefully checked in two Greek lexicons before I finished preparing this. Two of the main meanings are "simple" and "sincere," which I think probably bring out the point. If your eye is simple or sincere, if you just see things the way they are written, then you are not too clever or too philosophical. You don't know too many different ways of explaining the text away; you just take it as meaning what it says.

I previously explained that the second direction, *"Incline thine ear,"* means bow down your stiff neck, be willing to hear. There are certain normal barriers, and I have described two of them as *prejudice* and *preconception*. We think we already know what God ought to have said, so we are not willing to listen.

This third instruction speaks about simplicity or sincerity. I would suggest that the barriers to simplicity and sincerity are rationalization and sophistication. I become wary when I hear preachers quoting too many worldly experts, especially if they are trying to authenticate the Bible. I do not believe that the Bible needs to be authenticated by worldly experts. In the end, that doesn't build people's faith.

Sooner or later, as I said earlier, faith comes by hearing the Word of God (Rom. 10:17), and anything that distracts our attention too long from God's Word is not ultimately going to build our faith. We have to read the Bible with that single eye of simplicity and sincerity that says, "This is what God says, this is what He means, and I believe it the way it is written."

I think back to my own experience in hospital. There I was, a professor of philosophy with a knowledge of Latin and Greek, able to quote many long and learned books. As sick as I was, I was offered through God's Word a very simple, unsophisticated way of getting healed: taking God's Word as my medicine. Now, to a philosophic mind, that is pure nonsense! It is just ridiculous! You dismiss it. But, you see, I was sick, and philosophy hadn't healed me. So I was really faced with two clear alternatives: I could be clever and stay sick, or I could be simple and get healed. One thing I have always been glad about ever since—I became simple enough to get healed.

That brings out this point: If your eye is simple, if you're sincere, if you are not too profound, if you don't know too many arguments, if you can't quote all the theologians, then you have a much better chance to reach God. I am sorry to say it, but experience over many years has convinced me of that. Theology normally does not help people's faith.

Let me quote two passages from the writings of Paul to conclude this thought. Note that we are talking about a kind of simplicity that, in the eyes of the world, is foolish. Paul wrote the following on this subject:

The foolishness of God is wiser than men; and the weakness of God is stronger than men.   *(1 Cor. 1:25 KJV)*

He is speaking primarily about the cross. The cross was the weakest and most foolish thing that you could conceive of in the culture of that time, but out of the weakness of the cross comes the almightiness of God. Out of the foolishness of the cross comes the unsearchable wisdom of God. So we have to turn to something very weak and very foolish to receive God's wisdom and God's strength.

A little further on in 1 Corinthians, Paul said something very interesting. Because I realize that he was speaking to people with a philosophic background just like I acquired through my studies, I can appreciate it so well.

Let no man deceive himself. If any man among you seemeth to be wise in this world, let him become a fool, that he may be wise.   *(1 Cor. 3:18 KJV)*

You see, between us and God's wisdom is a valley, a place of humility. We have to lay aside worldly wisdom. We have to become fools in the eyes of the world in order that we may really enter into God's wisdom.

At that point, I was confronted with an alternative. I could go on being wise in the world and stay sick, or I could do something that was foolish in the eyes of the world and get healed. I actually have to say, I was much wiser to be foolish and get healed than I would have been to be clever and stay sick. That may sound confusing, but it is exactly what Paul was saying: "If you are wise in this world, you need to become a fool in order that you may be wise, because God's foolishness is much wiser than man's wisdom."

The application is this: *"Let them not depart from thine eyes."* Have a single, simple eye. Read the Bible the way it is written, and take it as meaning what it says.

CHAPTER FIVE

KEEP THEM IN YOUR HEART

We have already looked at the first three directions concerning how to receive God's medicine. Now we are coming to the fourth and final instruction about His words and sayings: *"Keep them in the midst of thine heart."*

This directive is very real to me for two reasons. The first is based on my own experience of being healed through this passage. The second reason is that for five years I was the principal of a college in East Africa that trained African teachers for African schools. Therefore, of course, I had to familiarize myself with some of the principles of teaching. One of the simple principles that we used to try to inculcate knowledge into our students was the principle of what we call the "ear gate" and the "eye gate." When you want to engage a child's total attention, you need to engage every available gate. It is not enough for the child just to hear; the child also needs to see. In fact, we also taught them that a child not only needs to hear and see, but must also become practically involved: hear, see, and do.

It blesses me to see that, in this passage in Proverbs, God anticipated the psychology of modern education theory by about 3,000 years. He said, *"'Incline thine ear....let* [my words and sayings] *not depart from thine eyes'*; then they will get into your heart." You see, the purpose of going through the ear gate and the eye gate is to reach that vital, central area of human personality that the Bible calls the heart. When their hearts are reached, students will do what they promise. But if their hearts are not touched, positive results will not be produced.

In order to be effective, some kinds of medicine that you take must be released into the bloodstream. You can take the medicine, but if it does not get to the bloodstream, it is not going to do what it is supposed to do. Well, God's medicine is only effective when it is released in the heart. The previous three directions are all concerned with the medicine getting where it will do what is promised, which is the heart. Then it says, *"Keep them in the midst of thine heart."*

We need to look on to the very next verse of Proverbs, which is one of the most profound verses in the Bible:

> *Keep thy heart with all diligence; for out of it are the issues of life.* (Prov. 4:23 KJV)

How profound that is: *"Out of [the heart] are the issues of life."*

My mind goes back again to East Africa. One of my students wrote this verse in her own vernacular language, which was called Lorlagoli. I knew just enough to be able to read what she had written on the dormitory wall. It said, "Guard your heart with all of your strength; for all the things in life come out of it." That is so simple, more simple in a sense than the King James Version.

The conviction never left me that all the things in life do come out of your heart. In other words, what you have in your heart will determine all that you experience in your life. If you have the right thing in your heart, your life will go right. If you have the wrong thing in your heart, your life will go wrong.

However, it is what is in your heart that determines the course of your life. So God says, "If My medicine and My words and My sayings are going to do what I have promised, they must get into your heart, and you must keep them there. 'Keep them in the midst of thine heart,' not just on the periphery of your heart, but in the middle. Keep them in the central place of your whole life and personality. They are going to affect the whole way that you live."

To conclude this teaching about God's Word being our medicine, I would like to turn to a parallel statement in the New Testament. Hebrews 4:12 speaks about the nature of

God's Word and how it acts within us. In order to make it vivid, I am going to quote two translations so we can pick out certain differences between the versions. First is the King James Version:

> *For the word of God is quick, and powerful, and sharper than any twoedged sword, piercing even to the dividing asunder of soul and spirit, and of the joints and marrow, and is a discerner of the thoughts and intents of the heart.*

The New American Standard Bible reads as follows:

> *For the word of God is living and active and sharper than any two-edged sword, and piercing as far as the division of soul and spirit, of both joints and marrow, and able to judge the thoughts and intentions of the heart.*

If I were to choose one word that sums this up, I think it would be the word "penetrating." God's Word penetrates. In fact, it penetrates where nothing else can penetrate. We are used to the concept of the surgeon's knife with its sharp, pointed blade that can penetrate so delicately into human tissue. But the Word of God penetrates into another realm. It divides between soul and spirit, the very innermost areas of our personalities. Things within ourselves that we cannot fully understand about ourselves, the Word of God reveals to us. It separates between joint and marrow. It touches the spiritual areas of us, and it touches the physical areas. There is no area of our lives that is out of its reach.

If you have a disease of the marrow or a disease of the joints, this Scripture says that maybe there's no human medicine or human instrument that can deal with it, but the Word of God can get there. If you have inner personality problems for which the psychiatrist does not have a solution, the Word of God will get there. God's Word penetrates.

What is important is that we take God's Word the way He Himself requires that we take it. We must take it with our undivided attention and with a humble, teachable attitude. We must lay down our barriers of prejudice and preconception and look at it with a single, sincere, wholehearted eye. We do not want to quibble, we do not want to theorize too much. We must take it as meaning what it says. We must lay down the barriers of rationalization and sophistication, and then we can let it enter and do its work.

CLOSING PRAYER

Heavenly Father,

I thank you for those who have been reading this book who have spiritual and physical needs that can only be solved by the Word of God. I pray that this word will enter in and do what is necessary in them: create faith, bring healing, bring deliverance, bring peace and joy and harmony. All of this I pray in the name of Jesus. Amen.

GOD'S REMEDY FOR REJECTION

Contents

CHAPTER ONE

THE NATURE OF REJECTION

Almost all of us have experienced rejection at one time or another, but many of us have not understood its nature or its effects. The rejection may have been something relatively minor—or it may have been so devastating that it affected your whole life and all your relationships.

Here are some common examples: you were not chosen to play on a school sports team; your first boyfriend failed to show up for an important date and never gave you a reason; you were not accepted at the college of your choice; you were laid off from your job for no good reason—they said you were "redundant."

Far worse than these examples is the pain that comes because you never felt love from your father, because you sensed your mother didn't want you, or because your marriage ended in divorce.

Experiences such as these leave permanent wounds, whether you are aware of them or not. But I have good news for you! God can heal you from the wounds that come from rejection, help you to accept yourself, and enable you to show His love to others. However, before you can receive His help, you must recognize the nature of your problem.

Rejection can be defined as the sense of being unwanted. You desire people to love you, and yet you believe that they do not. You want to be part of a group, but you feel excluded. Somehow you are always on the outside looking in.

Closely related to rejection are the wounds of betrayal and shame. All produce similar responses in the wounded person, the feeling of not being wanted or accepted.

Sometimes rejection is so wounding and painful that the mind refuses to focus on it. Nevertheless, you know something is there—even though it is deeper than the mind, deeper than the reason, deeper than the memory. It is in your spirit. The book of Proverbs describes this:

A happy heart makes the face cheerful, but heartache crushes the spirit.   *(Prov. 15:13 NIV)*

The writer also told how a crushed spirit will affect a person:

A man's spirit sustains him in sickness, but a crushed spirit who can bear?   *(Prov. 18:14 NIV)*

A vibrant spirit helps a person through great difficulties, but a crushed spirit has a crippling effect in all areas of life.

Our society today is suffering from a progressive breakdown of interpersonal relationships. Quite possibly, you have been caught in the crossfire, and the result has been a wound of rejection. Let me suggest, however, that you should look for a silver lining to that dark cloud.

I believe the Devil has some foreknowledge. He knows God wants to use you, and he has struck his blow first. In a way, it is a kind of twisted compliment. It means that Satan is afraid of what you can become in Christ. So, do not be discouraged. In my experience, I have found that the people who have been the lowest often end up the highest. The Scriptures tell us, *"He who humbles himself will be exalted"* (Luke 18:14 NIV).

There is a verse in Matthew that I believe describes how Jesus feels toward you:

But when He saw the multitudes, He was moved with compassion for them...   *(Matt. 9:36a NKJV)*

The Greek word translated *"compassion"* is amazingly powerful. It implies a forceful, physical reaction in a person's body in the abdominal area. It is a reaction so strong that it demands a response. A person who is *"moved with compassion"* cannot stand by and observe. He must do something. Why was Jesus so moved?

> *...because they were weary and scattered, like sheep having no shepherd.* (Matt. 9:36b NKJV)

That is just how you may feel: weary, harried, frustrated, perplexed, fearful, anxious, burdened down. Jesus sees you, just as He saw the multitudes. He has compassion for you. He is longing to heal you where you hurt the most.

First, we must understand the true nature of rejection. How does rejection occur? What causes the wounding? When we answer these questions, then we can ask, How can wounds of rejection be treated?

About 1964, I often found myself ministering to people who were bound by addictions to substances such as nicotine or alcohol. Very quickly, however, I discovered that addictions such as these are merely twigs that have sprouted from a branch. Normally, the branch that supports them is some form of frustration. Therefore, the practical solution is to deal with the branch. When the branch of frustration is cut off, dealing with the twigs of addiction is relatively easy.

As I continued to wrestle with people's personal problems, I gradually worked my way down the trunk of the tree until I came to the part of the tree that lies below the surface—that is, the roots. It is here that God seeks to work in our lives.

> *And even now the ax is laid to the root of the trees. Therefore every tree which does not bear good fruit is cut down and thrown into the fire.* (Matt. 3:10 NKJV)

From where is the tree cut down? From the roots. When I got down below the surface, I made a discovery that surprised me at first. One of the most common roots of all personal problems is rejection. I reached this conclusion, not as a sociologist or as a psychologist, but as a preacher and a Bible teacher.

Have you ever seen a small child in his father's arms? One little hand clutches the lapel of his father's jacket while his head is pressed against that strong, protective chest. Pressures and tensions may be all around, but the child is not threatened. His face registers total security. He is where he belongs—in his Daddy's arms.

God designed human nature so that every baby born into the world would crave this kind of security. A child can never truly be satisfied, fulfilled, or secure without parental love, particularly love from a father.

Any person who has been deprived of this kind of love is inevitably exposed to the wound of rejection. Almost an entire generation of American fathers have failed their children. Thus, we have a generation of young people whose deepest, most basic problem is rejection.

To this picture of broken relationships between parents and children, we must add the statistics for failed marriages. Today, that covers about half of all marriages. Almost always, one or both parties emerge with a wound of rejection. Very often, there is the added pain of betrayed trust.

When we consider the pressures of today's society, particularly the breakup of family life, my conviction is that at least half of the people in the United States suffer from some form of rejection. No doubt God foresaw this special end-time crisis of broken relationships when He gave this promise in Malachi:

> See, I will send you the prophet Elijah before that great and dreadful day of the LORD comes. He will turn the hearts of the fathers to their children, and the hearts of the children to their fathers; or else I will come and strike the land with a curse. (Mal. 4:5–6 NIV)

The final outcome of rejection caused by broken relationships is a curse. However, for those who will turn to God through Jesus, He has provided healing from this curse.

What form will this healing take? What is the opposite of rejection? Acceptance, of course. This is precisely what God offers you when you come to Him through Jesus. *"He has made us accepted in the Beloved"* (Eph. 1:6 NKJV)—that is, in Jesus.

The original Greek word that is translated here as "accepted" is very powerful. It is much stronger than mere approval. In the New King James Version of Luke 1:28, the same Greek word is translated *"highly favored one."*

When you come to God through Jesus, you are as accepted and as highly favored as Jesus Himself is. Amazing as it may seem, God loves you in just the same way He loves Jesus. You become a member of His own family.

The first step in overcoming rejection is to recognize the problem. Once you recognize it, you can deal with it. You are not alone in this; God will help you recognize it.

Let me give you a practical illustration. During World War II, when I was a medical orderly in the desert in North Africa, I was working with a man who was a brilliant doctor. A bomb fell from an enemy plane and exploded somewhere near us. One of our soldiers was struck with a piece of shrapnel. He came into the medical station with this tiny, black puncture mark in his shoulder. As a result, I was very busy attending to him, cleaning his wound and trying to do the right thing, when I asked the doctor, "Shall I get out a dressing?"

The doctor said, "No, give me the probe." So, I handed him the little silver stick, and he put it in the wound and moved it around. Nothing happened for a few moments. Suddenly, the probe touched the little piece of shrapnel inside, and the patient let out a yelp. The doctor knew he had found the problem.

When I again asked if I should bring the dressing, the doctor replied, "No, bring me the forceps." He put the forceps in and removed the piece of shrapnel. Only then did he want to apply the dressing.

You may be putting a little dressing of religion over a wound that cannot heal because there is something inside that is causing it to fester. However, if you will open your heart to the Holy Spirit, He will reveal the source of the problem. If the Holy Spirit's probe touches a piece of shrapnel, yelp if you must, but don't resist! Ask Him to use His forceps to remove the problem. Then God can apply something that will really heal it.

As you read on, you will discover how you can move from rejection to acceptance. Along the way, you will also learn how to deal with betrayal and shame. After that, I will show you how to let God's divine love flow through you to other people.

I have dealt with many, many people who have successfully recognized and recovered from the wounds of rejection. You can be one of those people through God's grace.

CHAPTER TWO

THE CAUSES OF REJECTION

All human relationships are accompanied by the risk of rejection. Sometimes rejection comes during the school years. Perhaps you wore hand-me-down clothes, or you were of a different race, or you had a physical defect, so you were singled out for ridicule at your school. Many people are disturbed by those who are different. If they do not know how to identify with you, they reject you.

The most damaging kind of rejection comes when a child perceives rejection from a parent. There are, perhaps, three main situations that can cause this wound. First, a child may be unwanted during pregnancy. The mother may be carrying a child in her womb whom she really does not want. She may not say anything, but the attitude is in her heart. The child may have been conceived outside of marriage. She may come to resent and hate this thing that is coming into her life and that will create all kinds of problems for her. Such a child may be born with a spirit of rejection.

I discovered an amazing phenomenon in ministering to people in the United States. Very commonly, people in a certain age group seemed to have this sense of early rejection. When I traced it back, I discovered they had been born during the Great Depression. I came to understand that a mother at that time, with many mouths to feed, could hardly bear the thought of having to struggle with one more child. Her inner attitude wounded that child before it ever came forth from her womb.

A second situation is when a child's parents do not physically demonstrate their love for their child. Bumper stickers used to ask, "Have you hugged your child today?" That is a good question. A child who receives little physical affection or touch tends to become a rejected child.

Even if parents love their child, they may not know how to express their love. I have talked to people recently who say, "I suppose my father loved me, but he never knew how to show it. All his life, he never sat me on his knee; he never did anything to show me that he loved me." It may be that the child feels rejection from the mother, instead, but in either case the child thinks, "I'm unwanted."

If you talk to many children today who are bitter and rebellious toward their parents, they will tell you this: "Our parents gave us clothes and an education and a car and a swimming pool, but they never gave us time. They never gave us themselves."

This, I think, is one reason for the bitter reaction we saw in the 1960s of young people against the older generations. It was a reaction against loveless materialism. Many of those young people who became so bitter and rebellious were from rather privileged, wealthy homes. They had been given everything except love, which was the thing they wanted and needed most.

This form of rejection may also affect a child whose parents have divorced. Usually, it is the mother who is left to care for the children by herself. The child of such a divorce may have had a warm, loving relationship with the father, but suddenly the father is no longer there. His leaving creates an aching void in the child's heart.

If the father has gone off with another woman, the child's reaction is twofold: bitterness toward the father and hatred toward the other woman. What the child now has is a deep wound of rejection, something that says, "The person I loved and trusted the most has abandoned me. From now on I can never trust anyone."

Often, too, the mother, with many new responsibilities thrust upon her, may not be able to give the child the affection she formerly lavished upon him or her. In this case, the child experiences a double rejection: from the father and from the mother.

A third rejection-producing circumstance occurs when siblings perceive unequal affection from their parents, whether it is intentional or not. I have noticed that a family with three children may have a first child who is clever and knows all the answers. As the first child, he enjoys a natural priority. The next child comes along and is not so brilliant. Then the third child is cute and bright. The second child continually feels inferior to the others. Somehow, the parents are always praising the oldest child or the youngest, but they do not say much about the middle child. In many cases, that middle child feels rejected and unwanted. He or she thinks, "My parents love my older brother and my younger sister, but they don't love me."

On the other hand, instead of one child in the family experiencing rejection, sometimes one child receives an unfair measure of love and attention at the expense of the siblings. The other children, just by comparing themselves with that particularly favored child, feel rejected.

I remember a story about a mother who had several daughters but favored one above the rest. One day, she heard a sound in another room. Thinking it was the daughter she particularly loved, she called out, "Is that you, darling?" The discouraged voice of another daughter was heard in reply, "No, it's only me."

Then the mother realized the impact that her favoritism for the one daughter had left on the others. She repented and sought to repair the damaged relationships with all of her children.

Let me give you another example of how rejection can occur at a very young age and of the spiritual impact it can have on a child. Many years ago, I was conducting services at a church in Miami. While visiting one of the parishioners at home a few nights earlier, I had done something I rarely do. I said to the woman, "Sister, if I'm correct, you have the spirit of death in you."

She had every reason to be happy, but she never was. She had a good husband and children, yet she hardly ever smiled or looked happy. She was like a person in continual mourning. Although I very rarely make that kind of statement to anybody, I felt I had to say something to her that night.

I said, "I'm preaching on Friday night in Miami. If you come, I'll pray for you."

At the beginning of the meeting, I noticed her sitting in the front row. Once again, I did something I do not usually do. At a certain point in the service, I walked over to her and said, "You spirit of death, in the name of Jesus, I command you to answer me now. When did you enter this woman?"

And the spirit, not the woman, answered very clearly, "When she was two years old."

I said, "How did you get in?"

Again, it was the spirit that answered, "Oh, she felt rejected; she felt unwanted; she felt lonely."

Later that evening, the woman was delivered from the spirit of death, but for several days that incident kept coming back to my mind. It gave me a new understanding of the effect that rejection can have on a person's life. It is not merely evil in itself, but it also opens the door for various other negative, destructive forces to move in and gradually take over a person's life. Rejection truly is a root from which much that is harmful can grow.

Since that time, I have dealt with several hundred people who needed and received deliverance from the spiritual effects of rejection.

The woman in that example was obviously distressed, but rejection is not always outwardly visible. Rejection can be a hidden, inner attitude that we carry around. The problem lies in the area of the spirit. I have learned by experience that every negative emotion, reaction, and attitude have associated with them a corresponding spirit. Behind fear is a spirit of fear; behind jealousy is a spirit of jealousy; behind hate is a spirit of hate.

This does not mean that every person who experiences fear, for instance, has a spirit of fear. However, a person who fails to exercise self-control and habitually or unrestrainedly gives in to fear will probably open the way for a spirit of fear to enter. After that, the person is no longer in full control of himself or herself.

This also applies to other emotions such as jealousy or hate. In many cases, rejection opens the way for the other negative spirits to follow. As already stated, rejection is a root from which many destructive emotions and attitudes may grow.

Here is an example of how the process may work. A young girl feels rejected by her father and hates him because he is critical and unloving. This hatred deepens to a point where she can no longer suppress it.

When she becomes an adult, she marries and has children of her own. In due course, she finds herself hating one of her own children. Her hatred is vicious and unreasonable, but she cannot control it. This is a spirit of hate. When the father is no longer present, the hatred is directed against some other family member.

Another effect of the spirit of hatred may cause her to hate all men. She may even become a lesbian and avoid all healthy contact with men.

In the next chapter, we turn to a form of rejection that far too many people have experienced in deep, close relationships— betrayal of trust. I also describe how shame often accompanies this kind of experience.

CHAPTER THREE

BETRAYAL AND SHAME

Previously, we discussed some of the primary causes of rejection in early childhood. As we grow older, we expose ourselves to the possibility of even more rejection as the bonds of intimate, close relationships form in us. If we are rejected in one of these relationships, especially by a marriage partner, the pain is compounded because it involves broken trust, and thus it becomes betrayal.

Like most other ministers, numerous times I have counseled wives who felt that they had lost everything. They trusted their husbands and gave themselves unreservedly. Then their husbands left them. The wives felt betrayed. I have also talked to husbands who have been betrayed by their wives. I have also seen many other varieties of betrayal.

Have you been betrayed? How have you responded?

When someone betrays you, you may say, "I'll never open myself up again. No one will ever get another chance to hurt me like that." That is a natural reaction, but it is also dangerous. It will open you up to a second problem, defensiveness, which is the reaction of somebody who has been hurt once too often. Defensiveness says, "All right, I'll go through life, but I will never let anybody come near enough to hurt me like that again. I'll always keep a wall between me and other people."

Do you know who suffers? You do. Your personality shrivels, becoming incomplete. You grow as a tree does when its main trunk is lopped off—in a distorted manner. In Isaiah we find a vivid picture of what betrayal is like. The Lord was comforting His people Israel through Isaiah. God painted for them a picture of their condition as He saw it. He compared them to a wife who has been rejected by her husband. This same situation is distressingly all too familiar for millions of women today, yet the Lord still offers these same comforting words:

"Do not be afraid; you will not suffer shame. Do not fear disgrace; you will not be humiliated. You will forget the shame of your youth and remember no more the reproach of your widowhood. For your Maker is your husband—the LORD Almighty is his name—the Holy One of Israel is your Redeemer; he is called the God of all the earth. The LORD will call you back as if you were a wife deserted and distressed in spirit—a wife who married young, only to be rejected," says your God.   (Isa. 54:4–6 NIV)

The illustration reaches its zenith in the last verse with the image of a *"wife deserted and distressed in spirit—a wife who married young, only to be rejected."* Many of you may know how that feels.

Sometimes it is the other way around; sometimes the wife rejects her husband. Although we regard men as somehow being stronger than women, I know from the many cases with which I have dealt that a man who feels rejected by his wife can suffer inexpressible agony. He may feel he has failed as a man. In some ways, perhaps, it is harder for a man to experience that kind of hurt because he feels ashamed of it. Our society expects men to be impervious to emotional pain.

This vivid picture in Isaiah highlights two things that are commonly associated with betrayal in marriage. Through Isaiah, the Lord says, *"You will not suffer shame....You will not be humiliated."* To have given yourself without reservation to another person, to have poured out your love upon him, to have made yourself available to him, and then to discover that he has rejected you—the sum of all that can bring with it shame and humiliation.

You are suffering from shame if somehow you feel that you are not fit to meet other people or that you cannot look anyone straight in the face. People who are suffering from shame will often avert or lower their eyes when approached by another person. Shame is debilitating, and it keeps us from functioning as healthy human beings.

In addition to betrayal through divorce, two other common ways in which shame affects a person's spirit are through public humiliation and child abuse.

Public humiliation often happens in a school setting. For example, my wife and I were acquainted with a fine, young Jewish man—we will call him Max—who had accepted the Messiah but still had problems. As we were speaking with him one time, I detected a sense of shame. When we asked him about this, his mind went back to high school. At the end of the school year, the headmaster had announced in front of all the other students that Max was the only one who had failed and that he would have to repeat his classes the following year.

From that time on, Max was never exactly the person he ought to have been. He covered it up. He was very active and aggressive in order to prove he was the best. However, if you have to struggle all the time to prove you are as good as others, something is wrong. Max needed to recognize and acknowledge shame at work in his life.

Another way betrayal and shame come in is through sexual or physical abuse in childhood. Both are distressingly common in our society. A child may not be free to tell anyone else about it. Often it is a parent, grandparent, or another relative who is responsible for the abuse. The abused child never knows whether to trust that relative again. Thus, the person continually struggles with mixed attitudes: on the one hand, mistrust; on the other, the obligation to show respect. How can a child honor a parent who has abused him or her?

A person may go through life without ever resolving that tension. It remains a shameful secret. However, you can always open up to the Lord and tell Him all your hidden secrets. You never embarrass or shock Him, and He will never reject you. You can tell Him the worst thing that ever happened to you, and He will respond, "I knew it all along, and I still love you."

Even though God offers us full acceptance, our realization of His love is often blocked by the far-reaching consequences of rejection, betrayal, and shame, which I will describe in the next chapter.

101

THE RESULTS OF REJECTION

I believe the primary result of rejection is the inability to receive or communicate love. A person who has never experienced being loved cannot transmit love. Scripture expresses that truth this way:

We love because [God] first loved us.

(1 John 4:19 NIV)

It is the love of God that stimulates our love for Him in response. Love lies dormant until it is stimulated by another person. Without such interaction, love never comes to life.

Hence, if a person does not know the love of God or parents, an inability to love can be passed from generation to generation. For example, a little girl is born into a family where she does not experience love. She has a wound of rejection, so she cannot communicate love. She grows up, marries, becomes a mother, and has a daughter. Because she cannot communicate love to her daughter, her daughter has the same problem. Thus, this terrible problem is perpetuated from generation to generation.

In ministering to such people, I have often said, "At some point this thing must be stopped. Why not let it happen now so that you don't continue passing on rejection to the next generation? Is rejection the legacy you want to leave to your children?"

God spoke through Ezekiel that children should not be obligated to suffer for what their ancestors did wrong:

The word of the LORD came to me: "What do you people mean by quoting this proverb about the land of Israel: 'The fathers eat sour grapes, and the children's teeth are set on edge'? As surely as I live, declares the Sovereign LORD, you will no longer quote this proverb in Israel. For every living soul belongs to me, the father as well as the son—both alike belong to me. The soul who sins is the one who will die....He [who] *follows my decrees and faithfully keeps my laws. That man is righteous; he will surely live, declares the Sovereign LORD."* (Ezek. 18:1–4, 9 NIV)

Thus, even if your parents never showed you love, God does not want you or your children to suffer for their mistakes. By accepting God's provision, you can cut off that evil inheritance once and for all.

Besides an inability to show love, there are other secondary results of rejection. I would say rejection produces three kinds of people: the person who gives in, the person who holds out, and the person who fights back.

First, let's look at the person who gives in. This type of person thinks, "I just can't take this. Life is too much for me. There is really nothing I can do."

I have learned by experience in dealing with such people that it opens the way for a descending series of negative emotions or attitudes that goes like this:

rejection

⇩

loneliness

⇩

self-pity

⇩

misery

⇩

depression

⇩

despair or hopelessness

⇩

death or suicide

The final result is tragic. Many, of course, stop short of it, yet it is the logical outcome of the process that is set in motion by rejection. Whether it takes the form of death or of suicide depends on the emotional makeup of each person. Someone whose reactions are essentially passive will ultimately succumb to death. Rejection is, in fact, a contributing factor in many deaths that are attributed merely to natural causes.

A person who follows the path to death has an inner desire to die. Have you ever made a remark such as, "I'd be better off dead" or "What's the use of living?" That is a very dangerous way to speak. It is an invitation to the spirit of death to enter.

In contrast, a person with a more aggressive attitude will turn to suicide as a radical solution. Such people may also ask themselves, "What's the use of living?" However, they will add, "I might as well end it all."

Often, the more aggressive person sees suicide as a way to hurt those who have caused his pain. The inner thought pattern is something like this: "I'll get even with them. Now they'll suffer the way I have!"

The latest figures for suicides among young people in America are frightening. More than five thousand youths between the ages of five and twenty-four committed suicide in 1990, according to National Center for Health statistics.

In most cases, the undiagnosed root cause of these suicides was rejection. They probably could not express it in words, but deep down, these young people felt unwanted and unimportant.

Are you beginning to realize that you have some of the symptoms I have described? If you find you are losing control over your own responses, it may well be that you are not just struggling with your own negative attitudes. A demonic influence may be at work exploiting those attitudes.

Do not close your mind to this possibility. Coming to grips with your problem can be a big step toward overcoming it. In a later chapter, I will show you how to pray against this kind of evil influence.

The second personality pattern produced by rejection is the type of person who refuses to give in and builds some kind of defense. This is really a facade, something that covers up the inner agony and struggle.

Someone who is building up a defense for himself usually develops a kind of superficial happiness. The person appears to be outgoing and is probably talkative, but the voice has a hollow, metallic ring to it. A woman practicing this facade often overdoes her makeup. Her frequent gestures are exaggerated. Her voice is a little louder than is pleasant. She is desperately trying to appear happy, as though she is not hurt, as though nothing is wrong inside, as though her life is perfect. What she is really thinking inside is, "I've been hurt so badly that I'm never going to give another person the opportunity to hurt me like that again. I will not let anyone come close enough to hurt me."

This type of reaction is often the response to betrayal, as I mentioned earlier. There are uncounted thousands of such people in American society today.

The third type of person becomes a fighter—one who fights everything. The order in which his reactions to rejection develop is usually like this: first, resentment; second, hatred; and finally, rebellion. Rebellion and witchcraft are twins, according to Scripture:

For rebellion is as the sin of witchcraft.
(1 Sam. 15:23 NKJV)

The sin of witchcraft means participating in the occult, which is the search for false spiritual experiences. The occult includes such things as Ouija boards, horoscopes, fortune tellers, séances, drugs—that whole realm. This sin is really the expression of rebellion. It is turning from the true God to a false god. It is the breaking of the first commandment, *"You shall have no other gods before me"* (Exod. 20:3 NIV).

Basically, the generation of young people growing up in the 1960s went the way of resentment, hatred, rebellion, and very often the occult. As I mentioned earlier, it was not because they were denied material things. Rather, it was because they did not feel loved, which was the one thing they really wanted.

Next, we will find out what Jesus has done to heal the wounds of rejection.

CHAPTER FIVE

THE ULTIMATE REJECTION

Everything that God provides in the Gospel is based on fact. This can be summed up in three progressive *fs*—facts, faith, and feelings. The Gospel is based on three simple facts: Christ died for our sins according to the Scriptures, He was buried, and He rose again on the third day. First Corinthians 15:3–4 indicates that these facts are the basis of the whole Gospel. They are the *facts*.

Faith appropriates these facts. Faith begins with the facts; it accepts, believes, and acts on them. Then, after facts and faith are feelings.

It makes all the difference in your life whether your faith is based on facts or on feelings. If it is based on feelings, you will be a very inconsistent, unstable person. Your feelings may change as circumstances change, but the facts will never change. If we are to make progress as Christians, we have to learn to believe the facts, even when our feelings cause us to doubt them.

To receive God's provision for rejection, there are two basic facts you must lay hold of. First of all, God did not make a lot of different provisions for each of the various needs of humanity. Instead, He made one all-inclusive provision that covers all the needs of all people: the sacrificial death of Jesus on the cross.

Second, what took place on the cross was an exchange that God Himself had planned. All the evil consequences of our sins came upon Jesus so that, in return, all the benefits of Jesus' sinless obedience might be made available to us. For our part, we have done nothing to deserve this, and we have no merits or rights by which we can claim it. It proceeded solely out of the unfathomable love of God.

Therefore, it is futile to approach God on the basis of some merit or virtue that we may imagine we possess. Nothing we have to offer of ourselves can be compared with the merit of the sacrifice that Jesus offered on our behalf. In contrast to the pure, holy Son of God dying in payment for our sins, *"all our righteous acts are like filthy rags"* (Isa. 64:6 NIV).

This wonderful revelation has been summed up in a simple couplet:

> How sovereign, wonderful, and free
> The love of God for sinful me!

As you read the following verses, you will discover various aspects of the exchange that took place on the cross.

Christ redeemed us from the curse of the law by becoming a curse for us, for it is written: "Cursed is everyone who is hung on a tree." He redeemed us in order that the blessing given to Abraham might come to the Gentiles.
(Gal. 3:13–14 NIV)

God made him who had no sin to be sin for us, so that in him we might become the righteousness of God.
(2 Cor. 5:21 NIV)

For you know the grace of our Lord Jesus Christ, that though he was rich, yet for your sakes he became poor, so that you through his poverty might become rich.
(2 Cor. 8:9 NIV)

He [Jesus] suffered death, so that by the grace of God he might taste death for everyone. *(Heb. 2:9 NIV)*

Do you see the exchange? Christ took our curse so that we might have His blessing. He took our sin in order that we might have His righteousness. He took our poverty so that we might have His wealth. He took our death in order that we might have His life. Isn't that beautiful?

This exchange also has implications for us concerning shame and rejection. The writer of Hebrews said,

*Let us fix our eyes on Jesus, the author and perfecter of our faith, who for the joy set before him endured the cross, scorning its **shame**.* (Heb. 12:2 NIV, emphasis added)

Jesus was well aware of the shame and public humiliation that He would experience on the cross. In fact, one of the primary objectives of crucifixion was to shame the person. As the person hung naked on the cross, spectators walked by, made derogatory remarks, and sometimes even did obscene things, which I will not describe.

In a prophetic vision, Isaiah glimpsed the sufferings of Jesus seven centuries before they actually took place:

I offered my back to those who beat me, my cheeks to those who pulled out my beard; I did not hide my face from mocking and spitting. (Isa. 50:6 NIV)

Jesus willingly endured mocking for us on the cross. What does God offer us in return? Again, we turn to Isaiah:

Instead of their shame my people will receive a double portion, and instead of disgrace they will rejoice in their inheritance. (Isa. 61:7 NIV)

In place of the word *"disgrace,"* I would say *embarrassment* or *humiliation*. Instead of personal shame, embarrassment, and humiliation, God offers us honor and joy. Hebrews 2:10 further tells us that through the suffering and death of Jesus, God purposed to bring *"many sons to glory"* (NIV). Joy, honor, glory—all are offered to us in the place of shame and humiliation. Now we come to the deepest wound of all—rejection. Jesus endured a double rejection: first by men and then by God Himself. Isaiah clearly portrayed the rejection of Jesus by His fellow countrymen:

*He was despised and **rejected** by men, a man of sorrows, and familiar with suffering. Like one from whom men hide their faces he was despised, and we esteemed him not.* (Isa. 53:3 NIV, emphasis added)

Still worse things were to happen to our Savior. The last moments of Jesus on the cross are described in Matthew:

From the sixth hour [midday] *until the ninth hour* [three o'clock in the afternoon] *darkness came over all the land. About the ninth hour Jesus cried out in a loud voice, "Eloi, Eloi, lama sabachthani?"—which means, "My God, my God, why have you forsaken me?" When some of those standing there heard this, they said, "He's calling Elijah." Immediately one of them ran and got a sponge. He filled it with wine vinegar, put it on a stick, and offered it to Jesus to drink. The rest said, "Now leave him alone. Let's see if Elijah comes to save him." And when Jesus had cried out again in a loud voice, he gave up his spirit. At that moment the curtain of the temple was torn in two from top to bottom.* (Matt. 27:45–51 NIV)

For the first time in the history of the universe, the Son of God prayed but the Father did not answer Him. God averted His eyes from His Son. God stopped His ears at His cry. Why? Because, at that time, Jesus was identified with our sin. The attitude of God the Father toward Jesus had to be the attitude of God's holiness toward our sin—the refusal of fellowship, a complete and absolute rejection. Jesus did not endure that for His own sake, but instead to make His soul a sin offering for us.

It means a lot to me that Jesus spoke in Aramaic at that agonizing moment on the cross. I have witnessed this behavior when visiting people in the hospital. When people are under real pressure, desperately sick, maybe at death's door, they often revert to the language they first learned in childhood. I have observed this many times, but I remember it so vividly with my first wife, Lydia. As she breathed her last, she whispered, *"Tak for blodet; tak for blodet,"* which means "Thank You for the blood" in Danish, her mother tongue.

This passage gives such a clear picture of the humanity of Jesus: as He suffered intense pain and agony, His mind went back to the language He had spoken in His childhood home. He cried out in Aramaic.

Think of that awful darkness. Think of the loneliness, the sense of being absolutely abandoned—first by man, then by

God. You and I may have experienced some measure of rejection, but never has it been in that measure. Jesus drained the cup of rejection to its bitter dregs. He should have been able to live several hours longer on the cross, but He died of a broken heart. What broke His heart? The ultimate rejection.

And then, look at the consequence, which was so dramatic, so immediate:

> *At that moment the curtain of the temple was torn in two from top to bottom.*

What does that mean? Simply that the barrier between God and man had been removed. The way was opened for man to come to God without shame, without guilt, without fear. Jesus took our rejection so that we might experience His acceptance. That is the meaning of the torn curtain. The rejection by His Father was more than Jesus could bear. But, thank God, the result for us is direct access to God.

Look now at how God has worked out and completed our acceptance:

> *Praise be to the God and Father of our Lord Jesus Christ, who has blessed us in the heavenly realms with every spiritual blessing in Christ. For he chose us in him before the creation of the world to be holy and blameless in his sight. In love he predestined us to be adopted as his sons through Jesus Christ, in accordance with his pleasure and will—to the praise of his glorious grace, which he has freely given us in the One he loves.* (Eph. 1:3–6 NIV)

What was God's eternal purpose, even before creation? That we might become His children, His sons and daughters. That could only be achieved through the substitutionary death of Jesus on the cross. When Jesus bore our sins and suffered our rejection, He opened the way for our acceptance. For just that time, Christ lost His status as God's Son in order that we might gain status as God's sons and daughters.

The New King James Version offers a special insight into this passage: *"To the praise of the glory of His grace, by which*

He has made us accepted in the Beloved" (v. 6). That is the remedy for rejection—the realization that Jesus bore your rejection so that you might have His acceptance.

Ponder the depth of that revelation! We are the objects of God's particular loving care and attention. We are number one on His list of things to take care of in the universe. He does not push us away into a corner and say, "Wait over there. I'm busy. I don't have time for you now." And never does some angel say, "Don't make a noise. Daddy is sleeping."

God says, "Come in. You are welcome. I am interested in you. I love and want you. I've been waiting a long time for you."

In the parable of the prodigal son in Luke 15:11–32, God's heart toward us is represented by the father, who longed for his son to return so much that he was out watching. No one had to come and tell him, "Your son is coming home." The first one to know it was the father. God's attitude toward us in Christ is like that father's. We are not rejects; we are not second-class citizens; we are not slaves.

When the Prodigal came back, he was willing to be a servant. He intended to say, *"Father…make me like one of your hired men"* (Luke 15:18–19 NIV). But as the Prodigal confessed his sins, his father cut his words off and never allowed him to say, "Make me one of your hired servants."

On the contrary, the father said, "Bring out the best robe. Put shoes on his feet, a ring on his finger. Kill the fatted calf! We're going to have a good time. *'For this son of mine was dead and is alive again; he was lost and is found'* (v. 24 NIV)."

The whole household was turned upside down to welcome the Prodigal as he returned. It is like that in heaven. Jesus said, *"There will be more rejoicing in heaven over one sinner who repents than over ninety-nine righteous persons who do not need to repent"* (Luke 15:7 NIV). That is how God welcomes us in Christ.

Here, then, are the two facts you need to lay hold of: First of all, Christ bore our rejection on the cross, along with all of the shame and betrayal, agony and heartache. In fact, He died of a broken heart. Second, we are accepted because of His rejection. We are *"accepted in the Beloved."* It was an exchange. Jesus bore the evil so that we might receive the good. He carried our sorrows so we might have His joy.

111

Sometimes, all you need is to grasp these two facts. Several years ago at a big camp meeting, as I was on my way to a preaching assignment, I literally bumped into a lady who was going rapidly in the opposite direction. Breathlessly, she said, "Oh, Brother Prince, I was praying that if God wanted me to speak to you, we would meet."

"Well," I said, "we've met! What's the problem? I can give you about two minutes because I'm due to preach." She started to talk, but after about half a minute, I interrupted her. "Wait, I know what your problem is. I don't need to hear any more," I said. "Your problem is rejection. I've got the answer. Listen. I want you to pray these words out loud after me."

I did not tell her in advance what I was going to say. I simply prayed extemporaneously, and she followed me phrase by phrase.

> Father God,
>
> I thank You that You love me; that You gave Jesus, Your Son, to die on my behalf; that He bore my sin; that He took my rejection; that He paid my penalty. Because I come to You through Him, I am not rejected; I am not unwanted; I am not excluded. You really love me. I am really Your child. You are really my Father. I belong in Your family. I belong to the best family in the universe. Heaven is my home. I really belong. Oh, God, thank You, thank You.

After we finished, I said, "Amen, good-bye, I have to go," and took off.

About a month later, I got a letter from the lady. After describing the encounter, she said, "I want to tell you, those two minutes you spent with me and the prayer that I prayed have completely changed the whole of my life. I've been a different person ever since."

As I read her letter, I understood what had happened to her at the moment of praying: she had passed from rejection to acceptance.

God's family is the best family. There is no family quite equal to the family of God. Even if your own family did not care for you, your own father rejected you, your mother never had time for you, or your husband never showed you love, bear in mind that God wants you. You are accepted; you are highly favored; you are the object of His special care and affection. Everything He does in the universe revolves around you.

Paul said to the Corinthians—who were not exactly top-class Christians—"*All this is for your benefit*" (2 Cor. 4:15 NIV). Everything God does, He does for us. You will not get conceited when you realize that—instead, it will humble you. There is no room left for conceit when you see the grace of God.

It is most significant that, before His crucifixion, Jesus' last prayer with His disciples was for those who followed Him then as well as for those who would follow afterward. (See John 17:20.) That prayer concerned our relationship with God as our Father and ended this way:

> *Righteous Father, though the world does not know you, I know you, and they know that you have sent me. I have made you known to them...*   (John 17:25–26a NIV)

How did Jesus make God known to us? As Father. The Jews had known God as Yahweh for fourteen centuries, but the only Person who could introduce Him as Father was His Son. Six times in this prayer for His disciples, Jesus addressed God as Father (vv. 1, 5, 11, 21, 24, 25).

When Jesus prayed, "*...and* [I] *will continue to make you known...*" (v. 26b NIV), He was saying that He would continue to reveal God as Father. Then we come to the purpose of this revelation:

> *...in order that the love you have for me may be in them and that I myself may be in them.*   (v. 26c NIV)

I understand this to mean that because Jesus is in us, God has exactly the same love for us as He has for Jesus. We are as dear to God as Jesus Himself is. However, there is also another aspect to this. Because Jesus is in us, we can love God in the same way that Jesus loves Him.

This represents the ultimate purpose of the earthly ministry of Jesus: to bring us into the same love relationship that exists between the Father and the Son. This has two aspects: not only does the Father have the same love for us that He has for Jesus, but also we can reciprocate with the same love for the Father that Jesus has.

The Beloved Apostle told us, *"There is no fear in love. But perfect love drives out fear"* (1 John 4:18 NIV). As we develop this love relationship with God, it leaves no room for guilt, for insecurity, or for rejection.

Perhaps you have unhappy memories of a human father. God intended every father to demonstrate what He Himself is, but many fathers have failed. Yet you still have a heavenly Father who loves you, who understands you, who thinks the best of you, and who plans the best for you. He will never abandon you, never misunderstand you, never take sides against you; nor will He ever reject you.

For some, the simple declaration of acceptance in Christ and the fatherhood of God resolves the problem of rejection. But for others, that may not be enough to solve the issue. If you feel that your situation is not yet resolved, you may need further help. Follow on with me in the next chapter as I explain certain practical steps you can take to make God's provision effective in your life.

CHAPTER SIX

HOW TO APPLY THE REMEDY

By this point, you have allowed the Holy Spirit to insert His probe into your wound, and He has exposed the foreign body that was causing the pain and the infection. Are you now ready to accept God's remedy? If so, there are five successive steps you need to follow.

Step 1. Recognize the nature of your problem and call it by its right name—rejection. God always has to bring us to the moment of truth, even though it may seem devastating and extremely painful, before we can receive His help.

Step 2. Take Jesus as your pattern.

> *Because Christ suffered for you, leaving you an example,*
> *that you should follow in his steps.*   *(1 Pet. 2:21 NIV)*

How did Jesus meet rejection? For three-and-a-half years, He had completely given His life to doing good, to forgiving sin, to delivering demon-oppressed people, to healing sickness. At the end of that period, the Roman ruler offered a choice to Jesus' own people, the Jews. He was willing to release from prison either Jesus of Nazareth or a criminal named Barabbas, who was guilty of political insurrection and murder.

By one of the most amazing and tragic decisions in all of human history, the people rejected Jesus and chose Barabbas. So, the mob cried out, "Away with Jesus! Crucify Him! We don't want Him. We'll have Barabbas, the rebel and the murderer." (See Luke 23:13–25.)

In response, Jesus prayed for those who had crucified Him,

Father, forgive them, for they do not know what they are doing. (v. 34 NIV)

The second step, therefore, is to forgive. This is not an easy thing to do. In fact, left to yourself, you are incapable of doing so. However, you are not left to yourself. As you come to this moment, the Holy Spirit is right there with you. If you will yield to Him, He will give you the supernatural grace you need.

You may say, "But the person who hurt me is dead, so why do I need to forgive him?" Whether he is dead or alive is not important. It is for your sake that you are forgiving, not for the other person.

I know a fine, young, Christian man who heard this message. He realized that for years he had carried bitterness, resentment, anger, and rebellion against his father, who was dead. He took his wife on a journey of several hundred miles to the cemetery where his father was buried. Leaving his wife in the car, he went alone to his father's grave. He knelt there and for the next several hours emptied out all his poisonous attitudes. He did not get up until he knew he had forgiven his father. When he walked out of that cemetery, he was a different person. His wife testifies today that she has a brand-new husband. His father had died, but his resentment had remained very much alive.

There is something especially important about parent-child relationships. Young people in particular need to remember this.

The only one of the Ten Commandments with a promise directly attached to it is this:

Honor your father and your mother, as the LORD your God has commanded you, so that you may live long and that it may go well with you. (Deut. 5:16 NIV)

You can be sure of this: if you do not honor your parents, your life will never go well; but if you do, God will favor you with a long, blessed life. (See Ephesians 6:2–3.)

You may say to me, "My mother was a prostitute; my father was an alcoholic. Do you expect me to honor them?" Yes, I do:

not as a prostitute and not as an alcoholic, but as your mother and father. It is God's requirement.

When I was newly saved and baptized in the Holy Spirit, I thought I knew so much more than my parents. Mark Twain once quipped that when he came back home after he had been away for a number of years, he was surprised at how much his parents had learned in the meantime! Well, I was like that, but one day God showed me this principle: If you want it to go well with you, you have to learn to honor your parents. My parents have both passed away now, but I thank God that I really learned to show them honor. I think that is one reason why it goes well with me.

I have seen both sides of this principle. I have seen the people who honored their parents and were blessed, and I have seen the people who refused to do it, and their lives never really went well for them. Their lives were never totally blessed of God.

The failure to forgive is one of the most common barriers to God's blessing. This principle also applies to the relationship between husbands and wives. I remember talking to a lady who had come to me for prayer and deliverance. I said to her, "You are going to have to forgive your husband."

She said, "After he ruined fifteen years of my life and ran off with another woman?"

I said, "Well, do you want him to ruin the rest of your life? If so, just keep on resenting him, because that will do it."

Remember, it is not the one who is resented that suffers the most. It is the one who resents. As somebody said about the man with the ulcer: "It's not what the man is eating; it's what's eating the man."

Forgiveness is not an emotion; it is a decision. Do not say, "I can't." In actuality, you are saying, "I won't." If you can say, "I won't," you can also say, "I will." Your fleshly nature may not be able to forgive, but you can choose to forgive by asking God to work His forgiveness in and through you. When the Holy Spirit enables you (and He will), you *can* forgive—if you *will*.

Step 3. Make a conscious decision to get rid of the bad fruit that rejection has produced in your life, such as bitterness, resentment, hatred, and rebellion. Remember that young man in the cemetery! These things are poison. If you nourish them in your heart, they will poison your whole life. They will cause you deep emotional problems and quite likely physical problems also. Say with a decision of your will: "I lay down bitterness, resentment, hatred, and rebellion."

Counselors say to cured alcoholics, "Resentment is a luxury you can no longer afford." That is true for all of us. No one can afford resentment. It is too expensive.

Step 4. In this step you simply need to receive and believe what God has already done for you.

> [God] *has made us **accepted in the Beloved**.*
> *(Eph. 1:6 NKJV, emphasis added)*

When you come to God through Jesus, you discover that you are already accepted. God has no second-class children. He does not just tolerate you. He loves you. He is interested in you. He cares for you. Look at these beautiful words in Ephesians:

> [God] *chose us in* [Christ] *before the foundation of the world, that we should be holy and without blame before Him in love, having predestined us to adoption as sons by Jesus Christ to Himself, according to the good pleasure of His will, to the praise of the glory of His grace, by which He has made us accepted in the Beloved.* *(vv. 4–6 NKJV)*

God's purpose from eternity was to make us His children, which He accomplished through the death of Jesus for us on the cross. The only thing you need to do is to believe that God wants you to be His child. When you come to God through Jesus, He has already accepted you.

Step 5. Accept yourself. Sometimes this is the hardest step of all. I tell Christians, "Never belittle yourself. Never criticize yourself. You did not make yourself. God made you."

Ephesians 2:10 tells us, *"We are God's workmanship"* (NIV). The Greek word translated here as *"workmanship"* is *poiema,* from which we derive the English word *poem.* It suggests an artistic achievement. We are God's masterpieces. Of all God created, He has devoted the most time and care to us.

Amazingly enough, He went to the scrap heap for His material! You may be looking back over a record of failures and false starts—over a broken marriage, over children who went wrong, over financial disaster. You may label yourself a failure, but God calls you, "My son, My daughter." You can accept yourself because God has accepted you. When you come to God in Jesus, you become a new creation.

> *Therefore, if anyone is in Christ, he is a new creation; old things have passed away; behold, all things have become new. Now all* [this is] *of God, who has reconciled us to Himself through Jesus Christ.* (2 Cor. 5:17–18 NKJV)

You can no longer evaluate yourself on the basis of the way you lived before you came to Christ, because you have become a new creation since then. Now, your only true standard of self-evaluation is what God says about who you have become in Jesus. As you repeatedly declare who you are in Christ according to God's Word, you will begin to override the old, negative self-talk and learn to accept yourself.

Have you followed through those five steps? If so, it is time now for you to claim your release and to pray a prayer that will set the seal on what you have learned about God's acceptance of you.

You can pray simply in your own words. But if you are not quite sure what to say, here is a pattern prayer that you may make your own:

Lord Jesus Christ,

I believe that You are the Son of God and the only way to God. You died on the cross for my sins, and You rose again from the dead. I repent of all my sins, and I forgive every other person as I would have God forgive me. I forgive all those who have rejected me and hurt me and failed to show me love, Lord, and I trust You to forgive me.

I believe, Lord, that You do accept me. Right now, because of what You did for me on the cross, I am accepted. I am highly favored. I am the object of Your special care. You really love me. You want me. Your Father is my Father. Heaven is my home. I am a member of the family of God, the best family in the universe. I am accepted. Thank You! Thank You!

One more thing, Lord. I accept myself the way You made me. I am Your workmanship, and I thank You for what You have done. I believe that You have begun a good work in me and You will carry it on to completion until my life ends.

And now, Lord, I proclaim my release from any dark, evil spirit that took advantage of the wounds in my life. I release my spirit to rejoice in You. In Your precious name, Amen.

This is the moment to be released from any evil spirit that may have been tormenting you. If you feel some force struggling against the prayer you have just prayed, that is an evil spirit. Quite possibly a word may form in your mind—rejection, resentment, self-pity, hatred, death, or other similar names. That is the Holy Spirit revealing the identity of your enemy. Renounce it by name, and then release it. No matter what way it manifests itself, you must expel it. Breathe it out, sob it out, or scream it out—but get it out!

This is the moment you have been longing for. Don't worry about your dignity right now! Accept all the help the Holy Spirit gives you.

As you experience release, begin to praise God out loud: "Lord, I thank You. Lord, I praise You. Lord, I love You! Thank You for liberation. Thank You for setting me free. Thank You for all You have done for me."

Thanking God sets the seal on your release. Now you are ready for your new life of freedom.

CHAPTER SEVEN

ACCEPTANCE IN GOD'S FAMILY

One more important step remains in achieving complete acceptance: finding acceptance by God's people. This means discovering your place in the body of Christ. As Christians, we are never isolated individuals. We are brought into a relationship with our fellow believers. That relationship is one of the ways in which our acceptance is worked out in our day-to-day living. Acceptance by our Father in heaven is the first step and the most important. However, acceptance also has to find expression in our relationships with our fellow believers. Christians collectively constitute one body, with each Christian a member of that body. As Paul wrote,

> *Just as each of us has one body with many members, and these members do not all have the same function, so in Christ we who are many form one body, and each member belongs to all the others.*   *(Rom. 12:4–5 NIV)*

Since we are members of one body, and each of us belongs to all the others, we can never find full satisfaction, peace, or acceptance apart from the other members.

> *Now the body is not made up of one part but of many. If the foot should say, "Because I am not a hand, I do not belong to the body," it would not for that reason cease to be part of the body. And if the ear should say, "Because I am not an eye, I do not belong to the body," it would not for that reason cease to be part of the body.*   *(1 Cor. 12:14–16 NIV)*

You are a part of the body. You may be a foot, a hand, an ear, or an eye. However, you are incomplete without the rest of the body, and the rest of the body is incomplete without you. That is why it is so important to find your place in the body.

> *The eye cannot say to the hand, "I don't need you!" And the head cannot say to the feet, "I don't need you!" On the contrary, those parts of the body that seem to be weaker are indispensable, and the parts that we think are less honorable we treat with special honor.*   *(vv. 21–23 NIV)*

Thus, none of us can say to our fellow believers, "I don't need you." We all need one another. God created the body so that the members are interdependent. None of them can function effectively alone. That applies to each one of us. That applies to you. You need the other members, and they need you. Finding your place in the body will make your acceptance a real, day-to-day experience.

Another picture the New Testament gives of Christians is that of a single family unit. We are all members of one and the same family. The great Prayer that Jesus taught His disciples begins with these two significant words: *"Our Father"* (Matt. 6:9). That tells us two things. First, we have a Father who is God. That means we are accepted vertically by God. But the first word is *our* and not *my,* which tells us that we are members of a family, with a lot of other children in that family. Our acceptance becomes effective horizontally only when we find and fit into our place in the family. Thus, we find vertical acceptance with God and horizontal acceptance in God's family.

> *Consequently, you are no longer foreigners and aliens, but fellow citizens with God's people and members of God's household* [or members of God's family].   *(Eph. 2:19 NIV)*

The alternative is to be foreigners and aliens. We do not like those words, *foreigners* and *aliens*. I immigrated to the United States in 1963, and I did not become a citizen until 1970. For seven years, I was an alien in this country. Most people who become citizens at birth have no idea what it is like to be an alien.

Every January I had to fill out a form for the Department of Justice, notifying them of where I was residing. They had to be able to find me if they had questions about me—or if they wanted to deport me. I also could not vote in federal or local elections.

If I went out of the country, on my return I had to join a special line, separate from U.S. citizens, to have my passport checked. Then, along with my passport, I had to present a little green card, stating that I was a resident alien.

There are distinctions and differences between citizens and foreigners. You do not really belong as long as you are an alien. However, God says, "You are no longer an alien. You do belong. You are inside. You are part of My family." Yet that only becomes real to you when you find your place in the family. The psalmist wrote,

God sets the lonely in families...

(Ps. 68:6a NIV)

Are you lonely? Millions of people are. They have not realized that God provides families for the lonely.

...he leads forth the prisoners with singing; but the rebellious live in a sun-scorched land.   *(v. 6b NIV)*

God's purpose is to bring you into a family. In doing so, He breaks the chains that bind you, and He brings you into happiness. Only people who refuse God's leadership have to dwell in a scorched land.

You may wonder just how you should become a part of God's family. You can join groups with many different names— church, fellowship, mission, and so on. The name is not important. But it is not always easy to find the kind of group that will make you truly accepted. In my book *The Marriage Covenant,* I have listed nine questions that anybody seeking such a group should ask before he or she joins:

1. Do they honor and uplift the Lord Jesus Christ?
2. Do they respect the authority of Scripture?

3. Do they make room for the moving of the Holy Spirit?
4. Do they exhibit a warm and friendly attitude?
5. Do they seek to work out their faith in practical, day-to-day living?
6. Do they build interpersonal relationships among themselves that go beyond merely attending services?
7. Do they provide pastoral care that embraces all your legitimate needs?
8. Are they open to fellowship with other Christian groups?
9. Do you feel at ease and at home among them?

If the answer to all or most of these questions is affirmative, you are getting warm. Continue to seek God, however, until you receive definite direction from Him. Keep in mind that you probably will not find the perfect group.

Now you know the way to escape from your loneliness and your sense of being on the outside looking in. Become part of a living organism, a living body. Find your place and your function, and you will experience fulfillment.

At the end of *The Marriage Covenant,* I suggest a prayer to be prayed by anyone longing to find his or her place among God's people. I am including it here. If it expresses how you feel, read it through, and then put it in your own words. That way you can make it your prayer.

> Heavenly Father,
>   I have been lonely and unfulfilled, and I acknowledge it. I long to *"dwell in your house"* (Psalm 84:4 NIV), to be part of a spiritual family of committed believers. If there are any barriers in me, I ask You to remove them. Guide me to a group where this longing of mine can be fulfilled, and help me to make the needed commitment to them. In Jesus' name, Amen.

If you have sincerely prayed that prayer, I promise you that something is going to happen in your life. God is going to move. He will give you new direction and new associations. He will open new doors for you. He will bring you out of that parched land and cause you to be a member of His family and a part of His body.

CHAPTER EIGHT

THE FLOW OF DIVINE LOVE

In briefly reviewing the information we have covered, we have learned that many people suffer from the spiritual wounds of rejection, betrayal, and shame. Specific causes include parental neglect, divorce, public humiliation, and child abuse.

Jesus provided healing for our wounded spirits through a series of exchanges on the cross. He was rejected by God and man in order that we might be accepted by God and God's family. He suffered shame so that we might share in His glory. He died our death in order that we might receive His life.

Recognizing what Christ has done may bring release to some; others may need to take further steps. These are:

1. Let the Holy Spirit help you identify how or where you have been wounded by rejection.
2. Forgive the people who have harmed you.
3. Lay down the destructive fruits of rejection such as resentment, bitterness, hatred, and rebellion.
4. Accept that God has accepted you in Christ.
5. Accept yourself.

The primary result of rejection is the inability to receive love from others and to communicate love to them. That is why rejection is one of the greatest hindrances to divine love. God works in our lives to bring us to the knowledge of divine love.

Here I am not referring to the love that God shows toward us but to the way in which God's love first flows into us and then out through us to the world at large. In this process, there are two successive phases: first, God's love is *outpoured;* then God's love is *outworked.* The first phase is a tremendous supernatural experience; the second is the gradual, progressive formation of godly character.

It is illuminating to contrast this kind of love with mere human love. In my youth, I especially admired the writings of William Shakespeare. Shakespeare was preoccupied with two human experiences, love and death. He hoped that love would somehow provide an escape from death.

There appeared in his sonnets someone who came to be known as "the dark lady." She was apparently the object of Shakespeare's passionate affection but did not fully requite it. In one sonnet, he tried to convince her that though she might grow old, his love through his poetry would make her immortal.

Shall I compare thee to a summer's day?
Thou art more lovely and more temperate:
Rough winds do shake the darling buds of May,
And summer's lease hath all too short a date:
Sometime too hot the eye of heaven shines
And often is his gold complexion dimmed;
And every fair from fair sometimes declines,
By chance or nature's changing course untrimmed;
But thy eternal summer shall not fade,
Nor lose possession of that fair thou ow'st;
Nor shall death brag thou wander'st in his shade,
When in eternal lines to time thou grow'st:
 So long as men can breathe or eyes can see,
 So long lives this, and this gives life to thee.

That was the best his love could offer her—the immortality of his poetry. Sure enough, it has lived on for four hundred years, but the lady died.

Shakespeare had a very high expectation of love, and I would say he was probably disappointed. Having gone that way myself, I think I understand his disappointment.

For twenty-five years, I searched for something permanent and satisfying in poetry, philosophy, and the world, with all its pleasures and intellectual challenges. The more I looked, the less satisfied I became. I had no idea what I was looking for. However, when the Lord revealed Himself to me and baptized me in the Holy Spirit, I knew instantly that this was what I had been seeking all the time. I had attended church services for twenty years, but no one had ever told me about it. God poured into my heart an overwhelming love that finally, completely satisfied me.

Now we will explore what happens when we love people with God's version of love—not Shakespeare's, but God's. In Romans, we read this tremendous statement:

And hope does not disappoint us, because God has poured out his love into our hearts by the Holy Spirit, whom he has given us. (Rom. 5:5 NIV)

Hope, or love, is never disappointed when it is fixed in God because the love of God has been poured out into our hearts— the totality of God's love. God withholds nothing. He just turns the bucket upside down and pours out the whole thing when He gives us the Holy Spirit.

During World War II, when I served in the British army as a medical orderly or attendant, I was overseas for four-and-a-half years, mainly in North Africa, and then in what was at that time Palestine. I spent one year in the Sudan, which is a bleak, dry, desert land. To the natural human mind, no perception of the Sudan or of the Sudanese people is very attractive. However, I had been baptized in the Holy Spirit, and God had shown me that He had a destiny for me there. He began to give me a supernatural love for the Sudanese.

The army stationed me for a short while at a railway junction in the northern Sudan called Atbara. I was in charge of a small reception station for military patients. I think it had three beds. I worked in liaison with a civilian doctor in the city, but I was my own boss for the first time in my military career. For the first time, too, I had a bed to sleep in. Additionally, among the issued equipment in this reception station were long, white nightgowns. At that time, I had spent about three years sleeping in my underwear, and I was tired of it. So, I availed myself of the facilities, put on a flannel nightgown, and slept in a bed.

One night, as I lay in bed, the Spirit of God came upon me while I was in intercessory prayer for the people of the Sudan. The prayer had nothing to do with my natural feelings toward them at all, but I could not sleep. I was driven by an inner urgency, which I know was the prompting of the Holy Spirit. I found myself praying with a supernatural love far above the level of anything I could achieve by my own reason or emotion.

Sometime in the middle of the night, I got out of bed and began to pace the floor. Suddenly, I was aware that my white nightgown was actually shining. I realized that for those brief moments, I had become identified with our great heavenly Intercessor, the Lord Jesus.

Later, the army transferred me to a small hospital in a miserable place in the Red Sea hills, where the local tribal people were called Hadundawa. They were a wild, fierce people who knew no religion but Islam. About one hundred years previously, they had fought a brief war against the British. At that time, the British soldiers had nicknamed the Hadundawa "fuzzy-wuzzies" because the men fixed their woolly hair with mutton fat in a bushy style that stood out about eight inches from their scalps.

All my fellow soldiers were discontented, but I spent eight of the happiest months of my life there because God had given me His love for those people. As a result, I had the privilege of winning to the Lord the first member of the Hadundawa tribe who had ever professed faith in Christ. When I left, it broke my heart to say good-bye to that man and that place.

In the Sudan at that time, I experienced some small measure of the outpoured love of God for those people. Later, however, I came to understand that this needed to be made complete by God's love developed in my character.

About a year later in Palestine, when I met my first wife, Lydia, and saw the girls she was caring for, the Lord again filled my heart with His wonderful love. At that time, neither Lydia nor I had any thoughts of marriage, but eventually we were married. God had once again poured out His supernatural love in my heart, but it still did not make me the kind of person I ought to have been. I was often selfish, irritable, impatient, self-centered, and insensitive, none of which exemplified Christ's character or image.

I came to understand that a supernatural experience of the outpoured love of God is wonderful, but much more needs to be done to form our characters. God has to take us beyond the supernatural outpouring of love to the formation of a character that consistently expresses His love. That is a process, a long process, and it requires God's patience to take us through it.

In this process of character formation, the wonderful Word of God plays a vital part.

> *The man who says, "I know him," but does not do what he commands is a liar, and the truth is not in him. But if anyone obeys his word, God's love is truly made complete in him. This is how we know we are in him: Whoever claims to live in him must walk as Jesus did.*   *(1 John 2:4–6 NIV)*

Notice how this verse mentions the Word of God, not the Spirit of God. We are not talking about a supernatural experience but about the slow, steady formation of character that develops through consistently obeying the Word of God. If we faithfully follow Christ's guidance by walking as He did in obedience to the Scriptures, God's love will gradually be brought to completion, or maturity, in us.

That verse is like the two faces of a coin. On the one side, the proof of our love for God is that we obey His Word. It is in vain to claim that we love God when we do not obey His Word. On the other side, as we obey His Word, God works out His love in our characters. These two aspects cannot be separated because they make up a whole.

The process of character building has seven successive phases, according to the apostle Peter:

> *But also for this very reason, giving all diligence, add to your faith virtue, to virtue knowledge, to knowledge self-control, to self-control perseverance, to perseverance godliness, to godliness brotherly kindness, and to brotherly kindness love.*   *(2 Pet. 1:5–7 NKJV)*

We start with the foundation: *"Giving all diligence, add to your faith virtue."* The starting point with everything God does is faith. There is no other place to begin. But after God has given us faith, there has to be a process of character development.

Let us follow these seven successive steps of character building as we find them in 2 Peter 1:5–7.

"Add to your faith virtue." For the word *"virtue,"* I like the alternate translation of "excellence." Excellence is the mark of a Christian. Never be sloppy in anything you do. If you were a janitor before you were saved, be a better janitor afterward. If you were a teacher before, be a better teacher after. If you were a nurse, be a better nurse. We must add excellence to our faith.

For five years, I was principal of a teacher training college in Kenya. My primary purpose was to win my students to Christ. When they professed Christ and were baptized in the Holy Spirit, they would sometimes say to me, "You can go easy on me now" or "You are going to expect less of me because I am a Christian."

I would reply, "On the contrary, I expect much more of you now. If you could be a teacher without Christ and the baptism, you ought to be twice as good a teacher when you have Christ and the baptism. I am going to expect more, not less."

God honored my commitment to excellence. The third year I was in charge of that college, the graduating class consisted of fifty-seven well-trained men and women. In the final examinations, every student passed in every subject. A representative of the education department of the Kenyan government who was responsible for teacher training colleges came. He congratulated me personally and said, "In all our records, we have never had results like these."

It was because I followed the Scriptures' demand for excellence. Our examination results impressed the secular authorities more than any doctrinal statement we might have issued. Christianity is no excuse for being sloppy. In fact, the sloppy Christian is denying his faith.

"To [excellence add] *knowledge."* Primarily, this means the knowledge of God's will and the knowledge of His Word. Secular knowledge is often important to acquire, especially in developing the necessary skills for your vocation, but even more important is learning what God's will is for your life in every circumstance, which can be discovered by thoroughly studying His Word.

"To knowledge [add] *self-control."* There is a point beyond which you cannot go in character development if you do not learn to control yourself, your emotions, your words, your appetites, and all the things that motivate you.

"To self-control [add] *perseverance."* Stick it out! Again, there is a point beyond which you will never advance if you do not learn to persevere. Otherwise, every time you are about to attain the next stage of development, you will give up.

"To perseverance [add] *godliness."* Godliness, or holiness, is developed by allowing the Holy Spirit to control your temperament and every aspect of your being.

"To godliness [add] *brotherly kindness* [or love]."* This becomes our corporate testimony to the world. Jesus said, *"By this all will know that you are My disciples, if you have love for one another"* (John 13:35 NKJV).

"To brotherly kindness [add] *love"*—divine, agape love. This is the consummate, ideal, perfect kind of love that God has for us. It begins when the Holy Spirit pours out God's love in our hearts. However, it comes to its culmination in the development of our characters. The difference between brotherly love and divine love is that in brotherly love, we love our fellow Christians who love us; in divine love, we love those who hate us, persecute us, and are altogether unloving and unlovable.

This brings us right back to the issue of rejection. What is the evidence that you are healed of this wound? Can God give you divine love for the person who has rejected you? Can you go back to an unloving parent and say, "I love you"? Can you say a prayer for your former spouse and ask for God's blessing on him or her? It is the most unnatural thing in the world, but then God's love is supernatural—far above anything that proceeds out of our own efforts.

This is perhaps the greatest of all the blessings that follow from the healing of the wounds of rejection, betrayal, and shame. You can become a vessel of God's love to others who have been wounded just as you were.

THE MARRIAGE
COVENANT

Contents

FOREWORD

Soon after I came to know the Lord Jesus as my Savior and Messiah in 1970, I came into contact with real Christians whose marriages were a constant testimony to His Lordship in their lives. At about the same time, I became acquainted with the teachings and ministries of Derek Prince, Charles Simpson, and others. As a single woman, my prayer to God was, "Set me under authority, in the place You have for me, that I may serve You in the best way and help to prepare for the coming of Your Kingdom."

My prayers were answered several years later, in a way that I had not anticipated, when God chose me to be Derek's wife, his new "*help meet*" (Gen. 2:18 KJV). Derek's first wife, Lydia, was an extraordinary woman who laid down her life and her own successful ministry in Jerusalem for her husband. When Derek married her in 1946, she was a respected spiritual leader there with an established work of her own.[1] However, she accepted willingly the behind-the-scenes role of intercessor, homemaker, supporter—that of a true wife.

When I first came into close personal contact with Derek, I was impressed by the way he lives out his teaching in his personal conduct; he practices what he preaches. I have come to see that much of his present ability to minister to the needs of God's people has its roots in the relationship he and Lydia had with one another for almost thirty years and in their relationship, as a unit, with the Lord.

---

[1] Lydia's own dramatic story is told by Derek in the book, *Appointment in Jerusalem*, published just before her death in 1975.

Most of the material contained in *The Marriage Covenant* was developed and taught before I came into Derek's life. Yet, in the same period of time, while I was living in Jerusalem completely out of touch with his ministry and teaching, the Holy Spirit was speaking to me along the same lines about the real meaning of covenant. My study led me to Genesis chapter 15. I identified with the experience of Abraham as he entered into a deep, personal, life-changing relationship with God—a relationship so profound that we still know our God as "the God of Abraham." It was a life of total commitment.

During the same period, I was also reflecting on the role of women in the body of our Lord. I saw that God had created Eve for the sole purpose of meeting Adam's need, that man was not complete without his God-given mate. It seems to me that in contemporary Western society and in much of the church, too many women are endeavoring (often loudly) to do something they were never created to do: to succeed in life as independent, solitary entities. For a number of years, I myself sought fulfillment in that way as a career woman. But when I entered into a relationship with Jesus, my life was redirected. I began to see that under these circumstances it is women who are the losers, along with the men who are not able to achieve the wholeness God intended for them in union with their mates.

I realize that it is not possible for every man and every woman to find that ideal mate, and that it certainly is better to be alone with the Lord than to be unequally yoked with an unbeliever. For many, there is no other choice than to remain single. The quality of the single life, with which I am well acquainted, can be determined by the quality of the relationship with God and the relationship with other Christians. Commitment seems to be the key—commitment to God, to His will for your life, and commitment to that part of the body of Christ with which you are connected.

It seems appropriate that this book is being published just as Derek and I are joining our lives in the covenant of marriage. At the same time, I am joining myself to the part of the body with which he is associated in the United States, and he with the part of the body to which I belong in Jerusalem. We believe we are conforming to God's preordained plan as we each lay down our lives for the other, that we may merge into one new entity under the lordship of Jesus. We know that, as with everything in the spiritual life, this must be walked out on a day-to-day basis. I believe that this book contains not only the pattern, but the practical instruction on how to do so.

I pray that applying the principles of this book will lead you, whether you are a man or a woman, into the wholeness that God wills for you, in covenant relationship with Himself and with His people.

Ruth Prince

CHAPTER ONE

MARRIAGE IS A COVENANT

Is there a secret to a successful marriage? Why do some couples succeed and others fail? Is it all just a matter of chance? One thing is certain: if there is a secret that ensures a successful marriage, millions of couples in our contemporary culture have never found it. In almost every country in Western civilization, the proportion of divorces to marriages has soared dramatically in the last few decades. In the United States, we have reached a situation where there is approximately one divorce for every two marriages. Fifty years ago, a person familiar with American life would never have dreamed that such a situation could arise in so short a period.

However, the ratio of divorces to marriages does not tell the whole story. Many marriages that have not yet ended in the final shipwreck of divorce nevertheless find themselves in very troubled and unhappy circumstances. In some cases, there is open strife and disharmony, usually involving all those who live under the one roof, both parents and children. In other cases, although things appear fairly calm on the surface, underneath there are the festering sores of bitterness, unforgiveness, and rebellion. Sooner or later, these are liable to erupt in the form of some mental or emotional breakdown, the cause of which may never be precisely diagnosed.

Those who are specifically concerned with mental health have suggested that about one out of every four persons in America today either needs or will need some form of psychiatric care. Psychiatric wards in many hospitals are overflowing, and professional psychiatrists are in ever increasing demand. This has a direct bearing on the condition of marriage and the home, because it is generally agreed that the majority of mental and emotional problems can be traced back to tension and disharmony in the home, primarily in marriage relationships. Thus, the progressive deterioration of mental and emotional health is one of many symptoms in contemporary society, all of which point to the most urgent social problem of our day—the breakdown of marriage and the home.

The reaction of certain contemporary sociologists to this situation has taken the form of passively accepting the inevitable. Some have even gone so far as to assert that the concept of marriage was a mistake in the first place, and that it is no longer relevant in our present advanced state of social progress. However, many of the so-called experts who make such pronouncements are themselves the product of unhappy homes; not a few also have the record of at least one unsuccessful marriage in their own lives. We may therefore have grounds to inquire whether their statements to the effect that marriage is irrelevant or outmoded do not merely put them on the level of the fox in Aesop's fable. He had tried desperately to reach a cluster of luscious grapes, but failed. His final comment was, "They're probably sour anyway!"

In the face of this confused situation and these conflicting opinions, I want to state, clearly and briefly, my own personal conviction. I believe that there is a secret that can ensure a successful marriage. Furthermore, I believe that this secret is revealed in the pages of one unique book—the Bible.

Before I proceed to explain what this secret is, it will be appropriate for me to give a little of my own personal background. This could be interpreted as presenting my credentials and qualifications for addressing this subject.

PERSONAL BACKGROUND

I was educated at two of Britain's most famous educational institutions—Eton College and Cambridge University. Prior to World War II, I pursued a career in philosophy, and in 1940 I was elected to a Fellowship (i.e., a resident professorship) in this field at King's College, Cambridge. However, the impact of World War II interrupted my academic career.

In 1941, while serving as a hospital attendant in the British Army, I had a dramatic, life-changing encounter with God—something that was totally out of line with my previous philosophic theories and preconceptions. Out of this encounter, I formed two conclusions that I have never since had reason to change: first, that Jesus Christ is alive; second, that the Bible is a true, relevant, up-to-date book. These two conclusions radically and permanently altered the whole course of my life.

When I was in Jerusalem in 1946, I married a Danish lady, Lydia Christensen, who was the "mother" of a small home for girls, which she had founded there. Through my marriage to Lydia, in one day I became the adoptive father of eight girls, of whom six were Jewish, one was Arab, and one was English. Also at this time, I studied for two years at the Hebrew University in Jerusalem. Lydia and I and our eight girls continued living in Jerusalem throughout the upheavals that marked the birth of the State of Israel. We thus came face-to-face, as a family, with the grim realities of siege, famine, and war. Later we moved, still as a family, to Britain.

In the years that followed, I served in various capacities in various lands: as a pastor in Britain; as an educator in Kenya; as a Bible teacher and conference speaker in Europe, Canada, the United States, New Zealand, Australia, and other countries. Throughout all my travels, Lydia was always by my side. Sometimes, after we had been ministering together in public, people would make the comment, "The two of you work together as if you were one person."

In Kenya, Lydia and I adopted our ninth child—an African baby girl. We successfully completed the raising of all our nine girls. All but our youngest have married and have presented us with many grandchildren.

After thirty years, my marriage with Lydia was terminated by her death. Our life together had always been an open book—not only to our children, but also to countless people who, through the years, came to our home for counseling and prayer. Of all those who knew us in this way, I question whether there are any who would not agree that our marriage was happy and successful. Certainly it had its fair share of tensions and problems—more than would normally be experienced by a couple who spend their whole lives in one familiar setting. But the success of a marriage does not depend upon the absence of tensions and problems; it depends upon a special quality of relationship that needs to be developed between husband and wife.

In the pages that follow, it is my intention to share with you the secret of how to build a relationship of this kind. I trust that the brief outline of my life to this point will be sufficient to demonstrate that my convictions are not just a set of abstract theories that have never been put to the tests of real life.

Perhaps I should add that at the moment of writing this I am about to remarry. Coincidentally, I met my second wife, Ruth, like my first, in Jerusalem. I enter this second marriage with a quiet trust that God will also crown this marriage with His blessing, as Ruth and I meet the conditions that He has revealed in Scripture.

MARRIAGE IS A "MYSTERY"

In Ephesians 5:22–32, Paul explained the Christian view of marriage. He concluded by saying, *"This mystery is great"* (NAS). Thus, he acknowledged that marriage is a mystery. In Paul's time, the word *mystery* had a more specific meaning than it does today. Then, it had religious associations. It denoted a form of knowledge that conferred valuable benefits but was restricted to a special group who were bound together by their religious practices. For a person to have access to this knowledge, he had first to be initiated into the group.

Thus, Paul's use of the word *mystery* to describe the marriage relationship suggests two things: first, that there is a little-known form of knowledge that can make marriage what it ought to be; second, that a person can only acquire this knowledge by undergoing certain tests and meeting certain conditions. It is the main purpose of this book to initiate the reader into these tests and conditions.

In the book of Deuteronomy, when the children of Israel were ready to enter into their promised inheritance in the land of Canaan, Moses reviewed for them the kind of lifestyle God had planned for them in their new environment. He promised them, on God's behalf, that if they would keep God's law, they would be abundantly blessed in every area of their lives. In particular, Moses told them that their homes would be like *"heaven upon...earth"* (Deut. 11:21 KJV). He painted a beautiful picture of contentment and unbroken harmony. Such was the level of home life God had planned for His people.

About twelve hundred years later, through the prophet Malachi, God took stock of Israel's conduct since they had entered into their inheritance. In general, they had failed to meet God's conditions and therefore had not enjoyed the level of life He had planned for them. In His assessment, God pinpointed a number of specific areas of failure. One was in the Israelites' home lives and specifically in their marriages. Here is what the Lord said concerning this:

> *And this is another thing you do: you cover the altar of the LORD with tears, with weeping and with groaning, because He no longer regards the offering or accepts it with favor from your hand. Yet you say, "For what reason?" Because the LORD has been a witness between you and the wife of your youth, against whom you have dealt treacherously, though she is your companion and your wife by covenant.*
> *(Mal. 2:13–14 NAS)*

Obviously, Israel's failure in this respect was not due to lack of religion. They were *"cover*[ing] *the altar of the LORD with tears."* Yet, for all their prayers, their marriages were failures. We are quite often confronted with a similar situation today. People may be very busy with religious activities and yet be unable to make a success of their marriages. Their religion does not enable them to succeed at home. Indeed, excessive preoccupation with religion outside the home, by one or both parties, is sometimes an important factor in the failure of a marriage.

The essence of Israel's failure is contained in the closing phrase of Malachi 2:14: *"though she is...your wife by covenant."* Israel had come to view marriage as a relationship for which they might set their own standards, one which they were free to initiate or terminate on their own terms. God reminds them, however, that He views marriage quite differently. According to His unchanging purpose, marriage is a covenant, which is the secret that alone ensures the success of the marriage relationship. Once this secret is forgotten or ignored, marriage inevitably loses its sanctity. With the loss of the sanctity of marriage, it also loses its strength and stability. Much of what we see in our contemporary civilization is closely parallel to the condition of Israel in Malachi's day, and the root cause is the same—a wrong view of marriage.

JESUS' STANDARD OF MARRIAGE

After Malachi, the next and fuller revelation of marriage comes to us through Jesus. The essence of His teaching on marriage is contained in a conversation He had with some Pharisees:

And some Pharisees came to Him, testing Him, and saying, "Is it lawful for a man to divorce his wife for any cause at all?" And He answered and said, "Have you not read, that He who created them from the beginning MADE THEM MALE AND FEMALE, and said, 'FOR THIS CAUSE A MAN SHALL LEAVE HIS FATHER AND MOTHER, AND SHALL CLEAVE TO HIS WIFE; AND THE TWO SHALL BECOME ONE FLESH'? Consequently they are no longer two, but one flesh. What therefore God has joined together, let no man separate." They said to Him, "Why then did Moses command to GIVE HER A CERTIFICATE OF DIVORCE AND SEND her AWAY?" He said to them, "Because of your hardness of heart, Moses permitted you to divorce your wives; but from the beginning it has not been this way. And I say to you, whoever divorces his wife, except for immorality, and marries another woman commits adultery. (Matt. 19:3–9 NAS)

We may sum up the teaching of Jesus in this passage in four successive statements:

1. The form of marriage that had become accepted in Israel under Judaism was below the level of God's will.

2. God's real purpose for marriage was expressed when He originally created man and woman.

3. In the initial union of man and woman, they were so perfectly joined together that they lost their separate identities and became *"one flesh."*

4. It is the purpose of Jesus to restore marriage in the lives of His disciples to the original standard revealed at creation.

If we consider the account in Genesis chapters 1 and 2 of the creation and union of Adam and Eve, one fact is emphasized throughout: God Himself was directly and personally involved. It was His decision, not Adam's, that Adam should have a mate; it was He who formed Eve from Adam; it was He who presented her to Adam; and it was He who established the terms of the covenant relationship in which He united them.

Therefore, it is correct to say that, all through the Old Testament, marriage was viewed as a covenant relationship. However, the concept that developed under Judaism was on a lower level than what had found expression at creation. Under Judaism, the covenant relationship was viewed as being merely horizontal—between a man and a woman. But the covenant relationship established at creation had two dimensions: horizontal and vertical. Horizontally, it related Adam and Eve to each other, but vertically, it related the two of them together to God.

"A CORD OF THREE STRANDS"

A passage in Ecclesiastes expresses in allegorical terms the difference between these two levels of marriage:

Two are better than one because they have a good return for their labor. For if either of them falls, the one will lift up his companion. But woe to the one who falls when there is not another to lift him up. Furthermore, if two lie down together they keep warm, but how can one be warm alone? And if one can overpower him who is alone, two can resist him. A cord of three strands is not quickly torn apart.
(Eccl. 4:9–12 NAS)

The principle from which Solomon started, *"Two are better than one,"* agrees with the reason that God gave originally for providing a mate for Adam: *"It is not good for the man to be alone"* (Gen. 2:18 NAS). Solomon went on to give three examples that clearly illustrate this principle: when two are together and one falls, the other can help him up; if two lie down together, they keep each other warm; if two are attacked, together they can drive off the attacker. But the last example that Solomon gave is different: *"A cord of three strands is not quickly torn apart."* In this case, the strength is supplied not merely by two together, but by three together.

We may use Solomon's pictures to illustrate the difference we have observed between the concept of marriage under Judaism and the concept of marriage that was initiated by God Himself at creation. Solomon's first three examples of *"two...together"* illustrate the concept of marriage on the human plane, a horizontal relationship, merely between a man and a woman. But Solomon's fourth picture, the *"cord of three strands,"* illustrates marriage as it was conceived at creation—a binding together of three persons: a man, a woman, and God. The relationship between the man and the woman is still on the human plane, but when God is added to the relationship, it introduces a new dimension. He becomes an integral part of the marriage.

One of the most revolutionary features of the teaching of Jesus was His standard of marriage. He refused to settle for anything less than the original purpose of God. For this reason, Solomon's picture of *"a cord of three strands"* not only illustrates the pattern of marriage established at creation, it also portrays just as accurately the pattern of marriage for believers today who are united through their faith in Christ. The three strands are the man, the woman, and God. The principle that binds them inseparably together is covenant. What Solomon says of a cord thus formed is still true today; it *"is not quickly torn apart."*

Some time ago, I was speaking in New Zealand on this picture of Christian marriage as *"a cord of three strands."* At the end of my talk, a man came up and introduced himself. "I am a professional rope maker," he said. "My business is making ropes. I want to tell you that what you have said is absolutely true in the practical realm. The strongest rope is a threefold rope."

Then he went on to give me the following explanation: The largest number of strands that can all touch one another is three. If you take away one and leave only two, obviously you weaken the rope. But if you add an extra strand and make four, you do not add to the strength of the rope because all the strands no longer touch one another. If you have a rope of three strands, one—or even two—of the strands may be under pressure and start to fray. But as long as the third strand holds, the rope will not break.

This rope maker's explanation made the picture of Christian marriage as a threefold cord so vivid for me that I went on meditating on it for days. In my mind's eye, I could see the rope under such tremendous strain that two of its strands began to fray. But the third strand remained strong and held out until the strain was eased and the two frayed strands could be bound up.

"That's exactly how it is," I said to myself, "in a truly Christian marriage! There come times of strain when both husband and wife may begin to weaken and feel unable to hold out. But God Himself is that third strand, and He holds on until the strain is eased and both husband and wife can be healed and restored."

In our comparison of Christian marriage to *"a cord of three strands,"* we have said that the principle that intertwines the strands and holds them together is covenant. Clearly, this makes covenant an essential element of a successful marriage. And yet, although covenant is one of the central themes of biblical revelation, it is very little understood by most Christians today. Therefore, we will now go on in chapter 2 to examine the nature of covenant as it is revealed in Scripture. Then in chapter 3, we will explain in practical terms just how covenant works to unite a man and a woman in marriage and to hold them together.

In chapters 4 and 5, respectively, we will examine how covenant also serves as the essential binding force in two other vitally important relationships: between God and the individual Christian, and between fellow Christians in their relationship to one another.

Finally, in chapter 6, "The Point of Decision," we will give practical direction to those who feel their need of bringing their personal relationship into line with the principles explained in this book.

CHAPTER TWO

THE NATURE OF COVENANT

What is there in a covenant that gives to marriage a strength and stability not otherwise possible? What is the essence of covenant? The nature of covenant is one of the jealously guarded secrets of Scripture. It is a pearl that God will not cast to the careless. (See Matthew 7:6.) It is something holy that God will not unveil to the impure. In Psalm 25:14, David said, *"The secret of the LORD is for those who fear Him, and He will make them know His covenant"* (NAS). The secret of covenant must be approached in the reverent fear of God. It is withheld from those who approach with any other attitude.

Furthermore, an understanding of covenant requires careful, thorough study of Scripture. It takes time and concentration. In Proverbs 2:4, Solomon stated that those who desire discernment and understanding must *"seek her as silver, and search for her as for hidden treasures"* (NAS). This implies strenuous effort. Just as the earth does not yield up her treasures to the superficial observer, so Scripture yields up the true understanding of covenant only to those who are willing to go below the surface and to devote time and study to their search.

I say this by way of introduction to the study of covenant that we will now undertake in this chapter. At first, it may seem somewhat hard and laborious. But if we pursue it with patience and diligence, it will ultimately yield up treasures of infinite worth. These treasures will be the subject of the succeeding chapters.

THE DEFINITION OF COVENANT

There are two basic words in Scripture for covenant. The Greek word used in the New Testament is *diatheke*. The Hebrew word, used in the Old Testament, is *b'rit* (or *b'rith*). This Hebrew word occurs in the name of the well-known Jewish organization *B'nai B'rith,* which means, literally, "Sons of Covenant." Each of these words—*diatheke* in Greek and *b'rit* in Hebrew—is regularly translated by two different English words: *covenant* and *testament*. The English word used in each case varies according to the context.

In English, we do not normally think of *covenant* and *testament* as being the same. We limit the word *testament* to a legal document that, as Scripture points out, comes into force only after the death of the one who made the testament. (See Hebrews 9:16–17 KJV.) On the other hand, we do not usually think of a covenant as being necessarily associated with the death of the parties to the covenant. However, in the concepts of Scripture, this distinction between *testament* and *covenant* is not valid. In Scripture a covenant is a testament, and a testament is a covenant.

We are all aware, of course, that the Bible has come to us in the form of two testaments—the Old Testament and the New Testament. However, our understanding is increased if we substitute the word *covenant* for *testament* in each case, and speak of the Old Covenant and the New Covenant. It is a fact of tremendous significance that God's entire written revelation to man is contained in the form of two covenants. Thus, the concept of covenant is central to the whole of divine revelation. If we do not understand the nature of covenant, how far can we hope to understand the real meaning of God's message to us?

What, then, is the meaning of the word *covenant*? It is not easy to give a precise and simple definition. It is suggested that the root meaning of the Hebrew word *b'rit* is "to bind," but that is not certain. It is certain, however, that a covenant is binding. The root meaning of the Greek word *diatheke* is "to set something out in order." It suggests, therefore, the setting forth of specific terms and conditions. It has more of a legal association than its Hebrew counterpart *b'rit*.

In Scripture, we find two different types of covenants. One is on the horizontal plane, a covenant between two human beings. This more nearly approaches the concept of a contract. For instance, in 1 Kings 5:12 (NASB), we read about Solomon making a covenant with Hiram, the king of Tyre. (The KJV here translates *b'rit* with the word *"league."*) By this covenant, Solomon and Hiram committed themselves to mutual friendship and established the conditions upon which Hiram would supply Solomon with material and labor for the building of the temple.

Although this form of covenant was only on the human level—between two kings—it is interesting to note that later on, when God declared through the prophet Amos that He would bring judgment on the kingdom of Tyre, one reason that He gave was that *"they...did not remember the covenant of brotherhood"* (Amos 1:9 NAS)—that is, the covenant made between Solomon and Hiram. So we see that, even on the human level, God considers the breaking of a covenant a very serious matter and one that will bring judgment on the guilty party.

COVENANT: THE BASIS OF RELATIONSHIP

However, beyond that, the main use of covenant in Scripture is not as a contract between two human beings on the horizontal plane, but as a relationship sovereignly initiated by God Himself, with man, in which the two parties are not on the same level. Essentially, a covenant expresses a relationship that God Himself sovereignly initiates out of His own choice and decision. He defines the terms on which He is prepared to enter into that relationship with man. We need to emphasize that the initiative is wholly with God and the terms are set exclusively by God. Man's part is simply to respond to God's offer of a covenant and to accept the relationship that the covenant brings with it. Man does not set the terms nor does he ever initiate the relationship. You have to be something of a Presbyterian or a Calvinist to understand this aspect of covenant. Historically, it is the Calvinist stream of Protestantism that has always laid special emphasis on covenant. In so doing, they have preserved a thread of truth that is very important. I would venture to say that we cannot fully understand our relationship with God unless we understand the scriptural concept of covenant.

In the last analysis, every permanent relationship of God with man is based on a covenant. God never enters into a permanent relationship apart from a covenant. In Psalm 50:1–5, the psalmist gave a prophetic preview of the Lord coming in power and glory at the close of this age to gather His people to Himself. In so doing, he clearly defined those whom God will acknowledge as His people:

> *The Mighty One, God, the LORD, has spoken, and summoned the earth from the rising of the sun to its setting.* [This is a call to the whole earth.] *Out of Zion, the perfection of beauty, God has shone forth. May our God come and not keep silence; fire devours before Him, and it is very tempestuous around Him.* [This is a clear prophecy of the coming of the Lord in power, glory, and judgment.] *He summons the heavens above, and the earth, to judge His people* [this is the judgment of God's people, before the judgment seat of Christ—not the judgment of the unbeliever, but the judgment of the believer; not the judgment of condemnation, but the judgment for reward]: *"Gather My godly ones to Me, those who have made a covenant with Me by sacrifice."* [This verse tells us to whom God's call is addressed.] (NAS)

The Hebrew word here translated *"godly one"* is *hasid*. It is the word that gives us *hasidic* Judaism—the most intense and dedicated form of orthodox Judaism. A *hassid* is a person whose life is totally wrapped up in God. He is a person who exists only for God.

However, the psalmist here defined the *"godly ones"* as the true *hasidim*, as *"those who have made a covenant with Me by sacrifice"*—more literally, "those who cut My covenant on the basis of a sacrifice." The Hebrew speaks of "cutting" a covenant, rather than merely making one. It suggests the action of the knife that puts the sacrifice to death. *"My"* covenant means specifically the covenant that God Himself initiated, the eternal covenant. There is only one basis on which God makes a covenant—the basis of a sacrifice. Without a sacrifice, there can be no covenant.

Years ago, about 1944, when I first began to study the Bible in Hebrew, the Holy Spirit prompted me to do something unusual. I armed myself with three colored pencils—blue, green, and red—and I set out to underline three different themes with a special color for each. The themes were: covenant, sacrifice, and the shedding of blood. Blue was for covenant, green for sacrifice, and red for the shedding of blood. In that way, I stumbled into a revelation because I discovered that wherever I had the blue, I had the green; and wherever I had the green, I had the red. In other words, wherever there is a covenant, there must be a sacrifice; and wherever there is a sacrifice, there must be the shedding of blood.

This agrees with the description of God's people in Psalm 50:5: "Those who cut My covenant on the basis of a sacrifice." Two things are essential for entering into a permanent relationship with God: a covenant and a sacrifice. Without a covenant, there can be no relationship with God; without a sacrifice, there can be no covenant.

Historically, the way that men entered into covenant with God before the new covenant in Jesus Christ was very remarkable, and many people are not familiar with it. Jeremiah describes it well. This is a period in Israel's history when the nation was backslidden and rebellious in their relationship to God, and they had done something God forbade them to do— they had made slaves out of their fellow Israelites. When God reproved them for this through the prophet Jeremiah, they made a show of repentance and entered into a covenant in which they agreed to release their slaves. But then, to add to their sin, they broke their covenant and took the slaves back. The only part of this incident that concerns us just now is the procedure by which they entered into the covenant. This has a significance that goes far beyond this particular moment in the history of Israel. It is described in Jeremiah 34:18–20, where God said,

And I will give the men who have transgressed My covenant, who have not fulfilled the words of the covenant which they made before Me, when they cut the calf in two and passed between its parts—the officials of Judah, and the officials of Jerusalem, the court officers, and the priests, and all the people of the land, who passed between the parts of the calf—and I will give them into the hand of their enemies. (NAS)

This provides an important addition to our understanding of the process of making a covenant. Not merely did making a covenant require a sacrifice, but the sacrifice had to be dealt with in a special way. The animal that was killed as the sacrifice was cut into two parts, and the two parts were placed opposite one another with a space in between. Then the people who were making the covenant passed between the two parts of the sacrifice. This was the act by which they entered into the covenant.

GOD'S COVENANT WITH ABRAM

Keeping in mind this procedure for making a covenant, we'll turn to Genesis 15:7–18, which describes how the Lord entered into a covenant with Abram (his name had not yet become Abraham):

And He said to him, "I am the LORD who brought you out of Ur of the Chaldeans, to give you this land to possess it." And he said, "O Lord GOD, how may I know that I shall possess it?" So He said to him, "Bring Me a three year old heifer, and a three year old female goat, and a three year old ram, and a turtledove, and a young pigeon." Then he brought all these to Him and cut them in two, and laid each half opposite the other; but he did not cut the birds. And the birds of prey came down upon the carcasses, and Abram drove them away. Now when the sun was going down, a deep sleep fell upon Abram; and behold, terror and great darkness fell upon him. And God said to Abram, "Know for certain that your descendants will be strangers in a land that is not theirs, where they will be enslaved and oppressed four hundred years. But I will also judge the nation whom they will serve; and afterward they will come out with many possessions. And as for you, you shall go to your fathers in peace; you shall be buried at a good old age. Then in the fourth generation they shall return here, for the iniquity of the Amorite is not yet complete." And it came about when the sun had set, that it was very

dark, and behold, there appeared a smoking oven and a
flaming torch which passed between these pieces. On that
day the LORD made a covenant with Abram, saying, "To
your descendants I have given this land, from the river of
Egypt as far as the great river, the river Euphrates. (NAS)

The passage opens with the Lord making a promise to
Abram that He will give him the land of Canaan for his possession. Abram responds with a question: *"How may I know?"* In
reply, the Lord proceeds to make a covenant with Abram. In
other words, God's final commitment to do anything is in a
covenant. When God has entered into a covenant, there is no
more that He can do to commit Himself. Covenant represents
final, irrevocable commitment. Once God has made the covenant with Abram, He no longer speaks in the future tense. He
does not say, "I will give." He says, *"I have given."* The covenant has settled it—finally and forever.

The procedure by which the Lord entered into the covenant
with Abram corresponds exactly to that described in Jeremiah
34:18–20. Abram had to take the sacrificial animals, kill them,
and divide them into two pieces. Then it appears that, in due
course, the Lord and Abram passed between the pieces of the
sacrifice. By that strange act, the Lord entered into a covenant
commitment with Abram.

Now let us look at some of the details of this transaction.
Every one of them is illuminating. Verse 11 reads, *"And the*
birds of prey came down upon the carcasses, and Abram drove
them away." These words bring back very vivid memories to
me.

During World War II, while serving with the British forces
in Egypt, I lay for one full year sick and in hospital, with a condition that apparently the doctors were not able to heal. In desperation, I turned to the Bible to see what it had to say.
Ultimately, after reading the whole Bible through, I came to the
conclusion that God had provided healing for me through the
death of Jesus Christ on the cross, that it was a part of the
covenant God had made with me through Christ. But as I
sought to lay hold of this truth, my mind was continually as-
sailed with all sorts of fits of depression, doubt, and darkness.

As I lay there, wrestling to appropriate my covenant benefits in Christ and fighting off these moods of depression and
doubt, I happened to read this passage in Genesis chapter 15,
and I saw that it was Abram's job to drive the birds of prey
away. God ordained the sacrificial objects, but to keep them intact was Abram's job. Likewise, I saw that God had provided the
sacrifice in Christ for me, but it was my job to keep those satanic birds from preying on the sacrifice and robbing me of my
benefits. So I saw there was a period in which I would have to
keep driving the birds away. No matter how many times doubt
or unbelief or fear would attack me, it was my privilege and my
responsibility to keep those sacrificial objects intact. They were
not to be desecrated by the satanic birds of prey that wanted to
feed on them and take away from my inheritance.

Then it says in verse 12, *"Now when the sun was going
down, a deep sleep fell upon Abram; and behold, terror and great
darkness fell upon him."* This was a very profound spiritual experience in which Abram, as a mature, committed believer,
went through *"terror and great darkness."* Does your theology
make room for that? Do you know that some of the greatest
saints of God go through periods of spiritual darkness? It is not
necessarily a mark of immaturity or weakness to go through
darkness. In fact, God cannot trust the immature and weak with
that kind of experience. He knows just how much each one of us
can endure. Abram did not go through the darkness because he
was weak or uncommitted, but he went through it because it
was part of his total spiritual experience. His darkness was a
preview of what his descendants were to suffer in Egypt. As
their father, he had to share a measure of their suffering.

In verses 13 through 16, the Lord explained to Abram what
was going to happen to his descendants in Egypt and how ultimately He would intervene and deliver them and bring them
back to the land of Canaan. Then in verse 17, a new dimension
was added to Abram's experience: *"And it came about when the
sun had set, that it was very dark, and behold, there appeared a
smoking oven and a flaming torch which passed between these
pieces."* To the normal darkness of night was added the black-
ness of smoke belching from an oven. Frequently in Scripture,
an oven or a furnace typifies intense suffering. In Isaiah 48:10,

God said to Israel, *"Behold, I have refined you, but not as silver; I have tested you in the furnace of affliction"* (NAS).

This applies at times to all of God's people. If you should ever find yourself in the furnace, remember that is where God refines you and tests you. How you react in the furnace will determine your destiny. You are not necessarily in the furnace because you are weak or backslidden or because you have failed God. You are in the furnace because the furnace does things for you that nothing else can do. In Malachi 3:3, God warns the sons of Levi, His priests, that He will refine them as gold and silver are refined. Precious metals are never purified without intense heat.

In the midst of this overwhelming darkness to which Abram was subjected—a darkness that was both natural and supernatural—there was *"a flaming torch which passed between these pieces"* (v. 17). What a depth of meaning there is in that! The flaming torch was a manifestation of the Spirit of God, corresponding to the *"seven lamps of fire...which are the seven Spirits of God"* (Rev. 4:5 NAS) that John saw before the throne in heaven. It was at this moment—the moment of deepest darkness—that the Lord, in the appearance of the flaming torch, made His commitment to Abram. He passed between the pieces and, in so doing, He entered into the covenant.

Let me return again for a moment to my experience in the hospital in Egypt. It was at that time of darkness in my own life that the truth of this incident in Genesis chapter 15 became so vivid to me. I learned that there are times of utter darkness when the Holy Spirit will illuminate only one thing, the emblems of the sacrifice, because that is all we need to see. The sacrifice is the emblem of the covenant, and the covenant is God's final, irrevocable commitment.

You may pass through a time when you can see nothing but the one fact that Jesus died for you. That is all you need to know. Everything is included in that. Romans 8:32 tells us, *"He who did not spare His own Son, but delivered Him up for us all, how will He not also with Him freely give us all things?"* (NAS). There are times when that is all you can hold on to. It is the covenant made in the sacrificial death of the Lord Jesus Christ.

That is how the Lord and Abram entered into covenant. As I understand it, each passed in turn between the pieces of the sacrifices. Isn't it amazing that Almighty God would do that with a man? It staggers my mind that, in a certain sense, God would come all the way down from heaven to pass between those pieces of slain animals to make His commitment to Abram. I am overwhelmed to realize that God would go to such lengths to make His personal commitment to a man.

VALID ONLY THROUGH DEATH

But why was a sacrifice necessary? Why was that the only way to enter into a covenant? The answer is that the sacrifice symbolized the death of each party to the covenant. As each party walked between the pieces of the slain animal, he was saying, in effect, "That is my death. That animal died as my representative. He died in my place. As I enter into this covenant, I enter by death. Now that I am in covenant, I have no more right to live." That explains why both Hebrew and Greek make no distinction between *covenant* and *testament*.

The necessity of death to make a covenant valid is emphasized in Hebrews:

For where a covenant is, there must of necessity be the death of the one who made it. For a covenant is valid only when men are dead, for it is never in force while the one who made it lives. (Heb. 9:16–17 NAS)

These words leave no room for misunderstanding. The one who enters into a covenant enters into it by death. As long as a person remains alive, he is not in covenant. It is impossible to be in covenant and remain alive. The death of the sacrificed animal is physical, but it symbolizes another form of death for the one who offers the sacrifice and passes through the pieces. The one who does this hereby renounces all right, from that moment, to live for himself. As each party passes through the pieces of the sacrifice, he says, in effect, to the other: "If need be, I will die for you. From now on, your interests take precedence over my own. If I have anything you need but cannot supply, then my supply becomes your supply. I no longer live for myself; I live for you."

In God's sight, this act of making a covenant is no empty ritual. It is a solemn and sacred commitment. If we trace through history the course of events that resulted from the Lord's covenant with Abram, we see that each party had to make good the commitment that the covenant represented.

Some years later, when Abram had become Abraham, God said to him: "I want your son Isaac, your only son. The most precious thing you have is no longer yours, because you and I are in covenant. It is mine." To his eternal credit, Abraham did not falter. He was willing to offer up even Isaac. Only at the last moment did the Lord intervene directly from heaven and stop him from actually slaying his son. (See Genesis 22.)

However, that is not the end of the story. God had also committed Himself to Abraham. Two thousand years later, God, in His turn, fulfilled His part of the covenant. To meet the need of Abraham and his descendants, God offered up His only Son. But this time, there was no last-minute reprieve. On the cross, Jesus laid down His life as the full price of redemption for Abraham and all his descendants. That act was the outcome of the commitment that God and Abram had made to each other on that fateful night, two thousand years earlier, when they passed between those pieces of the sacrifice. All that followed from then on in the course of history was determined by their covenant.

The commitment that is made in a covenant is that solemn, that total, and that irrevocable.

CHAPTER THREE

UNION BETWEEN MAN AND WOMAN

In the first chapter, we saw that marriage on the highest plane is *"a cord of three strands"* (Eccl. 4:12 NAS)—a covenant among a man, a woman, and God. In chapter 2, we discovered that a covenant requires a sacrifice; otherwise, it is not valid. In this chapter, we will apply these principles specifically to a marriage in which believers are united through their faith in Christ.

The sacrifice upon which the covenant of Christian marriage is based is the death of Jesus Christ on our behalf. He is the sacrifice through which, by faith, a man and a woman can pass into the relationship of marriage as God Himself ordained that it should be. Just as the Lord and Abram passed between the pieces of the slain animals, so in marriage a man and woman pass through the death of Jesus Christ on their behalf into a totally new life and a totally new relationship that would have been impossible without the death of Jesus Christ. The covenant of Christian marriage is made at the foot of the cross.

There are three successive phases in the outworking of this relationship. First, a life is laid down. Each lays down his life for the other. The husband looks back at Christ's death on the cross and says: "That death was my death. When I came through the cross, I died. Now I am no longer living for myself." The wife likewise looks at the cross and says the same: "That death was my death. When I came through the cross, I died. Now I am no longer living for myself."

Henceforth, each holds nothing back from the other. Everything the husband has is for the wife. Everything the wife has is for the husband. No reservations, nothing held back. It is a merger, not a partnership.

Second, out of that death comes a new life. Each now lives out that new life in and through the other. The husband says to the wife: "My life is in you. I am living out my life through you. You are the expression of what I am." Likewise, the wife says to the husband: "My life is in you. I am living out my life through you. You are the expression of what I am."

Third, the covenant is consummated by physical union. This in turn brings forth fruit that continues the new life that each has been willing to share with the other. In the whole realm of living creatures, God has ordained this basic principle: Without union, there can be no fruit. Covenant leads to shared life and fruitfulness; life that is not shared remains sterile and fruitless.

This approach to marriage, which sees it in terms of a covenant, is very different from the attitude with which most people today enter into marriage. Basically, the attitude of our contemporary culture is, "What can I get? What is there in this for me?" I believe that any relationship approached with this attitude is doomed to end in failure. The one who approaches marriage as a covenant does not ask, "What can I get?" Rather, he asks, "What can I give?" And he goes on to answer his own question: "I give my life. I lay it down for you, and then I find my new life in you." This applies equally to each party—to the husband and to the wife. To the natural mind, this sounds ridiculous. Yet it is, in fact, the secret of real life, real happiness, and real love.

In this new relationship, each party has a special contribution to make. It is noteworthy that in every passage of the New Testament that deals with the mutual obligations of husband and wife, the writer always begins by explaining the special responsibilities of the wife. This is true whether the writer is Peter (a married man) or Paul (an unmarried man). It would seem that, in some sense, the wife is the pivot upon which the whole relationship turns. Unless she plays her part, there is no way that the husband on his own can make the relationship work. We will begin, therefore, by looking at the wife's contribution.

THE WIFE'S CONTRIBUTION

In Proverbs 31:10–31 (NAS), Solomon painted one of the most beautiful portraits to be found anywhere in the Bible, that of *"an excellent wife"* (v. 10 NAS). The King James Version translates this *"a virtuous woman."* Neither translation fully expresses the force of the original. What Solomon really had in mind, I believe, is a woman who knows what it is to be a woman—a woman who knows how to make the fullest and richest expression of her womanhood; a woman who succeeds as a woman.

He opened his description with a question: *"An excellent wife, who can find?"* (v. 10). This would indicate that such a woman is rare. Since I was privileged to share thirty years of my life with a woman who answered to Solomon's description, I can never read this passage without tears of gratitude coming into my eyes.

It is outside the scope of this book to examine every detail of the portrait that Solomon painted. But I want to point out one simple fact that is very significant: the beginning, the middle, and the end of the picture all focus on her husband. In other words, the supreme achievement of an excellent wife is her husband. Everything else she achieves apart from that is of secondary value. This is how a woman should measure her achievement as a wife. She is not living out her own life now. Her life is in her husband. She sees her success in him. She rejoices in his achievements more than in her own.

In verse 11, notice the first statement about this excellent wife: *"The heart of her husband trusts in her, and he will have no lack of gain."* He does not have to go out in the world and make himself a millionaire to prove himself. His wife's approval is sufficient for him. Many men strive unceasingly for success in business or other fields primarily out of a desire to prove themselves. Usually their root problem is that they never had the assurance of approval in their own homes—first from their parents, and later from their wives. Consequently, they go through life with a driving urge to gain approval and prove themselves. But a man who has the right kind of wife need not depend on anyone else for approval. Hers is enough. Everybody else may misunderstand him, and may even betray him, but he knows there is one person on whom he can totally rely. That is his wife. To be a wife of this kind is a very high achievement for a woman.

The husband's trust in this *"excellent wife"* is based on one simple but vitally important fact: *"She does him good and not evil all the days of her life"* (v. 12). For thirty years, I had that total assurance concerning Lydia. She would never do me evil. She would disagree with me, perhaps admonish me. We might argue or hold different opinions. But I always knew where I stood with her. She was one hundred percent on my side. Without that, I could never have become what I am today.

Let us move on now to verse 23, the central section of this description: *"Her husband is known in the gates, when he sits among the elders of the land."* Again the focus is on her husband. He is a recognized leader among his people, sitting in the gate, the place of honor and authority. Solomon's language is so expressive: *"Her husband is known."* In other words, he is known as her husband. Without her support, he would not have been able to hold the position of honor. This principle holds true in most cases where we see a successful, confident, respected man. A great part of what we are really seeing is his wife's success.

Then, in verses 28 and 29, the description closes with the focus on her family—first her children, but finally her husband once more:

> *Her children rise up and bless her; her husband also, and*
> *he praises her, saying: "Many daughters have done nobly,*
> *but you excel them all."*   *(vv. 28–29)*

So this description of the *"excellent wife"*—the truly successful woman—begins with, centers in, and concludes with her husband. He is her supreme achievement, beside which every other achievement is secondary.

What reward does he, on his part, have to offer her? *"He praises her."* How important that is! Husbands, if you have a wife like this, there is no salary that is adequate for her. You have nothing to pay her with except praise. And you can afford to be lavish with that form of payment because the more you pay, the more you receive in return. So take time to praise your wife. Tell her how sweet she is. Tell her how good her food tastes. Tell her how much you enjoy seeing the home so clean. Tell her how pretty she looks. Tell her how much you love her.

Take time to do it. It is a good investment. You will get back many times over everything you put in.

For my part, as I have already indicated, I can look back over thirty years of happy and successful marriage with Lydia. If I have one major regret, it is that I did not tell her often enough how much I loved her. I did love her, and she knew it. But I did not tell her as often as I should have. If I could live that part of my life again, I would tell her ten times as often.

Let us return again for a moment to the wife's part. How can a wife achieve this kind of success with her husband? I would say that she has two main responsibilities, closely related to each other. The first is to uphold her husband; the second is to encourage him.

In 1 Corinthians 11:3, Paul said that *"the man* [husband] *is the head of a woman* [wife]" (NAS). In the natural body, final responsibility for decision and direction rests with the head. Yet the head cannot hold itself up. It depends upon the rest of the body to do this. Without the support of the rest of the body, primarily the neck, the head alone cannot fulfill its function.

This applies to the marriage relationship. As head, the husband has final responsibility for decision and direction. But he cannot fulfill this function on his own. He is dependent upon the body to uphold him. In a sense, the wife's responsibility may be likened to that of the neck. She is the one closest to her husband, on whose support he must continually rely. If she fails to uphold him, there is no way that he can function as he should. Just as there is no other part of the body that can take the place of the neck in upholding the head, so there is no other person who can give to the husband the support that he needs from his wife.

The wife's second main responsibility is to encourage her husband. A man should be able to look to his wife for encouragement at all times, particularly when he least deserves it. If Lydia had only encouraged me when I deserved it, it would not have been what I needed. I needed encouragement most when I deserved it the least. I needed somebody who had faith in me when no one else did. I didn't need a sermon. I didn't need a counselor. I needed someone to trust me.

Encouraging is not an easy thing for a wife to do—especially in times of pressure. It is much easier to reproach or criticize. In fact, encouraging is a ministry that must be cultivated. I believe that many times a wife can transform a bad marriage and an unsuccessful husband into a good marriage and a successful husband, if she will learn how to encourage. But that always means self-denial. We cannot encourage others when we are primarily interested in ourselves. If you and your husband are both feeling miserable, what are you going to do? Tell him how miserable you are, or encourage him? To encourage him requires self-denial. But that is the essence of the marriage covenant. You are no longer living for yourself.

This brings us back to our starting point: covenant commitment. This alone can provide the grace and the power that each party in a marriage needs to make it successful. Good advice or a set of rules are not sufficient by themselves to do this. There are a number of excellent books available today that offer counsel and instruction from a Christian viewpoint on how to have a successful marriage. But in the last resort, Christian marriage will not work without the supernatural grace of God; and this grace is received only as husband and wife yield themselves to God and to one another in covenant commitment.

THE HUSBAND'S CONTRIBUTION

Now we will consider the husband's contribution to the marriage covenant. A good starting place is provided by the words of Paul in 1 Corinthians 11:7: *"For a man ought not to have his head covered, since he is the image and glory of God; but the woman is the glory of man"* (NAS).

It is the closing statement that we are concerned with just now: *"the woman* [wife] *is the glory of man* [husband]." This simply takes the same principle that has been applied to the wife and applies it to the husband as well. We have already seen that the success of the wife is manifested in the husband. Now, Paul tells us, the wife is the evidence of the husband's success. She is his glory, his greatest achievement. Uniquely and supremely, she is a living demonstration of the quality of her husband.

A well-known evangelist was once asked about a fellow believer, "What kind of a Christian is he?" "I can't tell you yet," he replied, "I haven't met his wife!" That was a wise answer. Personally, I would never form an estimate of a married man until I had come to know his wife, because she is his glory. If she is radiant and restful and secure, her husband has earned my respect. But if, on the other hand, she is frustrated and nervous and insecure, I have to conclude that there is some area of failure in the husband.

This relationship of the wife to her husband as his glory is beautifully illustrated by a parable from the heavenly bodies: the relationship of the moon to the sun. The moon is the glory of the sun. The moon has no glory of its own. Its only beauty comes from reflecting the radiance of the sun.

Some years ago, in the NASA center in Houston, Texas, I had the opportunity to see a fragment of rock from the moon's surface that had been brought back to earth by the astronauts. For a while, I gazed at it in awe. Finally, I bowed my head in reverent worship of the Creator as I began to understand the perfect wisdom of His design. The moon rock is dull and unattractive in itself. It has no brilliance or radiance of its own. Yet it is the most highly reflective material that man has yet discovered. Why? The reason, of course, is that it was designed by the Creator for one supreme purpose—to reflect the radiance of the sun. This it will continue to do, so long as nothing comes between it and the sun. But if some other body—for example, the earth—comes between the moon and the sun, the result is manifested in the moon. It loses its light.

All this is a parable that illustrates a much more wonderful work of the Creator's genius—the marriage relationship. The wife is like the moon. She has no glory of her own. Her function is to reflect her husband. When he shines on her, she glows. But if the full, open fellowship between them is broken—if something comes in between—the result is manifested in the wife. She loses her light.

Those of us who are husbands would do well to check from time to time on our performance in this regard. We should be ready to see our wife's condition as a reflection of our own. We males are often quick to notice some area of weakness in our wives—even perhaps to be unkind or critical about it. Yet it may well be that the problem we see so clearly in our wife is, in reality, but the reflection of a corresponding problem that has gone unrecognized in ourselves.

What should a husband look for in his wife? What should he accept as evidence that he is fulfilling his responsibility toward her? If I had to answer this question in one word, the word I would choose would be security. When a married woman is truly secure—emotionally secure, financially secure, socially secure—in most cases that is sufficient evidence that her relationship with her husband is good and that he is fulfilling his obligations toward her. But if a married woman is subject to frequent or continuing insecurity, almost invariably this can be traced to one of two causes: either her husband is not fulfilling his obligation to her, or something has come in between them that prevents the wife from receiving what her husband has to give her.

What are the main practical ways in which a husband should fulfill his responsibility toward his wife? I would suggest that they can be summed up in two words: to protect and to provide.

A husband's primary practical responsibility is to protect his wife. She should feel secure. She should know that she has a covering. It is unfair to ask women to take many of the responsibilities that are thrust upon them today. They may prove to be very efficient; they may even outdo men; but they lose their femininity. In most cases, the true, underlying cause is that the husband has abdicated from his responsibility to protect his wife. A wife should always know that she has someone to stand between her and every blow, every attack, every pressure.

A husband's second practical responsibility is to provide for his wife. Scripture is very clear about this. *"But if anyone does not provide for his own, and especially for those of his household, he has denied the faith, and is worse than an unbeliever"* (1 Tim. 5:8 NAS). The word *"provide"* has a wide application. A husband should see that there is no area of need in his wife for which he has not made provision—whether the need be physical or emotional, cultural or spiritual.

However, one major area in which a husband is responsible to provide for his wife is that of finance. Normally, he should accept full responsibility for her financial needs. A man who does not do this when he can will almost inevitably forfeit some measure of authority in his home. It is hard to separate the earning of money from the right to make decisions about the way the money is spent. But the making of such decisions should be a function of headship. If a wife earns as much as, or more than, her husband, it is hard for him to retain effective headship.

We know, of course, that there are exceptions to this. There are husbands who become incapacitated and unable to work. In such cases, the responsibility for financial provision may fall upon the wife. The marriage vow makes allowance for such cases as this; it covers "in sickness" as well as "in health." However, it is wrong when unfortunate exceptions such as this become the normal rule.

Briefly, now, we may sum up the mutual responsibilities of husband and wife in this covenant relationship of marriage. The main responsibilities of the husband are to protect and to provide. The main responsibilities of the wife are to uphold and to encourage. However, the proper fulfillment of these responsibilities can never be achieved by mere unaided human effort or willpower. It takes something more than that; it takes the supernatural, all-sufficient grace of God. This kind of grace comes only as husband and wife together commit themselves to God and to one another in solemn, covenant relationship. It is the act of commitment that releases God's grace.

The outcome of this commitment is a new kind of life and relationship, one that can never be experienced by those who have not first met the conditions. We will go on now to see what is the distinctive character of this new life.

UNION LEADS TO KNOWING

The result of covenant commitment between a man and a woman can be summed up in one word: knowing. A man and a woman come to know each other in a depth and a degree that is not possible in any other way. The verb "to know" in the original language of Scripture has a meaning both wider and deeper than its English counterpart. In Genesis 4:1, it says, *"And Adam knew Eve his wife; and she conceived, and bare Cain"*

(KJV). (The New American Standard Bible says, *"The man had relations with his wife Eve."* However, the King James retains the correct, literal meaning of the original Hebrew.) This is the first time that the word *know* is used in Scripture after the Fall. It is also the first recorded occasion that a man and a woman came together in sexual union.

However, the writers of the Old Testament were very precise and discriminating in the way in which they used the verb "to know" to describe sexual intercourse between a man and a woman. Wherever a man came together with a woman in a covenant union that had the seal of God's approval, Scripture says that he *knew* her. But where it was an illicit relationship, one that God had not endorsed and did not approve, Scripture says that he *lay with* her. The implication is that it is possible for a man to have sexual intercourse with a woman and yet not to *know* her. I believe that this is fully borne out in experience. Indeed, a man may have promiscuous sexual intercourse with fifty women, and yet never *know* one of them.

What, then, is the essential difference between merely "lying with" a woman and "knowing" a woman? The answer can be given in one word: commitment. The essence of sexual immorality is that a man and a woman seek physical and emotional satisfaction from each other, but they have not made a permanent commitment to each other. The pleasure that they obtain in this way is stolen. They have not paid the due price for it.

This brings out how much importance God attaches to commitment. Sexual intercourse that is not preceded by permanent, mutual commitment is immorality. "Premarital sex" is the fancy title given to it in contemporary society. *Fornication* is the blunt word used in Scripture. On the other hand, *marriage* is sexual union that is preceded by legitimate, mutual commitment. The difference in God's attitude toward these two relationships is clearly brought out in Hebrews 13:4: *"Let marriage be held in honor among all, and let the marriage bed be undefiled; for fornicators and adulterers God will judge"* (NAS). In this context, *"fornicators"* are to be understood as those who indulge in sexual relationships without covenant commitment. *"Adulterers"* are those who have made a marriage commitment, but then indulge in sexual relationships that violate their commitment. In both cases, the essence of the sin is a wrong attitude toward covenant commitment.

We return to God's ultimate purpose for marriage: that a man and a woman come to know each other. I suppose that the full depth of this truth can only be appreciated by those who have been privileged to experience it. Such knowledge between a man and a woman is neither temporary nor static. It is not merely intellectual, as we normally understand knowledge in contemporary terminology, nor is it merely sexual. It is a total, unreserved opening up of each personality to the other. It embraces every area—physical, emotional, intellectual, and spiritual. If the marriage pursues its God-ordained course, the mutual knowledge of husband and wife will become fuller and deeper as the years pass.

It is my personal conviction that the greatest wonder of all God's creative achievement is expressed in human personality. Jesus taught that one human soul is worth more than the whole world. (See Mark 8:36–37.) I believe this is a true, objective evaluation. The whole created universe, in all its grandeur and greatness, is of less intrinsic worth than one human personality. The marvel of marriage is that, through it, two human personalities are permitted to know each other in all their uniqueness, permitted to explore the sacred, innermost depths of each other. But just because marriage in this sense is so wondrous and so sacred, God has protected it with His demand for covenant commitment.

There are countless facets to the way in which a man and his wife may come to know one another. For instance, the very way in which they look at one another is different from the way in which they look at other people, or other people look at them. One of my favorite (but unclassified) occupations is watching a husband and wife when they are not aware that anyone is watching them. What I always look at is their eyes. (Someone has said that the eye is the window of the soul.) Give me time to observe the looks that a husband and wife exchange between themselves, and I will form a pretty accurate estimate of how successful their marriage is.

A wife has a way of looking at her husband that tells him almost everything without saying anything in words. For instance,

"It's time *you* took care of the kids." Or, "You shouldn't have spent so long talking to that other woman." Or, "If we go home now, we can have an hour together by ourselves." For this reason, Scripture indicates that a married woman should never permit herself to look at any other person in the way that she looks at her husband.

This is very vividly illustrated by an incident in the life of Abraham. Abraham was a great man of faith, but he had certain very human weaknesses. On two occasions, in order to save his own life, he was prepared to let his wife Sarah be taken into the harem of a gentile king. He was slow to realize that divine destiny had linked him irrevocably with Sarah and could never be fulfilled through any other woman. Abraham's weakness in this respect should serve as a warning to husbands in this age. In 1 Peter 3:7, Christian husbands are reminded that their wives are, with them, *"fellow heir[s] of the grace of life"* (NAS). The phrase *"fellow heir"* indicates a joint inheritance, one that neither party can legally claim apart from the other. There are areas of God's inheritance for married couples that neither can enter without the other. These areas are reserved solely for couples who can move together in mutual love and harmony. This principle applies as much to Christian husbands today as it did in Abraham's relationship to Sarah.

The second of the two occasions on which Abraham was prepared to part with Sarah was in the court of Abimelech, king of Gerar. (See Genesis chapter 20.) Abraham persuaded Sarah to say that she was his sister—which was true, but not the whole truth—and to conceal the fact that she was also his wife. As a result, Abimelech took her into his harem, intending to make her his wife. However, God intervened supernaturally to preserve Sarah. In a dream, He revealed to Abimelech that Sarah was really Abraham's wife and warned him that if he took her, he would pay for it with his own life. Abimelech, who was apparently a God-fearing man, immediately returned Sarah to Abraham and compensated him with substantial gifts for the wrong that he had done.

In conclusion, however, Abimelech addressed a word of reproof and warning to Sarah: *"And unto Sarah he said, Behold, I have given thy brother a thousand pieces of silver: behold, he is*

171

to thee a covering of the eyes, unto all that are with thee, and with all other: thus she was reproved" (Genesis 20:16 KJV). We may sum up the essence of Abimelech's reproof to Sarah in this way: "When you are married, you may never look at another man in the way that you look at your husband. He is a covering of the eyes to you." There is a way in which a woman opens up her eyes to her husband that is both scriptural and very sacred. She should never deliberately let any other man look into her eyes the way her husband does.

Obviously, there is another side to this: just as a married woman has no right to look in this way at a man who is not her husband, so a married man has no right to receive such a look from a woman who is not his wife. To his credit, it would seem that Abimelech recognized this.

At any rate, this warning given to Sarah by Abimelech expresses, in a simple but vivid way, the essence of the relationship into which a man and woman enter through the covenant of marriage. Through their covenant commitment to each other, they come to know one another in a way in which neither of them should ever know any other person and no other person should ever know either of them. The purpose of the marriage covenant is to preserve this unique and sacred knowledge between husband and wife and to keep it from being violated by any other relationship.

CHAPTER FOUR

UNION WITH GOD

The marriage covenant is not merely sacred in its own right. It is sacred also because it typifies other relationships of great spiritual significance. The first and the most important of these is the relationship that God desires to have with His people.

GOD, THE HUSBAND OF HIS PEOPLE

In various passages of the Old Testament, God compared His relationship with Israel to that of a husband with a wife. He traced this relationship back to the covenant that He made with Israel at Mount Sinai after He had delivered them out of Egypt. Thus, God's relationship as a husband to Israel, like the human relationship of a man with his wife, is based on a covenant that He entered into when He made them His people. This is clearly brought out in Jeremiah:

"Behold, days are coming," declares the LORD, "when I will make a new covenant with the house of Israel and with the house of Judah, not like the covenant which I made with their fathers in the day I took them by the hand to bring them out of the land of Egypt, My covenant which they broke, although I was a husband to them," declares the LORD. (Jer. 31:31–32 NAS)

God said here that when He brought Israel out of Egypt and made a covenant with them, He entered into the relationship of a husband to them by that act. However, by unfaithfulness and

173

idolatry, Israel violated their covenant and forfeited their right to this relationship with God as their Husband. Nevertheless, rather than finally rejecting Israel for their unfaithfulness, God here declares that, at the close of this age, He will make a new covenant with them and thus once again become their Husband.

In Hosea 3:1, we again find God's relationship with Israel pictured as that of a husband to his wife: *"Then the LORD said to me, 'Go again, love a woman who is loved by her husband, yet an adulteress, even as the LORD loves the sons of Israel, though they turn to other gods and love raisin cakes'"* (NAS). By his continuing love for his wife Gomer, in spite of her unfaithfulness, the prophet Hosea became a type of God's continuing love for Israel, as their Husband, which did not cease even though they were persistently unfaithful on their side of the relationship.

In Hosea, as in Jeremiah, there is a prophetic promise that God will eventually bring Israel back into covenant with Himself and thereby restore His relationship to them as their Husband. God declared the following:

> *"And it will come about in that day,"* declares the LORD, *"that you will call Me Ishi* [my Husband] *and will no longer call Me Baali* [my Master]." *(Hos. 2:16 NAS)*

Then, in Hosea 2:18, God spoke of the new covenant that He would make with them. In verses 19 and 20, He pictured the result of this covenant as the restoration of His marriage relationship to them:

> *And I will betroth you to Me forever; yes, I will betroth you to Me in righteousness and in justice, in lovingkindness and in compassion, and I will betroth you to Me in faithfulness. Then you will know the LORD.* *(NAS)*

There is special significance in the closing statement of verse 20: *"Then you will know the LORD."* We have already seen that, in the natural, covenant brings a man and a woman into a union in which they come to know each other as they never could without such a commitment. Here the principle is applied to Israel's restored relationship to God. Through their covenant

174

commitment they would come to *"know the LORD"* as they had never known Him before.

Briefly, then, we may sum up the Old Testament picture of God's relationship to Israel as follows: The covenant that God made with Israel at Mount Sinai is viewed as establishing a marriage relationship between God and Israel, through which He became their Husband. Subsequently, through unfaithfulness and idolatry, Israel violated the covenant and forfeited their right to this relationship. God did not finally reject Israel on this account, nor did His love for them cease. Therefore, His ultimate purpose was to establish a new covenant with them through which He would once again enter into the relationship of a husband to them. This new covenant, unlike the first, would be eternal. It would never be violated. Through it, Israel would come to know the Lord with a totally new depth of intimacy, such as they had never hitherto experienced.

The New Testament more fully unveils the nature of this new covenant. It is based not on the sacrifice of animals, but on the atoning death of Jesus Christ, the Son of God. This is the covenant into which all those of whatever race or background who acknowledge Jesus as Savior and Lord have already entered. Consistent with the pattern already established in the Old Testament, this new covenant in Christ is viewed as bringing believers into a relationship with God that is analogous to the marriage relationship between husband and wife.

In Ephesians 5:25–33, Paul said that Christ redeems and sanctifies His church in order that He may present it to Himself as a bride is presented to her husband, *"holy and blameless"* (v. 27 NAS). Paul went on to apply this truth in a practical way to the natural relationship between husband and wife, but he closes by saying: *"This mystery is great; but I am speaking with reference to Christ and the church"* (v. 32 NAS). In other words, the relationship between Christ and the church is analogous to that between a husband and his wife.

ONE SPIRIT WITH GOD

In First Corinthians, Paul applied this picture not merely to the relationship of God to His people as a whole, but also to the relationship that God desires to have with each individual believer:

> *Or do you not know that the one who joins himself to a harlot is one body with her? For He says, "THE TWO WILL BECOME ONE FLESH." But the one who joins himself to the Lord is one spirit with Him.* (1 Cor. 6:16–17 NAS)

As usual with the writers of Scripture, Paul was very frank. He was speaking about the sexual union between a man and a woman. He said that a man who has sexual relations with a harlot makes himself *"one body"* with her. Then he went on to say that a believer can have a similar kind of union with God in which he becomes *"one spirit"* with God. Plus, the relationship that God invites each believer to have with Him is precisely parallel, on the spiritual plane, to the sexual union which, on the physical plane, a man may have with a woman.

In the last chapter, we have already seen the essential difference between the marriage union, which is pure and holy, and fornication, which is sinful. The difference is that the marriage union is preceded by mutual covenant commitment on the part of the man and the woman. In fornication, on the other hand, a man and a woman seek sexual satisfaction from each other, without being willing to make a covenant commitment to each other.

The language Paul used in 1 Corinthians 6:16–17 clearly justifies us in applying this principle also to the relationship between God and the believer. God desires spiritual union with each believer. At the same time, however, it is certain that God will never violate His own laws. He will never be a party to "spiritual fornication." Therefore, union with God in this sense depends upon, and must be preceded by, covenant commitment to God. Until a believer is ready to make the total, unreserved commitment to God that covenant requires, he can never have this full spiritual union with God that is the purpose of redemption.

Earlier, in examining Psalm 50:5, we saw how God defines His *"godly ones"* (NAS). They are those "who cut a covenant with Him on the basis of a sacrifice." The lesson is the same as that of 1 Corinthians 6:16–17. There is no way to the intimacy of union with God, which is godliness, except through covenant commitment. Without such commitment, a person can never truly be a *"godly one."* He can never be truly united with God.

This explains the pathetic condition of many people in our churches today. They desire a relationship with God. They may even lay claim to such a relationship. Nevertheless, their desire is unfulfilled; their claim is unjustified. The reason is that they have never made that solemn, unreserved, personal commitment to God that is the only basis upon which He will receive them into the relationship that they desire.

Such persons may indeed have made a decision at an evangelistic campaign. They may have gone forward in a church and shaken the pastor by the hand. They may have even gone through a religious ritual, such as baptism or confirmation. But all these acts—and many others too numerous to list—are of no avail unless they bring people into a vital, committed, covenant relationship with God. Short of this, there can be no true intimacy with God. He does not commit Himself to the uncommitted.

LIFE'S PURPOSE IS KNOWING GOD

For those, however, who are willing to enter into this type of covenant commitment to God, the reward is great. It is beautifully expressed by the words that Jesus addressed to the Father in John 17:3: *"And this is eternal life, that they may know Thee, the only true God, and Jesus Christ whom Thou hast sent"* (NAS). I once heard a paraphrase that rendered the verse, "And this is the purpose of eternal life, that they may know Thee, the only true God." Here, indeed, is the ultimate purpose of all life—to know the one true God. Out of this knowledge there comes eternal life, divine life, the life of God Himself, shared with the believer.

However, knowledge of this kind is not merely intellectual. It is not merely theology or doctrine. It is not knowing about God. It is actually knowing God Himself—knowing Him directly and intimately; knowing Him as a Person. It is a person-to-person relationship. It is a spiritual union.

Knowing God in this way is exactly parallel, on the spiritual plane, to the way in which a man may come to "know" a woman as his wife, and a woman may come to "know" a man as her husband. The use in Scripture of the same word to describe each type of relationship is no accident. It reveals the deep, underlying similarity that exists between the two relationships. In the natural, a man and a woman can never truly "know" one another unless they first make an unreserved, covenant commitment to each other. In the spiritual, a believer can never truly "know" God unless he has first made an unreserved, covenant commitment to God. The same principle applies on each plane: without covenant there can be no union; and without commitment there can be no covenant.

Does commitment of this kind sound too intense for you? Too intimate? Too absolute? In the last resort, each of us must make his own decision about this. But let me say that, for myself, I could never be interested in some watered-down, religious substitute for the real thing. Rather, I echo the words of David:

O God, Thou art my God; I shall seek Thee earnestly; My soul thirsts for Thee, my flesh yearns for Thee, in a dry and weary land where there is no water. *(Ps. 63:1 NAS)*

To the soul that is truly thirsty, there can be only one source of ultimate satisfaction: it is God Himself. To stop at less than true union with Him is to miss the real purpose of living. It is to remain forever frustrated, forever unfulfilled.

In Isaiah 1:22, God told rebellious, backslidden Israel, *"Your silver has become dross, your drink diluted with water"* (NAS). The same could be said to many churches today. Everything has lost its purity, its true character. We are asked to accept something adulterated and impure, a counterfeit of the real thing.

In the natural, if somebody were to offer me wine diluted with water, my response would be, "Spare yourself the trouble; keep the whole thing!" But today, in the church and in society, we are mixing everything with water. We dilute it, we water it down, we lower the standards. Our silver no longer has its proper value; our wine no longer has its proper flavor.

In such a spiritual climate, it takes a person of considerable strength of character to settle for nothing less than God's best. Such a person must be willing to say, "Others may do it the way they please, I will do it God's way. I want a real relationship with God. I want a marriage that works, a home that glorifies God, children that grow up happy and secure. Yes, I want these things—and I am willing to pay the price!"

God has made the price quite clear: it is a covenant commitment—on the vertical plane, to God Himself; on the horizontal plane, to our mates.

CHAPTER FIVE

UNION WITH GOD'S PEOPLE

In the two preceding chapters, we have seen that covenant is the indispensable condition for true union. In chapter 3, we saw how this principle applies to the union between a man and a woman, which we call marriage. In chapter 4, we saw how it applies also to the union of each believer with God, which on the spiritual plane is analogous to the marriage union. In this chapter, we will examine how the same principle applies to yet another relationship of vital importance: the relationship of God's people to one another.

COVENANT MAKES A "PEOPLE"

In the Old Testament, we find that from the time God entered into a covenant with Abraham, his descendants (through the line of Isaac and Jacob) were set apart from all other members of the human race. From that time forth, they were known as *"the seed of Abraham"* (2 Chron. 20:7 KJV). However, the outworking of God's purpose required that the covenant be established a second time, not with Abraham individually, but with all his descendants collectively. This took place at Mount Sinai after the Exodus. Thereafter, they were designated by a new title in the singular form: a *people* (Hebrew *'am*). This indicated that through entering into the covenant they had become a new, collective unit.

The process by which God entered into His covenant with Israel is described in Exodus, beginning in chapter 19. Here, God declares the purpose for which He was bringing Israel into covenant relationship with Himself:

Now then, if you will indeed obey My voice and keep My covenant, then you shall be My own possession among all the peoples, for all the earth is Mine; and you shall be to Me a kingdom of priests and a holy nation.   (Exod. 19:5–6 NAS)

We need to understand that, from then on, Israel was set apart unto God as a special people, not by any intrinsic righteousness of their own, but by the covenant God made with them. It is important to see that their holiness was the outcome of the covenant, not the reason for it. To express this another way: God did not enter into a covenant with Israel because they were holy; rather, He made them holy by entering into a covenant with them.

In our preceding chapter, we saw that on the basis of this covenant God assumed toward them the relationship and the responsibility of a husband. The covenant established a relationship between God and Israel analogous to that between a husband and a wife. It gave them a unique relationship to God in the same way that marriage gives a woman a unique relationship to her husband.

However, the only basis on which Israel had a right to continue in this unique and special relationship with God was by remaining faithful to the covenant. For this reason, God prefixed the declaration of His purpose for them by the word *if*. "*If you will indeed obey My voice and keep My covenant, then you shall be My own possession among all the peoples...and a holy nation.*" Israel's continuing unique relationship to God was, therefore, bound up with their abiding by the terms of the covenant. For this reason, when Israel lapsed into idolatry, their prophets frequently categorized their sin as adultery. It was analogous to that of a wife who had failed to abide by her marriage commitment to her husband.

From the time that God established this covenant with Israel, a careful distinction was made by the Old Testament writers in their usage of two related Hebrew words: *goy* (nation) and *'am* (people). All nations, including Israel, are *goyim* (plural of *goy*)—"nations." But Israel alone is also *'am*—a "people." That which singles Israel out by this distinctive title from all other nations is their unique covenant relationship with God.

In the New Testament, the same distinction is maintained by the use of two different Greek words: *ethnos* (nation), which corresponds to the Hebrew *goy,* and *laos* (people), which corresponds to the Hebrew *'am.* The Greek *ethnos,* in its plural form *ethne,* is translated alternatively "nations" or "gentiles." It is important to understand that the word *gentiles* normally does not refer to people who are not Christians, but rather refers to people who are not Israelites.

This analysis of the distinctive words used both in Hebrew and in Greek for "people" and "nation" has been necessary to establish one vital basic principle of Scripture: it takes a covenant (*b'rit*) to constitute a people (*'am*). An ethnic group that has no collective covenant with God is merely a "nation," but an ethnic group that has a collective covenant with God is, by that fact, a "people."

COVENANT RELATIONSHIPS: VERTICAL AND HORIZONTAL

If we turn back once more to the passage that begins in Exodus chapter 19 where God enters into a covenant with Israel, we discover a second, related principle: the same covenant that brought Israel into a unique relationship with God also, by that fact, brought them into a unique relationship with one another. The main purpose of the subsequent chapters of Exodus (chapters 10 through 23) was to define the specific, practical ways in which God required them, from then onward, to relate to one another. As members of one covenant people, they had special obligations to each other, different from those that they had to members of other nations who had no covenant relationship either with God or with Israel.

We may state this principle more generally, as follows: Those who have a covenant relationship with God necessarily also have a covenant relationship with each other. The relationships established by a covenant extend in two directions: vertical and horizontal. The covenant that brings us into union vertically with God must of necessity also bring us into union horizontally with all who have entered into the same covenant with God. We have no right to claim the benefits of covenant relationship with God, while at the same time refusing to accept our obligations toward those who share the same covenant with

Him. The same covenant that brings individuals into union with God also brings them into collective union with one another. It establishes them collectively as a "people" who are set apart from all other collective units of humanity.

These principles concerning covenant established in the Old Testament are carried over, unchanged, into the New Testament. When Jesus celebrated the Last Supper with His disciples and shared with them the bread and the wine, He brought them into a covenant relationship with Himself by that act. After He had handed them the cup and told them all to drink of it, He said, *"This is My blood of the covenant"* (Matt. 26:28 NAS). They not merely shared the cup of the covenant with Him; they also shared it with each other. The same solemn act that brought each of them into covenant with Jesus, at the same time brought them all into covenant with one another. From then on, their covenant relationship was not merely vertical, to Jesus; it was also horizontal, to each other.

This is borne out in 1 Corinthians, where Paul was explaining the significance of the Lord's Supper. He emphasized this horizontal relationship between all who partake of the one loaf and the one cup:

> *Is not the cup of blessing which we bless a sharing in the blood of Christ? Is not the bread which we break a sharing in the body of Christ? Since there is one bread, we who are many are one body; for we all partake of the one bread.*
>
> *(1 Cor. 10:16–17 NAS)*

Peter also declared that the new covenant in Christ has the same effect as God's previous covenant with Israel: it establishes all who enter into it as a collective *"people"*:

> *But you are A CHOSEN RACE, A royal PRIESTHOOD, A HOLY NATION, A PEOPLE FOR God's OWN POSSESSION, that you may proclaim the excellencies of Him who has called you out of darkness into His marvelous light* [Peter is quoting the very words spoken by God to Israel in Exodus 19:5–6]; *for you once were NOT A PEOPLE, but now you are THE PEOPLE OF GOD; you had NOT RECEIVED MERCY, but now you have RECEIVED MERCY.* *(1 Pet. 2:9–10 NAS)*

We have already seen in two cases that the end purpose of covenant is union. The purpose of the marriage covenant is to bring a man and a woman into union with each other. The purpose of the covenant between God and the individual believer is to bring the believer into union with God. This principle applies with equal force to the third case—the covenant between believers. Its purpose is to bring all believers into union with each other.

After Jesus had shared the bread and wine of the new covenant with His disciples, He went on to share with them the intimate discourse recorded in John chapters 14 through 16. This teaching came to its climax with His High Priestly Prayer for them in John chapter 17. This prayer, in turn, culminates with His plea to the Father that all who believe in Him *"may be one, just as We are one"* (John 17:22 NAS). In this context, we understand that this plea constitutes the outworking of the covenant that He had established with them earlier that evening. The end purpose of the covenant is union of the same nature and quality as what exists between the Father and the Son. Until we, as believers, have come into this unity, we have not fulfilled our covenant obligations—either to Christ or to one another.

We have already pointed out that when God made His covenant with Israel at Mount Sinai, He immediately explained to the Israelites the obligations that the covenant would impose upon them in their relationships and dealings with one another. These obligations are set out, in specific and practical terms, in Exodus chapters 20 through 23. In a corresponding way, the New Testament sets forth, for all who enter into the new covenant in Christ, the ways in which they are obligated, by their covenant commitment, to relate to one another. It is outside the scope of this book to examine in detail all the mutual obligations of believers toward each other. However, we may form a general picture of these obligations by picking out phrases such as *"each other"* or *"one to another"* wherever they occur in the New Testament and listing the various mutual obligations that are thereby indicated.

All who have entered into the new covenant in Christ are required to behave in the following ways toward one another:

- Wash one another's feet (John 13:14).
- Love one another (John 13:34, et al).
- Build up one another (Romans 14:19).
- Accept one another (Romans 15:7).
- Admonish one another (Romans 15:14, et al).
- Greet one another (Romans 16:16, et al).
- Serve one another (Galatians 5:13).
- Bear one another's burdens (Galatians 6:2).
- Show forbearance to one another (Ephesians 4:2).
- Forgive one another (Ephesians 4:32).
- Be subject to one another (Ephesians 5:21).
- Teach one another (Colossians 3:16).
- Comfort one another (1 Thessalonians 4:18).
- Encourage one another (Hebrews 3:13).
- Stimulate one another to love and good deeds (Hebrews 10:24).
- Confess their sins to one another (James 5:16).
- Pray for one another (James 5:16).
- Be hospitable to one another (1 Peter 4:9).
- Be clothed with humility toward one another (1 Peter 5:5).

Only insofar as we, as believers, discharge these mutual responsibilities toward one another are we fulfilling the terms of the new covenant.

Although the obligations of the new covenant are stated somewhat differently from those of the covenant made at Mount Sinai, the basic principle is the same: those who enter into a covenant with God are, by that very act, necessarily brought into covenant with one another. The obligations of each covenant extend in two directions: vertically, between the covenant people and God and horizontally, between the members of the covenant people.

ONLY DEATH VALIDATES THE COVENANT

Another principle that applies universally in each covenant is that the covenant is valid only on the basis of the sacrifice. This general principle is stated, as we saw in chapter 2, in Hebrews:

For where a covenant is, there must of necessity be the death of the one who made it. For a covenant is valid only when men are dead, for it is never in force while the one who made it lives. (Heb. 9:16–17 NAS)

In the next three verses, the writer of Hebrews applied this principle specifically to the covenant between God and Israel that was mediated by Moses at Mount Sinai:

Therefore even the first covenant was not inaugurated without blood. For when every commandment had been spoken by Moses to all the people according to the Law, he took the blood of the calves and the goats, with water and scarlet wool and hyssop, and sprinkled both the book itself and all the people, saying, "THIS IS THE BLOOD OF THE COVENANT WHICH GOD COMMANDED YOU." (vv. 18–20 NAS)

In each case, the death of the sacrifice represented the death of those who entered by it into the covenant. The animals sacrificed by Moses merely reminded Israel of the principle that covenant was valid only through death and prefigured a different kind of sacrifice that had not yet been offered. On the other hand, the death of Jesus on the cross was substitutionary. He died as the personal representative of all who were to enter into the covenant with God through Him. Jesus identified Himself with each of them in death, that each in turn might identify himself with Jesus. As this two-way identification is worked out through the ongoing commitment of each believer, the death of Jesus becomes, effectively and experientially, the death of the believer. This principle is clearly stated by Paul in 2 Corinthians:

For the love of Christ controls us, having concluded this, that one died for all, therefore all died; and He died for all, that they who live should no longer live for themselves, but for Him who died and rose again on their behalf. (2 Cor. 5:14–15 NAS)

Paul's conclusion is both clear and logical. It is summed up in the words *"therefore all died."* If we accept Christ's death as our death, then we must *"consider* [ourselves] *to be dead"* (Rom. 6:11 NAS). Therefore, we are no longer free to live for ourselves. This, too, has a two-way application: vertically, toward the Lord and horizontally, toward the Lord's people. When the Lord and Abram entered into covenant with each other, each voluntarily abrogated the right to live only for himself. Each, by the "cutting" of the covenant, said, in effect, to the other: "That is my death. As I enter into this covenant, I enter by death. Now that I am in covenant, I have no more right to live."

The same relationship that was established that memorable night, person-to-person, between the Lord and Abram is reestablished among all who, through the death of Jesus, are brought into covenant with each other. Each of us reaffirms the mutual covenant of which the Lord and Abram are the prototype, the original pattern. Each says to the other: "That is my death. As I enter into this covenant, I enter by death. Now that I am in covenant, I have no more right to live."

In 1 John, the outworking of the death that alone makes our covenant valid is applied by the apostle specifically to our relationship with our fellow believers:

> *We know love by this, that He laid down His life for us; and we ought to lay down our lives for the brethren. But whoever has the world's goods, and beholds his brother in need and closes his heart against him, how does the love of God abide in him?*   (1 John 3:16–17 NAS)

The phrase *"we ought to"* expresses an obligation—one that we cannot evade if we claim to be partakers of the same covenant. When John spoke about laying down our lives, he was not speaking solely—or even primarily—about undergoing physical death. He made this quite clear, because in the next verse he applied it to making our worldly goods available to our fellow believers. If we are not willing to do this where there is a legitimate need, then we are not willing to *"lay down our lives."* Laying down our lives means being ready to share with our covenant brothers and sisters both what we are and what we have. If we are not willing to do this, our covenant commitment is not genuine.

THE NEW LIFESTYLE—KOINONIA

In the Greek vocabulary of the New Testament, one very important word describes the distinctive lifestyle into which we are initiated through the new covenant. It is *koinonia*. The noun *koinonia* is derived from the adjective *koinos* (common). Literally and basically, *koinonia* is "having in common." Insofar as two or more persons have things in common, they have *koinonia*. If there are any areas where they do not have things in common, in those areas they do not have *koinonia*. It was said of the early church in Jerusalem, *"All things were common property to them"* (Acts 4:32 NAS). That was *koinonia*.

In the majority of English translations of the New Testament, *koinonia* is translated *"fellowship."* However, in some versions it is not translated by a single English word, but by a phrase, such as "to be in union with" or "to share in common life." Because there is no one English word that fully expresses its meanings, in this chapter we will continue to use the word in its Greek form, *koinonia*.

Koinonia is the outworking of true unity. The perfect example of *koinonia* is the relationship between God the Father and God the Son. In John 10:30, Jesus said, *"I and the Father are one"* (NAS). This unity between the Father and the Son is the basis of their *koinonia*. Its outworking was described by Jesus in John 16:14–15 where He said of the Holy Spirit, *"He shall take of Mine, and shall disclose it to you"* (NAS). But then He immediately explains, *"All things that the Father has are Mine"* (NAS). In other words, Jesus said, "All that is Mine I have, not in my own right, but on the basis of My unity with the Father."

In John 17:10, Jesus stated the same again in His prayer to the Father: *"All things that are Mine are Thine, and Thine are Mine"* (NAS). This is perfect *koinonia*—the having of all things in common.

In this sense, the Gospel is an invitation from the Father and the Son to all members of the human race to share with them the perfect *koinonia* that they share with each other. In 1 Corinthians 1:9, Paul said, *"God is faithful, through whom you were called into fellowship [koinonia] with His Son, Jesus Christ our Lord"* (NAS). It is important to distinguish between means and ends. So many forms of religious activity are means rather than ends. They are not valuable in themselves, but only insofar as they enable us to achieve ends, which alone are valuable in themselves. *Koinonia*, however, is not merely a means—it is an end. It is, in fact, the supreme end of all worthwhile religious activity.

John likewise declared that the end purpose of the Gospel is to bring all who respond to its message into the same eternal *koinonia* that the Father and the Son enjoy between themselves:

> *What we have seen and heard we proclaim to you also, that you also may have fellowship [koinonia] with us; and indeed our fellowship [koinonia] is with the Father, and with His Son Jesus Christ. And these things we write, so that our joy may be made complete.* (1 John 1:3–4 NAS)

"What we have seen and heard" is the eyewitness testimony of Christ's apostles, preserved for us in the pages of the New Testament. These verses, therefore, disclose the central purpose for which God caused the gospel record to be preserved and transmitted. It is that all who believe and obey may have opportunity to share in the perfect, eternal *koinonia*, which is the lifestyle of heaven.

THE PRICE OF KOINONIA

However, *koinonia* is not cheap. There is a price to pay. The cost is set by two unvarying requirements. The first is commitment; the second is a way of life that is called *"walk*[ing] *in the light"* (1 John 1:7).

Covenant, as we have seen, is the door to unity. Only those who are willing to make the total, unreserved commitment of a covenant can ever come into true unity with each other. This applies alike in the relationship between husband and wife, between the believer and God, and between believers in fellowship together.

Thereafter, this commitment is worked out through walking in the light. John said, *"But if we walk in the light as He*

Himself is in the light, we have fellowship [koinonia] with one another" (1 John 1:7 NAS). Walking in the light is the only way to experience *koinonia*. Wherever Scripture speaks of *koinonia*, it acknowledges only one standard—that of God Himself. It is expressed here by the phrase, *"as He Himself is in the light."* God is willing to lift humanity up to His own level of *koinonia*, but He is not willing to lower the standard of *koinonia* to that of unredeemed humanity—or even of backslidden Christendom.

At the same time, the phrase *"in the light"* sets boundaries to what may be shared in *koinonia*. Anything that contravenes divine law in the realm of morals or ethics is not *"in the light."* On the contrary, it is darkness. An obvious example is in the area of sexual relationship. It is in accordance with divine law for a husband and wife to have sexual relationship with each other. This is fully *"in the light."* But for either of them to have sexual relationship with any other person is contrary to divine law. It is no longer *"in the light."*

Subject to this reservation, however, walking in the light is a relationship of total, continuing honesty and openness between all who are in *koinonia*. Nothing may be hidden or misrepresented or held back. The essence of the relationship is the same whether it is between a husband and wife or among a group of believers who are committed to each other. We may sum it up in the words that we used in chapter 3 to describe the husband/wife relationship: a total, unreserved opening up of each personality to the others.

Thus, the limits of *koinonia* are governed by two factors: divine law and absolute honesty. Divine law sets the boundaries; whatever contravenes divine law is no longer *koinonia*. It is darkness, not light. But within those boundaries, the light must be full and unrestricted. Wherever dishonesty or insincerity or selfish reservations creep in, the light begins to dim. *Koinonia* is no longer on the divine level.

What shall we say of Christians who seek fellowship one with another, but are not willing to meet these requirements? Logically, we must say the same as we would of a man and a woman who seek a sexual relationship but are not willing to meet the requirements for marriage. The result that they achieve is not *koinonia*, but fornication. This is equally true whether it be on the physical plane between a man and a woman, or on the spiritual plane between Christians who seek a permanent relationship with each other. Those who refuse God's requirements are, by His standards, guilty of fornication. That there is such a thing as spiritual fornication is attested by the Old Testament, whose prophets charged Israel with this very sin repeatedly.

The results of such wrong, uncommitted relationships between Christians in a group are very similar to those that develop between a man and a woman in a wrong sexual relationship. These results are hurt, bitterness, strife, broken relationships, unfulfilled promises, and unsatisfied yearnings. When we judge by results, we are compelled to acknowledge that in many sections of professing Christendom today, there is little evidence of true *koinonia,* but abundant evidence of wholesale spiritual fornication.

Our purpose in this chapter has been to set forth as clearly as possible the scriptural remedy for this tragic situation. It lies in a return to God's requirements: covenant commitment that is walked out *"in the light."*

CHAPTER SIX

THE POINT OF DECISION

I n the preceding chapters, we have dealt with three of the most important relationships there are in life. In order of priority, they are: our personal relationships with God, our marital relationships (if we are married), and our relationships with God's believing people. In each of these areas, we have seen the type of relationship that God has made available to those who will believe and obey Him.

Perhaps you have come to realize that you have been living on too low a level in one or more of these areas. You are ready to move up to a new level, but you are not sure how to do it. Let me remind you, therefore, that in every case you will find that there is one simple but essential requirement. It is expressed by a word that we have used many times in this book: *commitment*.

COMMITMENT TO GOD

Let me speak first about the area of your personal relationship with God. You may be a churchgoer, or at least have a church background. You may be familiar with the accepted phrases used by religious people. You may actually have experienced moments of uplift or inspiration when you knew that God was real.

Alternatively, you may be a person with no church background. Although you are not an adherent of any definite religion, there is a hunger in your heart that you long to satisfy.

Or again, you may not belong to either of these categories. You may have come to this moment by some unique route of your own. That really is not the issue just now. What matters is that you have come to a point where you long for an intimate, personal relationship with God—something so deep and real that you will never again need to question it. You are ready, therefore, to make a sincere, wholehearted commitment of yourself to God through Jesus Christ.

The natural way for you to make your commitment is by prayer. In this way, you give expression to what is in your heart; in the process of verbalizing it, you give it content. You make your commitment specific. A prayer of this kind is like crossing a bridge. It takes you over into new territory. From this moment on, you will not be relying on something vague and undefined in the shadowy realm of your mind. After praying, you will know what you are committed to. You will also know when and where you made your commitment. Your ongoing relationship with God will henceforth have a definite starting point—something fixed in a time-space world—a point of decision.

My counsel is that you put the book down right now and pray! If you feel able to pray in your own words, then do so. But if you find that difficult, here is a prepared prayer that you may use:

> God,
>
> You have put a desire in my heart to know You in a real and personal way. Even if I do not fully understand everything, I believe what the Bible says about Jesus Christ: that He took my sins upon Himself, died in my place, and rose again from the dead. In His name, I ask You now to forgive all my sins and to receive me as Your child. Sincerely, and with my whole heart, I commit myself to You—all I am and all I have. Take me as I am, and make me what You want me to be. In faith, I believe You do hear this prayer, and You do receive me. I thank You.
>
> In Jesus' name, amen.

Once you have prayed your prayer of commitment, do not begin to reason or speculate. In simple faith, take God at His Word. He has promised to receive you if you come to Him through Jesus Christ. Thank Him, therefore, that He has done what He promised. Keep on thanking Him! The more you thank Him, the more your faith will grow.

From now on, make it your main aim to cultivate your new relationship with God. This will give you a simple standard by which to evaluate the various influences and activities in your life. Do they strengthen your relationship with God, or do they weaken it? Make more and more room for the things that strengthen it, less and less for those that weaken it. Specifically, there are two ways to strengthen the relationship that are particularly important.

First, make your commitment known to those around you. You will not need to be aggressive or to put on religious airs. But as opportunities come in the normal course of daily life, make it known in a quiet but firm way that Jesus is now in full control of your life.

Second, set aside a period of each day for God. Spend part of this period reading your Bible and part of it praying—that is, talking to God in a sincere and natural way. In this way, you will maintain an ongoing two-way communication with God. As you read your Bible, God speaks to you. As you pray, you speak to God.

Probably you will not achieve instant "sainthood"! If you fail from time to time, do not become discouraged. Simply acknowledge your failures to God and ask Him to forgive you. *"If we confess our sins, He is faithful and righteous to forgive us our sins and to cleanse us from all unrighteousness"* (1 John 1:9 NAS). If other people are affected by your failures, you may need to ask them also for forgiveness. But do not give up! Remember, commitment is a two-way street. Not only are you committed to God; He is also committed to you. And He is omnipotent!

COMMITMENT TO YOUR MATE

The second area that we have dealt with—in order of priority—is your relationship to your mate, your husband or wife, as the case may be. (Of course, if you are not married at present and not expecting to marry, this section does not directly concern you.)

You may already have been a committed believer before you read this book. Or again, you may just have prayed a prayer of commitment after reading the previous section. But either way, you are now face-to-face with the fact that your marriage is not what it ought to be. Perhaps you have realized for the first time what it could be. You have come to understand that. For committed believers, marriage is *a cord of three strands* (Eccl. 4:12 NAS)—a covenant between you, your mate, and God. But it will take your personal commitment to make the covenant effective and thus to release into your marriage the vital element that has hitherto been missing: the all-sufficient, supernatural grace of God.

Ideally, you and your mate should both make the commitment at the same time, to God and to each other. However, it sometimes happens that one party is ready before the other. So if you are ready, but your mate is not, make your commitment now and trust God to bring your mate to the same point that you have already reached—the point of decision. Then, when that happens, you can renew your commitment together.

If you feel able to pray in your own words, do so. Otherwise, here is a prepared prayer that you may use to make a covenant commitment to your mate before God:

> Father God,
> I come to You in the name of Jesus, my Savior and Lord. I thank You that You redeemed me through the blood of Jesus and that I belong to You. I thank You for my marriage. I thank You for my mate. At this moment, I want to commit myself to You, to my marriage, and to my mate. I am ready, Lord, to lay down my life and live it out through my mate, seeking my mate's good before my own, rejoicing in my mate's blessing and my mate's success, counting it as mine, living now in the life of my mate. Father God, accept this commitment in the name of Jesus. Set the seal of your Holy Spirit upon it. Bless our marriage and our home in a new way from this day forward.
> In Jesus' name, amen.

In our previous section, "Commitment to God," we recommended certain simple steps to make that commitment effective. For the most part, the same principles apply to the commitment you have now made to your mate and to your marriage.

First of all, make sure that your priorities are in right order. Quite probably, this may necessitate some adjustments. After your personal relationship to God, the next most important area of your life is your marriage and your home. Evaluate your various activities accordingly. Make more and more room for those that strengthen your marriage and your home, less and less for those that have the opposite effect.

In connection with your personal relationship with God, we pointed out the need to set aside time to maintain two-way communications with Him. The same applies to your relationship with your mate. Open, continuing communication between the two of you is vital. It will take time—more time, probably, than you have been giving to it. Remember, the way you allocate your time is the surest indication of your real priorities. You may say that your marriage is important to you, but if you allow disproportionate amounts of time to other activities, you are really giving them priority over your marriage.

Someone coined the saying, "The family that prays together stays together." There is a great deal of truth in it. For thirty years, Lydia and I prayed and read the Bible together almost every day—usually twice a day. Often, God spoke to us in a very intimate way in these times of communication with Him and with each other. They were one of the principle factors in the success of our marriage.

Sometimes, I have observed that husband and wife find it difficult to pray out loud in each other's presence. It seems hard to break through the "sound barrier." But work at it! Be patient with one another. The benefits will far outweigh any initial embarrassment or sense of strangeness. When you and your mate can freely talk to God in each other's presence, it is sure proof that God has really become a member of your family—and that is what He longs to be.

One last word on this subject. Never again rely solely on your own effort and ability to make your marriage a success. No marriage can ever be what God intends it to be apart from God's supernatural grace. The commitment you have now made to your mate and your marriage has made that grace available to you in a measure that you have never known before. Avail yourself of it freely! God has told us, *"My grace is sufficient for you, for power is perfected in weakness"* (2 Cor. 12:9 NAS). God's grace and power will see you through every difficulty that arises. If you feel perplexed, discouraged, or inadequate, trust God for an extra measure of grace and power, just then and there. Expect to see Him work—in ways, perhaps, you could never have imagined. Expect to see Him change whatever needs to be changed—you, your mate, the whole situation. He will not fail you.

COMMITMENT TO GOD'S PEOPLE

The third area of relationship that we have dealt with in this book is that which we have called *koinonia*—the sharing of your life with God's people. For true spiritual fulfillment, you need this kind of relationship. Without it, you can never be all that God intends you to be. This is equally true for single people and for married couples. All of us need to be part of something larger than ourselves.

In 1 Corinthians 12:13–27, Paul compared individual believers to the various parts that make up a single body. He explained that no part can function effectively on its own. Each needs the others. *"And the eye cannot say to the hand, 'I have no need of you'; or again the head to the feet, 'I have no need of you'"* (v. 21 NAS). As individual believers, we can only achieve true fulfillment and wholeness by entering into a committed relationship with other believers in such a way that we can, together with them, function as a single body.

A relationship of this kind is not optional. It is essential for our own spiritual well-being. Let us look once more at a verse that has been quoted earlier: *"But if we walk in the light as He Himself is in the light, we have fellowship [koinonia] with one another, and the blood of Jesus His Son cleanses us from all sin"* (1 John 1:7 NAS).

The introductory *"if"* confronts us with two related facts of spiritual experience. First, the primary evidence that we are walking in the light is that we have *koinonia* with one another. If we do not have this relationship of *koinonia* with other believers, it is normally evidence that we are not walking fully in the light. Second, if we are not in the light of *koinonia*, we no longer experience the continuous cleansing of the blood of Jesus, which alone can keep us pure and free from sin.

Our responsibility for regular fellowship with a group of committed believers is stated again in Hebrews 10:24–25:

And let us consider how to stimulate one another to love and good deeds, not forsaking our own assembling together, as is the habit of some, but encouraging one another; and all the more, as you see the day drawing near. (NAS)

Here again, we have two related truths: first, we are responsible for stimulating and encouraging one another; second, we can do this only if we do not forsake *"our own assembling."* This last phrase obviously takes it for granted that all of us will be related to a group that we can properly call "our own assembly."

The essential step that brings us into this kind of relationship is the same that brings us into proper relationship with God or with our mates. It is commitment—not just to another individual, however, but to a group who are themselves united in mutual commitment. If you have already made the first two commitments dealt with in this chapter—to God and to your mate—you should follow that with this third form of commitment to a group of fellow believers.

Unfortunately, it is not always easy in contemporary Christendom to find a group of people who are practicing real, mutual commitment on a sound, scriptural basis. However, if you acknowledge to God your need to identify with such a group and then go on to seek Him diligently for His direction, you can be confident that He will show you what to do. Remember that God has promised to reward those who seek Him (Heb. 11:6). If you are sincere and earnest in seeking Him, you will receive your reward.

As a guideline to recognize the kind of group that will fulfill your need, here are nine questions you should ask before you make any definite commitment:

• Do they honor and uplift the Lord Jesus Christ?
• Do they respect the authority of Scripture?

- Do they make room for the moving of the Holy Spirit?
- Do they exhibit a warm and friendly attitude?
- Do they seek to work out their faith in practical day-to-day living?
- Do they build interpersonal relationships among themselves that go beyond merely attending services?
- Do they provide pastoral care that embraces all your legitimate needs?
- Are they open to fellowship with other Christian groups?
- Do you feel at ease and at home among them?

If the answer to all or most of these questions is "yes," you are getting warm. Continue to seek God, however, until you receive definite direction from Him. Remember that you will not find the perfect group. Furthermore, even if you did, you could not join it, because after you did, it would no longer be perfect!

Finally, here is a word of encouragement, but also of warning:

God makes a home for the lonely; He leads out the prisoners into prosperity, only the rebellious dwell in a parched land. (Ps. 68:6 NAS)

If you are *"lonely,"* God will place you in a spiritual *"home"*—a family of Christian brothers and sisters united in mutual commitment to one another. If you are a *"prisoner"* of circumstances or evil forces, God will deliver you and bring you out into freedom. But—and here is the warning—if you are *"rebellious,"* you will continue to *"dwell in a parched land."*

Ultimately, the only barriers that can keep you from finding the kind of *koinonia* you need will be your own inner attitudes of pride, selfishness, or unyielding individualism. Ask God to show you if there are any such barriers in your life and, if they do exist, to break them down.

In Psalm 27:4, David gave utterance to the deepest longing of his soul:

One thing I have asked from the LORD, that I shall seek: that I may dwell in the house of the LORD all the days of my life. (NAS)

Do these words of David express the deep longing of your soul? If so, why not echo them in a prayer of your own?

Once again, if you feel able to pray in your own words, do that. But if you prefer a prepared prayer, you may use the following:

Lord,

I am lonely and unfulfilled, and I acknowledge it. I long to dwell in Your house—to be part of a spiritual "family" of committed believers. If there are any barriers in me, I ask You to remove them. Guide me to a group where this longing of mine can be fulfilled, and help me to make the needed commitment to them.

In the name of Jesus, amen.

GOD'S PLAN FOR YOUR MONEY

CONTENTS

CHAPTER ONE

GOD'S ALL-INCLUSIVE PLAN

You may be surprised to learn that God has a plan for your money. You may have the idea that money is too sordid for spiritual people. Like some of us, you may have grown up with a religious background that referred to money as "filthy lucre."

However, this is not a biblical view of money. In contemporary culture, money plays a large role in each of our lives. If God does not have a plan for our money, then a major part of living is not under His control. In turn, this will inevitably affect other areas of our lives. The truth is that many Christians whose lives are not really under God's control, try to solve their problems by becoming more spiritual. However, many times the answer is to be more practical.

If you are not handling your finances in line with God's plan, then your whole life is out of joint. No matter how spiritual you may be in other areas, you will never know the real blessing and reign of God in your life until you bring your money into line with the will of God as revealed in His Word. You see, the Bible clearly reveals that God does have a plan for our money.

As a teacher of God's Word, it is my responsibility to share with you God's plan for your money just as I would share His plan for any other area of your life. In Acts, Paul said this:

You know that I have not hesitated to preach anything that would be helpful to you but have taught you publicly and from house to house....For I have not hesitated to proclaim to you the whole will of God.   *(Acts 20:20, 27 NIV)*

In other words, Paul was saying that he had declared to them the whole will of God, and that he had taught everything in the Word of God that would be helpful to God's people. The whole will of God includes His will for our money. It is part of the total counsel, or plan, of God.

I want to point out in a general way that God really does have a plan that covers every area of our lives. In Romans 12:1, Paul said,

Therefore, I urge you, brothers, in view of God's mercy, to offer your bodies as living sacrifices, holy and pleasing to God—this is your spiritual act of worship. (NIV)

Notice that spiritual worship includes our bodies; it moves right into the physical world. Some people think the body is not spiritual. Being spiritual includes doing the right thing with your body—presenting it to God as a living sacrifice. Paul continued in the next verse,

Do not conform any longer to the pattern of this world, but be transformed by the renewing of your mind. Then you will be able to test and approve what God's will is—his good, pleasing and perfect will. (v. 2 NIV)

God's will is unfolded in three successive phases by three beautiful words. The will of God is *"good,"* *"pleasing"* (or *"acceptable"* KJV) and *"perfect."* These three words represent three phases in our perception of the will of God.

When we first begin to perceive God's will, we discover that it is good. God never wants anything bad for any of His people. Then we learn His will is pleasing or acceptable. The more we perceive it, the more we want to embrace it. Finally, as we move on in the perception and the application of God's will, we realize it is perfect or complete. The whole, complete will of God covers all areas of your life—and that includes your money.

Paul pointed out two essential steps to finding God's will. First, surrender yourself without reservation to God. Paul said to place your body on God's altar *"as [a] living sacrifice."* He was comparing it with the Old Testament sacrifices in which the animals that were offered were first killed and then placed on the altar. In this manner, they were set apart for God. Paul said that you must do the same with your body: put it on the altar of God's service without reservation. The only difference is that you do not kill the body, but rather present it as a living sacrifice.

The second essential step to finding God's will is learning to think God's way. Paul called it being renewed in your mind. This means changing your whole outlook, including the way you think, your values, your standards, and your priorities. Only as your mind is renewed can you perceive what is God's will.

I want to point out something else that is very important about your money. Do not underestimate your money, belittle it, or think it is unspiritual or unimportant. What does your money really represent? I suggest that it represents four very important aspects of you: your time, your strength, your talents, and, quite possibly, your inheritance.

Your inheritance may be money or other valuable things, like houses or lands, that were passed on to you from people who loved and cared for you when their lives came to an end. Perhaps you went to college and had a fairly elaborate education. All those years of education are represented by your money because if you did not have the education, you could not make the money that you do. Or you might have special talents or abilities that are not in the academic field, that are more practical in nature. Those talents and abilities are represented in your money. Certainly, too, your money represents your time. If you work eight hours a day, five days a week, that is forty hours of your life invested in the money you earn.

When you invest your money, you are investing a major part of yourself for good or bad. I hope you can begin to see how important it is that you invest yourself through your money in what is good and in accordance with God's will and plan.

God's plan for your life, including your money, is summed up in one beautiful word: *prosperity*. This is stated in 3 John 2, where the writer said to a fellow Christian,

> *Beloved, I pray that in all respects you may prosper and be in good health, just as your soul prospers.* (NAS)

Notice the key word there is *"prosper."* It covers three areas: your physical health, your soul, and your finances or material needs. In each area, the revealed will of God is prosperity or success. God wants you to succeed in the area of your soul, in the area of your physical body, and in the area of your finances.

Failure, defeat, frustration, and poverty are not the will of God. I grew up in a religious tradition where being holy meant you had to be poor. I respect people who hold that view, but it is not a scriptural one.

CHAPTER TWO

GOD OR MAMMON?

We need to see that our personal attitudes toward money are very important. This can be stated as the following principle: Your attitude toward money actually reveals your attitude toward God Himself.

I want to quote to you the words of Jesus on the subject. In the Sermon on the Mount, we find Jesus stated the following about this topic:

> No one can serve two masters; for either he will hate the one and love the other, or he will hold to one and despise the other. You cannot serve God and mammon.
>
> (Matt. 6:24 NAS)

First, let us look for a moment at the meaning of the word *"mammon."* One of the modern translations says, *"You cannot serve both God and Money"* (v. 24 NIV), but that does not fully express it because mammon is more than just money. Mammon is an evil, spiritual power that grips men and enslaves them through the medium of money. Mammon is not money itself, but the spiritual power that works in the world and the lives of millions of people through their attitudes toward money.

Jesus said you cannot serve God and mammon. Then He said, *"Either [you] will hate the one and love the other, or [you] will hold to one and despise the other."* In each case, Jesus naturally put God first, mammon second. Either you will hate God and love mammon, or you will hold onto God and despise mammon. That is a serious thought. If you love mammon, you hate God. On the other hand, if you hold onto God and your life is committed to Him, you will despise mammon. This attitude is not hating money, but loathing that satanic force that enslaves men and women through money. You will detest it, and you will not let it dominate you. You cannot maintain a position of neutrality on this subject. We must acknowledge in our lives the claim of one or the other. It is not a choice of whether we will serve, it is only a choice of whom we will serve—either God or mammon.

Jesus said it is a question of priorities:

But seek first His [God's] *kingdom and His righteousness; and all these things shall be added to you.* (v. 33 NAS)

Jesus did not say we have to be without *"these things"*— food, clothing, and other material goods—but He said we must not put these things first. We must put the kingdom of God and His righteousness first in our lives on a consistent basis—that is, commitment to God, His kingdom, and His purposes. Jesus said if we do not run after mammon and make it our god, but if we serve the true God and seek His kingdom and righteousness, then God will see to it that all the material and financial things we need are added to us.

Pursuing money is such an awful strain and leads to so much frustration. Do not chase after money. That is what Jesus said. Let money pursue you. If you have followed the right course in your life, then the money will be added to you. You do not have to lie awake at night or spend hours hatching plans to get rich.

Having followed that principle for more than forty years, by the grace of God, I can attest that God is faithful. Sometimes my faith has been tested. Sometimes I have had to deny myself things that the world esteems very highly. But as I look back at all I have gone through, I have to say God has been totally faithful.

The principle of putting God first runs all the way through the Bible. In the third chapter of Proverbs, we find that two beautiful verses affirm this principle:

Honor the LORD with your wealth, with the firstfruits of all your crops; then your barns will be filled to overflowing, and your vats will brim over with new wine.
(Prov. 3:9–10 NIV)

The *"barns"* and the *"vats"* are all of your material needs. They will be abundantly supplied and will overflow when you honor God with your wealth. The way in which you honor God with your wealth is by giving Him the *"firstfruits."* This means setting aside the first (or best) portion for God. We either honor or dishonor God with our money. There is no neutral ground.

Let me say, lovingly, God does not want your tips! When the offering plate comes around at church, do not drop a quarter in. That is insulting God. As a matter of fact, for most people today, giving a dollar is an insult to God. You would slip a dollar into the hand of the restaurant parking lot valet who parks your car. Do not treat God like that because you are insulting and dishonoring Him.

Similarly, the Scripture points out that putting money ahead of God is also idolatry:

> *Therefore put to death your members which are on the earth: fornication, uncleanness, passion, evil desire, and covetousness, which is idolatry.* (Col. 3:5 NKJV)

Notice Paul said that covetousness is idolatry. When you seek money first, you are making money your god, which is rightly called idolatry. The Lord said to Israel, *"Thou shalt have none other gods before me* [or *'besides Me'* AMP]" (Deut. 5:7 KJV). In our contemporary culture, far more people have made money their god than the true God. They are guilty of idolatry.

Notice that, in Colossians, Paul put covetousness side by side with many other unpleasant things such as fornication and uncleanness. Most churches would not accept people who live in fornication (sexual immorality), but, frankly, our churches are full of people who are guilty of covetousness and idolatry.

Another Scripture, 1 Timothy 6:9–11, carries a warning against making money your god and desiring to be rich:

> *But those who desire to be rich fall into temptation and a snare, and into many foolish and harmful lusts which drown men in destruction and perdition. For the love of money is a root of all kinds of evil* [money is not evil; the love of money is], *for which some have strayed from the*

211

faith in their greediness [or covetousness], *and pierced themselves through with many sorrows.* [Now here is the remedy or alternative:] *But you, O man of God, flee these things* [covetousness, love of money, materialism] *and pursue righteousness, godliness, faith, love, patience, gentleness.* (NKJV)

No vacuum can exist in our lives. If we are to be clear of the love of money, we must pursue something else. Something else must take its place. Paul said, *"Pursue righteousness, godliness, faith, love, patience, gentleness."*

Faith is necessary to break with the control of mammon in your life. At some point or other, you are going to have to do something to release yourself from the domination of mammon.

Personally, I can look back on a point in my life when I gave to the Lord's work everything I owned financially and materially. I gave up a prestigious, well-paying job with a tremendous future and stepped out in naked faith with nothing to uphold me but the promises of God. When I did so, the control of mammon over my life was broken. I refused to be a slave of mammon.

CHAPTER THREE

OFFERING IS PART OF WORSHIP

G od wants us to see our money as something holy that we offer in worship to Him, and that without this offering, our worship is incomplete. We will start with examples from the Old Testament.

In Exodus 23:14–15, God gave regulations for every male among the children of Israel to come up to Jerusalem three times a year. They were to offer worship and to celebrate before God in the temple. Here is part of the regulations He gave:

> *Three times a year you are to celebrate a festival to me. Celebrate the Feast of Unleavened Bread; for seven days eat bread made without yeast, as I commanded you. Do this at the appointed time in the month of Abib, for in that month you came out of Egypt. No one is to appear before me empty-handed.*   *(NIV)*

This was part of God's ordinance for worship and celebration in the temple. Israel had to come up at God's appointed time and in God's appointed way, and no Israelite was to appear before Him empty-handed. Every Israelite had to have an offering for God as part of the celebration and worship.

In Psalm 96:8–9, the psalmist said to all of God's people,

> *Give to the LORD the glory due His name; Bring an offering, and come into His courts. Oh, worship the LORD in the beauty of holiness!*   *(NKJV)*

The Scripture says, *"Bring an offering, and come into His courts,"* but do not come without an offering. Here are three important facts about the offering of finances, or anything else, to God.

- Bringing an offering gives glory to God. The psalmist said, *"Give to the LORD the glory due His name; Bring an offering."* How are we to give glory to God? By bringing an offering.

- Bringing an offering gives us access to God's courts. We have no right to claim access to God if we do not come with an offering. In Exodus 23:15, God said, *"No one is to appear before me empty-handed."* If you want to appear before God and come into His courts, you must bring an offering.

- Bringing an offering is a God-appointed part of our worship. The psalmist continued, *"Oh, worship the LORD in the beauty of holiness!"* This tells us that our worship is not complete until we bring our offering to God.

We saw earlier that when we give our money to God, we are giving a very important part of our lives. We are giving Him our time, our strength, and our talents. Most of us put the major portion of our efforts into the work that brings our income. When we offer God the appointed share of our income, we are offering ourselves to God. And there is nothing more holy we can offer to God than ourselves.

God says, in effect, "If you want to come into My courts, to appear before Me, to give glory to Me, and to worship Me in the beauty of holiness, then bring your offering." Bringing an offering, worship, and holiness are all very closely connected in God's plan for our lives.

Another important point that many of God's people do not fully understand is that God keeps a record of what His people offer. God has an account book for every one of us. To illustrate this, we need to read the seventh chapter of Numbers. This chapter describes what the twelve princes of the tribes of Israel offered to God. Each prince offered exactly the same, yet each of their offerings is described in detail, item by item. God did not say, "The second prince offered the same as the first" or "All twelve princes each offered this." Rather, the record goes through every item in the offering of each prince. The Bible is a very economical book in that it does not waste any space. When God enumerates identical offerings in this passage, He is illustrating for us how very carefully He records what we offer to Him.

Here is the account of the first prince:

When the altar was anointed, the leaders [or princes] brought their offerings for its dedication and presented them before the altar. For the LORD had said to Moses, "Each day one leader is to bring his offering for the dedication of the altar." [For twelve days this process of offering went on.] The one who brought his offering on the first day was Nahshon son of Amminadab of the tribe of Judah. His offering was one silver plate weighing a hundred and thirty shekels, and one silver sprinkling bowl weighing seventy shekels, both according to the sanctuary shekel, each filled with fine flour mixed with oil as a grain offering; one gold dish weighing ten shekels, filled with incense [that would be worth thousands of dollars today]; one young bull, one ram and one male lamb a year old, for a burnt offering; one male goat for a sin offering; and two oxen, five rams, five male goats and five male lambs a year old, to be sacrificed as a fellowship offering. This was the offering of Nahshon son of Amminadab.

(Num. 7:10–17 NIV)

God kept an absolute record of what each leader offered and then caused it to be preserved in Scripture in minute detail. We need to take note of the degree of importance God places on our offerings.

The New Testament teaches us that Jesus Himself watches how we give. We read the following in Mark 12:41–44:

Jesus sat down opposite the place where the offerings were put and watched the crowd putting their money into the temple treasury. Many rich people threw in large amounts. But a poor widow came and put in two very small copper coins, worth only a fraction of a penny. Calling his disciples to him, Jesus said, "I tell you the truth, this poor widow has put more into the treasury than all the others. They all gave out of their wealth; but she, out of her poverty, put in everything—all she had to live on."   *(NIV)*

Jesus thought it worthwhile to sit and watch what and how the people offered. He does the same today. We may not see Him, but He is watching how and what we give.

There are two important points here: first, Jesus looked at what everybody gave and estimated its true value; second, God gauges what we give by what we keep. Jesus stated that the one who put in the least in actual amount gave the most because she had nothing left. Bear in mind that when God measures what you give, He looks at what you retain for yourself.

One final point is that one day all of us will have to answer for ourselves to God:

So then, each of us will give an account of himself to God.
    (Rom. 14:12 NIV)

That lies ahead for every one of us. And the phrase in the original Greek, "to give account," is used primarily in reference to financial matters. So, every one of us is going to give a financial accounting to God.

CHAPTER FOUR

HOW TO PUT GOD FIRST

We have seen that God wants us to view our money as something holy. We mistakenly tend to think of money as something dirty or unworthy. However, money is a part of us. When we offer our money, we are offering a major part of ourselves to God. We need to offer our money in worship to God, and our worship is only complete in this way.

We will now consider a simple way to put God first in handling our money that is both practical and scriptural. To honor God in our finances, we must first seek God's kingdom and His righteousness and then honor the Lord with our firstfruits. The key word is *first* all the way through. If we put money first rather than God, then we are idolaters.

A simple, practical, and scriptural way to put God first with your money is by consistently setting aside for God the first tenth of your income. This practice is traditionally known as tithing. *Tithe* comes from an Old English word meaning "the tenth" and is used in the King James Version. Tithing is the regular practice of setting apart the first tenth of your total income for God. When you do that, you have laid a foundation for honoring God with your money.

Tithing goes back to Abraham. Some Christians think that tithing was first instituted under the Law of Moses, but that is incorrect. Tithing is at least four hundred years older than the Law. Genesis 14:12–17 records that Abraham had just won a great battle over certain kings and, in winning the battle, he had gathered a great quantity of booty. The narration continues as follows:

*Then Melchizedek king of Salem brought out bread and
wine. He was priest of God Most High, and he blessed
Abram, saying, "Blessed be Abram by God Most High,
Creator of heaven and earth. And blessed be God Most
High, who delivered your enemies into your hand."*

(Gen. 14:18–20 NIV)

Melchizedek was the priest of the Most High God, or God's
representative in the earth at that particular time, and he
blessed Abraham. How did Abraham respond? Abraham gave
Melchizedek a tenth of everything he had gained in victory.

It is important to see that Abraham is presented in the New
Testament as a father and a pattern to all subsequent believers.
Romans 4:11–12 states,

*So then, he [Abraham] is the father of all who be-
lieve....And he is also the father of the circumcised who not
only are circumcised but who also walk in the footsteps of
the faith that our father Abraham had before he was circumcised [which is at the time Melchizedek met him].*

(NIV)

In order to be children of Abraham, we must walk in the
steps of Abraham's faith. This includes handling our money the
way Abraham handled his money. In the fourth chapter of Romans, Paul continued,

*Therefore, the promise comes by faith, so that it may be by
grace and may be guaranteed to all Abraham's offspring—
not only to those who are of the law but also to those who
are of the faith of Abraham. He is the father of us all.*

(v. 16 NIV)

Abraham is our father when we walk in the footsteps of his
faith. And when we develop the same kind of faith he had, we
will include the areas of finances and material possessions just
as his faith did.

Now let us consider Jacob, Abraham's grandson. Jacob became a refugee because of the way he had tricked Isaac, his father, and Esau, his brother. He left the land of inheritance and

went off to seek his fortune in Mesopotamia. When he set out, all he had in his hand was one staff. This is what Jacob said in Genesis 28:20–22:

> Then Jacob made a vow, saying, "If God will be with me and will watch over me on this journey I am taking and will give me food to eat and clothes to wear so that I return safely to my father's house, then the LORD will be my God and this stone that I have set up as a pillar will be God's house, and of all that you give me I will give you a tenth."
>
> *(NIV)*

Here we find tithing again. In essence, Jacob said, "That's the basis of my relationship with God. He provides my needs, and in return, I give Him back a tenth of all that He provides for me."

Then we read Jacob's testimony twenty years later in Genesis 32:9–10:

> Then Jacob prayed, "O God of my father Abraham, God of my father Isaac, O LORD, who said to me, 'Go back to your country and your relatives, and I will make you prosper [notice that key word 'prosper'],' I am unworthy of all the kindness and faithfulness you have shown your servant. I had only my staff when I crossed this Jordan, but now I have become two groups."
>
> *(NIV)*

Jacob had tremendous wealth, a very large family, and every need had been supplied. What was the reason? His faithfulness in tithing. He left with one staff, and he came back with abundance. The key was that he gave God the first tenth of everything that God provided for him.

As we further examine tithing among God's people in the Old Testament, we find that under the Law of Moses, the tithe simply belonged to God. There was no question about this fact, which is verified in the following Scripture:

> A tithe of everything from the land, whether grain from the soil or fruit from the trees, belongs to the LORD; it is holy to the LORD [the tithe is holy]....The entire tithe of the herd

and flock—every tenth animal that passes under the shepherd's rod—will be holy to the LORD.   (Lev. 27:30, 32 NIV)

The entire tithe is holy to the Lord. In Deuteronomy 14:22, God said, *"Be sure to set aside a tenth of all that your fields produce each year"* (NIV). That is tithing.

Many Christians are not aware of this, but in the New Testament, tithing reappears in the priesthood of Jesus. Hebrews 6:19 speaks about *"the inner sanctuary behind the curtain"* (NIV) and tells us,

> *Jesus, who went before us, has entered on our behalf. He has become a high priest forever, in the order of Melchizedek.*   *(v. 20 NIV)*

So, Jesus is our High Priest in the order of Melchizedek.

In the next chapter of Hebrews, the writer explained the part tithing played in the priesthood of Melchizedek and in the high priesthood of Jesus:

> *Just think how great he* [Melchizedek] *was: Even the patriarch Abraham gave him a tenth of the plunder! Now the law requires the descendants of Levi who become priests to collect a tenth from the people—that is, their brothers— even though their brothers are descended from Abraham. This man, however, did not trace his descent from Levi, yet he collected a tenth from Abraham and blessed him who had the promises.* [Notice the emphasis on the tenth.] *And without doubt the lesser person is blessed by the greater.* [Abraham was lesser than Melchizedek because he was blessed by Melchizedek.] *In the one case* [the case of the Lord], *the tenth is collected by men who die; but in the other case, by him who is declared to be living.*
> *(Heb. 7:4–8 NIV)*

The priesthood of Melchizedek is an eternal priesthood because the one who is in this priesthood never dies. The writer states Jesus lives forever as a High Priest after the order of Melchizedek. And in His priesthood He receives the tithes of His people.

We can see that tithing has a continuous history from Abraham onwards: from Abraham to Jacob, to the nation of Israel, and then to the ministry of Jesus as our High Priest. According to Scripture, when we set aside our first tenth and offer our tithe to Jesus, we are actually acknowledging that Jesus is our High Priest according to the priesthood of Melchizedek. This is one of the ways we are able to honor Him and acknowledge Him as our High Priest.

CHAPTER FIVE

GOD CHALLENGES US

Now we will consider how God Himself actually challenges us to put Him to the test by following the scriptural examples of tithing. This complete challenge is given in Malachi 3:7–12. God was speaking to Israel:

> *"Ever since the time of your forefathers you have turned away from my decrees and have not kept them. Return to me, and I will return to you," says the LORD Almighty. "But you ask, 'How are we to return?' Will a man rob God? Yet you rob me. But you ask, 'How do we rob you?' In tithes and offerings."* *(NIV)*

Notice that withholding God's appointed portion is called robbing God. Most of us would never rob another human being, but we might be guilty of robbing God.

God then told Israel the result of robbing Him and the remedy:

> *"You are under a curse—the whole nation of you—because you are robbing me.* [Now here is the remedy:] *Bring the whole tithe into the storehouse, that there may be food in my house. Test me in this," says the LORD Almighty, "and see if I will not throw open the floodgates of heaven and pour out so much blessing that you will not have room enough for it."* *(vv. 9–10 NIV)*

Upon what condition did God promise the blessing? When we bring the whole tithe into the storehouse. He says, "Test Me.

See if I'll do what I've promised." God requires us to test Him with our finances; in other words, we must act in faith.

Finally, He went on to speak of further results:

"I will prevent pests from devouring your crops, and the vines in your fields will not cast their fruit," says the LORD Almighty. "Then all the nations will call you blessed, for yours will be a delightful land," says the LORD Almighty.

(vv. 11–12)

God says that if you will honor Him in that way that He will pour out such a blessing you will not find room to contain it. He will prevent the pests (the devourer) from eating up anything that is yours. All nations will look at you and say you are a blessed people and will recognize that God has truly blessed and prospered you. All this is promised as a result of bringing the whole tithe into the storehouse.

Let me summarize four points from this passage in Malachi:

- For more than one thousand years, God kept a record of Israel's giving. He had required them to give the tithe to Him more than a thousand years earlier. Then, at a certain point, He told them He had kept a record, and they had been robbing Him. So, remember, God keeps a record.

- Keeping back God's portion is robbery—not robbery of man, but robbery of God, and it brings a curse upon those who do it.

- Faithful tithing brings a blessing, and through the results God is glorified in the blessing that comes on His people.

- Tithing is a test of our faith and of God's faithfulness. But please take note, it must be done in faith.

Let us consider what the storehouse is in this passage. I want to illustrate this from the natural. A storehouse is basically two things: first, it is the place we get the food we eat; and second, it is the place we obtain seed to sow for future harvests. As Christians, we receive our spiritual food from a certain source or sources, and we probably receive seed to sow in the lives of others from the same source. I suggest that wherever that source is for you is your storehouse and where you need to bring your tithe. If you belong to a local church that supplies those needs, then by all means that is your storehouse. Be faithful to tithe there. But many Christians today are not privileged in that way. They must consider what is the source of their food and the seed that is sown.

Let me share a little parable, which I will not seek to interpret. Normally, you do not eat in the Holiday Inn and pay your bill at Howard Johnson's. Meditate on this, and you will understand it for yourself.

Now, we must understand that tithing is not the end of giving to God, it is the beginning. Tithing lays a foundation for our systematic, continual giving to God. The Bible also speaks of giving in two other main categories: offerings and alms. We really do not offer our tithe to God because it is His legal portion. But, beyond our tithe, what we give are offerings. Look at all the options Israel had for giving, as stated in Deuteronomy 12:6:

> *Bring your burnt offerings and sacrifices, your tithes and special gifts, what you have vowed to give and your free-will offerings, and the firstborn of your herds and flocks.*
>
> *(NIV)*

Six specific kinds of offerings are mentioned:

1. burnt offerings
2. sacrifices
3. special gifts
4. what you have vowed
5. freewill offerings
6. the firstborn of your herds and flocks

In other words, there is a very wide range of different kinds of offerings that we can give to God. But we do not offer our tithe; we simply return to God that which is His scriptural portion. In addition to offerings, there are what the Bible calls *"alms"* (Matt. 6:1, et al KJV), or what is known today as charity. This is not what we give to God, but what we give to the needy, the poor, and the afflicted. The Bible has a lot more to say about giving to the poor than many Christians have heard. This is what Jesus said in Luke 12:32–34:

> *Do not be afraid, little flock, for your Father has been pleased to give you the kingdom. Sell your possessions and give to the poor. Provide purses for yourselves that will not wear out, a treasure in heaven that will not be exhausted, where no thief comes near and no moth destroys. For where your treasure is, there your heart will be also.* (NIV)

Where you put your money is where your heart is. You cannot have your money in one place, your heart in another. Jesus says to act like children of a King. Your Father has given you the kingdom so you can afford to be generous. Give to the poor and lay up treasure for yourself in heaven.

In Ecclesiastes 11:1–2, there is another marvelous picture of what we do when we give to the poor:

> *Cast your bread upon the waters, for after many days you will find it again. Give portions to seven, yes to eight, for you do not know what disaster may come upon the land.* (NIV)

I hope you can see that point. When you give to the poor, then you are laying up insurance with God. The writer says, *"Give...to seven"*—that's your duty—and *"to eight"*—go a little beyond duty, *"for you do not know what disaster may come upon the land."* In other words, if you do what God says with your money, God will take care of you when the disaster comes. That is His guarantee, and that is your insurance. Giving is an insurance against bad times.

Consider the testimony of Oswald J. Smith, who was pastor of the People's Church in Toronto, Canada, for many years. During the Great Depression, hundreds of men came to his office every day to ask for financial help from the church. He said they gave aid to hundreds, but he said he always checked with each man whether that man had been faithful when he had an income to give the tithe to God. He reported that in all his experience, no man who came for help had ever been faithful in tithing. He concluded that God took care of all those who faithfully tithed.

CHAPTER SIX

THE GRACE OF GIVING

A s we continue our study, we want to consider the spiritual key to the only kind of giving that is truly acceptable to God. It is expressed in one simple and beautiful word: *grace*. We are not talking about giving by law or commandment, but in the New Testament we are talking about giving that comes out of grace. Paul spoke about this grace in the great Giving Chapter found in 2 Corinthians. Writing to the Christians in Corinth, he exhorted,

> *But just as you excel in everything—in faith, in speech, in knowledge, in complete earnestness and in your love for us—see that you also excel in this grace of giving.*
> *(2 Cor. 8:7 NIV)*

The Corinthian church was well equipped with spiritual gifts and graces. It also had a good attitude of love. But Paul said, "Be sure you don't miss out on this other tremendously important grace, the grace of giving."

In this chapter that deals with giving, the word *grace* occurs seven times. It is the key word. Unless we understand grace and how grace motivates giving, we really cannot understand God's plan for our money as revealed in the New Testament.

The Bible speaks of both law and grace. Law is external, written on stone tablets in front of our eyes. It says, "Do this. Don't do that." But the law is not inside us; the old nature is. This rebel nature resists what is written on the tablets of the law outside.

However, grace is different. Grace is internal. It works from within, not from without. It is written on the heart, not on tablets of stone. (See 2 Corinthians 3:3.) It is written there only by the Holy Spirit. No other agent can write the grace of God in our hearts but the Holy Spirit.

We need to see how the New Testament contrasts law and grace. In John 1:17, we read the following:

For the law was given through Moses; grace and truth
came through Jesus Christ. (NIV)

The law came through Moses, but grace comes only through Jesus Christ. If we want grace, it is made available to us only through Jesus Christ. Furthermore, it is made available only through the cross and what Jesus did on the cross. From the cross, grace has been released and made available to the human race. This is true also in the area of finance. What Jesus did on the cross made provision for our prosperity. 2 Corinthians 8:9 states,

For you know the grace of our Lord Jesus Christ, that
though he was rich, yet for your sakes he became poor, so
that you through his poverty might become rich. (NIV)

Notice the key word there at the beginning: *grace*. It is not law; it is grace. We cannot earn it. Grace is manifested here in an exchange. Jesus was rich, but He became poor out of His grace in order that we, through His grace, being poor, might become rich with His riches. Jesus exhausted the poverty curse of the broken law so that in return, through grace, we might receive the wealth of the kingdom of God. God's grace is through Jesus Christ and through the cross.

Also concerning grace, the New Testament reveals that grace is received only through faith. The very essence of grace is that it cannot be earned. There is nothing we can ever do that will deserve the grace of God. Paul said this in Ephesians 2:8–9:

For it is by grace you have been saved, through faith—and
this not from yourselves, it is the gift of God—not by
works, so that no one can boast. (NIV)

Notice the order: *"by grace...through faith...not by works."* I am not teaching you about a plan by which you can earn your money. I am teaching about something that you can receive only by grace through faith. In Galatians 5:6, Paul said the following:

> *For in Christ Jesus neither circumcision nor uncircumcision means anything, but faith working through love.* (NAS)

Faith is the only way we can appropriate the grace of God. The faith that appropriates God's grace works by love. This is the spiritual key to right giving. I want to state it very clearly: the spiritual key to right giving is grace (not law, but grace) received through Jesus and through the cross, by faith, and working by love.

I want to emphasize that the Bible's principles of finance, as unfolded in the New Testament, can only be apprehended by faith. You must respond to this message with faith. Further, faith means that we act. Faith without actions is dead (James 2:20). What do we do? We give. We give before we have received. That is contrary to the thinking of the carnal mind. The carnal mind says, "I can't afford to give." Faith says, "You can't afford not to give because that is the key to receiving." In Luke 6:38, Jesus said,

> *Give, and it will be given to you; good measure, pressed down, shaken together, running over, they will pour into your lap. For by your standard of measure it will be measured to you in return.* (NAS)

What happens first? Do we receive, or do we give? We give. Give, and it will be given back. We give to God, and God causes men to give back to us. That is God's control over the situation.

Then Jesus brought out this second principle: *"By your standard of measure it will be measured to you in return."* If you want to receive generously, then Jesus says you have to give generously.

That is remarkable. In actual fact, you have the key to your financial prosperity in your hands. It is the key of faith, responding to God's grace. You can do two things. First, you can take the initiative by giving. You do not have to wait, you can give. Second, you can set the proportion that you wish to receive, because the proportion that you give determines the proportion that you receive. You do not have to sit passively wishing or hoping. You can begin to act in faith with your finances according to God's revealed plan in the New Testament. Upon doing this, your finances then become God's responsibility.

CHAPTER SEVEN

FIRST GIVE YOURSELF

Our next Scripture comes from the eighth chapter of 2 Corinthians. I suggest that you take time to read chapters eight and nine through several times with careful consideration to get the full impact of the passage. The entire theme of both chapters is finances. Whoever said the Bible does not have much to say about money?

Paul was writing to the Corinthians about the Macedonian churches, and he was telling how the Holy Spirit moved on the Macedonians to be generous in their giving. Then he drew a lesson from that. In 2 Corinthians 8:2–5, we read,

> *Out of the most severe trial, their overflowing joy* [the Macedonian churches'] *and their extreme poverty welled up in rich generosity. For I testify that they gave as much as they were able, and even beyond their ability. Entirely on their own, they urgently pleaded with us for the privilege of sharing in this service to the saints. And they did not do as we expected, but they gave themselves first to the Lord and then to us in keeping with God's will.* (NIV)

The important sentence there is, *"They gave themselves first to the Lord."* What is the first thing we have to give to the Lord? Not our money, but ourselves. That is how it must begin with each of us. Do not give your money to God if you have not given yourself. You must begin with yourself. You cannot buy a good relationship with God. Actually, God can get on all right without your money. It is for your benefit that God requires you to give, but He has an order. He wants you first. Then, out of the giving of yourself, by His grace, the kind of giving the New Testament talks about will naturally flow.

In Romans 12:1–2, we see this same principle:

Therefore, I urge you, brothers, in view of God's mercy, to offer your bodies as living sacrifices, holy and pleasing to God—this is your spiritual act of worship. Do not conform any longer to the pattern of this world, but be transformed by the renewing of your mind. Then you will be able to test and approve what God's will is—his good, pleasing and perfect will.   (NIV)

The key to finding God's will, and that includes God's will for your money, is offering yourself as a living sacrifice. That means making yourself totally and unreservedly available to God for His service. When you do that, your mind is renewed by the Holy Spirit, and you begin to think a different way. As you begin to think differently, then you can find God's will in its three successive phases: good, pleasing, and perfect. As you find God's will, you should begin to discover that God's plan for your money is included in His will. God's plan for your life covers every facet of living.

Nothing exists for which He has not made provision, and for which He does not accept responsibility. But you must meet Him on His terms. Do not start by giving your money; start by giving yourself. Present yourself and all that you are to the Lord as a living sacrifice on the altar of His service. Then your mind will begin to grasp the fullness of God's provision and plan for you.

I have walked in this way for more than forty years, and I want you to know that there are still many areas of God's perfect will for my life into which I have not fully entered. But as far as finances are concerned, I have applied the principles I am sharing with you to my own life and can testify that they work.

Once we have given ourselves to God, the giving of our money (or whatever other gifts we may offer to God) completes and establishes our righteousness. It is very important to see that what you do with your money can establish you forever in

God's righteousness. In 2 Corinthians 9:9, Paul quoted from the book of Psalms in the Old Testament:

As it is written: "He has scattered abroad his gifts to the poor; his righteousness endures forever." (NIV)

Notice the order: the righteous man first gives himself to God and then gives liberally to others. It is said of him, *"His righteousness endures forever."* His giving of his money establishes him forever in the righteousness of God.

I would like to quote from the psalm that Paul quoted:

Blessed is the man who fears the LORD, who finds great delight in his commands [that includes His commands concerning money]....*Wealth and riches are in his house, and his righteousness endures forever. Even in darkness light dawns for the upright, for the gracious and compassionate and righteous man. Good will come to him who is generous and lends freely, who conducts his affairs with justice. Surely he will never be shaken; a righteous man will be remembered forever* [the key to this unshakable righteousness is handling your finances rightly, graciously, with compassion and generosity]....*He has scattered abroad his gifts to the poor, his righteousness endures forever.* (Ps. 112:1, 3–6, 9 NIV)

The theme of this psalm is that right dealing with our finances establishes us forever in the righteousness of God. I think the converse is also obviously true. If we do not handle our money rightly, we will never be established in the righteousness of God. The way we handle our money is very decisive.

Let me give you a beautiful teaching of Jesus found in Matthew 6:19–21:

Do not store up for yourselves treasures on earth, where moth and rust destroy, and where thieves break in and steal. But store up for yourselves treasures in heaven, where moth and rust do not destroy, and where thieves do not break in and steal. For where your treasure is, there your heart will be also. (NIV)

Right giving insures that God will provide for us in this world, but that is not the ultimate. The ultimate is that we are laying up treasure in heaven in proportion to what we give on earth. Our provision is on earth, but our treasure is in heaven. Where you invest is where you are concerned. If you want to be more concerned for the kingdom of God and if you want to have a greater zeal for the things of God, then I will tell you one way to achieve that end: invest more. The more you invest, the more concerned you will be. *"Where your treasure is, there your heart will be also."*

CHAPTER EIGHT

A TWO-WAY RELATIONSHIP

T he first gift we need to give to God is ourselves. We cannot offer God anything that is acceptable to Him until we have offered ourselves. However, once we have truly given ourselves to God, as Paul said in Romans 12, whatever we give in faith completes and establishes our righteousness. Paul quoted Psalm 112:9 in this connection when he spoke about a certain righteous man: *"He has scattered abroad his gifts to the poor, his righteousness endures forever"* (NIV). In fact, the theme of Psalm 112 is how generosity and compassion and right giving establish enduring righteousness that will never be eliminated.

We will now consider giving as a two-way relationship between God and the giver. First, let us consider giving as a proof of our love for God. In 2 Corinthians 8:7–8, we find the following:

> *But just as you excel in everything—in faith, in speech, in knowledge, in complete earnestness and in your love for us—see that you also excel in this grace of giving. I am not commanding you, but I want to test the sincerity of your love by comparing it with the earnestness of others.* (NIV)

A complete Christian, or a complete Christian church, must be able to excel in the grace of giving. Paul emphasized that this is not law, but rather grace.

Paul had been speaking to the Corinthians about the generosity of the Macedonian Christians. Then he said, "Now I want to see if your love is really sincere, and I'll find out by measuring what you give with what the Macedonian Christians gave." That is pretty plain talk. Paul sincerely loved the Corinthian

Christians. They were his spiritual children and the fruit of his ministry. But now he said he wanted to find out whether their love for God was sincere or whether it was just talk, and the way he could find out was by seeing how much they gave. The standard with which he compared them was the Macedonian Christians, who gave with amazing generosity out of their poverty. The Macedonians had proven their love. Now Paul was telling the Corinthians, "The ball is in your court. How about you? How are you going to respond to this challenge to prove your love to God?"

A little further on in the same chapter, Paul said,

> *Therefore show these men* [the representatives of the churches who had come] *the proof of your love and the reason for our pride in you, so that the churches can see it.*
> *(2 Cor. 8:24 NIV)*

Some people's giving is so secret that nobody knows about it. I wonder if it is secret because they would be embarrassed if anybody did know. But Paul said that giving to God does not have to be done in secret. He told the Corinthians to do it in front of everybody. They were to let everybody see their commitment to the Lord. He had boasted about them, had been proud of them, and it was very important to him that they prove their love in this vital matter of giving.

Our giving proves our love for God as well as for our fellow believers. This was very plainly stated by the apostle John in 1 John 3:16–18:

> *This is how we know what love is: Jesus Christ laid down his life for us. And we ought to lay down our lives for our brothers.* [We ought to do to others as Jesus did for us.] *If anyone has material possessions and sees his brother in need but has no pity on him, how can the love of God be in him? Dear children, let us not love with words or tongue but with actions and in truth.*
> *(NIV)*

Laying down our lives for our brothers includes helping them with our material resources if they are in need and we are in a position to help. There is a saying in our contemporary culture

235

that I think is pretty good: "Put your money where your mouth is." That is exactly what John was saying. He was saying, "You've said it, now do it! Don't love just *'with words or tongue but with actions and in truth.'"*

John continued with an amazing statement about love in action:

> *This then is how we know that we belong to the truth, and how we set our hearts at rest in his presence whenever our hearts condemn us. For God is greater than our hearts, and he knows everything.* (vv. 19–20 NIV)

So, if we are feeling condemned and wondering whether we are accepted by God, John said our generosity will set our hearts at rest. That is exactly what Paul was saying when he was quoting Psalm 112, *"He has scattered abroad his gifts to the poor, his righteousness endures forever"* (v. 9 NIV).

We have two alternatives when it comes to love: one is just in words and in tongue; the other is in actions and in truth. One of the ways to answer that challenge is by what we do with our finances. We will prove whether our love is just in word and in tongue, or whether it is in action and in truth by the measure of our generosity.

As I have already stated, giving to God is a two-way relationship. The first aspect of the relationship is our attitude to God. We prove our love for God by giving to Him.

The second aspect of the relationship is God's response to us. The New Testament teaches that right giving is a cause of God's special love for us. God loves the world, but He loves some people in a special way. One class of people He loves specially are those who give generously and happily:

> *Each man should give what he has decided in his heart to give, not reluctantly or under compulsion, for God loves a cheerful giver.* (2 Cor. 9:7 NIV)

Do you want to be loved of God? One way is to give cheerfully. God loves a cheerful giver. The Greek word that is translated *"cheerful"* is the word from which we derive the English word *hilarious*. God loves a hilarious giver. Have you ever thought of giving with hilarity?

Having spent five years in East Africa, I can remember scenes in African churches where the people gave with hilarity. By our American standards, they were extremely poor. Most did not have money, but they would give in kind: coffee beans, corn, eggs, or chickens. I remember seeing the African women walking up to the front of the church with a couple of ears of corn or even a live chicken balanced on top of their heads. (They carried everything on top of their heads.) They would put it down at the altar, go back, and be touched by God again and come running up with another gift. I do not think I have ever seen people more happy than those simple people. They were hilarious givers.

Why should people be hilarious when they give? Let me give you three reasons:

1. First, it is the supernatural grace of the Holy Spirit. Remember, giving is grace, not law. The Holy Spirit is the Spirit of Grace, and when we line ourselves up with what the Holy Spirit can bless, He comes upon us with supernatural grace. When He does, people get happy in a way they cannot be happy in the natural.

2. Second, giving calls down God's favor on us. The Bible says God's favor is like a shield and like a cloud of the latter rain. Giving is the catalyst for the precipitation of His blessings upon us.

3. Third, hilarious giving releases us from slavery to mammon. *"Mammon"* (Matt. 6:24 KJV) is that evil, satanic power that enslaves men and women through money. When we begin to give hilariously, we are saying to mammon, "Away with you. You're not going to dictate to me. You're not going to dominate my thinking. I'm going to give with joy because I'm giving to God, and God loves a cheerful giver."

CHAPTER NINE

GIVING IS SOWING

A nother aspect of giving is sowing seed. In 2 Corinthians 9:6–7, Paul said, *"Remember this: Whoever sows sparingly will also reap sparingly, and whoever sows generously will also reap generously. Each man should give what he has decided in his heart to give"* (NIV).

In talking about giving our money, Paul used the metaphorical figure of sowing and reaping. This analogy is taken from agriculture, but he was not talking about a farmer and his farm. He was talking about the Christian and his giving to God and the kingdom of God. Certain basic principles of agriculture must be followed if you want to succeed in agriculture. The possibility of success exists, but achieving success depends upon your following the principles, or laws, of agriculture.

When we think of giving as sowing (in agricultural terms), we understand that we should expect an increase from our giving, but only in proportion to what we sow. For example, when sowing seed, a farmer sows one bushel of wheat. When harvested, his wheat crop yields a biblical proportion, an increase of a hundredfold. By that proportion of increase, he receives one hundred bushels of wheat. That is an easy calculation. If he sows ten bushels and his proportionate increase is one hundred times the amount sown, he receives one thousand bushels. In other words, the original investment of seed sown determines the amount that is harvested or reaped. Paul said the same is true with giving money to God and His kingdom.

Let me give a simple example: A person gives five dollars. The proportion of increase is ten. What is he going to receive back? Fifty dollars. If he gives fifty dollars and the proportion of increase is the same, he is going to get back five hundred dollars. The degree of generosity with which he gives determines the proportionate size of the return that he will receive back.

Almost everybody can understand the principle of proportion in agriculture, but so few people understand it in the finances of the kingdom of God. The Bible makes it very clear that the same kinds of laws that apply in agriculture also apply in the finances of the kingdom of God. This is a principle of sowing and of reaping.

In order to obtain the increase, a farmer must follow certain basic rules. I would suggest that the following non-exhaustive guidelines that are employed in agriculture are also applicable in the area of giving. First, the farmer must choose good, suitable soil and the right kind of crop for the right kind of soil. Second, he must make proper preparation of the soil. Third, he must take proper care of the crop as it grows. If he does not meet these conditions, he will not receive the increase that he ought to receive. His failure to receive will not be because there is anything wrong with the laws of agriculture, but because he has not applied some of the basic rules.

A farmer does not walk down the street of the town casting his seed into the gutter on either side of the street and then expect a harvest. You might say that is absurd. But I have observed many Christians doing something that is analogous with their money. They cast it away without care or prayer in places where it will never bring an increase. Then they wonder why God does not bless their finances.

We need to follow certain basic rules just like the basic principles the farmer follows. We do not sow in the gutter; we choose good soil. We make sure the soil is properly prepared, and we try to see that there is care taken of the crop as it grows.

What are the things that we should look at when we consider giving to a church or a ministry or an organization? I will give you four questions that I think you need to ask:

1. Is the ministry anointed and fruitful? Is it bringing forth real fruit for the kingdom of God?

2. Is it ethical? Is it ethical in the way it appeals for money? Is it ethical in the way it handles money? Is it a good and faithful steward of the money in God's kingdom?

3. Is it aligned with Scripture? Is what they are doing in obedience to scriptural principles? That is very important, because God blesses what is in line with His Word.

4. Are the leaders prayerful, industrious, and efficient? The Bible makes it very clear that God hates sloppiness, waste, and extravagance. That does not mean we have to be stingy, but it does mean we cannot afford to be extravagant. We should not support extravagance in any ministry.

I would like to offer you some other practical safeguards in connection with investing your money in the kingdom of God. When people of this world invest their money, they like to get good advice from someone who is proficient in investments. I think God's children should be equally careful in their own way. Let me give you four safeguards:

1. Be prayerful. Never give except after prayer.

2. Avoid impulsive, emotional giving. I have seen countless sums of money squandered by people who gave out of emotion and impulse. There are people going around deliberately exploiting God's people to get money. There is no group of people in the world easier to exploit than American Christians. They are generous but, frankly, they are so often impulsive.

3. Maintain contact with whatever individual or organization you are supporting. Get reports. Find out what is happening. Check on the fruit.

4. Stay within the proportion of your faith. Allow God to increase it in a natural way. If you are accustomed to thinking in terms of ten dollars, it is probably unrealistic to think immediately in terms of one thousand dollars. Faith grows in a natural way. If you have been thinking in terms of ten dollars, progress to fifty. When you are comfortable with fifty, then move up to a hundred.

Finally, there are four results of wise sowing of your money. They were stated by Paul in 2 Corinthians 9:10:

Now he [God] *who supplies seed to the sower and bread for food will also supply and increase your store of seed and will enlarge the harvest of your righteousness.*   *(NIV)*

The four results of wise sowing are the following:

1. Bread for you to eat. You will get back all that you need for your own life.

2. You will get more seed to sow in God's harvest field. If you have been giving fifty dollars, you will find that you can move up to one hundred dollars. That is seed to sow back into God's harvest field, not to squander on your own selfishness.

3. You will get an increased store for sowing. Your barn will get bigger. You will have more to give.

4. You will get an increased harvest from increased sowing. It says there, "[God] *will enlarge the harvest of your righteousness.*"

I want to tell you that learning to give prayerfully, in a scriptural way, and in the guidance of the Holy Spirit is exciting, not a dreary duty. It is exciting to see how God will come to your help and extend and increase your faith. God wants you to invest in His kingdom. If you will seek God's counsel, He will make you a successful investor.

CHAPTER TEN

GOD'S LEVEL IS ABUNDANCE

Thus far, we have established six important facts in connection with giving. First, the key to right giving is grace. Grace comes only through Jesus, through the cross, and is received only by faith.

Second, we must first give ourselves. We cannot buy God's favor. He requires that we first surrender ourselves to Him before our gifts become acceptable. Third, giving completes and establishes our righteousness.

Fourth, giving is a proof of the sincerity of our love, both for God and for our fellow believers. Fifth, giving calls down God's favor and love upon us. God loves a hilarious giver.

Sixth, giving is sowing in God's harvest field. The same principles that apply to agriculture apply to giving. The Lord wants us to understand and employ these principles so that we may be blessed, we may have enough food for ourselves, we may have seed to sow, our barns for storage may be enlarged, and our harvest may increase.

Finally, we need to see that the level of God's provision for His people is abundance. One of the most powerful verses in the New Testament states this:

> *And God is able to make all grace abound to you, so that in all things at all times, having all that you need, you will abound in every good work.*   *(2 Cor. 9:8 NIV)*

Again, notice it is by grace—not by law. The principle of grace is stated in 2 Corinthians 8:9:

For you know the grace of our Lord Jesus Christ, that
though he was rich, yet for your sakes he became poor, so
that you through his poverty might become rich.   *(NIV)*

You need to keep those two references in your mind: 2 Corinthians 8:9 and 9:8. The first speaks about the grace of the Lord Jesus Christ that on the cross He became poor with our poverty so that we might by faith share His riches. In the second one, Paul told the level of the grace that is released to us through the cross:

God is able to make all grace abound to you, so that in all
things at all times, having all that you need, you will
abound in every good work.   *(2 Cor. 9:8 NIV)*

If you analyze the latter verse, you will find two key words: the word *"abound"* and the word *"all."* *"Abound"* occurs twice and *"all"* occurs five times in that one verse. In no way could the language be more emphatic. When speaking about the level of God's provision for His people, it says, *"all grace...so that in all things at all times, having all that you need, you will abound in every good work."* (The last word in English is *"every,"* but in the Greek it is the same word as *"all."*) If you have all that you need in all things at all times to abound to every good work, there is absolutely no room for unsupplied need anywhere in your life.

Let us consider for a moment the meaning of *abundance*. By its Latin origin, *abundance* speaks of "a wave that overflows." Your swimming pool has abundance when it overflows. Your sink has abundance when it spills over. A thing has no abundance until it overflows. Jesus said, *"Out of the abundance of the heart the mouth speaks"* (Matt. 12:34 NKJV). When your heart overflows, it overflows through your mouth.

What does it mean to have overflowing provision? Let me illustrate it very simply. You need fifty dollars worth of groceries, but you only have forty dollars. So when you go to the grocery store, you are shopping out of insufficiency. If you have fifty dollars and you need fifty dollars worth of groceries, you are shopping out of sufficiency. You have just enough. But if you need fifty dollars worth of groceries and you go to the store with sixty dollars, you are shopping out of abundance. You have more than enough; there is an overflow.

God's provision is on that level. God does not merely offer us just enough. If we, by faith, appropriate His grace, then the level of His provision is abundance. We have more than enough for all our needs and for ourselves.

You need to take notice that the final purpose of abundance is *"every good work"* (2 Cor. 9:8 NIV). It is not selfish indulgence; it is being able to do good works.

Why does God want His children to have abundance? His specific, practical reason is contained in Acts 20:35, where Paul quoted Jesus:

> *The Lord Jesus himself said: "It is more blessed to give than to receive."* (NIV)

Receiving has a blessing, but giving has a greater blessing. God has no favorites among His children. He wants all His children to enjoy the greater blessing of giving. God makes His abundance available to us so that we may not be limited to the blessing of receiving, but that we may also be in a position to enjoy the greater blessing of giving.

To complete what I have been teaching about giving, I want to add a word of warning. If you want to enter into what I have been teaching, you will have to express your faith in action. It will not be enough just to give mental assent to what I am saying. You cannot merely say, "Well, that was good teaching. Isn't that wonderful! God wants me to prosper. He wants me to have abundance." Nothing will change in your life if you go no further than that. At some point, you must express this teaching, if you believe it, in your actions by faith.

In James 2:26, it says, *"As the body without the spirit is dead, so faith without deeds* [or actions] *is dead"* (NIV). You can believe everything but have nothing unless you add action to your faith. You must act in faith.

If you want this kind of abundance, which comes by grace, not by law, then you must act in faith, and that means you must give first. The words of Jesus in Luke 6:38 express this idea:

*Give, and it will be given to you. A good measure, pressed
down, shaken together and running over, will be poured
into your lap. For with the measure you use, it will be
measured to you.* (NIV)

Do you want it to be given to you? Then you must give first.
That is faith. If you are not willing to act in faith, you will not
set in motion the processes that will bring God's prosperity and
God's abundance into your life.

We need to bear in mind that usually a time interval between sowing and reaping occurs. The farmer does not sow one
day and reap the next. He has to let the seed fall into the ground
and apparently die. Then when it has fallen into the ground and
died, the harvest comes up. This important lesson was expressed
by Paul in Galatians 6:9:

Let us not become weary in doing good [and that includes
doing good with our money], *for at the proper time we will
reap a harvest if we do not give up.* (NIV)

Paul said in that passage that we must wait for God's appointed time for the harvest. It will come if we do not give up.
But if we become impatient or lose our faith or turn away from
these principles, then God does not guarantee the harvest. We
must live and act in faith in every area of our lives, including
our money.

DOES YOUR TONGUE NEED HEALING?

Contents

CHAPTER ONE

DEATH OR LIFE?

The title for this study is a question: *Does Your Tongue Need Healing?* As we follow this theme, you may be in for some surprises!

Let me begin by pointing out something very significant about the way in which the Creator designed the human head. Every person has seven openings in his or her head, the number in Scripture that often denotes completeness. We have three pairs of openings: two eyes, two ears, and two nostrils. But the Creator restricted the seventh opening to one, the mouth. I have often asked people, "How many of you wish you had more than one mouth?" But I have never met anyone who did. Most of us have all we can do to use one mouth properly. This one opening causes us more problems than all the other six together!

If you take a Bible concordance and look up all the words related to that one opening, such as *mouth, tongue, lips, speech, words,* and so on, you will be amazed how much the Bible has to say about this subject, and it is with good reason. There is no area in our personalities more directly related to our total well-being than the mouth and tongue.

DEATH OR LIFE?

In the first section of this study, I wish to share a number of passages of Scripture that all emphasize the vital importance of the mouth and the tongue. Then, in subsequent sections, I will deal with principles that arise out of these Scriptures. First, we will consider Psalm 34:11–13:

*Come, my children, listen to me; I will teach you the fear of
the LORD. Whoever of you loves life and desires to see many
good days, keep your tongue from evil and your lips from
speaking lies.* (NIV)

The inspired Word of God offers to teach us, as God's children, the fear of the Lord. I have a series of audio cassettes that point out that there is nothing in all of Scripture to which there is attached greater blessing, fruitfulness, and assurance than the fear of the Lord. So, when the Scripture offers to teach us the fear of the Lord, it is offering something of infinite value and worth. By implication, the psalmist said here that *"life"* and *"many good days"* go with the fear of the Lord. In Scripture, life in its fullness and the fear of the Lord are always associated together. The measure in which we have the fear of the Lord is the measure in which we enjoy true life.

Practically speaking, where does the fear of the Lord begin? It is very clear. The psalmist said, *"Keep your tongue from evil and your lips from speaking lies."* In other words, the first area of our lives in which the fear of the Lord will be practically manifested is our tongues and our lips. If we can keep our tongues from evil and our lips from speaking lies, then we can move on into the fullness of the fear of the Lord.

Out of the fear of the Lord comes *"life"* and *"many good days."* The fear of the Lord, life, good days, and the proper use and control of our tongues and our lips are all bound together. We cannot really have good lives if we do not control our tongues and our lips.

Proverbs 13:3 states the following:

He who guards his lips guards his [soul], *but he who
speaks rashly will come to ruin.* (NIV)

Your soul is your whole personality. It is the real you. This is the area where weakness will be manifested first and where the Enemy will gain access first. If you want to guard your soul, you must guard your lips. But if you speak rashly, you will come to ruin. The alternatives are very clear. If you control the tongue, then you have protection, but if your tongue gets out of control and you are not master of your words, then the end is ruin. It is so clear; there are no blurred edges.

The whole book of Proverbs is full of these principles. Consider Proverbs 21:23:

> *He who guards his mouth and his tongue keeps himself from calamity.* (NIV)

Again, the vital area that you must protect is your mouth and your tongue. Once again, the alternatives are black and white. There is no gray. If you guard your mouth and tongue, then you guard your soul and your life. You are safe. But if you fail to do that, the alternative is *"calamity." Calamity* is a very strong word, and I believe the Bible uses it deliberately. The failure to guard our lips and our tongues will ultimately bring us to calamity.

There are two other passages in the book of Proverbs concerning the use of the tongue that are particularly significant.

> *A wholesome tongue is a tree of life: but perverseness therein is a breach in the spirit.* (Prov. 15:4 KJV)

Where the King James Version says, *"a wholesome tongue,"* the literal Hebrew says, "the healing of the tongue." This clearly indicates that our tongue can need healing. I believe the tongue of every sinner needs healing. The tongue is one area where sin is always manifested in every life. There are some areas in which a sinner may not offend. But the tongue is one area in which every sinner offends, and it must be healed.

"The healing of the tongue *'is a tree of life.'"* Notice again the close connection between life and the correct use of the tongue. The alternative is, *"Perverseness therein is a breach in the spirit."* Perverseness means "the wrong use." The misuse of the tongue is a breach, or a leak, in the spirit.

I remember once being in a service where a visiting preacher prayed for a certain person and said, "Lord, fill her with the Holy Spirit."

But the pastor who knew her said, "Don't, Lord; she leaks."

Many get filled and blessed, but it runs out through their tongues. You must keep a tight reign on your tongue if you are going to contain the blessing of the Lord. It is one thing to be blessed; it is another thing to contain the blessing. The healing of the tongue is a tree of life that brings life to us and to others. It works inwardly and outwardly.

> *Death and life are in the power of the tongue, and those*
> *who love it will eat its fruit.* (Prov. 18:21 NAS)

The alternatives are always so clear. It is either death or life. They are both in the power of the tongue. If we use our tongues properly, they will be trees of life. But if we use our tongues improperly, then the result will be death. Whichever way we use our tongues, we can be sure we will eat the fruit. Each one of us eats the fruit of his own tongue. If the fruit is sweet, we will eat sweet fruit. If the fruit is bitter, we will feed on bitter fruit. God has ordained it that way.

The tongue is the decisive member. Death and life are in the power of the tongue.

CHAPTER TWO

THE HEART OVERFLOWS THROUGH THE MOUTH

Our theme will be made a little more relevant by an illustration. During World War II, I was a hospital attendant with the British army in North Africa. At one time, I was appointed the NCO in charge of a small reception station in the desert that catered only to dysentery patients.

Each morning, the doctor under whom I worked would summon me, and we would go on rounds of our patients who were all lying there on stretchers right on the sand. I noticed that every morning the doctor always greeted each patient with the same two sentences. The first one was, "Good morning, how are you?" The second one was, "Show me your tongue."

It was not long before I realized that the doctor paid very little attention to the answer to his question, "How are you?" He always moved on immediately to the next question, "Show me your tongue." When the patient stuck his tongue out, the doctor looked very carefully at it. Then he formed his estimate of the patient's condition, much more from looking at his tongue than from the answer the patient actually gave to the question, "How are you?"

That stuck with me, and later, as I moved on into the ministry, many times it occurred to me that God does much the same with us as that doctor did with his patients. God may ask us, "How are you?" and we may give him an estimate of our condition. But I think the next thing that God says, metaphorically, is, "Show me your tongue." And when God looks at our tongues, then He forms His own estimate of our true spiritual condition.

The state of your tongue is a very sure guide to your spiritual condition.

Now we will make a Scriptural application of this. Many passages establish the principle that there is a direct connection between the heart and the mouth. Jesus stated, in Matthew 12:33–37,

> *Either make the tree good, and its fruit good; or make the tree bad, and its fruit bad; for the tree is known by its fruit. You brood of vipers* [He's speaking to the religious leaders of His time], *how can you, being evil, speak what is good? For the mouth speaks out of that which fills the heart. The good man out of his good treasure brings forth what is good; and the evil man out of his evil treasure brings forth what is evil. And I say to you, that every careless word that men shall speak, they shall render account for it in the day of judgment. For by your words you shall be justified, and by your words you shall be condemned.* (NAS)

Jesus here established the direct connection between the heart and the mouth using parabolic language. He referred to the heart as the tree and to the words that come out of the mouth as the fruit. And the kind of words that come out of your mouth will indicate the condition of your heart. He said, for instance, *"The good man out of his good treasure* [in his heart] *brings forth* [good words]; *and the evil man out of his evil treasure* [in his heart] *brings forth* [evil words]." You will notice Jesus used the word *"good"* three times, and He used the word *"evil"* three times. If the heart is good, then out of the mouth will come words that are good. But if the heart is evil, then out of the mouth will come words that are evil. In Matthew 7:17–18, Jesus expressed the following in similar language:

> *Every good tree bears good fruit; but the bad tree bears bad fruit. A good tree cannot produce bad fruit, nor can a* [rotten] *tree produce good fruit.* (NAS)

The nature of the tree inevitably determines the kind of fruit. Conversely, when we see the kind of fruit, we know the nature of the tree. The tree is the heart, and the fruit is the mouth. If the heart is good, the words that come from the mouth will be good. But if the words that come from the mouth are evil, we know that the heart is evil. You cannot have bad fruit from a good tree, nor can you have good fruit from a bad tree. There is an absolute, inescapable connection between the state of the heart and the state of the mouth.

We may deceive ourselves about the state of our hearts with all sorts of ideas about our own goodness, purity, or righteousness, but the sure and unfailing indicator is what comes out of our mouths. If what comes out of our mouths is corrupt, then our hearts are corrupt. There can be no other conclusion.

I did educational work for five years in East Africa. One of the tribes I worked with was the Marigoli tribe. I was amazed to discover that the same word in that language meant "heart" and "voice." I used to wonder how to determine which one the person meant. Does he mean "your heart" or "your voice"? But as I pondered it, I began to see the real insight in the use of that particular language. In reality, the voice indicates the heart. The voice tells with words what is the condition of the heart. This is the same as what Jesus said: you cannot have bad words out of a good heart, and you cannot have good words out of a bad heart.

When we come to God with an estimate of our own spiritual condition, I think God is prone to respond the same way that the doctor did with his dysentery patients in the desert. You might say, "God, I'm a very good Christian. I really love you, and I go to church." But God says, "Show me your tongue. When I've seen your tongue, I'll know the real condition of your heart."

I want to illustrate this by taking two prophetic pictures from the Old Testament: the first is of Christ Himself, the Messiah, and the second is of the bride of Christ, the church. Notice, in each case, the feature that is emphasized first and foremost is the condition of the lips and the mouth. Psalm 45:1–2 gives us a beautiful, prophetic picture of the Messiah:

> *My heart overflows with a good theme; I address my verses to the King; My tongue is the pen of a ready writer.* [And then these are the words that the writer addresses to the King, to the Messiah:] *Thou art fairer than the sons of*

men; Grace is poured upon Thy lips; Therefore God has blessed Thee forever. *(NAS)*

Here is a picture of the Messiah in His grace, His beauty, and His moral purity. What is the first aspect of that beauty that is manifested? His lips. *"Grace,"* it says, *"is poured upon Thy lips."* Then it says, *"Therefore God has blessed Thee forever."*

Two very important principles are given here. First, the grace of the Messiah is manifested primarily in His lips. Second, God has blessed Him forever because of the grace of His lips. When Jesus appeared in human form and men were sent to arrest Him, they came back without Him, and were asked, *"Why didn't you bring him in?"* Their answer was, *"No one ever spoke the way this man does"* (John 7:45–46 NIV). The grace that poured from His lips marked Him out as the Messiah.

In the Song of Solomon, there is a prophetic picture of Christ and His bride and the relationship between them. Song of Solomon 4:3 is addressed to the bride:

Your lips are like a scarlet thread, And your mouth is lovely. Your temples are like a slice of a pomegranate behind your veil. *(NAS)*

The first feature mentioned about the bride is her lips; *"Your lips are like a scarlet thread, and your mouth is lovely."*

The word *"scarlet"* there indicates sanctification through the blood of Jesus. The lips have been touched by the blood. As a result, the mouth is lovely. Notice that the face is hidden behind a veil: *"Your temples are like a slice of a pomegranate,"* but they are behind a veil. Still, the voice is heard through the veil. The other beauties are veiled, but the beauty of the voice comes out through the veil. The voice is the thing most manifested. In the same chapter of the Song of Solomon, we read,

Your lips, my bride, drip honey; Honey and milk are under your tongue, And the fragrance of your garments is like the fragrance of Lebanon. *(Song 4:11 NAS)*

Notice the two distinctive words used of the tongue of the bride: *"honey and milk."* They are also the two distinctive features of the Promised Land. The beauty of the Promised Land is seen in the bride and especially in her tongue and in her lips. There is a fragrance associated with these beautiful lips that penetrates the veil. Again, the clear form of the bride is not seen behind the veil, but her voice and her fragrance penetrate the veil due to the beauty of her lips. Her lips are like a thread of scarlet and her mouth is lovely.

Is that true of you and me as followers of Jesus? We need to ask ourselves this question.

CHAPTER THREE

THE BIBLICAL PICTURE OF THE TONGUE

W e have considered thus far the direct connection between our hearts and our mouths, as summed up in the words of Jesus in Matthew 12:34: *"Out of the overflow of the heart the mouth speaks"* (NIV). When the heart is filled, it overflows through the mouth, and that overflow tells us the real condition of the heart.

In the Old Testament, there are portraits of Christ and of Christ's bride. For Christ, the Messiah and His bride, the church, the first feature of the grace of God and spiritual and moral beauty is their lips and their speech.

We are now going to consider a biblical picture of the tongue itself. The epistle of James deals at length with this subject. First, consider some very searching remarks James made about the kind of religion that God accepts and also the kind that He does not accept. James spoke about the kind of religion that is not acceptable to God:

> *If anyone considers himself religious and yet does not keep a tight rein on his tongue, he deceives himself and his religion is worthless.*　　　　　　　　*(James 1:26 NIV)*

It does not matter how religious we may claim to be. We may attend church, sing hymns, and do all the other things that are expected of religious people. In themselves, all those things are good. We may do all those things, but if we do not keep our tongues under control, our religion is worthless and unacceptable

260

to God. May God grant that all religious people would face up to this issue.

On the other hand, James spoke about the kind of religion God accepts. Again, it is different from the practice of the average churchgoer today.

> *Religion that God our Father accepts as pure and faultless is this: to look after orphans and widows in their distress and to keep oneself from being polluted by the world.*
>
> *(James 1:27 NIV)*

The first positive requirement of pure religion is not churchgoing or even Bible reading. It is looking after and showing practical love to those who are in need, primarily orphans and widows.

Let me suggest, if you are in any way religious, that you take time to look in this mirror of the Word of God found in James 1:26–27. If you do not control your tongue, your religion is worthless. If you want to have a religion that is accepted by God, it must be demonstrated first and foremost in caring for those who are in need: the orphans and the widows.

I think again about the doctor in the desert when he asked his patients how they felt. He really was not too interested in the answer because the next thing he always said was, "Show me your tongue."

That is really what James was saying in these two verses. If you want to impress God with your religion, the first thing He will say is, "Show me your tongue." He is going to judge from your tongue whether your religion is valid and acceptable or not.

James used a number of pictures to illustrate the function of the tongue in our lives. First, James 3:2 says,

> *We all stumble in many ways. If anyone is never at fault in what he says, he is a perfect man, able to keep his whole body in check.*
>
> *(NIV)*

James was saying that if you can control your tongue, you can control your whole life. You are a perfect man if you can control your tongue. Then he goes on in the remainder of this passage to give some illustrations from the natural world. James 3:3–8 continues,

> *When we put bits into the mouths of horses to make them obey us, we can turn the whole animal. Or take ships as an example. Although they are so large and are driven by strong winds, they are steered by a very small rudder wherever the pilot wants to go. Likewise the tongue is a small part of the body, but it makes great boasts. Consider what a great forest is set on fire by a small spark. The tongue also is a fire, a world of evil among the parts of the body. It corrupts the whole person, sets the whole course of his life on fire, and is itself set on fire by hell. All kinds of animals, birds, reptiles and creatures of the sea are being tamed and have been tamed by man, but no man can tame the tongue. It is a restless evil, full of deadly poison.* (NIV)

James was bringing out the unique significance and influence of the tongue for the whole course of our lives. The first example he used was the bit in the horse's mouth. He said, "If we succeed in putting a bit in a horse's mouth, we can turn the whole animal around."

The horse, in the Bible, is usually a type of physical strength. James was saying that no matter how strong a horse is, if you can get control of its mouth with the bit, you can control the whole animal. The horse's strength is brought into subjection through the control of its mouth. The same is true with us. What controls our mouths controls the whole course of our lives.

The next example is perhaps a little more vivid. He compared the tongue to the rudder of a ship. A ship may be a great structure but be carried to and fro by the tremendously powerful forces of the winds and the waves. Yet in that ship there is only one decisive, small piece—the rudder. It is the use of the rudder that determines the whole course of the ship. If the rudder is used properly, the ship will arrive safely in the harbor. If the rudder is not used properly, the ship is likely to be shipwrecked.

James said it is the same in our lives. The tongue is the rudder. Our tongues control the course of our lives. If the rudder of the tongue is used properly, we will make it safely to our appointed destinations. But if our tongues are not used properly, we will be shipwrecked.

James also gave the example of a small spark that can start a forest fire. Every year in the United States, billions of dollars of damage is caused by forest fires, and they usually start just the way James said, with a small spark. The forest department of the United States has a very vivid poster that says, "Only you can prevent forest fires."

That is also true in the spiritual realm. The tongue is like a little spark that can cause a forest fire of vast proportions, causing billions of dollars of damage. Many churches and religious groups no longer exist because one tongue set a spark that burned up the whole thing, which could never be restored.

The final example James used is that of a source of lethal poison. He said the tongue is like a deadly element that can poison us by spreading infection through the whole system of our lives.

Consider those examples again: the bit in the horse's mouth, the rudder in the ship, the spark that starts a forest fire, and a poison that is injected into the life stream. The principle underlying each of these illustrations is the same: the tongue is a small part of the body, but it is able to cause inestimable damage that might never be undone.

James went on to point out, once more, the inconsistencies of religious people:

With the tongue we praise our Lord and Father, and with it we curse men, who have been made in God's likeness. Out of the same mouth come praise and cursing. My brothers, this should not be. Can both fresh water and salt water flow from the same spring? My brothers, can a fig tree bear olives, or a grapevine bear figs? Neither can a salt spring produce fresh water. (vv. 9–12 NIV)

James was saying exactly the same thing Jesus said. If the tree is good, the fruit will be good. If you have a fig tree in your heart, you will get figs out of your mouth. But if you have a vine in your heart, you will never get figs out of your mouth. What comes out of your mouth indicates what is in your heart.

It is the same, he said, with the flow of water. If the water that comes out of your mouth is fresh, then the spring that is in your heart is fresh. But if the water that comes out of your mouth is salty and brackish, then the spring of your heart is salty and brackish. So what comes out of the mouth inevitably indicates the true condition of the heart.

CHAPTER FOUR

WORDS DETERMINE DESTINY

T he essence of the different pictures that James used to illustrate the function of the tongue in our lives is the same: the tongue is something small in itself but capable of causing incalculable harm if left unchecked. Of the four particular pictures that I referred to (the bit in the horse's mouth, the rudder in the ship, a spark that starts a forest fire, and a source of poison that corrupts the whole life stream), the one that best illustrates the tremendous potential of the tongue is that of the rudder in the ship.

The rudder is visually just a small part of the ship that is down below the surface. You do not see it when you look at the ship sailing on the surface of the water. Yet that small part, which is not normally visible to the eye, determines the direction of the ship. If the rudder is used correctly, the ship will make it safely to its destined harbor. But if the rudder is misused, almost certainly the ship will suffer shipwreck. The rudder determines the course and the destiny of the entire ship.

The Bible says the tongue is like that in our bodies. When we look at people from outward appearances, normally we do not even see their tongues. Yet that small, unnoticed member is just like the rudder in the ship. The tongue's use determines the course of the person's life. It determines his or her destiny.

To continue our study, we want to consider an example from the history of Israel that drives home this lesson with inescapable clarity. The lesson to learn is this: Men determine their own destinies by the way they use their tongues.

The incident we are going to look at is found in the book of Numbers, chapters 13 and 14. The Israelites had come out of

Egypt and were on their way to the Promised Land. God arranged with Moses to send twelve men ahead of them to spy out the land: to find out its general character, the nature of the inhabitants, the kind of cities, the kind of fruit, and to bring back a report. One leader was chosen from each of the twelve tribes to go ahead into the land. They spent forty days walking through the land and then they came back with their report. The report they brought back is given to us in Numbers 13:26–28:

> *And they* [the twelve spies] *went and came to Moses, and to Aaron, and to all the congregation of the children of Israel, unto the wilderness of Paran, to Kadesh; and brought back word unto them, and unto all the congregation, and showed them the fruit of the land. And they told him, and said, We came unto the land whither thou sentest us, and surely it floweth with milk and honey; and this is the fruit of it.* [The fruit was so heavy that it took two men to carry one bunch of grapes on a staff between them. But this is what they said next:] *Nevertheless the people be strong that dwell in the land, and the cities are walled, and very great: and moreover we saw the children of Anak* [the giants] *there.*   *(KJV)*

When God gives you a promise, are you going to accept the promise at its face value, or are you going to accept it and then say *"nevertheless"*? That was a fatal word that caused the people to be disturbed and distressed.

Two of the spies, however, Caleb and Joshua, refused to go along with this negative attitude. In Numbers 13:30–31, we read this:

> *And Caleb stilled the people before Moses, and said, Let us go up at once, and possess it; for we are well able to overcome it. But the men that went up with him said, We be not able to go up against the people; for they are stronger than we.*   *(KJV)*

Let us take notice of the words that were used. Caleb said, *"We are well able to overcome it."* The other ten spies said, *"We be not able."* One set of spies said the positive: "We are able." The other set said the negative: "We are not able." As you follow the story, you will see that each group got exactly what they said. Each group's destiny was settled by their words.

> *And the LORD said, I have pardoned according to thy word: but as truly as I live, all the earth shall be filled with the glory of the LORD. Because all those men which have seen my glory, and my miracles, which I did in Egypt and in the wilderness, and have tempted me now these ten times, and have not hearkened to my voice; surely they shall not see the land which I sware unto their fathers, neither shall any of them that provoked me see it: but my servant Caleb, because he had another spirit with him, and hath followed me fully, him will I bring into the land whereinto he went; and his seed shall possess it.* (Num. 14:20–24 KJV)

By his positive confession, Caleb settled his destiny for the positive.

Numbers 14:26–32 continues,

> *And the LORD spake unto Moses and unto Aaron, saying, How long shall I bear with this evil congregation, which murmur against me? I have heard the murmurings of the children of Israel, which they murmur against me. Say unto them, As truly as I live, saith the LORD, as ye have spoken in mine ears, so will I do to you: your carcases shall fall in this wilderness; and all that were numbered of you, according to your whole number, from twenty years old and upward, which have murmured against me, doubtless ye shall not come into the land, concerning which I sware to make you dwell therein, save Caleb the son of Jephunneh, and Joshua the son of Nun. But your little ones, which ye said should be a prey, them will I bring in, and they shall know the land which ye have despised. But as for you, your carcases, they shall fall in this wilderness.* (KJV)

Notice the words, *"As ye have spoken in mine ears, so will I do to you."* God is saying, in effect, "You have settled what I will do to you by the words that you have spoken."

And the men, which Moses sent to search the land, who returned, and made all the congregation to murmur against him, by bringing up a slander upon the land, even those men that did bring up the evil report upon the land, died by the plague before the LORD. [They settled their own deaths. They spoke words of death, and death was the outcome.] *But Joshua the son of Nun, and Caleb the son of Jephunneh, which were of the men that went to search the land, lived still.*   *(vv. 36–38 KJV)*

Death and life are in the power of the tongue. How much more clearly could that be illustrated? The men who spoke negatively settled for death. The men who spoke positively received life. They settled their own destinies by what they spoke. The ones who said, "We are not able," were not able. The ones who said, "We are able," were able.

In the New Testament, our experience as Christians is directly compared to that of Israel in the Old Testament. We are warned that the same lessons apply to us. Hebrews 4:1–2 reads,

Therefore, since the promise of entering his rest still stands, let us be careful that none of you be found to have fallen short of it. For we also have had the gospel [the Good News] *preached to us, just as they did; but the message they heard was of no value to them, because those who heard did not combine it with faith.*   *(NIV)*

The same promise that God gave to Israel still stands for us—a promise of entering into the rest of God—but we must be careful that we do not fall short of it in the same way that they did in the Old Testament. Their problem was that they heard the message, a promise from God, but they added that one fatal word *"nevertheless."* Instead of focusing on the promise of God and boldly confessing their faith in God's promise and power, they focused on the negative. They looked at the giants and the walled cities and said, "We are not able." Thank God for two men who had the faith and the courage to say, *"We are well able"* (Num. 13:30).

When you face God's promise concerning a certain situation, what are you going to do with your tongue? Are you going to give assent to the promise of God? Are you going to identify yourself with the promise of God and say, "God said it; I'm able." Or are you going to be one of those who say, "Nevertheless, look at all the problems. God said it, but somehow I don't feel able." Remember, just as those spies settled their destinies with their tongues by the words that they spoke, so the same lesson applies to whoever has heard the Gospel. We likewise settle our destinies by the words that we speak.

Ten of the twelve spies focused on the problems, not on the promises. Two of the twelve spies, Joshua and Caleb, focused on the promises, not on the problems. Joshua and Caleb said, *"We are well able."* The other spies said, "We are not able." Each got exactly what they said. They all settled their own destinies by the way they used their tongues.

CHAPTER FIVE

DISEASES OF THE TONGUE

We have studied an example from the Old Testament that illustrates how *"death and life are in the power of the tongue"* (Prov. 18:21 NAS). We learned that the right use of the tongue will impart life, and, conversely, the wrong use will impart death.

Now we will consider certain specific diseases that affect our tongues. These six diseases that commonly infect our lives through the misuse of our tongues can, in some cases, be fatal if left unchecked.

DISEASE NUMBER ONE: *EXCESSIVE TALKING*

This disease is so common that people accept it as normal when it is not. *"When words are many, sin is not absent, but he who holds his tongue is wise"* (Prov. 10:19 NIV). Another version of the same Scripture verse reads, *"When there are many words, transgression is unavoidable, But he who restrains his lips is wise"* (NAS). In other words, if you say too much, you are bound to say something wrong. There is no alternative.

We are also warned in the Bible not to use too many words toward God Himself. This is a warning that most of us really need to hear. This admonition is found in Ecclesiastes 5:1–2:

> *Guard your steps when you go to the house of God. Go near to listen rather than to offer the sacrifice of fools, who do not know that they do wrong. Do not be quick with your mouth, do not be hasty in your heart to utter anything before*

God. God is in heaven and you are on earth, so let your
words be few.   *(Eccl. 5:1–2 NIV)*

Somebody said to me once, "Remember, it's just as much a
sin to sing a lie as it is to tell a lie." I have heard people sing
hymns of total consecration and surrender to God, such as, "All
to Jesus, I surrender." Then, when the offering plate comes
around, they drop in a quarter. The two actions are not consistent. If you are not going to give your life to God, do not tell
Him that you are surrendering all, because God is going to hold
you to account for the words you speak (or sing) in His presence.

A little further on in the same chapter, the Scripture indicates that an angel records what we say when we are speaking,
praying, or worshipping. One day, we are going to be confronted
by that angel and the record of what we have said. Then, the
Bible says, it will be too late to say "I didn't really mean it," because we will be held accountable for all we have said, sung, or
prayed. One day, those words are going to be held up before us,
and we are going to have to answer for them if we have been
insincere and have not really lived according to the things we
have said.

The next verse, Ecclesiastes 5:3, continues, *"As a dream*
comes when there are many cares, so the speech of a fool when
there are many words" (NIV). To use too many words is the mark
of a fool. The King James Version of Ecclesiastes 5:3 is even
more blunt: *"For a dream cometh through the multitude of busi-*
ness; and a fool's voice is known by multitude of words."

When you hear a person continually talking, you need no
other evidence: that person is a fool. *"A fool's voice is known by*
multitude of words." What is the root problem? I believe it is
restlessness. Compare that to what James said in James 3:8:
"No man can tame the tongue. It is a restless evil, full of deadly
poison" (NIV).

People who are always talking are restless people, and our
contemporary culture is filled with them. Have you ever been
with somebody who made your head swim by all the words that
came out of his or her mouth? What is the root problem? Restlessness. Excessive talking is a sure indication of someone whose
heart is not at rest.

DISEASE NUMBER TWO: *IDLE OR CARELESS WORDS*

In Matthew 12:36, Jesus said this:

But I tell you that men will have to give account on the day of judgment for every careless word they have spoken. (NIV)

One day, we are going to have to answer for every word we have spoken. We are going to have to answer for words that were idle, insincere, that we did not really mean, that we were not prepared to stand behind, or that were not worked out in our lives.

In the Sermon on the Mount, Jesus stated the following in Matthew 5:37:

Simply let your "Yes" be "Yes," and your "No," "No"; anything beyond this comes from the evil one.   (NIV)

That is an astonishing statement. If we say more than we mean, then the exaggeration (unnecessary emphasis or overdoing) in our speech comes from the Evil One.

Let me sum it up in just one simple word of advice: *If you don't mean it, don't say it.* If you will follow that one rule, I promise you, it will change your whole life. You will be a different person. If you will keep that rule for one year, I promise you that a year from now you will be a different and a much better person.

DISEASE NUMBER THREE: *GOSSIP*

Do not go about spreading slander among your people.
                            (Lev. 19:16 NIV)

Going about spreading slander—idle, untrue, exaggerated, malicious talk—is gossip. The very title of Satan in the New Testament, the word rendered *"devil,"* means "a slanderer" in Greek. That is its root meaning and the main description of Satan in the Bible. If you gossip or tell tales, you are actually doing the Devil's work for him. You are a representative of Satan. Not only must we be careful not to give out gossip, we have a responsibility not to receive gossip, also.

*The words of a gossip are like choice morsels; they go
down to a man's inmost parts.   (Prov. 18:8 NIV)*

How true that is of human nature. When we hear something about someone that is bad or shows them in a bad light,
something in the human heart rejoices. *"The words of a gossip
are like choice morsels."* Be careful that when one of those
choice morsels of gossip is placed in front of you, you do not
swallow it. They are poisoned. They taste sweet but they poison
us. And as we receive these morsels of gossip into our hearts,
our lives will become poisoned by them.

*A gossip betrays a confidence; so avoid a man who talks
too much.   (Prov. 20:19 NIV)*

See how closely these various diseases are related. If you
listen to a gossip, you become an accessory after the fact. If you
receive somebody who has stolen something and accept those
stolen goods from them, then in legal terms you become an accessory after the fact. So, if you entertain a gossip and listen to
their words, you become an accessory to the gossip. This is what
God says in Psalm 15:1–3:

*O LORD, who may abide in Thy tent? Who may dwell on
Thy holy hill? He who walks with integrity, and works
righteousness, and speaks truth in his heart. He does not
slander with his tongue, nor does evil to his neighbor, nor
takes up a reproach against his friend.   (NAS)*

There are various requirements for access to God's presence, in order to *"dwell on* [His] *holy hill."* We must walk with
integrity; we must work righteousness; we must speak the truth
in our hearts.

Then three things we must not do are listed. We must not
slander with our tongues, and we must not do evil to our neigh-
bors. Also, we must not take up a reproach, or receive a reproach, against our friends.

It is not enough that we do not slander; we must not receive
the slanderer. We must not take up a reproach against someone

whom we know. We must not eat those choice morsels of the gossip because they are poison, and many relationships are poisoned by eating them.

DISEASE NUMBER FOUR: *LYING*

We need to be careful that we use the right word to describe this disease of the tongue. Somebody has used the phrase, "evang–**e-l-a-s-t-i-c**–ally speaking." The evangelist sees two hundred people come forward in his crusade, and by the time the report is in his newsletter, it is five hundred. What is that— exaggeration or lying? It is really lying. I do not mention this to be critical of others. It is important that every one of us be very careful that we are not found guilty of lying.

In Proverbs 6:16–19, the writer tells of seven things that the Lord hates. *Hate* is a very strong word. This is what it says:

> *There are six things the LORD hates, seven that are detest-*
> *able to him: haughty eyes, a lying tongue, hands that shed*
> *innocent blood, a heart that devises wicked schemes, feet*
> *that are quick to rush into evil, a false witness who pours*
> *out lies and a man who stirs up dissension among broth-*
> *ers.*   (NIV)

Out of those seven specific things that the Lord hates, there are three that are related to the tongue: first, *"a lying tongue"*; second, *"a false witness"* (obviously that affects the tongue also); third, *"a man who stirs up dissension among brothers"* (and normally the way that dissension is stirred up is by words). So, out of seven things that the Lord hates, there are three that affect the tongue, and of those three, two are specifically connected with lying. This is stated again in Proverbs 12:22:

> *The LORD detests lying lips, but he delights in men who*
> *are truthful.*   (NIV)

In that verse, we have two sets of opposites. We have the word *detest* and the word *delight*. *"The LORD detests lying lips...he delights in men who are truthful."* There is nothing in between.

Then we have the other two opposites: *"lying"* and *"truthful."* Again, there is nothing in between. If it is not truthful, it is a lie. If it is a lie, the Lord detests it. If it is truthful, the Lord delights in it.

Our problem is that we have so many gray areas in our thinking. But I question whether those gray areas are found in Scripture. If traced to its source, every lie comes from the Devil. That is a frightening thought, but I will back it up with the words of Jesus Himself. Speaking to the religious leaders of His day (and bear in mind, they were very religious people), Jesus said,

> *You belong to your father, the devil, and you want to carry out your father's desire. He was a murderer from the beginning, not holding to the truth, for there is no truth in him. When he lies, he speaks his native language, for he is a liar and the father of lies.* (John 8:44 NIV)

Every time a lie passes through our lips, it comes from the Devil.

One more very important, frightening fact about the disease of lying is that unless the disease is arrested and healed, it is fatal.

> *But the cowardly, the unbelieving, the vile, the murderers, the sexually immoral, those who practice magic arts, the idolaters and all liars—their place will be in the fiery lake of burning sulfur. This is the second death.* (Rev. 21:8 NIV)

Notice the groups of people: *"the cowardly, the unbelieving, the vile, the murderers, the sexually immoral, those who practice magic arts, the idolaters and all liars."* The result of that disease is incurable. There is no way out: *"their place will be in the fiery lake of burning sulfur."* Once a person is consigned to that *"second death,"* it is ultimate. I repeat what I said: Unless this disease of lying is arrested and healed, it is sure to be fatal!

Revelation 22:15 speaks about the city of God:

> *Outside are the dogs, those who practice magic arts, the sexually immoral, the murderers, the idolaters and everyone who loves and practices falsehood* [or lies]. (NIV)

So, each of us must determine: Am I willing to be healed of this disease of lying, or am I prepared to lose my soul forever? Unless arrested and healed, the disease of lying is ultimately fatal.

DISEASE NUMBER FIVE: *FLATTERY*

Help, LORD, for the godly are no more; the faithful have vanished from among men. Everyone lies to his neighbor; their flattering lips speak with deception. May the LORD cut off all flattering lips and every boastful tongue.
(Ps. 12:1–3 NIV)

In this Scripture, David was speaking about a state of moral decline in the human race. I believe it is not unlike what we see around us today. Godly men are difficult to find. The faithful have vanished. What is the result? *"Everyone lies to his neighbor; their flattering lips speak with deception."* A judgment of God is pronounced by the Scripture upon these flattering lips: *"May the LORD cut off all flattering lips and every boastful tongue."*

In Proverbs 26:28, we are warned, *"A lying tongue hates those it hurts, and a flattering mouth works ruin"* (NIV). If we listen to and receive flattery, or if we become flatterers, the end is ruin. *"Whoever flatters his neighbor is spreading a net for his feet"* (Prov. 29:5 NIV).

After many years in the ministry, I have learned by practical experience that this is true. There are people who will speak flattering words, but they are not sincere. There is another motive behind it. And many times, if it had not been the grace of God, my feet would have been caught in that net of flattery. I would have been led into some commitment or some relationship that was outside the will of God. So bear that in mind: *"A flattering mouth works ruin,"* and *"Whoever flatters his neighbor is spreading a net for his feet."*

DISEASE NUMBER SIX: *HASTINESS OF SPEECH*

Do you see a man who is hasty in his words? There is more hope for a fool than for him. *(Prov. 29:20 NAS)*

This verse says if we are hasty in our words, our condition is worse than that of a fool. That is a solemn statement because the Bible has nothing good to say about the fool.

There is one example in Scripture of a man who was hasty in his words just once, and it tells of the price it cost him. The man was Moses. He was told by God to go ahead of the children of Israel, speak to a rock, and it would bring forth water. But he was so angry with the children of Israel that he said to them, *"You rebels, must we bring you water out of this rock?"* (Num. 20:10 NIV). Then, instead of speaking to the rock, he smote it. (See Numbers 20:7–12.) That act of disobedience, expressed in hasty words, cost him the privilege of leading the children of Israel into the Promised Land. This is described in Psalm 106:32–33:

> *They* [the children of Israel] *angered him* [Moses] *also at the waters of strife, so that it went ill with Moses for their sakes: because they provoked his spirit, so that he spake unadvisedly with his lips.*   *(KJV)*

Notice the diagnosis. A provoked spirit causes us to speak unadvisedly with our lips, and these hasty words cost us many privileges and blessings. If Moses had to pay that price for that one hasty statement, let us beware that we do not also say things hastily that will cost us dearly in the spiritual realm.

CHAPTER SIX

THE ROOT OF THE PROBLEM

G od has made a provision in Scripture for the healing of our tongues. The first step in acquiring this is to identify the root of the problem. The testimony of Scripture is clear and unequivocal: the root of every problem affecting our tongues is in our hearts.

In Matthew 12:33–35, Jesus said,

Make a tree good and its fruit will be good, or make a tree bad and its fruit will be bad, for a tree is recognized by its fruit. You brood of vipers, how can you who are evil say anything good? For out of the overflow of the heart the mouth speaks. The good man brings good things out of the good stored up in him, and the evil man brings evil things out of the evil stored up in him. (NIV)

The heart is the tree and the words are the fruit. The words that come out of the mouth indicate the condition of the heart. If the heart is good, the words will be good. If the heart is evil, the words will be evil. Our hearts are either good or evil all the way through. Whatever flows out of your mouth indicates the contents of your heart.

If you accidentally spill some water from a pail onto the kitchen floor and see that the water you spilled is dirty and greasy, you do not need to examine the water that is left in the bucket. You know it is dirty and greasy. The same applies to our hearts. If evil, impure, unbelieving, corrupt words come out of our mouths, then that indicates the same condition prevails in our hearts.

Compare the text from Matthew with James 3:9–12, where James spoke about the inconsistencies of religious people:

With the tongue we praise our Lord and Father, and with it we curse men, who have been made in God's likeness. Out of the same mouth come praise [or blessing] *and cursing. My brothers, this should not be. Can both fresh water and salt water flow from the same spring? My brothers, can a fig tree bear olives, or a grapevine bear figs? Neither can a salt spring produce fresh water.* (NIV)

James combined two pictures there. The one is of a spring of water; the other is of a tree. He said that an olive tree will never bear another kind of fruit, such as figs. The kind of tree indicates the kind of fruit. James was using the same picture as Jesus. The tree is the heart and the fruit is the words that come out of the mouth. He also used another picture, a spring of water. He says that if brackish, salty water comes out of a spring, you know the water in the spring is brackish and salty.

These two pictures are parallel but not identical. The two trees represent two natures. The corrupt tree is the old man or the old person. The good tree is the new man in Jesus Christ. The old man cannot bring forth good fruit. Jesus said that clearly many times. Out of that old, carnal nature will always come fruit that corresponds to that nature. The fountain, or the spring, represents something spiritual. A pure spring is the Holy Spirit. A corrupt, brackish, salty, impure spring is another spirit.

Therefore, we have two potential problems indicated by the mouth: first, the old, corrupt nature that has not been changed goes on producing corrupt fruit; and second, some kind of spirit, which is not the Holy Spirit, brings forth impure, brackish water. The essence of the teaching is the same in both: What is inside us, the condition of our hearts, determines what comes out of our mouths. So, the problem of the tongue takes us back inevitably to the problem of the heart.

We are confronted by the truth that Solomon spoke in Proverbs 4:23:

Above all else, guard your heart, for it is the wellspring of life. (NIV)

The word *"wellspring"* agrees with the picture that James used of a fountain or a spring that brings forth the kind of water that is characteristic of that spring. Another translation of Proverbs 4:23 says,

> *Watch over your heart with all diligence, for from it flow the springs of life.* (NAS)

Whatever flows out in your life or through your mouth originates in your heart. If the source is pure, what comes out will be pure. If the source is corrupt, what comes out will be corrupt.

With this, we can compare the words of Hebrews 12:15–16:

> *See to it that no one comes short of the grace of God; that no root of bitterness springing up causes trouble, and by it many be defiled; that there be no immoral or godless person like Esau, who sold his own birthright for a single meal.* (NAS)

Esau was entitled to the birthright, but he sold it and lost it. We can have a birthright or a promise from God, but if we do not conduct ourselves rightly, we will lose our birthright and our inheritance just like the ten spies who came with the negative report.

The reason why Esau acted like that is traced back to a root of bitterness in his heart. He was bitter against his brother Jacob. This root of bitterness in his heart brought forth bitter fruit in his life that corrupted his life and caused him to lose his birthright. (See Genesis 25:19–34.) Therefore, the root of the problem was in his heart.

Scripture warns us that if there is a root of bitterness in the heart of any one of us, others may be defiled by it. The corrupt, negative use of the tongue is infectious. The ten spies came back with a negative report. They corrupted the whole nation. The whole nation was infected with that negative disease. That is one reason why God treats it so seriously. It is an infectious disease.

There are other examples of evil roots in our hearts that express themselves through our tongues and cause problems that rob us of the blessings that God desires us to have. We can have roots of resentment, unbelief, impurity, or pride. Whatever the nature of the roots in our hearts, they will manifest themselves in the way we speak. We may want to be gracious and kind, but a root of resentment will poison our words with a kind of resentful spirit. We will try to say nice things, but they will not come out right. We may claim to be believers, but a root of unbelief will cause us to do as the ten spies and add our *"nevertheless"* to God's promises. The same is true of impurity and pride.

Let me remind you of the story about the doctor in the desert checking his dysentery patients. The first question was, "Good morning, how are you?" But he did not really care much about the answer to that question. The second request was, "Show me your tongue." How would you respond if God said to you, "Show me your tongue"?

CHAPTER SEVEN

FIRST STEPS TO HEALING

L et us look at three simple, practical, scriptural steps to dealing with the problem of your tongue. By following these three steps, you can be delivered from any diseases of your tongue.

STEP NUMBER 1: *CALL YOUR PROBLEM BY ITS RIGHT NAME: SIN*

It is important that we become honest. As long as we use some fancy, psychological terminology to cover, condone, excuse or pretend that our problems are not really there, nothing will happen. We must come to the moment of honesty. I have seen this many times in God's dealings, both with me and with many other people. When we come to the moment of truth, God moves in and helps us. As long as we try to excuse, cover up, or misrepresent our problems, God does nothing for us. Sometimes we say, "God, why don't you help me?" God replies (we may not hear Him, but God replies), "I'm waiting for you to be honest— honest with yourself and honest with Me."

That is the first and the most important step. Once you take that step, you are well on the way to the steps that follow. Call your problem by its right name: sin.

Religious people have many different ways of excusing or glossing over the misuse of their tongues. We think it does not matter much what we say, but God says it makes all the difference. In fact, you have seen that you settle your destiny by what you say. Jesus said, *"By your words you shall be justified, and by your words you shall be condemned"* (Matt. 12:37 NAS). It is a serious matter. Do not trifle with it. Come to the moment of truth and say, "I have a problem: it is sin." When you have come there, you are ready to take the second step.

STEP NUMBER 2: CONFESS YOUR SIN AND RECEIVE FORGIVENESS AND CLEANSING

First John 1:7–9 illustrates this clearly:

If we walk in the light as He Himself is in the light, we have fellowship with one another, and the blood of Jesus His Son cleanses us from all sin. If we say that we have no sin, we are deceiving ourselves, and the truth is not in us. If we confess our sins, He is faithful and righteous to forgive us our sins and to cleanse us from all unrighteousness. (NAS)

Again, we see the importance of being honest. The blood of Jesus does not cleanse in the dark. Only when we come to the light can we receive the cleansing of the blood of Jesus. If we are walking in the light, the blood of Jesus Christ continually cleanses us and keeps us pure from all sin. If we say that we have no sin, which I have pointed out to be the real problem, we are deceiving ourselves. The truth is not in us and we are not in the light. We are still in the dark where God's provision does not work.

Then we come to the alternative. If we confess our sins, come to the light, and acknowledge the real nature and the seriousness of our problems, then God *"is faithful and righteous to forgive us our sins and to cleanse us from all unrighteousness."* Two words are used, *"faithful"* and *"righteous."* God is faithful because He has promised, and He will keep His promise. God is righteous, and Jesus has already paid the penalty for our sins; therefore, He can forgive us without compromising His justice.

If we confess our sins, the guarantee of Scripture is that God, in faithfulness and in justice, will forgive us our sins and cleanse us from all unrighteousness. God not only forgives but, even more important, He cleanses. Once our hearts are cleansed, because the heart is the wellspring of life, we do not go on committing the same sins.

If you believe that your sins are forgiven but you find experientially that you have not been cleansed, I would like to question whether you have really been forgiven. The same God who forgives, also cleanses. The same Scripture that promises forgiveness also promises cleansing. God never stops halfway. If we meet the conditions, we get the whole packet. If we do not meet the conditions, we do not get half, we get nothing. *"If we confess our sins, [God] is faithful and righteous to forgive us our sins and to cleanse us from all unrighteousness."* Once our hearts are cleansed, then the problem will not be there. Remember, the condition of the heart determines what comes out of the mouth. A clean heart cannot produce unclean utterances. Unclean utterances indicate an unclean heart.

First, if we come to the light, confess, and turn to God with the problem, then God is faithful and righteous to forgive. The record of the past is blotted out, and all those things you wish you had never said are blotted out. Second, God cleanses your heart. Then, out of a clean, pure heart, what comes through your lips will be clean and pure. If your heart glorifies God, then your lips will glorify God. God solves the problem of the tongue and of the lips by dealing with the condition of the heart.

STEP NUMBER 3: *REFUSE SIN; YIELD TO GOD*

There is a negative and a positive that go together like the two opposite sides of the same coin. You must exercise your will both ways. You must say no to sin and yes to God. You must do both. You cannot say no to sin without saying yes to God, because you will be in a vacuum that will be filled again with the same problem. You cannot escape from sin without yielding to God.

In Romans 6:12–14, Paul said,

Therefore do not let sin reign in your mortal body that you should obey its lusts, and do not go on presenting the members of your body to sin as instruments of unrighteousness; but present yourselves to God as those alive from the dead, and your members [or the parts of your body] *as instruments of righteousness to God. For sin shall not be master over you, for you are not under law, but under grace.* (NAS)

When sin challenges you, say, "No, I will not yield to you; I will not yield the parts of my body. Above all, I will not yield that member that causes most of the trouble: my tongue. Sin, you cannot control my tongue any longer."

Then turn to God and say, "God, I yield my tongue to You, and I ask You to control the member that I cannot control."

Let us look at what James said:

For every species of beasts and birds, of reptiles and creatures of the sea, is tamed, and has been tamed by the human race. But no one can tame the tongue; it is a restless evil and full of deadly poison. (James 3:7–8 NAS)

You must accept the fact that you cannot tame or control your own tongue. Only one power can control your tongue for good: the power of God through the Holy Spirit. When you have been forgiven and cleansed and then are challenged again to use your tongue sinfully, you must say to sin, "You cannot have my tongue; I refuse it to you." Then you must say to the Holy Spirit, "Holy Spirit, I yield my tongue to you. I cannot control my tongue. I ask you to control my tongue for me."

Let us just briefly review those three steps. First, call your problem by its right name—call it sin. Second, confess your sin, and receive forgiveness and cleansing. Third, refuse to yield to sin; determine to yield to God. That is the climax of the process of deliverance and of healing. It is yielding to God the Holy Spirit that member that you can never control.

CHAPTER EIGHT

THE REASON YOU HAVE A TONGUE

We have already seen that the root of every problem affecting our tongues is in our hearts. Obviously, this means that in order to deal with problems affecting our tongues, we must first deal with the root problems in our hearts.

We considered the three steps we must take to deal with these root problems in our hearts that are manifested through our tongues. First, call your problem by its right name, which is sin. Come to the moment of truth. God will only deal with you on the basis of truth. God is the God of Truth. The Holy Spirit is the Spirit of Truth.

Second, confess and receive forgiveness and cleansing on the basis of the promise in 1 John 1:9:

If we confess our sins, [God] is faithful and righteous to forgive us our sins and to cleanse us from all unrighteousness. (NAS)

God not only forgives the past, He cleanses the heart so that the problem itself is dealt with at the root. Then there is a change in the fruit that comes out of the heart.

Third, refuse sin, and yield to God. Say no to sin and yes to God. Refuse sin, and yield to the Holy Spirit. The only power in the universe that can control your tongue effectively for good is the Holy Spirit.

Let us deal more fully with the positive aspect of this third step: yielding our tongues to God.

First, we need to understand the real reason why the Creator gave each of us a mouth with a tongue in it. There is an answer to this in Scripture but it is one of those interesting examples of truth in Scripture that can only be found by comparing two passages of Scripture and setting them side by side. As we do this, there comes a revelation that is not given to us solely in one of the two passages.

In this case, the two passages that I have in mind are taken from the Old and New Testaments. In the New Testament, the Old Testament passage is quoted in a way that brings out a meaning that is not apparent in the Old Testament. The Old Testament passage is Psalm 16:8–9:

I have set the LORD continually before me; because He is at my right hand, I will not be shaken. Therefore my heart is glad, and my glory rejoices; my flesh also will dwell securely. (NAS)

Please focus on the phrase, *"my glory rejoices."* On the Day of Pentecost, when the Spirit of God fell and the crowd gathered to know the reason, Peter preached his famous sermon. He referred to everything that happened in the life, the death, and the resurrection of Jesus. He quoted various passages from the Old Testament to prove that Jesus was indeed the Messiah and the Son of God. One of the passages he quoted was the one in Psalm 16:8–9. The quotation is found in Acts 2:25–26, where Peter said this:

For David says of Him, "I WAS ALWAYS BEHOLDING THE LORD IN MY PRESENCE; FOR HE IS AT MY RIGHT HAND, THAT I MAY NOT BE SHAKEN. THEREFORE MY HEART WAS GLAD AND MY TONGUE EXULTED; MOREOVER MY FLESH ALSO WILL ABIDE IN HOPE." (NAS)

Now, we put together these two key phrases: Psalm 16:9, *"my glory rejoices"*; and Acts 2:26, quoting the same passage, *"MY TONGUE EXULTED."* Where David said in the Psalm *"my glory,"* Peter, inspired and interpreted by the Holy Spirit, said *"MY TONGUE."* This tells us something very profound and important:

our tongues are our glory. You might ask why. The answer is because the Creator gave each of us a tongue for one supreme purpose—to glorify Him. The only reason for a tongue is that with it you and I may glorify God. That is why our tongues become our glory. It is the member by which, above all others, we may glorify the Creator. This leads to a consequence of great importance. Every use of our tongue that does not glorify God is a misuse because we were given our tongues to glorify God.

We can look at that well-known statement of Paul in Romans 3:23:

For all have sinned and fall short of the glory of God.

(NAS)

The essence of sin is not necessarily committing some terrible crime. The essence of sin is falling short of the glory of God or not living for God's glory. People might argue with that and say, "It's not true of me; I have never fallen short of the glory of God."

But I ask you to check the use of your tongue. Remember, the only reason you have a tongue is to glorify God. Every use of your tongue that does not glorify God is a misuse. I do not believe that there is one of us who could honestly say that we have always used our tongues for the glory of God. Therefore, we must acknowledge the truth of Paul's statement that we have all sinned and fallen short of the glory of God. If this is not true in any other area, then it is true in the area of our tongues.

Two different kinds of fire meet on the human tongue. First, there is a fire from hell that inflames the tongue of the natural, unregenerate, sinful man. James said,

The tongue also is a fire, a world of evil among the parts of the body. It corrupts the whole person, sets the whole course of his life on fire, and is itself set on fire by hell.

(James 3:6 NIV)

This fire in the human tongue comes from hell itself, and its fruit—its results and consequences—are hellish. But on the Day of Pentecost, when God brought into being the redeemed community that He wanted to use for His glory in the earth, another kind of fire came from another source. The fire of the Holy Spirit came from heaven, not from hell. It first operated in the tongues of those in the Upper Room. In other words, the fire of God from heaven drove out the natural tongue's fire of hell. The fire from hell was replaced by a fire that cleanses, purifies and glorifies God. Consider Acts 2:1–4:

> *When the day of Pentecost came, they were all together in one place. Suddenly a sound like the blowing of a violent wind came from heaven and filled the whole house where they were sitting. They saw what seemed to be tongues of fire that separated and came to rest on each of them* [Note that there was a tongue of fire for each one]. *All of them were filled with the Holy Spirit and began to speak in other tongues as the Spirit enabled them.*　　　(NIV)

Notice the Spirit operated first in their tongues. The fire of God from heaven gave them a new way to use their tongues. Then the Scripture makes it plain that everything they said after that, through the Holy Spirit, glorified God. They were using their tongues for the purpose God had given them tongues.

The key to this problem is yielding our tongues to the Holy Spirit. This is clearly stated by Paul in Ephesians 5:17–18:

> *Therefore do not be foolish, but understand what the Lord's will is.* [The next verse tells us the Lord's will:] *Do not get drunk on wine, which leads to debauchery. Instead, be filled with the Spirit.*　　　(NIV)

We need to put those two things together. It is sinful to get drunk on wine, but it is also sinful not to be filled with the Holy Spirit. The positive commandment is just as valid as the negative. Do not be drunk with wine, but be filled with the Holy Spirit. In a sense, it is two different kinds of drunkenness, if you can accept that, because on the Day of Pentecost, when the men and women were first filled with the Holy Spirit, the mockers said, "They're drunk." In a certain sense, they were inebriated, but with a totally different kind of inebriation. They were not drunk with wine, but they were filled with the Holy Spirit. Then Paul went on,

> *Speak to one another with psalms, hymns and spiritual songs. Sing and make music in your heart to the Lord, always giving thanks to God the Father for everything, in the name of our Lord Jesus Christ.*   *(vv. 19–20 NIV)*

Notice the word *"speak,"* which comes after the injunction, *"Be filled with the Spirit."* There are fifteen places in the New Testament where it speaks about people either being filled with or full of the Holy Spirit. And in every place, the initial manifestation came through the mouth. *"Out of the abundance of the heart the mouth speaks"* (Matt. 12:34 NKJV).

When you are filled with the Holy Spirit, the first manifestation will come out of your mouth, through your tongue. Instead of murmuring, complaining, criticizing, and giving vent to unbelief, Paul said that you will speak, sing, make music, and give thanks. The whole use of your tongue will be positive, not negative.

The solution to every problem of sin in our lives must be a positive one. It is not enough to give up sinning; we must have righteousness. It is not enough to deny your tongue to the Devil; you must yield your tongue to the Holy Spirit. Be filled with the Holy Spirit and speak: that is the remedy.

CHAPTER NINE

THE IMPORTANCE OF YOUR CONFESSION

We need to see how the right use of the tongue links us in a very special way to Jesus Christ as our High Priest. The high priesthood of Jesus is an eternal ministry that goes on continually in heaven. After He had dealt with our sins, died, risen again, and ascended into heaven, He entered into a ministry as our High Priest forever, always representing us in God's presence. He is our High Priest on the condition that we make the right confession with our tongues.

This is what the writer of Hebrews said:

> *Therefore, holy brethren, partakers of a heavenly calling, consider Jesus, the Apostle and High Priest of our confession.* (Heb. 3:1 NAS)

Note that last phrase. Jesus is the *"High Priest of our confession."* It is our confession that links us to Jesus as High Priest. If we merely believe but make no confession, then His high priesthood cannot operate on our behalf. It is on the basis of our spoken confession, not of our unspoken faith, that Jesus operates in heaven as our High Priest.

It is tremendously important that we make and maintain the right confession. The word *"confession"* means, literally, "to say the same thing as." In this usage, confession is saying the same thing with our mouths as God says in the Scripture. It is making the words of our mouths agree with the Word of God in the Scripture.

When we make the words of our mouths agree in faith with what God has said in the Bible, that enables Jesus to exercise His high priestly ministry as our representative in the presence of God. If we make the wrong confession, we frustrate His ministry. It depends on our making the right confession. It is our confession that links us to Jesus as our High Priest. This is brought out twice more in Hebrews. The first reference is in Hebrews 4:14:

> *Since then we have a great high priest who has passed through the heavens, Jesus the Son of God, let us hold fast our confession.* (NAS)

It is our confession that continues to link us to Jesus as our High Priest. And again, we read in Hebrews,

> *And since we have a great* [High] *priest over the house of God...let us hold fast the confession of our hope without wavering, for He who promised is faithful.*
> (Heb. 10:21, 23 NAS)

Every time the Bible speaks about Jesus as our High Priest, it says we must make, maintain, and hold fast the confession of our faith and our hope. It is our confession that links us to Jesus as our High Priest. If we do not maintain that confession, we frustrate His ministry on our behalf. Right confession is actually essential for salvation.

> *The word is nigh thee, even in thy mouth, and in thy heart: that is, the word of faith, which we preach; that if thou shalt confess with thy mouth the Lord Jesus, and shalt believe in thine heart that God hath raised him from the dead, thou shalt be saved. For with the heart man believeth unto righteousness; and with the mouth confession is made unto salvation.* (Rom. 10:8–10 KJV)

Again, as we have seen all the way through, there is a direct link between the heart and the mouth. Jesus said, *"Out of the overflow of the heart the mouth speaks"* (Matt. 12:34 NIV). Salvation depends on two things: exercising faith in our hearts and making the right confession with our mouths.

In the Bible, *salvation* is the great all-inclusive word for all the blessings and provisions of God that have been obtained for us through the death of Jesus Christ. It includes spiritual, physical, financial, temporal, and eternal blessings. All those blessings purchased by the death of Jesus are summed up in the word *salvation*.

To enter into the fullness of God's salvation in every area of our lives, we have to make the right confession. In every area, whatever it may be, we must say the same with our mouths as God says in His Word. When our confession agrees with the Word of God, we are moving into the full provision of God in salvation, and we have the ministry of Jesus as our High Priest operative on our behalf in heaven. With Him standing behind us on the basis of our confession, there is nothing that can hinder us or keep us from moving on into the fullness of our salvation. Our confession links us to Jesus as our High Priest. That is why what we say with our mouths determines our experience.

Let us return briefly to the illustration of the tongue as the rudder of the human life.

> *Or take ships as an example. Although they are so large and are driven by strong winds, they are steered by a very small rudder wherever the pilot wants to go. Likewise the tongue is a small part of the body.*   *(James 3:4–5 NIV)*

What the rudder is to the ship, the tongue is to the body or to the life. The right use of the rudder directs the ship properly. The wrong use brings shipwreck. The same is true with the tongue. The right use of the tongue brings success and salvation in its fullness. The wrong use brings shipwreck and failure.

The ship is steered with a very small rudder wherever the pilot wants to go. A great ocean liner may have a captain with many years of experience, but when he comes into a harbor, he is not permitted to berth that ship himself. It is an almost unvarying rule that the captain must take a pilot on board and allow the pilot to assume responsibility for the use of the rudder and the berthing of the ship.

You and I may feel we are capable of handling our lives, but there are situations in which we cannot manage. We must take a pilot on board and let him assume responsibility. Can you guess who the pilot is? Of course! The pilot is the Holy Spirit. Only the Holy Spirit can enable us always to use our tongues rightly and to make the right confession.

The Holy Spirit is the Spirit of Truth and the Spirit of Faith. When He motivates and controls our words and speech, they become positive. Our speech then honors God and brings the blessings of God into our lives. Every one of us needs the Holy Spirit to pilot our lives by controlling our tongues. He is the ultimate solution to the problem of the human tongue.

God permits us to come to a place of failure. He says, "None of you can control your own tongues." And then He says, "But I have a Pilot. Will you invite the Pilot on board?" All you need to do is simply respond with a prayer such as this:

> Holy Spirit, I really cannot control my tongue aright. Come in and take control. I yield to You. Give me a tongue that glorifies God. Amen.

How to Fast Successfully

CONTENTS

CHAPTER ONE

WHAT IS FASTING?

The theme of this study is "How to Fast Successfully." This subject does not readily lend itself to a sermon, but rather to some practical teaching on various aspects of fasting. Many people ask: "How do I fast? How long do I fast? How often should I fast? How should I break my fast?" The purpose of this study is to answer these questions and to clear up some misconceptions about fasting.

I think it is good to begin with a definition of fasting. The definition I have used several times is: Fasting is abstaining from food for spiritual purposes. Normally, fasting is not abstaining from fluids, but only from solid food. Although there were occasions in the Bible when people did fast without food or without water for as long as forty days, for this study we will consider fasting as abstaining from food for spiritual purposes.

Many of the people who have asked, "How do I fast?" have been Christians and members of churches for many years. Yet, apparently no one has ever taught them about fasting, even though the Bible has much to say about the subject. Since most of these people know something about prayer, it may be good to begin by pointing out a parallel between fasting and praying.

In the Sermon on the Mount in Matthew 6, when Jesus spoke first about praying and then about fasting, He used similar language in talking about both topics. The main difference is that when He talked about praying, He included a pattern prayer that we call the Lord's Prayer. But I think there is a basic parallel between fasting and praying, and I'll point out two aspects of it.

We all know we can pray as individuals, and most of us are also familiar with praying in groups. Group praying we usually refer to as a prayer meeting. Individual praying is what we do when we're by ourselves. I believe there is the same distinction in fasting: there is group fasting, where people fast together; and there is individual fasting, where a person fasts on his own.

We are also familiar with two kinds of prayer: regular prayer at a set time each day, and special times of prayer when the Holy Spirit leads us to take extra time beyond our usual pattern of prayer for a special need. The same, I believe, is true of fasting. I think fasting should be a regular practice in the life of every disciplined Christian. But beyond those regular times of fasting, there are times when the Holy Spirit leads us to give additional emphasis to fasting.

So we see that there is a parallel between praying and fasting. Just as there is individual prayer and collective prayer, so there is also individual fasting and collective fasting. Just as there are normal patterns of prayer and there are times of special prayer, so there should be normal patterns of fasting in the life of every Christian and there should be special times of fasting as the Holy Spirit leads.

CHAPTER TWO

SHOULD ALL CHRISTIANS FAST?

If we go to the Bible and to the history of Israel and the early church, we find that fasting was a regular part of the life of God's people. Under the old covenant, Israel was required by God to fast collectively at least once a year on the Day of Atonement and on other occasions. There are also records of individuals who fasted: Moses fasted, David fasted, Elijah fasted, and many of the kings of Israel led their people in fasting.

In the book of Acts, we have records of the early church fasting together in groups for special needs. Particularly when they were sending forth apostles, but also when they were appointing elders in local churches, the early church would collectively fast and pray for God's guidance. Reliable church tradition and recorded history also tell us that for several centuries the early church practiced fasting regularly on Wednesday and Friday of each week. These were the two days normally recognized for fasting.

The early Methodists under John and Charles Wesley regularly practiced fasting. It was a normal part of their procedure; however, I find that today many Methodists have never heard of it. In fact, John Wesley would not ordain a man to the Methodist ministry unless he would commit himself to fast every Wednesday and Friday until 4:00 P.M. In other words, Wesley regarded it as an absolutely normal part of any Christian minister's life and discipline. Personally, I believe that the restoration of this practice would change the lives and the influence of many ministries and ministers.

CHAPTER THREE

HOW SHOULD I PREPARE FOR A FAST?

The first thing that I would like to say about preparation concerns the mental attitude with which we go into a fast. This has a great deal to do with whether the fast is successful or not. I believe we should approach fasting with an attitude of positive faith: it is God's will for me to fast, and God will bless me when I do fast in accordance with His will. I believe it is God's will because Scripture reveals that it is. We do not need some special feeling or revelation about the fact that fasting is the will of God, because the Bible clearly indicates that it is. We do not need some special revelation that it is God's will for us to pray because it is plainly taught in the Bible. People who wait for a special revelation for something that is definitely stated in the Bible seldom get that special revelation and therefore miss the purpose of God.

Furthermore, I believe that God will reward us in fasting if we seek Him with right motives and in a scriptural way. The Bible clearly promises this. Jesus said,

> *But thou, when thou fastest, anoint thine head, and wash thy face; that thou appear not unto men to fast, but unto thy Father which is in secret: and thy Father, which seeth in secret, shall reward thee openly.* (Matt. 6:17–18 KJV)

That is a very clear promise. If you fast in the right way with the right motives, God will reward you openly. So if you fail to fast, bear in mind that you are depriving yourself of the reward, because God cannot give you the reward if you don't meet His conditions.

The writer of Hebrews set down a basic principle for approaching God and seeking anything from Him. Hebrews 11:6 states, *"But without faith it is impossible to please him: for he that cometh to God must believe that he is, and that he is a rewarder of them that diligently seek him"* (KJV). When we approach God, the Bible says we must approach Him on the basis of faith. There is no other basis on which to approach Him. Further, if we come to God on that basis, we must believe two specific things: first of all, that God is (that He exists), and second, that He is a rewarder of those who diligently seek Him. If you diligently seek God, He will reward you—that is guaranteed! He may not always reward you exactly the way you might have expected to be rewarded, but those who diligently seek God will never fail to receive a reward.

In Isaiah 58, we also have a series of promises to those who fast according to the will of God. I think it is worthwhile just looking at some of these statements. The Lord promised that all of these results will follow if fasting is done in a way pleasing to Him:

> *Then your light will break forth like the dawn, and your healing will quickly appear; then your righteousness will go before you, and the glory of the LORD will be your rear guard. Then you will call, and the LORD will answer; you will cry for help, and he will say: Here am I....The LORD will guide you always; he will satisfy your needs in a sunscorched land and will strengthen your frame. You will be like a well-watered garden, like a spring whose waters never fail. Your people will rebuild the ancient ruins and will raise up the age-old foundations; you will be called Repairer of Broken Walls, Restorer of Streets with Dwellings.* (Isa. 58:8–9, 11–12 NIV)

I have made a list of ten specific promises for those who fast according to the will of God:

- light
- health

- righteousness
- glory
- answered prayer
- continual guidance
- satisfaction
- refreshing
- work that endures
- restoration

To me, any Christian who does not desire those benefits is very foolish. They are specifically promised to those who fast in accordance with the will of God. When we begin to fast with a positive attitude of faith that we are doing what the Scripture teaches, that we are obeying the revealed will of God, and that God Himself will reward us, then we can expect the specific rewards that are listed in Isaiah 58.

We also need to have the right attitude toward our own bodies. Many Christians have a wrong attitude towards the body. They have the impression that the body is a necessary evil they have to live with and that it will be a good thing when they're out of it. In the meantime, they don't want to give too much thought or attention to the body, because they erroneously believe they are being unspiritual if they do. I don't find the Bible teaches that attitude towards the body. I'd like you to read just two verses in 1 Corinthians:

> *What? know ye not that your body is the temple of the Holy Ghost which is in you, which ye have of God, and ye are not your own? For ye are bought with a price: therefore glorify God in your body, and in your spirit, which are God's.* *(1 Cor. 6:19–20 KJV)*

The Bible teaches that the physical body is the temple of the Holy Spirit and that when Jesus died on the cross and shed His blood, He redeemed not only our spirits and our souls, but also our bodies. He bought the whole of us with the price of His shed blood. We belong to Him entirely—spirit, soul, and body.

God has a very real interest in and a very specific purpose for our bodies. The body is to be the temple of the Holy Spirit. It

304

is to be the place where the Holy Spirit dwells. The Bible tells us that God does not dwell in temples made by hands (Acts 7:48). We can build Him any church, any synagogue, any tabernacle we like, but God will not dwell there. God has chosen to dwell in the physical bodies of those who believe in Him. Thus, the believer's body has a very important function as a residence of the Holy Spirit.

I believe that it is pleasing to God that I keep that residence of the Holy Spirit in the best possible condition. It should be healthy and strong and able to do the things God wants done.

Furthermore, Paul told us about our physical members in Romans 6:13: *"Neither yield ye your members as instruments of unrighteousness unto sin: but yield yourselves unto God, as those that are alive from the dead, and your members as instruments of righteousness unto God"* (KJV). So the various members of my physical body are intended to be instruments (or an alternative reading is "weapons") that God can use. They do not belong to me; they belong to God. I am to yield them to God.

Now I think it is logical and obvious that God wants His weapons in good condition. He doesn't want them feeble and broken down. He wants our bodies to be healthy. He wants our members to be strong, effective, and active because they are the members of Christ and they are the instruments God uses for His purposes in the earth. In a certain sense, Christ has no body in the earth except ours. Our bodies are the instruments that He uses for His will in the earth, and I have become convinced that God expects us to keep our bodies strong and as healthy as we can.

I am convinced that fasting is a very practical way to make and keep our bodies healthy. I believe that many physical as well as other problems would be solved if Christians would learn to fast in a practical and healthy way. Part of what I'm going to teach is intended to help you fast with the maximum benefits for your body.

When I look at the way Christians in America treat their bodies, especially the kinds of things they feed them, I ask myself, "What shape would their cars be in if they treated them with as little understanding and as little respect as they treat their bodies?" I've come to the conclusion that most people's cars would not be running! Our bodies are much more forgiving and long-suffering than our cars.

Personally, I think it is simply common sense to treat your body with at least as much concern and intelligent care as you would treat your car. In fact, it should be more because $20,000 will buy a new car, but $20,000 will not begin to buy a new body. It can't even buy one eye. There is no monetary price to be set on a healthy body. One basic problem with Christians today is that they simply don't appreciate the importance of a healthy body.

In regard to physical aspects of fasting, some people should exercise caution. If you have certain types of physical problems such as diabetes or tuberculosis, or if you are on some kind of regular medication, you should consult your physician for advice about whether you should fast. There are some people who cannot practice fasting. For example, those who are diabetics have to maintain their blood chemistry at certain levels. In such cases, I believe that it is the responsibility of other Christians to fast for those who cannot.

CHAPTER FOUR

WHAT IS THE PURPOSE OF FASTING?

L et's talk about choosing objectives in fasting. Somebody said once, "If you aim at nothing, you can be pretty sure you'll hit it." We need to have an aim or an objective when we go into something like fasting.

We can find many good, scriptural reasons for fasting. I'll give you some, relating them to myself. First, one biblical purpose for fasting is to humble myself. David said, *"I humbled my soul with fasting"* (Ps. 35:13 NAS). We need to bear in mind that humility is not an emotion, not something vague, but rather it is specific. God will not humble us because He has told us to humble ourselves. I have proved by experience that if I fast with the right motives and in faith, I can humble myself.

When I humble myself, God exalts me. That principle runs throughout the Bible. *"Whosoever shall exalt himself shall be abased; and he that shall humble himself shall be exalted"* (Matt. 23:12 KJV). We have to make the choice. Do I want to be abased? Then I can exalt myself. Do I want to be exalted? Then I need to humble myself. I believe that the basic way for a believer to humble himself is by fasting.

Another motive for fasting is to come closer to God. The Scripture says that if you *"draw near to God...He will draw near to you"* (James 4:8 NAS).

A third reason for fasting is to understand God's Word more clearly. I have learned by experience over the years that when I'm seeking God in times of fasting, He gives me further, deeper understanding of His Word.

Another very important reason for fasting is to find God's will and to receive direction in your life. Ezra said, *"I proclaimed a fast there, at the river of Ahava, that we might afflict ourselves before our God, to seek of him a right way for us, and for our little ones, and for all our substance"* (Ezra 8:21 KJV). Again, it has been my experience and my testimony that when I humble myself in fasting and seek Him for direction and guidance, He does lead me in the right way. I've proved this in many situations where we have had to move from country to country and when we have had to make decisions between going to one field or another to work, to one type of ministry or another. I've found that if we take time to fast and pray, in humility, seeking God's direction, we receive what we pray for.

Another very common reason for fasting is to seek healing. Isaiah 58:8 says, *"Thine health shall spring forth speedily"* (KJV). This also applies to deliverance from evil spirits. Jesus said in one place about a certain type of evil spirit, *"This kind goeth not out but by prayer and fasting"* (Matt. 17:21 KJV). Before Jesus Himself entered into His ministry of healing and deliverance, He spent forty days fasting.

We also can fast when we need God's intervention in some particular crisis, or when some tremendous problem has arisen that we can't handle by ordinary means. There are many examples of this in the Bible. In 2 Chronicles 20, Jehoshaphat and the people of Judah found that they were facing an invading army that they could not meet with normal military methods. They humbled themselves before God, gathered together, fasted, and prayed. God dealt with the invading army. They didn't have to use a single weapon. God totally defeated their enemies for them, and I don't believe God has any favorites. I believe He's just as willing to intervene on our behalf when we seek Him in the same way.

A final reason for fasting is to intercede and pray on behalf of others. Many, many people come to me about their unsaved relatives and they ask, "What can I do to get my relatives saved?" I often ask them, "Have you ever fasted and prayed for your unsaved husband or for your unsaved son or daughter? Are you willing to make a personal sacrifice—do something that will cost you—on behalf of your loved one?" There are many testimonies from believers of how God has answered the prayer that is accompanied by fasting on behalf of unsaved relatives.

If you're going to have a special period of fasting—more than a day or so—or you have some special purpose for fasting, sometimes it is good to make a written list of what you are fasting about and date it. I'm glad that many years ago in the early 1950s I did that on several occasions. I still have the lists. In looking back over them, I see with amazement how many of the things that I fasted for God answered—and some of them were great things. To give you one example, I fasted and prayed for the salvation of my mother. Although it took many years, God saved her very definitely and very dramatically almost at the last moment. At about the last time I could be reassured she really understood the Gospel, she had a tremendous experience of salvation, so it pays to pray and to fast. When I look back on those lists now, I praise God for the marvelous answers to prayer. A prayer list might be a good idea in your ordinary prayer life. That's not to say that everybody needs to do it, but if you do, one day you'll praise God for the way He's answered your prayers.

CHAPTER FIVE

HOW LONG SHOULD I FAST?

Now we come to the question of choosing a length of time to fast. My advice is: Don't begin with a very long fast. Don't begin with a week, two weeks, or forty days. Some people do, and they achieve it, but I find it's better to start climbing the ladder from the bottom, rung by rung. The problem is, if you start with too long a period and don't achieve it, then you feel defeated. You may give up and never try again. I would suggest that normally it is better to begin at the bottom of the ladder and climb toward the top.

If you are not familiar with fasting, and you don't really feel equal to a big test, begin by omitting the last meal of the day. If you normally would eat your last meal about 6:00 or 6:30 P.M. and don't have any snacks afterwards until breakfast the next morning, you've actually fasted from lunch time to breakfast time, which is about eighteen hours. That's quite a substantial period to be without food by only missing one meal. That way you achieve a real fast without too drastic a change in your life pattern or too great an objective. If you succeed in that, the next time you may want to skip the last two meals: the noon meal and the evening meal. If you don't eat until breakfast then you have actually been twenty-four hours without food. Then when you begin to feel like a real soldier, you can omit all three meals one day, and you will have fasted from supper the previous night until breakfast the next day—about thirty-six hours.

Once you have achieved that and know you can do it, then I think it's time to seek the Lord as to whether He wants you to go on a longer fast. Again I would advise you not to take too big a step the first time. Take two or three days, or a week. If you spend a week fasting, that will probably have a substantial effect on the course of your life.

Looking back on my own career of ministry, I believe that if I had not practiced fasting many years ago, I would not be where I am today. I believe that fasting in many ways settled the course my life was to take. Again I come back to the Scripture I quoted once already, "[God] *is a rewarder of them that diligently seek him*" (Heb. 11:6 KJV). I say that not only on the basis of Scripture, but on the basis of personal experience!

Now, it's perfectly possible to fast for two or three weeks. In the Bible, quite a number of people fasted for forty days, and I know a good many people who are alive who have fasted for as long as forty days. But I do not believe that it is wise to make the length of time your main objective. It isn't really as important how long you fast as that you fast in the will of God, that your motives are right, and that you get the benefits that should be yours from fasting.

To sum up, I suggest that you begin on a small scale and gradually increase the length of your fasts.

CHAPTER SIX

WHAT HAPPENS DURING A FAST?

I have already spoken about your mental attitude, which is probably the most important thing in fasting. Now let's talk about what happens during a fast. This is an important section of our study, and there are a number of things I would like to suggest.

On a practical level, one important thing to do is to guard against constipation. If you know you are going to fast, make your last meal or two something that will prevent you from becoming constipated. Everyone has his own particular way of arranging for that, but some obvious things you can do are to eat more than the usual amount of fruit, salad, fruit juice, or maybe a type of bran cereal. That's something you can settle for yourself, but it is a detail that you ought to take into consideration.

During a fast, I very strongly recommend that you take extra time for Bible reading and for prayer. I put Bible reading first because, in my opinion, it is wise to make it a practice not to pray without first reading your Bible. When you read your Bible, it anoints your spirit, and it gets your mind in line with God's thoughts. Your prayer will normally be much more effective and focused after Bible reading.

If you are just fasting a couple of meals, you may feel that you do not have much time, but after all, you have the time you would normally have spent preparing and consuming two meals. Offer that time to the Lord. At least spend that time specifically in Bible reading and prayer.

Second, guard against spiritual attack. The real sacrifice in fasting is not going without food. Rather, it is the fact that when you really begin to seek God, pray, and fast for things that matter, Satan is going to turn extra spiritual forces loose against you. You may find that strange oppressions begin to come over you—doubt, fear, or loneliness. You may somehow feel yourself in a dark place, or you may lose some of the usual feelings of joy, peace, and happiness that you normally have as a Christian. Don't get worried if that happens. In fact, it's a kind of backhanded compliment from the Devil. It means that you are worrying him, and he's out to prevent you from achieving your objectives. Don't yield to these emotions. Don't let feelings dictate to you. Bear in mind the great basic truths of the Word of God: God is on your side; God loves you and is a rewarder of those who diligently seek Him (Heb. 11:6). This is true whether you feel it or not. Don't let feelings turn you away.

Another caution I would give is to avoid religious ostentation. I think we should look at Matthew 6:16: *"Moreover when ye fast, be not, as the hypocrites, of a sad countenance: for they disfigure their faces, that they may appear unto men to fast. Verily I say unto you, they have their reward"* (KJV). Don't put on a religious act. Don't let everybody know that you are fasting. Some people will have to know, but don't make a show of it. Don't make a display of it. Do it as quietly and as unostentatiously as possible.

Generally speaking, you will be able to carry on your normal daily duties and activities. My wife once went on a prolonged fast—over four weeks—when we lived in London, and during all that time she prepared all the meals for the family and always sat with us at the table, although she did not eat. Neither did she give up any of her other normal domestic activities. About the same time, I fasted for more than three weeks and still carried on my normal activities during that period. We used to hold five indoor meetings and three open-air meetings in our church every week at that time. I conducted and preached in every one of them. Normally speaking, with a few exceptions, fasting does not prevent you from doing the things you would ordinarily be doing. In fact, after a while you may be able to do them much better when you're fasting than when you're eating.

I would caution you not to make a show of your fasting. Just carry on your normal activities as much as possible.

313

CHAPTER SEVEN

WHAT ABOUT UNPLEASANT PHYSICAL REACTIONS?

Now we come to the question that always occupies people's minds—unpleasant physical reactions from fasting. Because of current lifestyles, most people will experience some type of physical reaction in the early stages of a fast. Some common ones are headaches—and they can be very severe—dizziness, and nausea. I'm no medical expert, but people who study reactions from a medical point of view say that, in most cases, what is happening is that the blood in your body that is normally taken up in the process of digestion is now liberated from that and begins to work in other areas to clear them up. For instance, if you are a heavy coffee drinker, you will normally get quite a severe headache when you fast. That is the coffee drinker's penalty for all the coffee he drinks. I'm not saying, don't drink coffee. I'm just saying there will probably be a reaction when you fast if you are a coffee drinker.

What most of us don't realize is that the process of digestion is very hard work. If you eat a heavy meal, much of your physical energy for the next hour or two is mainly taken up dealing with that meal. Consequently, the blood that is there cannot be used in other areas of your body. For instance, I think it is a matter of experience that if you go swimming too soon after a heavy meal, you may get cramps in your arms or legs. Why? Because all the blood is in the stomach being used for the digestive process. But by the time your food is digested, you can go swimming and you won't get cramps. In other words, the blood is liberated for other activities. If you're fasting for a day, you are liberating your blood to do a lot of cleanup jobs that badly need to be done, but that are never done when your blood has to spend its time digesting food.

In actual fact, to overeat is to reduce our physical energy. When you go beyond what you need in food, you are simply making your body do extra, unnecessary work digesting unneeded food. Then it isn't able to do the other things that need to be done. Personally, I have discovered by experience that I cannot preach my best after a heavy meal. I have to have at least an hour or two between a heavy meal and preaching because the blood isn't in my brain, it's in my stomach. My brain is fuzzy; it isn't equal to the job.

We said there may be various physical reactions from fasting in most people, especially in our modern way of life. If you can find the faith to do it, praise God for them. "Thank you, God, for my headache. I realize my blood is there doing something that needed to be done a long while ago!" Don't stop your fast. If you do, you have let the Devil defeat you.

Daniel said, *"I set my face unto the Lord God, to seek by prayer and supplications, with fasting"* (Dan. 9:3 KJV). When you fast, you need to set your face. You must make up your mind that you are going to do it. Don't leave open the possibility that you might have that meal after all because then the Devil will be at you all the time to eat. If you have made up your mind not to eat again today and dismiss that possibility from your mind, it's much easier.

At mealtime, you may feel real hunger pains. Actually, you really don't need food, but your stomach operates by habit. In about an hour, you will find the hunger pains will subside without your having eaten. It was just a habit. Your stomach was set like a clock to react that way at that time. If you want to fool your stomach, take a couple of glasses of water. When you fill your stomach up with water, it gets fooled. It thinks it has some food and stops protesting.

If these physical reactions become severe, you may have to give up everything else and lie down and rest. That is good for you, too. If you are in a position of employment where you can't do that, then you will have to choose another way or another day. If your reactions become so severe that you cannot endure them, then I would advise you to break the fast, take a little while to recover, and then try again. You may be quite surprised the next time. You'll hardly have any reaction.

Fasting uncovers both our spiritual and physical problems. When the problem is exposed, don't blame the problem on the fasting. Instead, thank God that the fasting has revealed the problem that was already there. If your problems are severe—whether emotional, spiritual, or physical—as a result of fasting, then I think you need to consult somebody with experience, either a pastor or physician.

CHAPTER EIGHT

HOW CAN I FAST WITH MAXIMUM PHYSICAL BENEFITS?

I f you want the maximum physical benefits from your fast, there are certain things that will help you. I will give you some very practical suggestions to help you benefit the most from your fast.

1. Get plenty of rest. In fact, take extra time to rest. You can pray just as well lying in your bed as you can on your knees.

2. Do some exercise, and try to get some fresh air. I find it very easy to pray when I'm walking; and when I'm walking, I'm getting fresh air and exercise—all three at once! It greatly increases both the spiritual and physical benefits of the fast. Usually in most people's experiences of fasting, the unpleasant reactions come to a climax in the second, third, or fourth day. If you get beyond that, then you come into a period where fasting really becomes exciting, exhilarating, and enjoyable. You may even find that your physical strength increases remarkably. My experience, not so much in the physical, but with mental activity, is that when I get to that stage in a fast, I can do in one hour work that would normally take me two or three hours. My mind is much clearer, although my body may still be protesting a little with the sense of weakness.

3. While you are fasting, it is normally wise to consume plenty of fluids, because that has the effect of flushing out your kidneys and generally cleaning out your body. What kind of

fluids? Well, I've come to believe that the best thing is pure water—and I don't mean the water that comes out of the tap, but the purified water that you can buy in the supermarket or from a firm that handles this product.

When you fast, you will invariably notice that your sense of taste becomes much keener, and you will perceive all sorts of horrid tastes in the drinking water that you hardly noticed when you were eating—particularly the taste of chlorine.

Although I strongly feel that it is wise to take just pure water, at the beginning of your fast, you may want to put some honey in the water. Take the water hot with a little lemon. Honey and lemon together are kind of purifying. If you don't feel that you want to stick to just water, there are various other fluids available such as broth, bouillon, or fruit juice.

Personally, again, I would advise people during fasting to avoid drinking tea or coffee since they both are very strong stimulants. You get more physical benefits from your fast if you do not consume these during your fast.

CHAPTER NINE

WHAT ARE THE DIFFERENT TYPES OF FASTS?

There are times when God does lead us to abstain from fluids, but this can be a dangerous area physically. The only examples I can find in the Bible of people fasting extensively without food or water are Moses and Elijah, who each fasted forty days. However, they were on a supernatural plane—in the immediate presence of God or under some supernatural power. I don't believe that is a normal pattern for us.

I believe the pattern for the length of time without fluids is found in Esther 4:16. Esther said to her uncle Mordecai, *"Go, gather together all the Jews that are present in Shushan, and fast ye for me, and neither eat nor drink three days, night or day"* (KJV). Three days, night and day, is seventy-two hours, and personally I would not advise anybody to go beyond seventy-two hours without fluids. If you try seventy-two hours without eating or drinking, I think you will find that you'll be on your knees at the end—if not spiritually, at least physically. However, I must say that I have twice been seventy-two hours without food or drink, and God blessed me in it. I would not recommend anybody to go beyond this length of time. To do so, I believe, is very dangerous physically. I think any doctor would confirm that.

I just need to mention another practical physical detail at this point. While you are fasting, your bowels may not move, but if you have avoided constipation to begin with, you don't need to worry about that. When you resume eating, your bowels will start functioning again. If you start eating in the right way, you will find that you have probably cleansed your bowels considerably and that they are in better condition than when you started fasting. If your bowels don't move during your fast, don't worry. Sometimes they will; sometimes they won't. Obviously, if you are fasting for a considerable period of time and they have already moved, there would be no further need for them to move, since no food has been digested.

There is also a biblical precedent for what I would call a partial fast. In other words, you eat something, but not much.

> *In those days I Daniel was mourning three full weeks* [that's twenty-one days]. *I ate no pleasant bread, neither came flesh* [that's meat] *nor wine in my mouth, neither did I anoint myself at all, till three whole weeks were fulfilled.* (Dan. 10:2–3 KJV)

That was not a complete fast, but it was what is called a partial fast. He didn't eat meat, and he didn't eat dessert—he just ate simple, basic food.

Daniel's fast was a kind of mourning. Fasting and mourning are very closely related in the Bible. There is a spiritual mourning that God has promised to bless: *"Blessed are those who mourn, for they shall be comforted"* (Matt. 5:4 NAS). There may be a time when you are led to a kind of partial fast, like Daniel.

A short time ago, I met a Catholic priest, a missionary in Japan, who had just come from a place here in the U.S. where a group of priests were praying and fasting for forty days on behalf of all the priests. This really was exciting to me. Some of the priests had been there the whole forty days, but others, like the missionary from Japan, had just been there a week. They had taken time off from everything else and were praying and seeking God, asking Him to bless all the priests in the Roman Catholic Church. He informed me that they were experiencing a tremendous blessing in this gathering. Let's bear in mind that none of this is out of date; it's all taking place today; and if the Protestants aren't doing it, then the Catholics are!

The incident just related brings up another point about fasting: if a group agrees to fast together, I think that if possible they should also meet together at least part of the time to pray and seek God as a group. There are things accomplished by praying together that often will not happen just by our praying on our own.

CHAPTER TEN

HOW ARE THE SABBATH AND FASTING RELATED?

A n important related facet of this message, which is slightly beyond fasting, is the matter of taking time for God. In Isaiah 58, we have already looked at the blessings that are promised to those who fast in accordance with the will of God. The first twelve verses of Isaiah 58 deal with fasting; the last two verses deal with keeping God's Sabbath, and I believe they are related. The following are the last two verses of Isaiah 58:

> *"If you keep your feet from breaking the Sabbath and from doing as you please on my holy day, if you call the Sabbath a delight and the Lord's holy day honorable, and if you honor it by not going your own way and not doing as you please or speaking idle words, then you will find your joy in the LORD, and I will cause you to ride on the heights of the land and to feast on the inheritance of your father Jacob." The mouth of the LORD has spoken.*
>
> *(Isa. 58:13–14 NIV)*

I believe it is no accident that those two verses come immediately after the twelve verses on fasting. Let me say that I do not believe that Christians are required to observe the Jewish Sabbath, nor do I believe that Sunday is the Sabbath. I believe that Saturday is the Sabbath and that Jews are required to observe it; but Christians, not under the Law, are not required to observe that Sabbath. That is my personal conviction.

In the epistle to the Hebrews, it says, *"There remains there-fore a Sabbath rest for the people of God"* (Heb. 4:9 NAS). The root idea of the Sabbath is resting and ceasing from our own activities. I believe that it is very profitable to unite together fasting with resting from our own works. The average American is either working, at home busy with his family, has a spare job, or is busy with some kind of recreation. Actually, there is a tremendous spiritual blessing from just relaxing and waiting upon God and not being busy with anything.

I find that this is a principle of the Bible. When God brought Israel into the Promised Land, He said, "Every seventh year, your land is to have a sabbath. For one year out of seven, don't sow it; don't do any work on the land; let it lie fallow." (See Leviticus 25:2–6.) All the time Israel was in the land, they failed to observe that. So God warned them, "If you don't do it when you are in the land, I will turn you out of the land, and the land will have its sabbath while you are out of it." I want you to read that warning of judgment:

> *I will scatter you among the nations and will draw out my sword and pursue you. Your land will be laid waste, and your cities will lie in ruins. Then the land will enjoy its sabbath years all the time that it lies desolate and you are in the country of your enemies; then the land will rest and enjoy its sabbaths. All the time that it lies desolate, the land will have the rest it did not have during the sabbaths you lived in it.* (Lev. 26:33–35 NIV)

In other words, Israel refused to keep the sabbath of the land, so God said, "All right, I'll turn you out of the land, and the land will have nothing but sabbaths all the time you are out of it, because you wouldn't observe the sabbath when you were in it."

I've come to see that God deals with Christians in the same way. We're so busy and so active doing things for God that when God says, "Take time off, relax, rest, get alone, get away from everything because I have things I need to tell you," we are often too busy to listen. I can think of men whom I could name—friends of mine—to whom God went on speaking and warning, but who would not listen. Finally, God said, "All right, you'll be in a hospital bed for twelve months. Then you'll have to rest!"

My personal conviction is that it's better to rest voluntarily than to be compelled to rest. I've made a personal decision to try to do that. I think there is a great deal of importance in taking time to relax, rest, and wait upon God, and often to combine that rest with fasting. Then your spirit and your stomach rest. Your whole body gets a rest, as well as your whole personality.

Let me point out to you that God ordained a combination of fasting and resting for the Day of Atonement. Leviticus records God's ordinances for that day:

> And this shall be a statute for ever unto you: that in the seventh month, on the tenth day of the month [that's the Day of Atonement], ye shall afflict your souls [by fasting], and do no work at all, whether it be one of your own country, or a stranger that sojourneth among you: for on that day shall the priest make an atonement for you, to cleanse you, that ye may be clean from all your sins before the LORD. It shall be a sabbath of rest unto you, and ye shall afflict your souls, by a statute for ever. (Lev. 16:29–31 KJV)

The priest had his part to do—he had to go into the Holy of Holies with the blood of the sacrifice and make propitiation for the sins of the people. However, the people had their part to do, and their part was twofold: (1) to fast, and (2) to abstain from all work.

I feel the Lord is emphasizing that we need to unite these two things again. When we fast, if possible, we need to take time off from every other activity—not necessarily a whole day, but half a day—and set that time aside for God. Let our busy minds stop turning over for a little while. We're so busy, even when we pray, that we never give God a chance to tell us what to do. Praying is not just telling God, it's also listening to God. Sometimes it takes a good many hours to get ourselves into the position where we can hear Him. So I believe that rest should be linked with fasting.

Let me give you one other Scripture where fasting is united with taking a sabbath. In the book of Joel, the people of God were faced with a tremendous crisis. They had no answer, so

God told them His answer through the prophet Joel: *"Sanctify ye a fast, call a solemn assembly, gather the elders and all the inhabitants of the land into the house of the LORD your God"* (Joel 1:14 KJV). A solemn assembly means a day when nobody does anything but seek God.

Years ago when we were in Jerusalem, during times of upheaval in the city, a curfew would be proclaimed, and the word they used at those times for curfew is the same word that is used in this passage for *"a solemn assembly."* A curfew is a time when no one is allowed out. Everybody has to stay at home. In other words, there is a voluntary restraint on all activities.

God tells us to sanctify a fast, proclaim a solemn assembly, stop our own activities, and set aside time for Him. In Joel 2:15–16, when God said, *"Blow the trumpet in Zion, sanctify a fast, call a solemn assembly: gather the people, sanctify the congregation, assemble the elders, gather the children"* (KJV), everyone was to stop all their own activities and take time to seek God.

CHAPTER ELEVEN

HOW SHOULD I BREAK A FAST?

O ne final concern as we close this study is with breaking a fast. This is a very important aspect of fasting. You may lose a lot of the benefits that are due you from fasting if you break your fast unwisely.

Some of us don't realize that the word *breakfast,* which we still use in the English language, means the meal that breaks a fast. However, some people eat so much so late at night that they never have a fast to break.

After fasting, always begin with a light meal, even if you have fasted only a short period of time. Don't begin with anything cooked or greasy or fat or heavy. Preferably, begin with a raw salad or fruit. My experience has been that if you begin with a salad—especially lettuce or raw greens—it does a tremendous purging job on your whole body. It's like a brush sweeping out your intestines. This has been my experience in breaking a fast this way.

The next thing to keep in mind is that the longer the fast, the more gradually you must break it. Somebody has said that you must take as long to break your fast as you spent fasting. I don't think that is completely accurate, but I have discovered when I have fasted for a long time (over three weeks) that my stomach was like a baby's. I had to be as careful about feeding myself after that fast as I would have been feeding a baby. It took me a week, at least, to get back to normal food.

This is where you are going to have to have real self-control. When you are in a fast, after about the first two or three days you don't feel hungry, but when you start to eat again, your hunger comes back. That is when you really must hold onto yourself. You may get mental pictures of all sorts of things you love eating, but you just can't give way because you can ruin many of the physical benefits of fasting by breaking your fast rapidly or unwisely.

One more point needs to be mentioned. As a result of fasting—even if it's only a couple of days—your stomach will have contracted. It is usually not wise to expand it again to the same extent. Most people in Western civilization have overexpanded stomachs. You will find that as you start eating after a fast, you will begin to feel full sooner than you would have before you fasted. Habit will make you go on eating the rest of the meal, but wisdom says, "Why not stop there? You've had enough."

Thus, fasting is a way also to change our eating habits, which many of us need to do. However, if you are planning to slim down or reduce, fasting alone will not do that normally. You will get a few pounds off, but you'll put them on just as quickly unless you combine it with a changed program of eating.

Chapter Twelve

In Summary

I n this study, we have covered many of the practical aspects of fasting. Briefly, in review, we defined fasting as abstaining from food for spiritual purposes. We saw that fasting is the revealed will of God and that He has promised to reward those who diligently seek Him through the scriptural way of fasting.

We also discovered several scriptural objectives for fasting:

- to humble ourselves
- to come closer to God
- to help us understand God's Word
- to find God's will and to receive direction in our lives
- to seek healing or deliverance from evil spirits
- to seek God's intervention in some particular crisis or some problem that cannot be handled by ordinary means
- to intercede and pray on behalf of others

We also pointed out that our motive for fasting is much more important than the length of time we spend fasting. For those who have not fasted before, it is wise to begin with a shorter time and build up to longer periods of fasting.

During our periods of fasting, we need to take extra time for Bible study and prayer, guard against spiritual attack, and avoid religious ostentation.

Because of the way we live today, we also pointed out that most people may experience some physical reactions during the early stages of a fast. Such reactions are usually a sign that our blood is doing a badly needed clean-up job on various parts of our bodies.

We also showed the parallel between fasting and the Sabbath, encouraging the combination of rest and relaxation with fasting and waiting upon God.

Finally, we covered how to break a fast so as to get the maximum physical benefits from it.

Fasting is both our duty and our privilege as Christians. Let us heed God's call to pray and fast, individually and corporately, trusting Him that He will fulfill His promise to reward those who diligently seek Him.

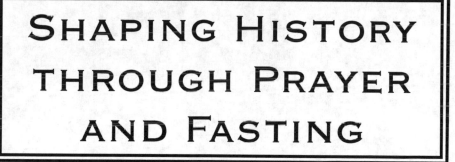

Shaping History through Prayer and Fasting

CONTENTS

By The President of The United States of America:

A Proclamation

For a Day of National Humiliation
Fasting and Prayer

Whereas, the Senate of the United States, devoutly recogniz-ing the Supreme Authority and Just Government of Almighty God, in all the affairs of men and of nations, has, by a resolu-tion, requested the President to designate and set apart a day for National prayer and humiliation:

And whereas, it is the duty of nations, as well as of men, to own their dependence upon the overruling power of God, to con-fess their sins and transgressions, in humble sorrow, yet with assured hope that genuine repentance will lead to mercy and pardon; and to recognize the sublime truth, announced in the Holy Scriptures and proven by all history, that those nations only are blessed whose God is the Lord:

And, insomuch as we know that, by His divine law, nations, like individuals, are subjected to punishments and chastisements in this world, may we not justly fear that the awful calamity of civil war, which now desolates the land, may be but a punish-ment inflicted upon us for our presumptuous sins, to the needful end of our national reformation as a whole People? We have been the recipients of the choicest bounties of Heaven. We have been preserved, these many years, in peace and prosperity. We have grown in numbers, wealth, and power as no other nation has ever grown. But we have forgotten God. We have forgotten the gracious hand which preserved us in peace, and multiplied and enriched and strengthened us; and we have vainly imagined, in the deceitfulness of our hearts, that all these blessings were pro-duced by some superior wisdom and virtue of our own. Intoxi-cated with unbroken success, we have become too self-sufficient to feel the necessity of redeeming and preserving grace, too proud to pray to the God that made us! It behooves us, then, to humble ourselves before the offended Power, to confess our national sins, and to pray for clemency and forgiveness.

Now, therefore, in compliance with the request, and fully concurring in the views of the Senate, I do, by this my proclamation, designate and set apart Thursday, the 30th day of April, 1863, as a day of national humiliation, fasting, and prayer. And I do hereby request all the People to abstain on that day from their ordinary secular pursuits, and to unite, at their several places of public worship and their respective homes, in keeping the day holy to the Lord, and devoted to the humble discharge of the religious duties proper to that solemn occasion.

All this being done, in sincerity and truth, let us then rest humbly in the hope authorized by the Divine teachings, that the united cry of the Nation will be heard on high, and answered with blessings, no less than the pardon of our national sins, and restoration of our now divided and suffering country, to its former happy condition of unity and peace.

In witness whereof, I have hereunto set my hand, and caused the seal of the United States to be affixed.

Done at the city of Washington this thirtieth day of March, in the year of our Lord one thousand eight hundred and sixty-three, and of the Independence of the United States the eighty-seventh.

Abraham Lincoln

By the President:
WILLIAM H. STEWARD, Secretary of State

The above proclamation is preserved in the Library of Congress as Appendix number 19 in volume 12 of the United States At Large. It was initiated by a resolution of the United States Senate, and was officially declared by President Lincoln on March 30, 1863.

Its message contains two related themes that challenge our careful consideration.

First, the proclamation acknowledges the unique blessings enjoyed by the United States, but suggests that these blessings have brought about an attitude of pride and self-sufficiency that are the root causes of a grave national crisis. Some of the phrases could apply with equal force to the condition of the nation today: "We have grown in numbers, wealth, and power as no other nation has ever grown....We have vainly imagined, in the deceitfulness of our hearts, that all these blessings were produced by some superior wisdom and virtue of our own....We have become too self-sufficient...too proud to pray to the God that made us!"

Second, the proclamation unequivocally acknowledges "the overruling power of God" in the affairs of men and nations. It indicates that behind the political, economic, and military forces of history, there are divine spiritual laws at work; and that by acknowledging and submitting to these laws, a nation may change its destiny, averting threatened disaster and regaining true peace and prosperity. In particular, the proclamation sets forth one specific, practical way in which a nation may invoke on its own behalf "the overruling power of God"— by united prayer and fasting.

The author of this proclamation, Abraham Lincoln, is generally regarded, both by Americans and by the world at large, as one of the shrewdest and most enlightened of American presidents. He was a man of sincere faith and deep convictions, but he never sought membership in any of the Christian denominations of his day. In no sense could he be considered as unbalanced or extreme in his religious views. Further, this proclamation was not merely the product of Lincoln's private convictions. It was requested by a resolution of the entire United States Senate.

How shall we assess the deep and unanimous convictions of men of this caliber? Shall we dismiss them as irrelevant or out-of-date? To do this would be merely the mark of unreasoning prejudice.

Rather, we owe it to ourselves to give honest and careful consideration to this proclamation and the issues that it raises. Is there a divine Power that overrules the destinies of nations? Can this Power effectively be petitioned by prayer and fasting?

It is to the examination of these questions that this book is devoted. An answer will be offered from four main sources: first, the teaching of Scripture; second, events of world history during or after World War II; third, the annals of American history; fourth, records of personal experience in the realm of prayer and fasting.

Derek Prince

CHAPTER ONE

THE SALT OF THE EARTH

"YE ARE THE SALT OF THE EARTH."—MATTHEW 5:13 (KJV)

Jesus is speaking to His disciples—to all of us, that is, who acknowledge the authority of His teaching. He compares our function on the earth to that of salt. His meaning becomes clear when we consider two familiar uses of salt in relation to food.

SALT GIVES FLAVOR

First of all, salt gives flavor. Food that in itself is unappetizing becomes tasty and acceptable when seasoned with salt. In Job 6:6, this is put in the form of a rhetorical question: *"Can that which is unsavory be eaten without salt?"* (KJV). It is the presence of salt that makes the difference, causing us to enjoy food that we would otherwise have refused to eat. As Christians, our function is to give flavor to the earth. The one who enjoys this flavor is God. Our presence makes the earth acceptable to God. Our presence commends the earth to God's mercy. Without us, there would be nothing to make the earth acceptable to God. But because we are here, God continues to deal with the earth in grace and mercy rather than in wrath and judgment. It is our presence that makes the difference.

This principle is vividly illustrated in the account of Abraham's intercession on behalf of Sodom, as recorded in Genesis 18:16–33. The Lord had told Abraham that He was on His way to Sodom to see if that city's wickedness had come to the point where judgment could no longer be withheld. Abraham then walked with the Lord on the way toward Sodom and reasoned with Him about the principles of His judgment.

First, Abraham established one principle that is the basis for all that follows: It is never the will of God that the judgment due to the wicked should come upon the righteous. *"Wilt thou also destroy the righteous with the wicked?"* (v. 23 KJV) Abraham asked. *"That be far from thee to do after this manner, to slay the righteous with the wicked: and that the righteous should be as the wicked, that be far from thee: Shall not the Judge of all the earth do right?"* (v. 25 KJV).

The Lord made clear in the ensuing conversation that He accepted the principle stated by Abraham. How important it is that all believers understand this! If we have been made righteous by faith in Christ, and if we are leading lives that truly express our faith, then it is never God's will that we be included in the judgments that He brings upon the wicked.

Unfortunately, Christians often do not understand this because they fail to distinguish between two situations that outwardly may appear similar, but that in reality are completely different in nature and cause. On the one hand, there is persecution for the sake of righteousness. On the other hand, there is God's judgment upon the wicked. The difference between these two situations is brought out by the following contrasted statements: Persecution comes from the wicked upon the righteous; but judgment comes from God, who is righteous, upon the wicked. Thus, persecution for righteousness and judgment for wickedness are opposite to each other in their origins, their purposes, and their results.

The Bible plainly warns that Christians must expect to suffer persecution. In the Sermon on the Mount, Jesus said to His disciples: *"Blessed are they which are persecuted for righteousness' sake: for theirs is the kingdom of heaven. Blessed are ye, when men shall revile you, and persecute you, and shall say all manner of evil against you falsely, for my sake"* (Matt. 5:10–11 KJV). Likewise, Paul wrote to Timothy, *"Yea, and all that will live godly in Christ Jesus shall suffer persecution"* (2 Tim. 3:12 KJV). Christians must therefore be prepared to endure persecution for their faith and their way of life, and even to count this as a privilege.

337

But by the same token, Christians should never be included in God's judgments upon the wicked. This principle is stated many times in Scripture. In 1 Corinthians 11:32, Paul wrote to his fellow believers, and he said, *"But when we [Christians] are judged, we are chastened of the Lord, that we should not be condemned with the world"* (KJV).This demonstrates that there is a difference between God's dealings with believers and His dealings with the world. As believers, we may expect to experience God's chastening. If we submit to the chastening and set our lives in order, then we are not subject to the judgments that come upon unbelievers, or the world in general. The very purpose of God's chastening us as believers is to preserve us from undergoing His judgments upon unbelievers.

In Psalm 91:7–8, the psalmist gave this promise to the believer: *"A thousand shall fall at thy side, and ten thousand at thy right hand; but it shall not come nigh thee. Only with thine eyes shalt thou behold and see the reward of the wicked"* (KJV). Here again the principle is seen. Whatever judgment comes as *"the reward of the wicked"* (what the wicked justly deserve) should never fall upon the righteous. No matter if God strikes the wicked on every side, the righteous in the midst of it all will not be harmed.

In Exodus chapters 7 through 12, it is recorded that God brought ten judgments of ever increasing severity upon the Egyptians because they refused to listen to His prophets Moses and Aaron. Throughout all this, God's people Israel dwelt in the midst of Egypt, but not one of the ten judgments touched them. In Exodus 11:7, the reason is graphically stated: *"But against any of the children of Israel shall not a dog move his tongue, against man or beast: that ye may know how that the LORD doth put a difference between the Egyptians and Israel"* (KJV). Judgment did not come upon Israel because the Lord *"put a difference"* between His own people and the people of Egypt. Even the dogs of Egypt had to acknowledge this difference! And the difference is valid to this day.

Continuing his conversation with the Lord concerning Sodom, Abraham attempted to ascertain the least number of righteous persons needed to preserve the whole city from judgment. He began with fifty. Then with a remarkable combination of reverence and perseverance, he worked his way down to ten. The Lord finally assured Abraham that if He found only ten righteous persons in Sodom, He would spare the whole city for the sake of those ten.

What was the population of Sodom? It would be difficult to arrive at an exact estimate. However, there are figures available for certain other cities of ancient Palestine that provide a standard of comparison. In Abraham's day, the walls of Jericho enclosed an area of about seven or eight acres. This would provide dwelling space for a minimum of five thousand persons or a maximum of ten thousand. But Jericho was not a large city by the standards of its day. The largest city of that period was Hazor, which covered about 175 acres and had a population estimated at between forty and fifty thousand. Later, in the period of Joshua, we are told that the total population of Ai was twelve thousand persons (Josh. 8:25). The Bible record seems to indicate that Sodom was a more important city in its day than Ai.

Taking these other cities into account, we could say that the population of Sodom in Abraham's day was probably not less than ten thousand. God assured Abraham that ten righteous persons could by their very presence preserve a city of at least ten thousand. This gives a ratio of one to a thousand. The same ratio of "one among a thousand" (KJV) is given in Job 33:23 and in Ecclesiastes 7:28, and both these passages suggest that the "one" is a person of outstanding righteousness, while all the remainder fall below God's standards.

It is easy to extend this ratio indefinitely. The presence of ten righteous persons can preserve a community of ten thousand. The presence of a hundred righteous persons can preserve a community of one hundred thousand. The presence of one thousand righteous persons can preserve a community of one million. How many righteous persons are needed to preserve a nation as large as the United States, with an estimated population of over 250,000,000? About 250,000 persons.

These figures are evocative. Does Scripture give us grounds to believe that, for example, a quarter of a million truly righteous persons, scattered as grains of salt across the United States, would suffice to preserve the entire nation from God's judgment and to ensure the continuance of His grace and mercy? It would be foolish to claim that such estimates are exact. Nevertheless, the Bible definitely establishes the general principle that the presence of righteous believers is the decisive factor in God's dealings with a community.

To illustrate this principle, Jesus used the metaphor of *"salt."* In 2 Corinthians 5:20, Paul used a different metaphor to convey the same truth: *"We are ambassadors for Christ"* (KJV). What are ambassadors? They are persons sent forth in an official capacity by a nation's government to represent that government in the territory of another nation. Their authority is not measured by their own personal abilities but is in direct proportion to the authority of the government that they represent.

In Philippians 3:20, Paul specified the government that, as Christians, we represent. He said, *"Our conversation* [literally, our citizenship] *is in heaven"* (KJV). Two translations render this, *"We are citizens of Heaven"* (PHILLIPS) and *"We...are citizens of heaven"* (NEB). Thus our position on earth is that of ambassadors representing heaven's government. We have no authority to act on our own, but as long as we carefully obey the directions of our government, the entire might and authority of heaven are behind every word that we speak and every move that we make.

Before one government declares war on another, its usual action of final warning is to withdraw its ambassadors. While we are left on earth as heaven's ambassadors, our presence guarantees a continuance of God's forbearance and mercy toward the earth. But when heaven's ambassadors are finally withdrawn, there will then be nothing left to hold back the full outpouring of divine wrath and judgment upon the earth.

This leads us to a second effect of the presence of Christians as *"the salt of the earth."*

SALT RESTRAINS CORRUPTION

A second function of salt in relation to food is to restrain the process of corruption. In the days before artificial refrigeration, sailors who took meat on long voyages used salt as a preservative. The process of corruption was already at work before the meat was salted. Salting did not abolish the corruption, but it held it in check for the duration of the voyage, so that the

sailors could continue to eat the meat long after it would otherwise have become inedible.

Our presence on the earth as Christ's disciples operates like
the salt in the meat. The process of sin's corruption is already at
work. This is manifested in every area of human activity—
moral, religious, social, political. We cannot abolish the corruption that is already there, but we can hold it in check long
enough for God's purposes of grace and mercy to be fully
worked out. Then, when our influence is no longer felt, corruption will come to its climax, and the result will be total degrada-
tion.

This illustration from the power of salt to restrain corruption explains Paul's teaching in 2 Thessalonians 2:3–12. Paul
warned that human wickedness will come to its climax in the
person of a world ruler supernaturally empowered and directed
by Satan himself. Paul called this ruler the *"man of sin"* (more
literally, "the man of lawlessness") and *"the son of perdition"* (v.
3 KJV). In 1 John 2:18, he is called *"antichrist."* In Revelation
13:4, he is called *"the beast."* This ruler will actually claim to be
God and will demand universal worship.

Emergence of this satanic ruler is inevitable. Paul said with
certainty, *"Then shall that Wicked* [lawless one] *be revealed"* (2
Thess. 2:8 KJV). Paul also declared in the same verse that the
true Christ Himself will be the One to administer final judgment upon this false Christ: *"Whom the Lord shall consume
with the spirit* [breath] *of his mouth, and shall destroy with the
brightness of his coming"* (v. 8 KJV).

Unfortunately some preachers have used this teaching
about Antichrist to instill into Christians an attitude of passivity and fatalism. "Antichrist is coming," they have said. "Things
are getting worse and worse. There is nothing we can do about
it." As a result, Christians have all too often sat back with
folded hands, in pious dismay, and watched the ravages of Satan
proceed unchecked all around them.

This attitude of passivity and fatalism is as tragic as it is
unscriptural. It is true that Antichrist must eventually emerge.
But it is far from true that there is nothing to be done about
him in the meanwhile. To this present moment, there is a force
at work in the world that challenges, resists, and restrains the

spirit of antichrist. The work of this force is described by Paul in 2 Thessalonians 2:6–7. Freely rendered in modern English, these verses might read as follows: "And now you know what holds him in check until he is revealed in his time. For the secret power of lawlessness is already at work: only he who now holds him in check will continue to do so until he is withdrawn or taken out of the midst" (author's paraphrase).

This restraining power, which at present holds back the full and final emergence of Antichrist, is the personal presence of the Holy Spirit within the church. This becomes clear as we follow the unfolding revelation of Scripture concerning the person and the work of the Holy Spirit. At the very beginning of the Bible, in Genesis 1:2, we are told, *"The Spirit of God moved upon the face of the waters"* (KJV). From then on throughout the Old Testament, we find frequent references to the activity of the Holy Spirit in the earth. However, at the close of His earthly ministry, Jesus promised His disciples that the Holy Spirit would shortly come to them in a new way, different from anything that had ever taken place on earth up to that time.

In John 14:16–17, Jesus gave this promise: *"And I will pray the Father, and he shall give you another Comforter, that he may abide with you for ever; even the Spirit of truth* [a title of the Holy Spirit]...*for he dwelleth with you, and shall be in you"* (KJV). We may paraphrase this promise of Jesus as follows: "I have been with you in personal presence three-and-a-half years, and I am now about to leave you. After I have gone, another Person will come to take my place. This Person is the Holy Spirit. When He comes, He will remain with you forever."

In John 16:6–7, Jesus repeated His promise: *"But because I have said these things unto you, sorrow hath filled your heart. Nevertheless I tell you the truth; it is expedient for you that I go away: for if I go not away, the Comforter will not come unto you; but if I depart, I will send him unto you"* (KJV). The picture is clear. There is to be an exchange of Persons. Jesus will depart, but in His place another Person will come. This other Person is the Comforter, the Holy Spirit.

In John 16:12–13, Jesus returned to this theme for the third time: *"I have yet many things to say unto you, but ye cannot bear them now. Howbeit when he, the Spirit of truth, is come, he will guide you into all truth"* (KJV). In the original Greek text, the pronoun *"he"* is in the masculine gender, but the noun *"Spirit"* is neuter. This grammatical conflict of genders brings out the dual nature of the Holy Spirit—both personal and impersonal. This agrees with the language used by Paul in 2 Thessalonians chapter 2 concerning the power that holds back the emergence of antichrist. In verse 6, Paul said, *"What is restraining him"* (RSV), and in verse 7, he said, *"He who now restrains [lawlessness]"* (RSV). This similarity of expression confirms the identification of this restraining power with the Holy Spirit.

The exchange of Persons promised by Jesus was effected in two stages: first, the ascension of Jesus into heaven; then, ten days later, the descent of the Holy Spirit on the Day of Pentecost. At this point in history, the Holy Spirit descended as a Person from heaven and took up His residence on earth. He is now the personal Representative of the Godhead resident on earth. His actual dwelling place is the body of true believers, called collectively "the church." To this body of believers Paul said in 1 Corinthians 3:16, *"Know ye not that ye are the temple of God, and that the Spirit of God dwelleth in you?"* (KJV).

The great ministry of the Holy Spirit within the church is to prepare a completed body for Christ. After completion, this body will in turn be presented to Christ as a bride is presented to a bridegroom. As soon as this ministry of the Holy Spirit within the church is finished, He will again be withdrawn from the earth, taking with Him the completed body of Christ. Thus we may paraphrase Paul's statement in 2 Thessalonians 2:7 as follows: "The Holy Spirit who now holds the Antichrist in check will continue to do so until he be withdrawn."

The opposition between the Holy Spirit and the spirit of antichrist is described also in 1 John 4:3-4: *"And every spirit that confesseth not that Jesus Christ is come in the flesh is not of God: and this is that spirit of antichrist, whereof ye have heard that it should come; and even now already is it in the world. Ye are of God, little children, and have overcome them: because greater is he that is in you, than he that is in the world"* (KJV).

In the world is the spirit of antichrist, working toward the emergence of Antichrist himself. In the disciples of Christ is the Holy Spirit, holding back the emergence of Antichrist. Therefore the disciples who are indwelled by the Holy Spirit act as a barrier, holding back the climax of lawlessness and the final emergence of Antichrist. Only when the Holy Spirit, together with the completed body of Christ's disciples, is withdrawn from the earth, will the forces of lawlessness be able to proceed without restraint to the culmination of their purposes in Antichrist. Meanwhile, it is both the privilege and the responsibility of Christ's disciples, by the power of the Holy Spirit, to *"overcome"* the forces of Antichrist and to hold them in check.

THE CONSEQUENCES OF FAILURE

As the salt of the earth, then, we who are Christ's disciples have two primary responsibilities. First, by our presence we commend the earth to God's continuing grace and mercy. Second, by the power of the Holy Spirit within us, we hold in check the forces of corruption and lawlessness until God's appointed time.

In fulfilling these responsibilities, the church stands as the barrier to the accomplishment of Satan's supreme ambition, which is to gain dominion over the whole earth. This explains why Paul said in 2 Thessalonians 2:3 that there must be *"a falling away first,* [before] *that man of sin* [Antichrist] *be revealed"* (KJV). The word translated *"falling away"* is literally "apostasy"—that is, a departure from the faith. So long as the church stands firm and uncompromising in its faith, it has the power to hold back the final manifestation of Antichrist. Satan himself fully understands this, and therefore his primary objective is to undermine the faith and righteousness of the church. Once he achieves this, the barrier to his purposes is removed, and the way is open for him to gain both spiritual and political control over the whole earth.

Suppose that Satan succeeds because we, as Christians, fail to fulfill our responsibilities. What then? Jesus Himself gave us the answer. We become salt that has lost its savor. He warned us of the fate that awaits such savorless salt: *"It is thenceforth good for nothing, but to be cast out, and to be trodden under foot of men"* (Matt. 5:13 KJV).

"Good for nothing"! That is severe condemnation indeed. What follows? We are *"cast out,"* or rejected by God. Then we

are *"trodden under foot of men."* Men become the instruments of God's judgment upon a saltless, apostate church. If we in the church fail to hold back the forces of wickedness, our judgment is to be handed over to those very forces.

The alternatives that confront us are clearly presented by Paul in Romans 12:21: *"Be not overcome of evil, but overcome evil with good"* (KJV). There are only two choices: either to overcome or to be overcome. There is no middle way, no third course open to us. We may use the good that God has put at our disposal to overcome the evil that confronts us. But if we fail to do this, then that very evil will in turn overcome us.

This message applies with special urgency to those of us who live in lands where we still enjoy liberty to proclaim and to practice our Christian faith. In many lands today, Christians have lost this liberty. At the same time, multiplying millions in those lands have been systematically indoctrinated to hate and to despise Christianity and all that it stands for. To people thus indoctrinated, there could be no greater satisfaction than to trample under their feet those Christians who are not already under their yoke.

If we will heed the warning of Jesus, and fulfill our functions as salt in the earth, we will have the power to prevent this. But if we default from our responsibilities and suffer the judgment that follows, the bitterest reflection of all will be this: it need never have happened!

CHAPTER TWO

A KINGDOM OF PRIESTS

G od has vested in us—His believing people on earth—
authority by which we may determine the destinies of
nations and governments. He expects us to use our
authority both for His glory and for our own good. If we fail to
do so, we are answerable for the consequences. Such is the message of Scripture, unfolded both by precept and by pattern. It is
confirmed by the personal experience of many believers and is
written across the pages of the history of whole nations. In later
chapters, we will examine specific instances of this, taken from
the events of recent world history and also from the annals of
American history. But first, in this chapter, we will study the
scriptural basis of this authority.

GOD'S WORDS IN MAN'S MOUTH

An outstanding example is provided by the career of the
prophet Jeremiah. In the opening ten verses of the first chapter
of Jeremiah, God declared that He had set Jeremiah apart as *"a
prophet unto the nations"* (1:5 KJV). Jeremiah, in response, pro-
tested his inability to fulfill this role, saying, *"I cannot speak: for
I am* [only a youth]" (v. 6 KJV). However, God reaffirmed His
call in stronger terms and concluded by saying, *"See, I have this
day set thee over the nations and over the kingdoms, to root out,
and to pull down, and to destroy, and to throw down, to build,
and to plant"* (v. 10 KJV).

What an exalted position for a young man, to be *"set...over
the nations and over the kingdoms."* This is authority on a higher
plane than the normal forces that shape secular politics. To judge

by outward appearances, the subsequent career of Jeremiah gave little indication of such authority. On the contrary, his message was almost universally rejected, and he himself was continually subjected to indignity and persecution. For several months, he languished in prison, and at various times, he was at the point of death, either by execution or by starvation.

Yet the course of history has vindicated the authority of Jeremiah and his message. His prophetic messages unfolded the destinies of Israel and of nearly all the surrounding nations in the Middle East, as well as those of nations in other areas of the earth. Twenty-five hundred years have passed. In the light of history, it is now possible to make an objective evaluation. Throughout all the intervening centuries, the destiny of every one of those nations has followed precisely the course foretold by Jeremiah. The more closely we compare their subsequent histories with the prophecies of Jeremiah, the more exactly do we find them to correspond. Thus Jeremiah was in very fact "set over those nations and over the kingdoms," and by the prophecies that he uttered, he became the actual arbiter of their destinies.

What was the basis of such tremendous authority? The answer is found in Jeremiah 1:9: *"And the LORD said unto me, Behold, I have put my words in thy mouth"* (KJV). The authority lay in God's words, imparted to Jeremiah. Because the words that Jeremiah uttered were not his own, but those that God gave him, they were just as effective in Jeremiah's mouth as they would have been in the mouth of God Himself. In all earth's affairs, the last word is with God. At times, however, God causes this word to be spoken through the lips of a human believer. Such a word may be spoken publicly in prophecy or in the authoritative exposition of Scripture. More often, perhaps, it is spoken within a prayer closet, in petition or in intercession.

It is important to observe that Jeremiah stood in a twofold relationship to the secular government of his day. On the natural plane, as a citizen of Judah, he was in subjection to the government of his nation, represented by the king and the princes. In no sense did he preach or practice political subversion or anarchy. Nor did he ever seek to evade or to resist decrees made by the government concerning him, even though these were at

347

times arbitrary and unjust. Yet on the spiritual plane to which God elevated him through his prophetic ministry, Jeremiah exercised authority over the very rulers to whom he was in subjection on the natural plane.

SHARING THE THRONE WITH CHRIST

Jeremiah's career illustrates a principle that is more fully unfolded in the New Testament: Every Christian has dual citizenship. By natural birth, he is a citizen of an earthly nation, and he is subject to all the ordinances and requirements of his nation's lawful government. But by spiritual rebirth, through faith in Christ, he is also a citizen of God's heavenly kingdom. This is the basis of Paul's statement, already referred to in our previous chapter: *"We...are citizens of heaven"* (Phil. 3:20 NEB).

As a citizen of heaven, the Christian is subject to the laws of the heavenly kingdom, but he is also entitled to share in its authority. This is the kingdom of which David spoke in Psalm 103:19: *"The LORD hath prepared his throne in the heavens; and his kingdom ruleth over all"* (KJV). God's kingdom is supreme over all other kingdoms and over all other forces at work on earth. It is God's purpose to share the authority of His kingdom with His believing people. In Luke 12:32, Jesus assured His disciples, *"Fear not, little flock; for it is your Father's good pleasure to give you the kingdom"* (KJV). The comfort of this assurance does not depend upon the strength or numbers of the flock, for it is a *"little flock,"* a company of *"sheep in the midst of wolves"* (Matt. 10:16 KJV). The certainty that the kingdom belongs to us is founded on the *"good pleasure"* of the Father, *"the purpose of him who worketh all things after the counsel of his own will"* (Eph. 1:11 KJV).

As Christians, our position in God's kingdom is determined by our relationship to Christ. Paul explained this in Ephesians 2:4–6, which is rendered in The New English Bible: *"But God, rich in mercy, for the great love he bore us, brought us to life with Christ even when we were dead in our sins; it is by his grace you are saved. And in union with Christ Jesus he raised us up and enthroned us with him in the heavenly realms."*

God's grace identifies us with Christ in three successive phases. First, we are *"brought...to life,"* or made alive. We share Christ's life. Second, we are *"raised...up,"* as Christ was raised up, from the tomb. We share Christ's resurrection. Third, we are *"enthroned"* in the heavenly kingdom. We share Christ's kingly authority on the throne. None of this is in the future. It is all stated in the past tense, as a fact already accomplished. Each of these three phases is made possible, not by our own efforts or merits, but solely by accepting in faith our union with Christ.

In Ephesians 1:20–21, Paul described the position of supreme authority to which Christ has been exalted by the Father: *"When he raised him from the dead, when he enthroned him at his right hand in the heavenly realms, far above all government and authority, all power and dominion, and any title of sovereignty that can be named"* (NEB). Christ's authority at God's right hand does not necessarily set aside all other forms of authority or government, but it takes preeminence over them. The same truth is expressed by the title twice given to Christ in the book of Revelation: *"Lord of lords, and King of kings"* (Rev. 17:14; see 19:16). Christ is the Supreme Ruler over all rulers and Governor over all governments. This is the position on the throne that He shares with His believing people.

How shall we comprehend the magnitude of what is thus made available to us? The answer is given in Paul's prayer in the preceding verses of Ephesians chapter 1:

> *That the God of our Lord Jesus Christ, the Father of glory, may give you a spirit of wisdom and of revelation in the knowledge of him, having the eyes of your hearts enlightened, that you may know...what is the immeasurable greatness of his power in us who believe, according to the working of his great might which he accomplished in Christ when he raised him from the dead and made him sit at his right hand in the heavenly places. (Eph. 1:17–20 RSV)*

This revelation cannot come by natural reasoning or by sense knowledge. It comes only by the Holy Spirit. He is the One who enlightens the eyes of our hearts and shows us two interwoven truths: first, that Christ's authority is now supreme over the universe; second, that the same power that raised Christ to that position of authority now works also *"in us who believe."*

In 1 Corinthians chapter 2, Paul further explained these truths that are revealed to Christians only by the Holy Spirit. He said, *"But we impart a secret and hidden wisdom of God, which God decreed before the ages for our glorification. None of the rulers of this age understood this; for if they had, they would not have crucified the Lord of glory"* (vv. 7–8 RSV). This *"secret and hidden wisdom"* reveals Christ as *"Lord of glory."* It is *"for our glorification,"* for it shows us that in our union with Him we share His glory. Paul continued, *"But, as it is written, 'What no eye has seen, nor ear heard, nor the heart of man conceived, what God has prepared for those who love him,' God has revealed to us through the Spirit"* (vv. 9–10 RSV). Paul again emphasized that knowledge of this kind is not imparted through the senses, nor is it forthcoming out of the inner resources of man's reason or imagination, except as these are illuminated by the Holy Spirit.

In verse 12, Paul summed this up: *"Now we have received, not the spirit of the world, but the spirit which is of God; that we might know the things that are freely given to us of God"* (KJV). One of the things thus given to us is our position in Christ at God's right hand. Paul here contrasted two sources of knowledge. *"The spirit of the world"* shows us the things of this world. Through this we understand our earthly citizenship, with all its rights and responsibilities. But *"the spirit which is of God"* reveals to us the kingdom of Christ and our place in it. Through this we understand our rights and responsibilities as citizens of heaven.

If, at times, our position with Christ on the throne seems remote or unreal, the reason is simple: we have not received the revelation that the Holy Spirit, through the Scriptures, makes available to us. Without this revelation, we can neither understand nor enjoy the benefits of our heavenly citizenship. Instead of reigning as kings, we find ourselves still toiling as slaves.

FROM SLAVES TO KINGS

From the beginning, it was God's purpose to share with man His dominion over the earth. In Genesis 1:26, the initial

350

purpose of man's creation is stated: *"And God said, Let us make man in our image, after our likeness: and let them* [the human race] *have dominion...over all the earth"* (KJV). Because of disobedience, Adam and his descendants forfeited their position of dominion. Instead of reigning in obedience as kings, they were subjugated as slaves to sin and to Satan.

However, the dominion that was lost to the whole race through Adam is restored to the believer in Christ. *"For if by one man's offence* [that is, the offense of Adam] *death reigned by one; much more they which receive abundance of grace and of the gift of righteousness shall reign in life by one, Jesus Christ"* (Rom. 5:17 KJV). The consequences of Adam's disobedience and of Christ's obedience are both already manifested in this present life. Death reigns now over unbelievers. Likewise, believers reign now in life by Christ. Through our union with Christ, we have already been raised up to share the throne with Him, and we are reigning there with Him now.

God's purpose in man's redemption reflects His original purpose in man's creation. God's redeeming grace lifts man from his position of slavery and restores him to his position of dominion. In the Old Testament, this is demonstrated in the deliverance of Israel from the slavery of Egypt. In Exodus 19:6, God declares to Israel the purpose for which He has redeemed them: *"And ye shall be unto me a kingdom of priests, and an holy nation"* (KJV). *"A kingdom of priests"* speaks of dominion restored—kingship in place of slavery. God offered Israel a double privilege: to minister as priests and to reign as kings. As we will see in later chapters of this book, some of the great saints of Israel, such as Daniel, entered into this high calling. For the most part, however, the nation failed to accept God's gracious promises.

In the New Testament, to those redeemed by faith in Christ, God renews the calling that He originally gave to Israel. In 1 Peter 2:5, Christians are called *"an holy priesthood."* As priests of the new covenant, their ministry is *"to offer up spiritual sacrifices, acceptable to God by Jesus Christ"* (KJV). The *"spiritual sacrifices"* offered up by Christians are the various forms of prayer—particularly worship and intercession. Then, in 1 Peter 2:9, Christians are further called *"a royal* [or kingly] *priesthood."* The phrase *"a royal priesthood"* exactly corresponds to *"a kingdom of priests"* in Exodus 19:6.

In the book of Revelation, the same phrase is again applied twice to those redeemed by faith in Jesus Christ. In Revelation 1:5–6, we read: *"Unto him* [Christ] *that loved us, and washed us from our sins in his own blood, and hath made' us kings and priests unto God and his Father"* (KJV). And again in Revelation 5:9–10: "[Thou] *hast redeemed us to God by thy blood...and hast made us unto our God kings and priests"* (KJV). In all, God's purpose to make His redeemed people *"a kingdom of priests"* is stated four times in Scripture—once in the Old Testament and three times in the New Testament. In all three instances in the New Testament, God's purpose is presented not as something yet to take place in the future, but as a fact already accomplished for us as Christians through our position in Christ.

WE RULE BY PRAYER

In Psalm 110:1–4, David painted a picture of Christ reigning as King and Priest together with His believing people. Every detail of the scene is significant and merits our careful attention. The inspired language and imagery David uses must be interpreted by reference to other related passages of Scripture.

In the first verse, we have the revelation of Christ as King, enthroned at the Father's right hand: *"The LORD said unto my Lord, Sit thou at my right hand, until I make thine enemies thy footstool"* (KJV). No other verse of the Old Testament is quoted more often in the New Testament than this. In three of the gospels, Jesus quoted the words of David and applied them to Himself (Matt. 22:44; Mark 12:36; Luke 20:42–43). They were likewise applied to Jesus by Peter in his sermon on the Day of Pentecost (Acts 2:34–35). The truth of Christ's kingship is similarly presented by David in Psalm 2:6, where the Father declares: *"Yet have I set my king upon my holy hill of Zion"* (KJV).

In verse 4 of Psalm 110, David's picture is completed by the revelation of Christ as Priest: *"The LORD hath sworn, and will not repent, Thou art a priest for ever after the order of Melchizedek"* (KJV). The whole teaching of the epistle to the

Hebrews concerning Christ's high priesthood is based on this verse of Psalm 110. The writer of Hebrews stressed that in Melchizedek there was the union of the two functions of kingship and priesthood. Melchizedek was *"priest of the most high God."* In addition, he was, by the very meaning of his name, *"King of righteousness, and after that also King of Salem, which is, King of peace"* (Heb. 7:1–2 KJV).

Such is the double ministry that Christ now exercises at the Father's right hand. As King, He rules. As Priest, He intercedes: *"He ever liveth to make intercession"* (v. 25 KJV).

Verse 2 of Psalm 110 describes the way in which Christ's kingly authority is exercised: *"The LORD shall send the rod of thy strength out of Zion: rule thou in the midst of thine enemies"* (KJV). This is the situation in the world today. The enemies of Christ have not been finally subdued, but are still actively at work, opposing His rule and His kingdom. However, Christ has been exalted and given authority over them all. Thus He rules now *"in the midst of* [His] *enemies."*

David spoke of *"the rod of thy strength."* It is by this that Christ rules. The *"rod"* in Scripture is the mark of a ruler's authority. When Moses stretched out his rod, the plagues of God came upon Egypt, and later the waters of the Red Sea parted before Israel. (See Exodus 7–14.) As high priest and head over the tribe of Levi, Aaron had a rod on which his name was inscribed. (See Numbers 17:3.) The same applies to Christ. His authority is made effective by the use of His name.

In the scene painted by David, the rod is not stretched forth by Christ's own hand, but is sent forth *"out of Zion."* All through Scripture, Zion denotes the place of assembly of God's people. Speaking to Christians, the writer of Hebrews says: *"But ye are come unto mount Sion...to the general assembly and church of the firstborn, which are* [enrolled] *in heaven"* (Heb. 12:22–23 KJV). By right of our heavenly citizenship, we take our place in this assembly that is gathered in Zion.

Here we play our part in the double ministry of Christ. As kings, we rule with Him. As priests, we share His ministry of prayer and intercession. We must never seek to separate these two functions from each other. If we would rule as kings, we must serve as priests. The practice of our priestly ministry is the key to the exercise of our kingly authority. It is through prayer and intercession that we administer the authority that is ours in the name of Jesus.

How wonderfully David's picture illustrates the church's ministry of prayer! In the world, the forces of evil are rampant on every hand, rejecting the authority of Christ and opposing the work of His kingdom. But *"in the midst"* (Ps. 110:2), the Christians assemble in divine order as kings and priests. Out of their assembly, the rod of Christ's authority, exercised in His name, is sent forth through their prayers. In every direction that the rod is extended, the forces of evil are compelled to yield, and Christ in turn is exalted and His kingdom advanced.

All Christians look forward to the day when Christ's enemies will have been finally and completely subdued, and He will be openly manifested and universally acknowledged as King. The Bible promises that that day will come. But we must not let the promised glory of the future blind us to the reality of Christ's present position at God's right hand. Christ rules even now *"in the midst of* [His] *enemies"* (v. 2 KJV), and we rule with Him. It is our responsibility to exercise the authority that is ours through His name, and in face of all the forces of evil to demonstrate that Christ is already *"Lord of lords, and King of kings"* (Rev. 17:14 KJV).

CHAPTER THREE

PRAYING FOR OUR GOVERNMENT

Christ is *"Lord of lords, and King of kings"* (Rev. 17:14 KJV). He is the Ruler of earth's rulers and the Governor over earth's governments. His authority over all earthly governments is made available in His name to the church—the assembly of His believing people. As Moses stretched forth his rod on God's behalf over Egypt, so the church by its prayers stretches forth Christ's authority over the nations and their rulers.

GOOD GOVERNMENT IS GOD'S WILL

In his first letter to Timothy, Paul instructed him in the proper administration and order of the local church, which he called God's house. (See 1 Timothy 3:14–15.) Paul also gave directions for the church's ministry of prayer:

> *I exhort therefore, that, first of all, supplications, prayers, intercessions, and giving of thanks, be made for all men; for kings, and for all that are in authority; that we may lead a quiet and peaceable life in all godliness and honesty. For this is good and acceptable in the sight of God our Saviour; who will have all men to be saved, and to come unto the knowledge of the truth.* (1 Tim. 2:1–4 KJV)

"First of all," Paul called for *"supplications, prayers, intercessions, and giving of thanks."* If we were to choose one term to cover all four activities, it would be prayer. The first duty of

Christians meeting in fellowship is prayer. It is also their primary outreach.

In the second verse, Paul said that prayer is to be offered *"for all men."* This agrees with the prophecy of Isaiah 56:7, where God says, *"Mine house shall be called an house of prayer for all people"* (KJV). God is concerned with *"all men"* and *"all people."* He expects His people to share His concerns. Contrast this with the narrow, self-centered prayers of many professing Christians! Someone offered the following as a parody of the average church member's prayer: "God bless me, my wife, my son John, and his wife. Us four. No more. Amen!"

After *"all men,"* the first specific topic for prayer is *"kings, and...all that are in authority."* In countries such as the United States, which have no monarchy, the word *"kings"* does not apply. In any case, whether there be a monarchy or not, the phrase *"all that are in authority"* indicates all those who are responsible for governing the nation. This may be summed up in the single word: the *government.*

Thus, the first specific topic of prayer ordained by God for His people meeting in fellowship is the government. Extensive experience has convinced me that the vast majority of professing Christians never give any serious consideration to this topic in prayer. Not merely do they not pray for the government *"first,"* they scarcely pray for it at all! They pray regularly for groups such as the sick, the shut-ins, preachers, missionaries, evangelists, the unconverted—anything and everybody but the one group that God puts first—the government. It is no exaggeration to say that many who claim to be committed Christians never pray seriously for the government of their nation as much as once a week!

When praying for the government, what specific petition are we exhorted to make? In the second verse, Paul answered, *"That we may lead a quiet and peaceable life in all godliness and honesty."* Does the kind of government we live under affect the way we live? Obviously it does. Therefore, if we desire a good way of life, logic and self-interest alike indicate that we should pray for our government.

This was brought home to me in a new way when I applied for United States citizenship. Like all who make application, I was required to study in outline the basic principles and purposes of the American Constitution. As I meditated on these, I asked myself, "What was the real objective of those who originally drafted that Constitution?" I concluded that their objective could be summed up with complete accuracy in the words of Paul: *"That we may lead a quiet and peaceable life in all godliness and honesty."* The authors of the Constitution had as their objective a state in which every citizen would be free to pursue his own legitimate interests without interference from other citizens or the government, but with the protection of the government and its officers. Judged by the language that they used, most, if not all, of those who drafted the Constitution viewed such a state as being possible only under the sovereign protection and favor of Almighty God. Christian citizens of the United States should forever be thankful that the basic charter of their nation agrees so exactly with the purposes and principles of government ordained by Scripture.

Continuing in 1 Timothy 2, Paul said in verse 3, *"For this is good and acceptable in the sight of God our Saviour."* The pronoun *"this"* refers back to the topic of verse 2, which we have summarized as "good government." If we replace the pronoun *"this"* by the phrase to which it refers, we arrive at the following statement: "Good government is good and acceptable in the sight of God." More simply still, "Good government is the will of God."

Here is a statement with the most far-reaching consequences. Do we really believe it? To judge by the words and actions of many Christians, they have little or no expectation of good government. They are more or less resigned to the fact that the government will be inefficient, wasteful, arbitrary, corrupt, unjust. For my part, I have studied this question long and carefully in the light of logic and of Scripture, and I have come to a deep conviction concerning God's will in this area: The will of God is good government.

WHY GOD DESIRES GOOD GOVERNMENT

Moving on to verse 4, we find that Paul stated the reason why good government is the will of God: God desires *"all men to be saved, and to come unto the knowledge of the truth."* God

357

desires the salvation of all men so intensely that He made it possible by the supreme sacrifice of history, the atoning death of Jesus Christ on the cross. Through faith in Christ's atonement, salvation has been made available to all men. However, for men *"to be saved,"* they must first *"come unto the knowledge of the truth"* concerning Christ's atonement. This is possible only if they have the Gospel preached to them.

Paul presented this issue very plainly in Romans 10:13–14: *"For whosoever shall call upon the name of the Lord shall be saved. How then shall they call on him in whom they have not believed? and how shall they believe in him of whom they have not heard? and how shall they hear without a preacher?"* (KJV). Unless the Gospel is preached to them, men cannot avail themselves of the salvation purchased for them by Christ's atonement.

We may sum up the logic of this very simply: God desires *"all men to be saved."* For this it is necessary for them to *"come unto the knowledge of the truth."* *"Knowledge of the truth"* comes only through the preaching of the Gospel. Therefore, God desires the Gospel to be preached to all men.

It remains only to trace the connection between good government and the preaching of the Gospel. We may do this by asking ourselves one simple question: Which kind of government makes it easier to preach the Gospel? Good government? Or bad government? To obtain an answer to this question, we may briefly contrast the effects of good and bad government, insofar as they relate to the preaching of the Gospel.

On the one hand, good government maintains law and order; it keeps communications open, preserves civil liberty, and protects freedom of speech and freedom of assembly. (It is noteworthy that nearly all these points are specifically covered by the Constitution of the United States.) In short, good government, without becoming involved in religious controversy, provides a climate in which the Gospel can be preached effectively.

On the other hand, bad government allows the breakdown of law and order, permits unsafe travel conditions and poor communications, and imposes unjust and arbitrary restrictions. In all these ways, although in varying degrees, bad government hinders the effective preaching of the truth. At its worst, bad government either restricts or totally suppresses the universal right of all men to believe in God and to express their faith by public worship and proclamation. In one degree or another, we see these conditions in countries under communist rule today.

Our conclusion, therefore, is that good government facilitates the preaching of the Gospel, while bad government hinders it. For this reason, good government is the will of God.

We are now in a position to present the teaching of 1 Timothy 2:1–4 in a series of simple logical steps:

1. The first ministry and outreach of believers as we meet together in regular fellowship is prayer.
2. The first specific topic for prayer is the government.
3. We are to pray for good government.
4. God desires all men to have the truth of the Gospel preached to them.
5. Good government facilitates the preaching of the Gospel, while bad government hinders it.
6. Therefore, good government is the will of God.

PRAYING WITH THE KNOWLEDGE OF GOD'S WILL

The final sentence of the above summary has the most far-reaching consequences for our prayers. In all effective praying, the decisive issue is the knowledge of God's will. If we know that what we are praying for is according to God's will, then we have faith to claim it. But if we are not sure of God's will, our prayers are wavering and ineffective. In James 1:6–7, James warned us that such wavering prayers will not be answered: *"For he that wavereth is like a wave of the sea driven with the wind and tossed. For let not that man think that he shall receive any thing of the Lord"* (KJV).

On the other side, John described the confidence that comes from the assurance of God's will: *"And this is the confidence that we have in him* [God], *that, if we ask any thing according to his will, he heareth us: and if we know that he hear us, whatsoever we ask, we know that we have the petitions that we desired of him"* (1 John 5:14–15 KJV).

John's teaching in this passage revolves around the knowledge of God's will. Provided that we know we are praying in full accord with God's will, we may know that *"we have"* whatsoever we prayed for. The use of the present tense *"we have"* does not necessarily indicate an immediate manifestation of the thing that we prayed for, but it does indicate an immediate assurance that the thing is already granted to us by God. Thereafter, the amount of time taken for its actual manifestation cannot affect this initial assurance.

This agrees with the teaching of Mark 11:24: *"Therefore I say unto you, What things soever ye desire, when ye pray, believe that ye receive them* [more properly, believe that you already received them], *and ye shall have them"* (KJV). Receiving comes at the very moment of praying. After that, the actual manifestation of that which we have received follows at the appropriate time.

With this preliminary explanation, it is now possible to apply to 1 John 5:14–15 the same kind of logical analysis that we have already applied to 1 Timothy 2:1–4. John's teaching in these verses may be summed up as follows:

1. If we know that we are praying for anything according to God's will, we know that He hears us.

2. If we know that God hears us, we know that we have the thing that we prayed for. (This does not necessarily indicate immediate fulfillment.)

To comprehend fully what we can accomplish by praying for our government, we need to combine the teaching of John with that of Paul. The result is as follows:

1. If we pray for anything knowing that it is according to God's will, we have the assurance that the thing is granted to us.

2. Good government is according to God's will.

3. If we know this and pray for good government, we have the assurance that good government is granted to us.

Why, then, do the majority of Christians have no assurance of good government? There can only be two reasons: either they do not pray at all for good government, or they pray for good government, but without the knowledge that it is God's will.

These conclusions drawn from Scripture have been confirmed by my personal observations. The great majority of Christians never pray seriously for good government at all. Of the few who do pray for good government, hardly any do so with the scriptural conviction that it is really God's will. Whichever of these explanations may apply in any given situation, the conclusion remains the same: God has made it possible for Christians by their prayers to insure good government. Christians who fail to exercise this God-given authority are gravely delinquent—both toward God and toward their countries.

Having been raised in Britain, I am frequently shocked by the way in which Americans habitually speak about the officers of their government. I do not know of any European nation where people would permit themselves to speak about their rulers with the disrespect and cynicism regularly heard in America. The irony of this is that, in an elective democracy, those who continually criticize their rulers are, in effect, criticizing themselves, since it is within their power by the processes of election to change those rulers and to replace them by others. This applies with double force to Christians in such a democracy who, in addition to the normal political machinery, also have available to them the God-given power of prayer by which to bring about the changes that they believe desirable, either in the personnel or in the policy of the government.

The truth is that Christians are not held responsible by God to criticize their government, but they are held responsible to pray for it. So long as they fail to pray, Christians have no right to criticize. In fact, most political leaders and administrators are more faithful in the discharge of their secular duties than Christians are in the discharge of their spiritual duties. Furthermore, if Christians would seriously begin to intercede, they would soon find less to criticize.

I am persuaded that the root of the problem with most Christians is not lack of will, but lack of knowledge. Let this fact first be clearly established: Good government is God's will. This will provide both the faith and the incentive that Christians need to pray effectively for their government.

CHAPTER FOUR

RULERS ARE GOD'S AGENTS

I n politics, as in many other fields of activity, men continually strive for promotion. Yet few seriously ask the question: Where does promotion come from? What power is it that exalts men to positions of authority or removes them from such positions?

PROMOTION COMES FROM GOD

In Psalm 75, the Bible deals very directly with this question:

> I said unto the fools, Deal not foolishly: and to the wicked, Lift not up the horn: lift not up your horn on high: speak not with a stiff neck. For promotion cometh neither from the east, nor from the west, nor from the south. But God is the judge: he putteth down one, and setteth up another.
>
> (Ps. 75:4–7 KJV)

The psalmist begins by warning men against their own self-confidence and arrogance. To *"lift...up the horn"* suggests the desire for personal aggrandizement. To *"speak...with a stiff neck"* suggest boastful self-assertiveness. These are not the ways to promotion. Indeed, promotion does not come from the earthly level. We may interpret the three directions east, west, and south as representing the various sources to which men are prone to look for political aggrandizement, such as wealth, education, social position, influential connections, and military power. For men to seek their own exaltation from sources such

362

as these is to *"deal...foolishly."* Promotion comes from God. He is the One who both raises men up and puts them down.

The record of the men who have hitherto held office as president of the United States is a remarkable confirmation that the source of political power is outside the men who themselves exercise it. This is well illustrated by a passage from the writings of President John F. Kennedy:

> This insight into the nature of governing affirms the lesson of our history that there is no program of vocational training for the presidency; no specific area of knowledge that is peculiarly relevant. Nor are qualities of great leadership drawn from any particular section of the country or section of society. Nine of our Presidents, among them some of the most brilliant in office, did not attend college; whereas Thomas Jefferson was one of the great scholars of the age and Woodrow Wilson the president of Princeton University. We have had Presidents who were lawyers and soldiers and teachers. One was an engineer and another a journalist. They have been drawn from the wealthiest and most distinguished families of the nation, and have come from poor and anonymous beginnings. Some, seemingly well endowed with great abilities and fine qualities, were unable to cope with the demands of the office, while others rose to a greatness far beyond any expectation. (1962, Parade Publications, Inc. 733 Third Ave. New York, N.Y.)

If we turn back to the records of the kings of Israel, we find none who achieved a more spectacular rise to greatness than David. Beginning life as a poor shepherd boy, he ended his days in victory and honor as the ruler of a powerful empire. Unlike many other men who have achieved political greatness, David recognized the source of his success. In a prayer to God uttered near the end of his life, he ascribed his greatness solely to God: *"Both riches and honour come of thee, and thou reignest over all; and in thine hand is power and might; and in thine hand it is to make great, and to give strength unto all"* (1 Chron. 29:12 KJV). Wise and happy is the ruler who acknowledges the true source of his power!

Daniel is another great character of the Bible who discovered the true source of political power. Challenged by King Nebuchadnezzar to reveal both the king's dream and its interpretation, he and his companions sought God in earnest prayer and received the answer by direct revelation (Dan. 2:17–19). In response, Daniel offered his prayer of gratitude and acknowledgment:

Blessed be the name of God for ever and ever: for wisdom and might are his: and he changeth the times and the seasons: he removeth kings, and setteth up kings: he giveth wisdom unto the wise, and knowledge to them that know understanding. (Dan. 2:20–21 KJV)

In the fourth chapter of Daniel, the prophet is again called upon to interpret a dream for King Nebuchadnezzar. Concerning this dream, Daniel told the king:

This matter is by the decree of the watchers, and the demand by the word of the holy ones: to the intent that the living may know that the most High ruleth in the kingdom of men, and giveth it to whomsoever he will, and setteth up over it the basest of men. (Dan. 4:17 KJV)

God wants men to acknowledge that He is the supreme ruler over all human affairs, and that earthly rulers are raised up by His decree. Not only so, but at times God actually raises up *"the basest of men"* as rulers.

HOW GOD USES HUMAN RULERS

Why should God raise up "base men" as rulers? The answer is supplied by the case of Nebuchadnezzar. God uses human rulers as instruments of judgment upon His own people. The Jewish nation had persistently offended God by religious backsliding and social injustice. After many warnings, God set over them the cruel, idolatrous King Nebuchadnezzar. In a series of judgments that progressively increased in severity, Nebuchadnezzar first removed many of the Jews as captives to Babylon and brought the nation under tribute. Finally, he destroyed the city of Jerusalem, together with the temple, and uprooted the whole nation out of their own land. Thus even in his baseness, Nebuchadnezzar was the instrument of God to bring judgment upon the backslidden and rebellious Jewish nation.

Yet Nebuchadnezzar is also a remarkable example of how God's grace and power can change an instrument of judgment into an instrument of mercy. When Daniel and his companions sought God in earnest prayer, God changed the heart of Nebuchadnezzar. On account of the special wisdom given by God to Daniel, Nebuchadnezzar raised him and his companions to positions of the highest power. Daniel's three companions became rulers of the province of Babylon, while Daniel himself became the prime minister of the entire Babylonian empire, with power second only to that of Nebuchadnezzar himself. This dramatic change, both in the personal attitude of Nebuchadnezzar and in the position of the Jews, was brought about by the prayers of Daniel and his companions.

The career of Daniel, like that of David, is in itself an example of God's ability to raise up a man from humble beginnings to a position of great political power. In his youth, Daniel had originally been taken to Babylon as a kind of political hostage. Yet within a short period, he was elevated to the position of prime minister. Even after the fall of the Babylonian empire, we still find Daniel occupying a position of influence and authority in the succeeding Medo-Persian empire, under the rulership of Darius and Cyrus.

We are given a glimpse of Daniel's prayer life in Daniel chapter 6. The story indicates that his practice of regular prayer was well known in the court of Darius. Motivated by jealousy, Daniel's rivals seized upon this as a means to incriminate him. They persuaded Darius to sign a decree by which, for the next thirty days, prayer was not to be offered to any person except Darius. The penalty for disobeying this decree was death by being cast into the lions' den. Daniel's response is recorded in verse 10: *"Now when Daniel knew that the writing was signed, he went into his house; and his windows being open in his chamber toward Jerusalem, he kneeled upon his knees three times a day, and prayed, and gave thanks before his God, as he did aforetime"* (KJV).

What a standard Daniel set for all who follow him in the ministry of intercession! What a pattern of dedication and persistence! His face was set toward Jerusalem. Three times every day he prayed for the restoration of the city and for the return of Israel from exile to its own land. His continuing intercession on behalf of his people was a personal commitment so solemn and so urgent, that not even the threat of death could deter him.

The outcome of Daniel's intercession is recorded in 2 Chronicles:

Now in the first year of Cyrus king of Persia, that the word of the LORD spoken by the mouth of Jeremiah might be accomplished, the LORD stirred up the spirit of Cyrus king of Persia, that he made a proclamation throughout all his kingdom, and put it also in writing, saying, Thus saith Cyrus king of Persia, All the kingdoms of the earth hath the LORD God of heaven given me; and he hath charged me to build him an house in Jerusalem, which is in Judah. Who is there among you of all his people? The LORD his god be with him, and let him go up. (2 Chron. 36:22–23 KJV)

In this way, God fulfilled the promises of Israel's restoration that He had previously given, both through Isaiah and through Jeremiah. The promise given through Isaiah is found in Isaiah 44:26–28, and that given through Jeremiah is found in Jeremiah 25:11–12.

Here indeed is a very clear example of God changing human governments in the interests of His own people. On the one hand, God brought judgment upon the king of Babylon and his people because they stood in the way of the return of the Jews to Jerusalem and the rebuilding of the temple. (The king of Babylon here referred to was a successor of Nebuchadnezzar.) On the other hand, God raised up in their place Cyrus and the Medo-Persian empire, and made them the instruments of mercy and restoration for the Jews and Jerusalem.

Behind these events that changed the course of world empires, there were two unseen spiritual forces at work: the Word of God spoken through His prophets, and the intercessory prayer of Daniel.

From these examples of God's dealings with the Jewish nation through the instrumentality of Nebuchadnezzar and Cyrus, certain important principles emerge:

1. God uses human rulers as instruments to fulfill His purposes in history, particularly as they relate to His own covenant people.

2. If God's people are disobedient and rebellious, God subjects them to cruel and evil rulers.

3. If through repentance and prayer God's people lay claim upon His mercy, He may bring about a change of government in one of two ways: either by removing an evil ruler and replacing him by a good one; or by changing the heart of a cruel ruler, so as to make him an instrument of mercy rather than of judgment.

"FOR YOUR SAKES"

These principles, derived from historical examples of the Old Testament, are confirmed by the teaching given to Christians in the New Testament. In 2 Corinthians 4:15, Paul said, *"For all things are for your sakes"* (KJV). God's dealings with the whole world have one supreme objective: the fulfillment of His purposes for His own people, related to Him through faith in Jesus Christ. Over all the events of the last two thousand years of world history, God has inscribed one all-inclusive heading, addressed to His people: *"For your sakes."*

In Romans, Paul applied this principle specifically to those who hold office in government:

> *Every person must submit to the supreme authorities. There is no authority but by act of God, and the existing authorities are instituted by him; consequently anyone who rebels against authority is resisting a divine institution, and those who so resist have themselves to thank for the punishment they will receive. For government, a terror to crime, has no terrors for good behaviour. You wish to have no fear of the authorities? Then continue to do right and you will have their approval, for they are God's agents working for your good. But if you are doing wrong, then you will have cause to fear them; it is not for nothing that they hold the power of the sword, for they are God's agents of punishment, for retribution on the offender. That is why you are obliged to*

submit. It is an obligation imposed not merely by fear of ret-
ribution but by conscience. (Rom. 13:1–5 NEB)

Out of this passage, we may select three statements that are particularly significant: *"There is no authority but by act of God," "They are God's agents working for your good,"* and, *"They are God's agents of punishment."* Paul addressed these words specifically to Christians. He stated that government is established by an act of God. How that government will affect Christians depends upon the attitude and conduct of the Christians. If they are walking in obedience to the will of God, then the government and its officers *"are God's agents working for* [their] *good."* But if Christians are disobedient and not walking in the path of God's will, then the government and its officers become *"God's agents of punishment."* This may all be summed up in one brief sentence: Christians get the kind of government they deserve.

What if Christians find themselves under a government that is evil? It may be corrupt, inefficient, wasteful, or again it may be actively cruel and oppressive towards Christians. How are Christians to react? God's Word gives them no liberty either to complain or to disobey. It does, however, impose upon them a solemn obligation to pray for their government. If they will humble themselves before God and meet His conditions, He will then hear their prayers and will *"for* [their] *sakes"* bring about a change of government that will ensure the fulfillment of His purposes and the best interests of His people.

WHAT GOD REQUIRES IN THOSE WHO RULE

Since it is within the power of Christians to determine by their prayers the kind of government they are to live under, it is important that we know what kind of government to pray for. What are God's main requirements in one who governs? The answer to this question is given by the Holy Spirit through the lips of David in 2 Samuel:

The spirit of the LORD spake by me, and his word was in my tongue. The God of Israel said, the Rock of Israel spake

368

to me, He that ruleth over men must be just, ruling in the
fear of God. And he shall be as the light of the morning,
when the sun riseth, even a morning without clouds; as the
tender grass springing out of the earth by clear shining af-
ter rain.   *(2 Sam. 23:2–4 KJV)*

Two simple requirements for a ruler are here stated: he must be just, and he must rule in the fear of God. No doubt there is a prophetic reference here to the kingdom of Christ, and these words will find their complete and final fulfillment only in Christ. Nevertheless, the general principle is firmly established and applied to every man who exercises government. God's two requirements are that he will be just and God-fearing. Whenever such a man is raised up to rule, God promises that blessings will follow: *"He shall be as the light of the morning, when the sun riseth, even a morning without clouds; as the tender grass springing out of the earth by clear shining after rain."*

The simplicity of God's requirements cuts across most of the motives and the pressures with which we are familiar in contemporary politics. In the United States and in Britain alike, there is firmly established a system of two-party government. In the United States, the two parties are Democrats and Republicans. In Britain, there are the Labor and Conservative parties. The names are different in the two countries, but the basic attitudes are similar.

Unfortunately, Christians in both countries often allow themselves to be more influenced by party sentiments or affiliations than by divine requirements. God does not promise blessing to a government upon the condition that it carry a particular party label—whether that label be Republican or Democrat, Conservative or Labor. God promises blessing to a government whose officers fulfill two great basic moral requirements. He demands that they be just and God-fearing. Wherever possible, Christians who respect God's requirements should make it a principle not to vote for any man who is not just and God-fearing, no matter what party label he may wear. If Christians ignore God's requirements and vote for men who are morally unworthy, they are actually inviting God to make those men, if elected, agents of His judgment against the very people who voted them into office.

In the United States particularly, the proportion of committed Christians within the total community is large enough to permit them to exercise a powerful influence over the type of men put forward as candidates for office. This was originally pointed out early in the nineteenth century by the great evangelist Charles Finney. Christians of all political backgrounds should agree upon one basic principle: to withhold their votes from any candidates who do not fulfill the moral requirements established by Scripture. If this principle were clearly established and firmly adhered to, each of the major political parties would be under pressure to put forward as their candidates only such men as fulfilled these requirements. The result would be to raise the standards of political conduct and government throughout the whole nation.

In other countries, and under other systems of government, God's people are not always in a position to apply this kind of political pressure. Nevertheless, they are still responsible to pray for the rulers of their nation, and in this way to exercise a decisive influence upon the course of government.

CHAPTER FIVE

SEEING HISTORY SHAPED
THROUGH PRAYER

For me, the power of prayer to shape history is no mere abstract theological formula. I have seen it demonstrated in my own experience on many occasions. In this chapter, I will relate four such occasions. To make them effective as illustrations, I have chosen situations in which different nations and different political factors were involved.

THE WAR IN NORTH AFRICA

From 1941 to 1943, I served as a hospital attendant with the British forces in North Africa. I was part of a small medical unit that worked with two British armored divisions—the First Armored Division and the Seventh Armored Division. It was this latter division that became celebrated as the "desert rats," with the emblem of the white jerboa.

At that time, the morale of the British forces in the desert was very low. The basic problem was that the men did not have confidence in their officers. I myself am the son of an army officer, and many of the friends with whom I grew up were from the same background. I thus had some valid standards of judgment. As a group, the officers in the desert at that time were selfish, irresponsible, and undisciplined. Their main concern was not the well-being of the men, or even the effective prosecution of the war, but their own physical comfort.

I recall one officer who became sick with malaria and was evacuated to a base hospital in Cairo. For his transportation to Cairo, he required one four-berth ambulance for himself, and a one-and-a-half-ton truck to carry his equipment and personal belongings. At the time, we were continually being reminded that trucks and gasoline were in very short supply, and that every effort must be made to economize in the use of both. From Cairo, this officer was then evacuated to Britain (a procedure that certainly was not necessitated by a mere bout of malaria). Some months later, we heard him on a radio broadcast relayed from Britain. He was giving a very vivid account of the hardships of campaigning in the desert!

At that period, our greatest hardship was the shortage of water. Supplies were very strictly rationed. Our military water bottles were filled every other day. This was all the water that we were allowed for every purpose—washing, shaving, drinking, cooking, etc. Yet the officers in their mess each evening regularly consumed more water with their whiskey than was allotted to the other ranks for all purposes combined.

The result of all this was the longest retreat in the history of the British army—about seven hundred miles in all—from a place in Tripoli called El Agheila to El Alamein, about fifty miles west of Cairo. Here the British forces dug in for one final stand. If El Alamein should fall, the way would be open for the Axis powers to gain control of Egypt, to cut the Suez Canal, and to move over into Palestine. The Jewish community there would then be subjected to the same treatment that was already being meted out to the Jews in every area of Europe that had come under Nazi control.

About eighteen months previously, in a military barrack room in Britain, I had received a very dramatic and powerful revelation of Christ. I thus knew in my own experience the reality of God's power. In the desert, I had no church or minister to offer me fellowship or counsel. I was obliged to depend upon the two great basic provisions of God for every Christian: the Bible and the Holy Spirit. I early came to see that, by New Testament standards, fasting was a normal part of Christian discipline. During the whole period that I was in the desert, I regularly set aside Wednesday of each week as a special day for fasting and prayer.

During the long and demoralizing retreat to the gates of Cairo, God laid on my heart a burden of prayer, both for the British forces in the desert and for the whole situation in the

Middle East. Yet I could not see how God could bless leadership that was so unworthy and inefficient. I searched in my heart for some form of prayer that I could pray with genuine faith and that would cover the needs of the situation. After a while, it seemed that the Holy Spirit gave me this prayer: "Lord, give us leaders such that it will be for Your glory to give us victory through them."

I continued praying this prayer every day. In due course, the British government decided to relieve the commander of their forces in the desert and to replace him with another man. The man whom they chose was a general named W. H. E. "Strafer" Gott. He was flown to Cairo to take over command, but he was killed when his plane was shot down. At this critical juncture, the British forces in this major theater of the war were left without a commander. Winston Churchill, then Prime Minister of Britain, proceeded to act largely on his own initiative. He appointed a more-or-less unknown officer, named B. L. Montgomery, who was hastily flown out from Britain.

Montgomery was the son of an evangelical Anglican bishop. He was a man who very definitely fulfilled God's two requirements in a leader of men. He was just and God-fearing. He was also a man of tremendous discipline. Within two months, he had instilled a totally new sense of discipline into his officers and had thus restored the confidence of the men in their leaders.

Then the main battle of El Alamein was fought. It was the first major allied victory in the entire war up to that time. The threat to Egypt, the Suez Canal, and Palestine was finally thrown back, and the course of the war changed in favor of the Allies. Without a doubt, the battle of El Alamein was the turning point of the war in North Africa.

Two or three days after the battle, I found myself in the desert a few miles behind the advancing Allied forces. A small portable radio beside me on the tailboard of a military truck was relaying a news commentator's description of the scene at Montgomery's headquarters as he had witnessed it on the eve of the battle. He recalled how Montgomery publicly called his officers and men to prayer, saying, "Let us ask the Lord, mighty in battle, to give us the victory." As these words came through that portable radio, God spoke very clearly to my spirit, "That is the answer to your prayer."

How well this incident confirms the truth about promotion that is stated in Psalm 75:6–7. The British government chose Gott for their commander, but God set him aside and raised up Montgomery, the man of His own choosing. God did this to bring glory to His own name, and to answer a prayer that, by the Holy Spirit, He Himself had first inspired me to pray. By this intervention, God also preserved the Jews in Palestine from coming under the control of the Axis powers.

I believe that the prayer that God gave me at that time could well be applied to other situations, both military and political: "Lord, give us leaders such that it will be for Your glory to give us victory through them."

THE BIRTH OF THE STATE OF ISRAEL

During 1947, the future of Palestine was brought before the General Assembly of the United Nations. At that time, the British still governed the country under a mandate that had been assigned to them by the League of Nations shortly after the end of World War I. On November 29, 1947, the United Nations voted to partition the country into two separate states, allotting a small area to an independent Jewish state and the rest of the country to the Arabs, with the city of Jerusalem under international control. The date set for the termination of the British mandate and the inception of the new political order in Palestine was May 14, 1948.

Almost immediately after the United Nations decision in favor of partition, the Arabs of Palestine, aided and abetted by infiltrators from the surrounding Arab nations, embarked on an undeclared war against the Jewish communities in their midst. Several main areas of the country were virtually taken over by armed groups of Arabs, with little or no semblance of normal civil government. By the early part of 1948, the Jewish community inside Jerusalem already presented the appearance of a beleaguered city. They were almost totally cut off from supplies of food and other commodities, and were in a condition bordering on starvation.

On the date set for the inauguration of the new Jewish state, all the surrounding Arab nations simultaneously declared war on it. Around six hundred and fifty thousand Jews, with the barest minimum of arms and equipment and without any officially constituted military forces, found themselves confronted on every frontier by a hostile Arab world, fifty million strong, who boasted well-trained armies and abundant military supplies. The leaders of the Arab nations publicly declared their intention to annihilate the newborn Jewish state and to sweep the Jews into the sea.

At this period, my wife Lydia and I were living with our eight adopted daughters in the center of Jewish Jerusalem. We occupied a large house on the southeast corner of a main intersection between King George Avenue and a street leading eastward to the Jaffa Gate of the old city. Lydia had been living in or near Jerusalem for the previous twenty years. She had been an eyewitness to a long series of earlier conflicts in that area between the Arabs and the Jews. She recalled that invariably the Jews had been poorly armed and ill-prepared to resist attack. In this critical hour, it seemed that the odds against the Jews were immeasurably greater than on previous occasions, and the results of defeat too terrible to contemplate.

Together Lydia and I searched the Scriptures for words of encouragement or direction from God. Each day, we became more and more convinced that we were living in the period of Israel's restoration, to which their prophets and leaders had looked forward over the long centuries of agony and exile. This was the time spoken of in Psalm 102:12–13: *"But thou, O LORD, shalt endure for ever….Thou shalt arise, and have mercy upon Zion: for the time to favour her, yea, the set time, is come"* (KJV).

We realized that we were seeing before our eyes the fulfillment of God's promise to Israel:

> *Fear not: for I am with thee: I will bring thy seed from the east, and gather thee from the west; I will say to the north, Give up; and to the south, Keep not back: bring my sons from far, and my daughters from the ends of the earth.*
>
> (Isa. 43:5–6 KJV)

These and other passages of Scripture convinced us that the restoration of the Jews to their land was the sovereign purpose of God being brought to fulfillment. If it was God's purpose to restore Israel, then it could not be His will for them to be driven out or destroyed. This gave us faith to pray for Israel's deliverance, based not on nationalistic prejudices, but on the scriptural revelation of God's will.

When Lydia and I were thus brought together by the Holy Spirit concerning God's will, our prayers fulfilled the condition stated in Matthew 18:19: *"Again I say unto you, That if two of you shall agree on earth as touching any thing that they shall ask, it shall be done for them of my Father which is in heaven"* (KJV). One day, as we were praying together, I heard Lydia utter this short prayer: "Lord, paralyze the Arabs!"

When full-scale fighting broke out in Jerusalem, our house was less than a quarter of a mile from the front line, which ran more or less along the west wall of the old city. In the first six weeks of fighting, we counted approximately 150 windowpanes that had been broken by bullets. For most of this period, our whole family lived in a large laundry room in the basement.

Because of the strategic location of our house, our backyard was taken over by the Haganah—the volunteer Jewish defense force that later developed into the official Israeli army. An observation post under the command of a young man named Phinehas was located in the yard. Because of this, we became quite well acquainted with a number of the young Jewish people—both men and women—who manned the post.

Early in June of 1948, the United Nations succeeded in imposing a four-week cease-fire, and there was a temporary lull in the fighting. One day during the cease-fire, some of our young Jewish friends were sitting in our living room, talking freely about their experiences in the initial period of fighting.

"There's something we can't understand," a young man said. "We go into an area where the Arabs are. They outnumber us ten to one and are much better armed than we are. Yet, at times, they seem powerless to do anything against us. It's as if they are paralyzed!"

Right there in our own living room, this young Jewish soldier repeated the very phrase that Lydia had uttered in prayer a few weeks previously! I have never since ceased to marvel at God's faithfulness. Not only did God literally answer Lydia's prayer to "paralyze the Arabs," but He also provided us with firsthand, objective testimony from a Jewish soldier in our own living room that this was what He had done! God's purpose to grant Israel continuing occupation of their land was, in this miraculous way, achieved with the loss of fewer lives than would otherwise have been the case.

It was the invading Arab armies, with all their superiority in arms and numbers, that were defeated and driven back. In the next twenty years, this initial victory of Israel was consolidated by equally dramatic victories in two succeeding wars. Today, the state of Israel has been firmly established and has achieved amazing progress in almost every area of its national life.

For Lydia and me, all of this had greater significance than the mere record of unusual military or political achievements. Each time we received some fresh news concerning Israel's continuing development and progress, we said to ourselves with deep inner satisfaction: "Our prayers played a part in that."

THE END OF STALIN'S ERA

From 1949 to 1956, I was pastor of a congregation in London, England. I retained a special interest in God's dealings with the Jewish people, which had first been kindled by my experiences in Jerusalem at the time of the birth of the state of Israel. Early in 1953, I received information from reliable sources that Josef Stalin, who at that time ruled the Soviet Union as an unchallenged dictator, was planning a systematic purge directed against the Russian Jews.

As I meditated on this situation, the Lord reminded me of Paul's exhortation to the gentile Christians concerning the Jews:

For as ye in times past have not believed God, yet have now obtained mercy through their unbelief: even so have these also now not believed, that through your mercy they also may obtain mercy.   (Rom. 11:30–31 KJV)

Somehow, I felt that God was laying at my door the responsibility for the Jews in Russia. I shared my feelings with the leaders of a few small prayer groups, in various parts of Britain, who also had a special concern for the Jews. Eventually, we decided to set aside one day for special prayer and fasting on behalf of the Russian Jews. I do not recall the exact date chosen but I believe it was a Thursday. All the members of our groups voluntarily committed themselves to abstain from food that day and to devote special time to prayer for God's intervention on behalf of the Jews in Russia. Our own congregation met that evening for group prayer devoted primarily to that topic.

There was no particularly dramatic spiritual manifestation in the meeting, no special sense of being "blessed" or emotionally stirred. But within two weeks from that day, the course of history inside Russia was changed by one decisive event: the death of Stalin. He was seventy-three years old. No advance warning of his sickness or impending death was given to the Russian people. Up to the last moment, sixteen of Russia's most skilled doctors fought to save his life, but in vain. The cause of death was said to be a brain hemorrhage.

Let it be clearly stated that no member of any of our groups prayed for the death of Stalin. We simply committed the situation inside Russia to God, and trusted His wisdom for the answer that was needed. Nevertheless, I am convinced that God's answer came in the form of Stalin's death.

In Acts chapter 12, a somewhat similar answer to the prayers of the early church is recorded. King Herod had the apostle James, brother of John, executed. Then he proceeded to arrest Peter and hold him for execution immediately after the Passover. At this point, the church in Jerusalem applied themselves to earnest, persistent prayer on Peter's behalf. As a result, God intervened supernaturally through an angelic visitation, and Peter was delivered out of the prison. In this way, the prayers of the church for Peter were answered, but it still remained for God to deal with King Herod.

In the closing verses of the chapter, Luke gives a vivid picture of Herod, arrayed in his royal apparel, making a speech to the people of Tyre and Sidon. At the end of his oration, the people applauded, shouting, *"It is the voice of a god, and not of a man"* (Acts 12:22 KJV). Puffed up with conceit at his own achievements, Herod accepted the applause. However, the record concludes, *"Immediately an angel of the Lord struck him down because he did not give God the glory"* (12:23 PHILLIPS), and in fearful internal agony he died. The outworking of the power of prayer in human history can at times be swift and terrible.

It remains to point out the consequences of Stalin's death. The planned purge of Russian Jews was not carried out. Instead, a period of change in internal Russian policy was initiated, so significant and far-reaching that it later came to be known as the era of "destalinization." In due course, Stalin's successor and former associate, Khrushchev, denounced Stalin as a cruel and unjust persecutor of the Russian people. Later, Stalin's daughter, who had been raised under the teaching of atheistic communism, fled from her native land and sought refuge in the country that her father had persistently abused. She further professed her faith in a crucified Jew, whose followers her father had cruelly persecuted.

KENYA'S BIRTH PANGS

From 1957 to 1961, Lydia and I served as educational missionaries in Kenya, East Africa. I was the principal of a teacher training college in western Kenya.

During this period, Kenya was still painfully struggling to recover from the bloody agonies of the Mau Mau movement, which had created bitter mistrust and hatred, not only between Africans and Europeans, but also among many of the various African tribes. At the same time, the country was being hastily prepared for the end of British rule and for national independence. This was eventually achieved in 1963.

In 1960, the Belgian Congo, which is to the west of Kenya, gained its independence. Without adequate preparation, the various African groups inside the Congo were unable to meet the demands of self-government, and were plunged into a protracted series of bloody internal wars. Many of the European residents of the Congo fled eastward into Kenya, bringing with them gruesome pictures of the strife and chaos they had left behind them.

Against this background, the forecasts of the political experts for the future of Kenya were dark indeed. It was generally predicted that Kenya would follow the unhappy course of the Congo, but with problems made even more serious by the internal antagonisms that were the legacy of Mau Mau.

In August 1960, I was one of a number of missionaries ministering at a week-long convention for African young people held in western Kenya. There were about two hundred young Africans in attendance, most of whom were either teachers or students. A considerable number of these were either students or former students from the Teacher Training College of which I was the principal.

The convention ended on a Sunday. In the final service that evening, we witnessed a fulfillment of Joel's prophecy, quoted by Peter:

And it shall come to pass in the last days, saith God, I will pour out of my Spirit upon all flesh: and your sons and your daughters shall prophesy, and your young men shall see visions, and your old men shall dream dreams.

(Acts 2:17 KJV)

A missionary colleague from Canada brought the closing address, which was translated into Swahili by a young man named Wilson Mamboleo, who had recently graduated from our Teacher Training College. The first two hours of the service followed a normal pattern, but after the close of the missionary's address, the Holy Spirit moved with sovereign power and lifted the meeting onto a supernatural plane. For the next two hours, almost the whole group of more than two hundred people continued in spontaneous worship and prayer without any visible human leadership.

At a certain point, the conviction came to me that, as a group, we had touched God, and that His power was at our disposal. God spoke to my spirit, and said, "Do not let them make the same mistake that Pentecostals have so often made in the past, by squandering My power in spiritual self-indulgence. Tell them to pray for the future of Kenya."

I began to make my way to the platform, intending to deliver to the whole group the message that I felt God had given me. On the way, I passed Lydia, who was sitting beside the aisle. She put out her hand and stopped me.

"What do you want?" I asked her.

"Tell them to pray for Kenya," she said.

"That's just what I'm going up to the platform for," I replied. I realized that God had spoken to my wife at the same time that He had spoken to me, and I accepted this as confirmation of His direction.

Reaching the platform, I called the whole group to silence and presented God's challenge to them. "You are the future leaders of your people," I told them, "both in the field of education and also in the field of religion. The Bible places upon you, as Christians, the responsibility to pray for your country and its government. Your country is now facing the most critical period in its history. Let us unite together in praying for the future of Kenya."

Wilson Mamboleo was with me on the platform, translating my words into Swahili. When the time came to pray, he knelt down beside me. As I led in prayer, almost every person present joined me in praying out loud. The combined volume of voices rising in prayer reminded me of the passage in Revelation 19:6: *"And I heard as it were the voice of a great multitude, and as the voice of many waters, and as the voice of mighty thunderings"* (KJV). The sound of prayer swelled to a crescendo, then suddenly ceased. It was as if some invisible conductor had brought down his baton.

After a few moments of silence, Wilson stood up and spoke to the congregation. "I want to tell you what the Lord showed me while we were praying," he said. I realized that God had given him a vision as he knelt beside me in prayer.

Wilson then related the vision he had seen, first in English and then in Swahili. "I saw a red horse approaching Kenya from the east," he said. "It was very fierce, and there was a very black man riding on it. Behind it were several other horses, also red and fierce. While we were praying, I saw all the horses turn around and move away toward the north."

Wilson paused for a moment, and then continued, "I asked God to tell me the meaning of what I had seen, and this is what He told me: 'Only the supernatural power of the prayer of My people can turn away the troubles that are coming upon Kenya!'"

For many days after that, I continued to meditate on what Wilson had told us. I realized that Wilson's vision was in some ways similar to one recorded in Zechariah 1:7–11. I asked Wilson whether he was familiar with this passage of Zechariah, and he replied that he was not. I gradually concluded that by this vision, God had granted us an assurance that He had heard our prayers for Kenya, and that He would intervene in some definite way on behalf of the country. Subsequent events in Kenya's history have confirmed that this was so.

During the period of British rule, Kenya was one of three states that made up British East Africa. The other two states were Uganda to the west and Tanganyika to the south. (Tanganyika was later renamed Tanzania.) Kenya eventually achieved her independence on December 12, 1963. The other two states had already achieved independence somewhat earlier. Immediately after independence was declared, a national government was duly elected in Kenya, with Jomo Kenyatta as the nation's first president.

In January 1964, there was an exact outworking in Kenya's history of the vision that Wilson had seen. A bloody revolution broke out in Zanzibar, off Kenya's east coast. This was led by an African from Uganda who had been trained in revolutionary tactics under Castro in Cuba. The revolution succeeded in overthrowing the Sultan of Zanzibar.

In the same month, a revolutionary movement gripped the national army of Tanzania. Its influence also spread to the army of Kenya. The aim was to overthrow the elected government in Kenya and to replace it by a military dictatorship under communist control.

At this critical point, Kenya's new president, Jomo Kenyatta, acted with wisdom and firmness. Enlisting the help of the British army, he suppressed the revolutionary movement in the Kenyan army and restored law and order throughout the country. Thus, the authority of Kenya's duly-elected government was preserved, and the communist attempt at a military takeover was completely foiled.

In Wilson's vision, the red horses that turned away from Kenya moved towards the north. Northward along the African coast from Kenya lies Somalia. The kind of communist military coup that failed in Kenya was successful in Somalia. Someone later described Somalia as "a communist military camp."

The other countries bordering on Kenya have likewise experienced serious political problems. To the south, in Tanzania, strong communist influence has brought about various limitations of political freedom. To the west, in Uganda, there has been a history of unstable governments and internal tribal clashes, with a very determined effort by the Moslems to gain control of the country and to make Islam the official religion of the nation. Yet in the midst of all this, Kenya has succeeded in combining order and progress with a high degree of political and religious liberty to a remarkable extent.

The attitude of Kenya's government toward Christianity has been consistently friendly and cooperative. Although President Kenyatta does not himself profess to be a Christian, he has officially invited the various Christian bodies in Kenya to teach the message of Christianity in every government school in the country. In many ways, Kenya has become a strategically located center from which trained national Christians are able to move out with the gospel message to all the surrounding countries.

Sometimes God uses unexpected means of getting information to us. In October 1966, I was in the office of a travel agency in Copenhagen, making arrangements for a flight to London. While I was waiting for my ticket to be prepared, I picked up an English edition of the *London Times*. There was a special sixteen-page supplement that dealt exclusively with Kenya. In essence, the theme of this supplement was that Kenya had proved to be one of the most stable and successful of nearly fifty new nations that had emerged on the continent of Africa since the end of World War II. As I turned each page of the supplement, I seemed to hear the inaudible voice of God within my spirit, saying, "This is what I can do when Christians pray with faith for the government of their nation."

When I decided to record God's dealings with Kenya, I wrote to Wilson Mamboleo in Nairobi. I outlined my recollection of the vision that God had given him in 1960, and asked him to indicate any ways in which I could make my account more accurate. I also asked him if he had any comments to make on the then present situation in Kenya. The following are some extracts from his reply, dated June 30, 1972:

> Thank you for your letter. It is the Spirit of the living God who has guided you to ask me to write these things....
>
> It is so wonderful how the Lord has worked. I and another brother who loves to pray have been uplifting you before the Lord in prayer and while we were doing so, I received your letter....
>
> Concerning my vision of 1960, I feel you have grasped it well, so there wouldn't be any need for an addition....
>
> At this time Kenya is leading a peaceful life. Economic development is steadily growing. Foreign investment is in a healthy structure. Business among the African people is booming in every town in the country. The success which is being achieved in Kenya is because of the stability of the present government led by His Excellency the President, "Mzee" Jomo Kenyatta.
>
> I can say that God chose this man to lead our nation at such a time as this, and I, as well as many other faithful Christians in the country, do pray for him, that God may grant him wisdom.
>
> Many people in the country do not have an answer who would be a successor to President Kenyatta, when his days on earth are over. In the eyes of men, there is no man of his caliber who will have such a commanding leadership, accepted by all his countrymen, as Kenyatta. However, I do believe, and this is what I tell those I meet, that "God will provide" a man—but only as a result of persistent prayer of the saints....
>
> We thank God that Kenya enjoys more freedom to worship God in the way a person is led, than the other neighboring states. In Tanzania, religion—and especially Christianity —is being suppressed. Open-air evangelistic meetings are not allowed unless one has a valid permit from the authorities....In Uganda, the military government led by General Amin, a Moslem, is urging all religious bodies to become ecumenical. Recently General Amin himself made a mixture of worship—Moslem prayers were conducted in a Christian church, when the General himself attended the prayers....
>
> The military government of Somalia is a socialist type of government. Somalia has close ties with the communist countries of the East—the Soviet Union and Red China. Large amounts of financial and material aids are given to Somalia,

just as Tanzania receives its aid from China (including military training and supplies of Chinese MIG fighters)....

Over these past years, the history of Kenya and the surrounding nations has demonstrated the exact outworking of the vision that God gave to Wilson in 1960. The intervention of God on behalf of Kenya came through a group of Christians who united together to pray, in accordance with Scripture, for the government and the destiny of their nation.

As you ponder on this record of God's faithfulness, call to mind the words with which Wilson's vision closed: "Only the supernatural power of the prayer of My people can turn away the troubles that are coming upon Kenya."

Is there not good reason to believe that these words apply just as much to your country and to mine?

CHAPTER SIX

FASTING INTENSIFIES PRAYER

I n the preceding chapter, various incidental references were made to the practice of fasting. It is now time to examine more systematically the teaching of Scripture on this subject. It will help to begin with a simple definition. We understand fasting to be the practice of deliberately abstaining from food for spiritual purposes. If abstinence from water (or other fluids) is also included, this is normally indicated by the context.

CHRIST'S TEACHING AND EXAMPLE

The best starting point for a study of the Christian discipline of fasting is to be found in the Sermon on the Mount. In Matthew 6:1–18, Christ gave instructions to His disciples on three related duties: giving alms, praying, and fasting. In each case, He placed His main emphasis upon the motive and warned against religious ostentation for the sake of impressing men. With this qualification, He assumed that all His disciples would practice all three of these duties. This is indicated by the language that He used concerning each.

In the second verse, He said, *"When thou doest thine alms"* (KJV). In verse 6, He said, *"When thou* [singular] *prayest"* (individually); and in verse 7, *"When ye* [plural] *pray"* (collectively). In verse 16, He said, *"When ye* [plural] *fast"* (collectively); and in verse 17, *"When thou* [singular] *fastest"* (individually). In no case did Christ say *if,* but always *when.* The inference is clear. Christ expected that all His disciples would regularly practice all three of these duties. In particular, the parallel between prayer and fasting is exact. If Christ expected

386

His disciples to pray regularly, then by the same token He expected them also to fast regularly.

Fasting was an accepted part of religious duty among the Jewish people in Christ's day. They had practiced it continuously from the time of Moses onward. Both the Pharisees and the disciples of John the Baptist fasted regularly. The people were surprised that they did not see the disciples of Jesus doing the same, and they asked Him the reason. Their question, and Christ's answer, are recorded in Mark:

> And the disciples of John and of the Pharisees used to fast: and they come and say unto him, Why do the disciples of John and of the Pharisees fast, but thy disciples fast not? And Jesus said unto them, Can the children of the bridechamber fast, while the bridegroom is with them? as long as they have the bridegroom with them, they cannot fast. But the days will come, when the bridegroom shall be taken away from them, and then shall they fast in those days. *(Mark 2:18–20 KJV)*

This answer of Jesus is given in the form of a simple parable. It is important to interpret the parable correctly. The *"bridegroom,"* as always in the New Testament, is Christ Himself. The *"children of the bridechamber"* are the disciples of Christ (about whom the question had been asked). The period *"while the bridegroom is with them"* corresponded to the days of Christ's ministry on earth, while He was physically present with His disciples. The period *"when the bridegroom shall be taken...from them"* commenced when Christ ascended back to heaven, and will continue until He returns for His church. In the meanwhile, the church, as a bride, is awaiting the return of the Bridegroom. This is the period in which we are now living, and concerning which Jesus says very definitely, *"And then shall they* [the disciples] *fast in those days."* In the days in which we now live, therefore, fasting is a mark of true Christian discipleship, ordained by Jesus Himself.

Fasting is endorsed not merely by the teaching of Jesus, but also by His own personal example. Immediately after being baptized in the Jordan by John the Baptist, Jesus was led by the

Holy Spirit to spend forty days fasting in the wilderness. This is recorded in Luke:

> *And Jesus being full of the Holy [Spirit] returned from Jordan, and was led by the Spirit into the wilderness, being forty days tempted of the devil. And in those days he did eat nothing: and when they were ended, he afterward hungered.* (Luke 4:1–2 KJV)

The record says that Jesus did not eat at all during these forty days, but it does not say that He did not drink. Also, it says, *"He afterward hungered,"* but it does not say that He was thirsty. The probable inference is, therefore, that He abstained from food, but not from water. During this period of forty days, Jesus came into direct spiritual conflict with Satan.

There is a significant difference in the expressions used by Luke to describe Jesus before and after His fast. At the beginning, in Luke 4:1, we read: *"And Jesus being full of the Holy [Spirit] returned from Jordan."* At the end, in Luke 4:14, we read: *"And Jesus returned in the power of the Spirit into Galilee"* (KJV).

When Jesus went into the wilderness, He was already *"full of the Holy Spirit."* But when He came out again after fasting, He *"returned in the power of the Spirit."* It would appear that the potential of the Holy Spirit's power, which Jesus received at the time of His baptism in Jordan, only came forth into full manifestation after He had completed His fast. Fasting was the final phase of preparation through which He had to pass, before entering into His public ministry.

The same spiritual laws that applied in Christ's own ministry apply also in the ministry of His disciples. In John 14:12, Jesus said, *"He that believeth on me, the works that I do shall he do also"* (KJV). By these words, Jesus opened the way for His disciples to follow in the pattern of His own ministry. However, in John 13:16, Jesus also said, *"The servant is not greater than his lord; neither he that is sent greater than he that sent him"* (KJV). This applies to the preparation for ministry. If fasting was a necessary part of Christ's own preparation, it must play a part also in the disciple's preparation.

THE PRACTICE OF THE EARLY CHURCH

In this respect, Paul was a true disciple of Jesus. Fasting played a vital part in his ministry. Immediately after his first encounter with Christ on the Damascus road, Paul spent the next three days without food or drink (Acts 9:9). Thereafter, fasting was a regular part of his spiritual discipline. In 2 Corinthians 6:3–10, Paul listed various ways in which he had proved himself a true minister of God. In verse 5, two of the ways that he listed are: *"in watchings, in fastings"* (KJV). *Watching* signifies going without sleep; *fasting* signifies going without food. Both were practiced at times by Paul to make his ministry fully effective.

In 2 Corinthians 11:23–27, Paul returned to this theme. Speaking of other men who set themselves up as his rivals in the ministry, Paul said, *"Are they ministers of Christ?...I am more"* (v. 23 KJV). He then gives another long list of ways in which he had proved himself a true minister of Christ. In verse 27, he said, *"In weariness and painfulness, in watchings often, in hunger and thirst, in fastings often"* (KJV). Here again, Paul joined watching with fasting. The plural form, *"in fastings often,"* indicates that Paul devoted himself to frequent periods of fasting. *"Hunger and thirst"* refers to occasions when neither food nor drink was available. *"Fastings"* refers to occasions when food was available, but Paul deliberately abstained for spiritual reasons.

The New Testament Christians not only practiced fasting individually, as a part of their personal discipline, but also practiced it collectively, as a part of their corporate ministry to God. This is attested to by Luke's account in Acts:

> *Now there were in the church that was at Antioch certain prophets and teachers; as Barnabas, and Simeon that was called Niger, and Lucius of Cyrene, and Manaen, which had been brought up with Herod the tetrarch, and Saul. As they ministered to the Lord, and fasted, the Holy [Spirit] said, Separate me Barnabas and Saul for the work whereunto I have called them. And when they had fasted and prayed, and laid their hands on them, they sent them away.* (Acts 13:1–3 KJV)

In this local congregation in the city of Antioch, five leading ministers—designated as prophets and teachers—were praying and fasting together. This is described as ministering to the Lord. The majority of Christian leaders or congregations today know very little of this aspect of ministry. Yet, in the divine order, ministry to the Lord comes before ministry to men. Out of the ministry to the Lord, the Holy Spirit brings forth the direction and the power needed for effective ministry to men.

So it was at Antioch. As these five leaders prayed and fasted together, the Holy Spirit revealed that He had a special task for two of them—Barnabas and Saul (later called Paul). He said, *"Separate me Barnabas and Saul for the work whereunto I have called them."* In this way, these two men were called out for a special task.

However, they were not yet ready to undertake the task. They still required the impartation of the special grace and power that were needed for the task that lay ahead. For this purpose, all five men fasted and prayed together the second time. Then, after the second period of fasting, the other leaders laid their hands on Barnabas and Paul, and sent them forth to fulfill their task.

Thus, it was through collective prayer and fasting that Barnabas and Paul received, first, the revelation of a special task, and second, the grace and power needed to fulfill that task. At the time they all prayed and fasted together, Barnabas and Paul—like the other three men—were recognized as prophets and teachers. But after being sent forth to their task, they were described as apostles. (See Acts 14:4, 14.) We may therefore say that the apostolic ministry of Barnabas and Paul was born out of collective prayer and fasting by five leaders of the church at Antioch.

In due course, this practice of collective prayer and fasting was transmitted by Barnabas and Paul to the congregations of new disciples that were established in various cities as a result of their ministry. The actual establishment of each congregation was accomplished through the appointment of their own local elders. This is described in Acts:

And...they returned again to Lystra, and to Iconium, and Antioch, confirming the souls of the disciples, and exhorting

them to continue in the faith....And when they had or-
dained them elders in every church, and had prayed with
fasting, they commended them to the Lord, on whom they
believed. (Acts 14:21–23 KJV)

In Acts 14:22, these groups of believers in each city are referred to merely as *"disciples."* But in the next verse, the writer
referred to them as *"church*[es].*"* The transition from
"disciples" to *"church*[es]*"* was accomplished by the appointment of the local leaders for each congregation, who were designated as *"elders."* In each case, when elders were appointed,
"they...prayed with fasting." It is therefore fair to say that the
establishment of a local church in each city was accompanied by
collective prayer and fasting.

Taken together, chapters 13 and 14 of the book of Acts indicate that collective prayer and fasting played a vital role in the
growth and development of the New Testament church. It was
through praying and fasting together that the early Christians
received direction and power from the Holy Spirit for decisions
or tasks of special importance. In the examples that we have
considered, these were: first, the appointment and sending forth
of apostles; second, the appointment of elders and the establishment of local churches.

HOW FASTING WORKS

There are various ways in which fasting helps a Christian to
receive direction and power from the Holy Spirit. In one sense,
fasting is a form of mourning. Psychologically, no one welcomes
the thought of mourning, just as, physically, no one welcomes the
thought of fasting. Nevertheless, there are times when both
mourning and fasting are beneficial. Mourning has its place
among the Beatitudes. In Matthew 5:4, Jesus said, *"Blessed are*
they that mourn: for they shall be comforted" (KJV). In Isaiah 61:3,
the Lord promised special blessings to those who *"mourn in*
Zion." He promised them *"beauty for ashes, the oil of joy for*
mourning, the garment of praise for the spirit of heaviness" (KJV).

Mourning in Zion is neither the self-centered remorse nor
the hopeless grief of the unbeliever. Rather, it is a response to

the prompting of the Holy Spirit through which the believer shares in a small measure God's own grief over the sin and folly of humanity. When we consider our own failures and short-comings as Christians, and when we look beyond ourselves at the misery and wickedness of the world, there is indeed cause for this kind of mourning. In 2 Corinthians 7:10, Paul contrasted the godly sorrow of the believer with the hopeless sorrow of the unbeliever: *"For godly sorrow worketh repentance to salvation not to be repented of: but the sorrow of the world worketh death"* (KJV). Godly mourning of this kind is followed in due season by the *"oil of joy"* and the *"garment of praise."*

Under the old covenant, God ordained for Israel one special day in each year in which they were to afflict their souls. This was the Day of Atonement. In Leviticus 16:31, the Lord instructed Israel concerning this day: *"It shall be a sabbath of rest unto you, and ye shall afflict your souls, by a statute for ever"* (KJV). From the time of Moses onward, the Jews have interpreted this as a command to fast. In Acts 27:9, it is this annual Day of Atonement that is referred to as *"the fast"* (KJV).

Nineteen centuries later, under its Hebrew name *Yom Kippur*, the Day of Atonement is still observed by Orthodox Jews all over the world as a day of fasting.

In two of his psalms, David also spoke of fasting in this way. In Psalm 35:13, he said, *"I humbled my soul with fasting"* (KJV). The word here translated *"humble"* is the same that is translated *"afflict"* in Leviticus 16, the chapter on the Day of Atonement. Again, in Psalm 69:10, David said, *"I wept, and chastened my soul with fasting"* (KJV). We may combine the various expressions used and say that fasting, as here practiced, is a form of mourning and a means to humble oneself and to chasten oneself.

Fasting is also a means by which a believer brings his body into subjection. In 1 Corinthians 9:27, Paul said, *"But I keep under my body, and bring it into subjection: lest that by any means, when I have preached to others, I myself should be a castaway"* (KJV). Our bodies, with their physical organs and appetites, make wonderful servants, but terrible masters. Therefore, it is necessary to keep them always in subjection. I once heard this well expressed by a fellow minister who said, "My stomach does not tell me when to eat, but I tell my stomach when to eat." Each time a

Christian practices fasting for this purpose, he is serving notice on his body: "You are the servant, not the master."

In Galatians 5:17, Paul laid bare the direct opposition that exists between the Holy Spirit of God and the carnal nature of man: *"For the flesh lusteth against the Spirit, and the Spirit against the flesh: and these are contrary the one to the other"* (KJV). Fasting deals with the two great barriers to the Holy Spirit that are erected by man's carnal nature. These are the stubborn self-will of the soul and the insistent, self-gratifying appetites of the body. Rightly practiced, fasting brings both soul and body into subjection to the Holy Spirit.

It is important to understand that fasting changes man, not God. The Holy Spirit, being God, is both omnipotent and unchanging. Fasting breaks down the barriers in man's carnal nature that stand in the way of the Holy Spirit's omnipotence. With these barriers removed, the Holy Spirit can work unhindered in His fullness through our prayers.

In Ephesians 3:20, Paul sought to express the inexhaustible potential of prayer: *"Now unto him that is able to do exceeding abundantly above all that we ask or think, according to the power that worketh in us"* (KJV). The *"power"* that works in and through our prayers is the Holy Spirit. By removing the carnal barriers, fasting makes a way for the Holy Spirit's omnipotence to work the *"exceeding abundantly above"* of God's promises.

There is indeed only one limit to God's omnipotence, and that is God's eternal righteousness. Fasting will never change the righteous standards of God. If something is outside the will of God, fasting will never put it inside the will of God. If it is wrong and sinful, it is still wrong and sinful, no matter how long a person may fast.

An example of this is in 2 Samuel chapter 12. David had committed adultery. Out of this, a child was born. God said that part of the judgment was that the child would die. David fasted seven days, but the child still died. Fasting seven days did not change God's righteous judgment on David's sinful act. If a thing is wrong, fasting will not make it right. Nothing will do that.

Fasting is neither a gimmick nor a cure-all. God does not deal in such things. God has made full provision for the total well-being of His people in every area of their lives—spiritual, physical, and material. Fasting is one part of this total provision. Fasting is not a substitute for any other part of God's provision. Conversely, no other part of God's provision is a substitute for fasting.

In Colossians 4:12, we read that Epaphras prayed for his fellow believers that they might *"stand perfect and complete in all the will of God"* (KJV). This sets a very high standard for all of us. One scriptural means provided for us to attain to this standard is fasting.

We may illustrate the relationship between fasting and the will of God by a simple diagram:

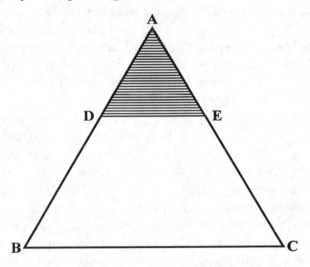

The whole triangle *ABC* represents the complete will of God for every believer. The truncated cone *DBCE* represents the area of God's will that may be appropriated by prayer without fasting. The smaller shaded triangle *ADE* represents the area of God's will that can be appropriated only by prayer and fasting combined.

If an objective is outside the area *ABC*, it is altogether outside God's will. There is no scriptural means by which we may obtain it. If an objective is in the area *DBCE*, we may obtain it by prayer without fasting. If an objective is in the area *ADE*, we may obtain it only by prayer and fasting combined.

Many of God's choicest provisions for His people lie within that top shaded triangle *ADE*.

CHAPTER SEVEN

FASTING BRINGS DELIVERANCE
AND VICTORY

I f we turn to the historical records of the Old Testament, we find a number of occasions where collective fasting and prayer brought forth dramatic and powerful intervention by God. We will examine four such occasions.

JEHOSHAPHAT CONQUERS WITHOUT FIGHTING

Our first example is found in 2 Chronicles 20:1–30. Jehoshaphat, king of Judah, received word that a very large army from the territories of Moab, Ammon, and Mount Seir was invading his kingdom from the east. Realizing that he had no military resources with which to meet this challenge, Jehoshaphat turned to God for help. His first decisive act is described in verse 3: *"Jehoshaphat...proclaimed a fast throughout all Judah"* (KJV). In this way, God's people were called to unite in public, collective fasting and prayer for divine intervention. Verse 13 indicates that men, women, and children were all included.

From the initial call to fasting, events followed in swift succession, leading up to a dramatic climax. The first result is recorded in verse 4: *"And Judah gathered themselves together, to ask help of the LORD: even out of all the cities of Judah they came to seek the LORD"* (KJV). Common danger had the effect of bringing all God's people together. The same emergency that threatened one community or one city threatened all alike. No doubt there were jealousies or rivalries between some of the represented cities. But in the face of the enemy invasion, these were set aside. God's people were called upon to protect their common inheritance rather than to promote their individual differences.

With the people of Judah thus assembled in one accord, Jehoshaphat led them in a prayer, reminding God of His covenant with Abraham and of His promises of mercy based on that covenant. Jehoshaphat's prayer received an immediate, supernatural response from God, which is described in verses 14 through 17. Through one of the Levites present, named Jahaziel, the Holy Spirit gave forth a powerful prophetic utterance, combining encouragement, assurance, and direction.

Jahaziel's prophetic utterance was received in turn with spontaneous worship and praise by Jehoshaphat and all the people. Thereafter, Jehoshaphat made provision for continuing, organized praise as he led his people forth to battle:

> *And Jehoshaphat bowed his head with his face to the ground: and all Judah and the inhabitants of Jerusalem fell before the LORD, worshipping the LORD. And the Levites...stood up to praise the LORD God of Israel with a loud voice on high....And when he [Jehoshaphat] had consulted with the people, he appointed singers unto the LORD, and that should praise the beauty of holiness, as they went out before the army, and to say, Praise the LORD; for his mercy endureth for ever.* (2 Chron. 20:18–19, 21 KJV)

The outcome is described in verses 22 through 30. There was no need for God's people to use any kind of military weapon. The entire army of their enemies destroyed themselves, leaving not a single survivor. All that God's people needed to do was to spend three days gathering the spoils and then to return in triumph to Jerusalem, with their voices raised in loud thanksgiving and praise to God. Furthermore, the impact of this tremendous, supernatural victory was felt by all the surrounding nations. From then on, no other nation dared to contemplate hostilities against Jehoshaphat and his people.

Three practical lessons can be learned from Jehoshaphat's victory. All three apply with equal force to Christians in this age.

396

First of all, the anti-Christian forces that are at work in the world today are just as hostile and just as formidable as the army that threatened Judah in the days of Jehoshaphat. These forces are united in hatred and opposition toward all who truly love and serve the Lord Jesus Christ. They are not concerned about internal denominational distinctions among Christians. They are not disposed to spare the Baptists at the expense of the Methodists, nor the Catholics at the expense of the Pentecostals. Therefore, this is no time for Christians to emphasize sectarian or denominational issues that have in the past divided us. Rather, it is time for all God's people to follow the example of Judah and to unite in fasting and prayer.

Second, the story of Jehoshaphat demonstrates the need for spiritual gifts. It was the gift of prophecy that gave both encouragement and direction to Judah in their hour of crisis. The supernatural gifts of the Holy Spirit are still needed just as much by the church today. Nor does the Bible suggest that God ever intended to withdraw these gifts from the church.

In 1 Corinthians 1:7–8, Paul thanked God on behalf of the Corinthian believers, saying, *"So that you are not lacking in any spiritual gift, as you wait for the revealing of our Lord Jesus Christ; who will sustain you to the end, guiltless in the day of our Lord Jesus Christ"* (RSV). Clearly, Paul both expected and desired that the spiritual gifts would continue to operate in the church right up to the return of Christ and the end of the age.

Likewise, in the book of Acts, Peter quoted the prophecy of Joel and applied it to our present age:

> *And it shall come to pass in the last days, saith God, I will pour out of my Spirit upon all flesh: and your sons and your daughters shall prophesy, and your young men shall see visions, and your old men shall dream dreams: and on my servants and on my handmaidens I will pour out in those days of my Spirit; and they shall prophesy.*
>
> *(Acts 2:17–18 KJV)*

These words of Joel, quoted by Peter, confirm those of Paul in 1 Corinthians. There is no suggestion that the supernatural gifts of the Holy Spirit are to be withdrawn from the church, but rather that they are to be more and more manifested, the nearer we come to the end of the age.

The third lesson to be learned from the story of Jehoshaphat is the supremacy of spiritual power over carnal power. In 2 Corinthians 10:4, Paul said, *"For the weapons of our warfare are not carnal, but mighty through God"* (KJV). There are two kinds of weapons: spiritual and carnal. Jehoshaphat's enemies relied on carnal weapons; Jehoshaphat and his people used only spiritual weapons. The outcome of the conflict demonstrates the absolute supremacy of the spiritual over the carnal.

What exactly were the spiritual weapons that Jehoshaphat used to such effect? They may be briefly summarized as follows: first, collective fasting; second, united prayer; third, the supernatural gifts of the Holy Spirit; fourth, public worship and praise. These weapons, scripturally employed by Christians in this present day, will gain victories as powerful and dramatic as they gained for the people of Judah in the days of Jehoshaphat.

EZRA OBTAINS SAFE CONDUCT BY GOD'S POWER

For our second example of collective fasting and prayer, we will turn to Ezra:

Then I [Ezra] proclaimed a fast there, at the river of Ahava, that we might afflict ourselves before our God, to seek of him a right way for us, and for our little ones, and for all our substance. For I was ashamed to require of the king a band of soldiers and horsemen to help us against the enemy in the way: because we had spoken unto the king, saying, The hand of our God is upon all them for good that seek him....So we fasted and besought our God for this: and he was entreated of us. (Ezra 8:21–23 KJV)

Ezra did something that you and I sometimes do. By testifying to the king, he put himself in a position where he had to live up to his own testimony. He had told the king: "We are the servants of the living God. Our God protects us and supplies all our needs." A little later, the way opened for Ezra to lead a company of returning exiles back to Jerusalem. They had to make a long journey through country infested by savage tribes and by bandits. In addition to their wives and children, they had with them the sacred vessels of the temple, worth hundreds of thousands of dollars. What a prey for bandits!

The question arose: How were they to be protected on their way from Babylon to Jerusalem? Should Ezra go to the king and ask him for an escort of soldiers and horsemen? No doubt the king would have granted this request, but Ezra felt ashamed to make it because he had already testified to the king that their God, the true and living God, would protect those who served Him.

At this point, Ezra and the returning exiles made a vital decision: they would not rely on soldiers and horsemen for their protection, but on the supernatural power of God. There would not have been anything morally wrong in accepting an escort from the king, but it would have been depending on carnal means. Instead, by collective prayer and fasting, they committed themselves to seeking their help and protection solely from the spiritual realm of God's power.

Ezra followed the same procedure as Jehoshaphat. As the leader of God's people, he *"proclaimed a fast."* The reason he gave for this was *"that we might afflict ourselves before our God, to seek of him a right way for us, and for our little ones, and for all our substance."* In chapter 6 of this book, we saw (both from the psalms of David and from the ordinances of the Day of Atonement) that fasting was recognized by the Jews, and approved by God, as a means whereby God's people might humble themselves before Him and acknowledge their total dependence upon Him. Ezra concluded by saying: *"So we fasted and besought our God for this: and he was entreated of us."*

The result of collective fasting and prayer for Ezra and his company was as decisive as it had been for Jehoshaphat and the people of Judah. The returning band of exiles completed their long and dangerous journey in perfect peace and safety. There was no opposition by bandits or savage tribes, no loss of persons or of property. Thus, the lesson demonstrated by Jehoshaphat was further confirmed by Ezra: Victory in the spiritual realm is primary. It is to be obtained by the employment of spiritual weapons. Thereafter, its outcome will be manifested in every area of the natural and material realm.

ESTHER TRANSFORMS DISASTER INTO TRIUMPH

Our third example of collective fasting and prayer is found in the fourth chapter of the book of Esther. Here is described the greatest crisis that has ever confronted the Jewish people in their entire history up to the present time—greater even than the crisis under Adolph Hitler. Hitler had only one-third of all the Jews at his mercy. The Persian emperor had the entire Jewish nation. A decree went out that they were all to be annihilated on a certain day. The name of the man who was Satan's advocate against the Jews was Haman.

This story has given rise to the feast that the Jews call *Purim*. *Purim* means "lots." The feast is so called because Haman cast lots to determine the day that should be appointed for the destruction of the Jews. In this case, casting lots was a form of divination. Haman was seeking guidance from occult powers. He relied on unseen spiritual forces to direct him in exterminating the Jews. This placed the whole conflict on the spiritual plane. It was not just flesh against flesh; it was spirit against spirit. Through Haman, Satan was actually challenging the power of God Himself. Had he succeeded in the destruction of the Jews, it would have been an everlasting reproach to the name of the Lord.

But when the decree for the destruction of the Jews went out, Esther and her maidens accepted the challenge. They understood that the conflict was on the spiritual plane, and their response was on the same plane. They agreed to fast three days, night and day, neither eating nor drinking. They arranged with Mordecai that he would gather together all the Jews in Shushan, the capital city, to unite with them in fasting for the same period. (Notice in Esther 4:16 that once again, in the hour of crisis, we find God's people *"gather*[ed] *together"* (KJV), just as in the days of Jehoshaphat.) Thus, all the Jews in Shushan, together with Esther and her maidens, fasted and prayed three days—seventy-two hours—without eating or drinking.

The outcome of their collective fasting and prayer is described in the succeeding chapters of the book of Esther. We may summarize it briefly by saying that the whole policy of the Persian empire was completely changed, in favor of the Jews.

Haman and his sons perished. The enemies of the Jews throughout the Persian empire suffered total defeat. Mordecai and Esther became the two most influential personalities in Persian politics. The Jews in every area experienced a unique measure of favor, peace, and prosperity. All this can be directly attributed to one cause: the collective fasting and prayer of God's people.

NINEVEH SPARED; SAMARIA DESTROYED

We have taken our first three examples of collective fasting and prayer from the history of Israel. For our fourth and final example, we will turn to a gentile nation. The book of Jonah records God's dealings with the city of Nineveh, the capital of Assyria, at that time the most powerful empire in the ancient world. The Bible pictures Nineveh as a cruel, violent, idolatrous city, ripe for divine judgment. God called Jonah to go and warn Nineveh that judgment was about to fall.

Jonah refused to go at first. He was a citizen of the northern kingdom of Israel. He knew that the Assyrian empire was at that time the national enemy of his own people. Judgment upon Nineveh would relieve the Assyrian threat to Israel. Conversely, mercy toward Nineveh would increase the danger to Israel. Therefore, Jonah was reluctant to carry any message to Nineveh that might avert God's impending judgment upon that city.

However, at the second call, after undergoing the severe discipline of God, Jonah went to Nineveh. His message was very simple: *"Yet forty days, and Nineveh shall be overthrown"* (Jonah 3:4 KJV). The response of the people of Nineveh was immediate and dramatic. It is described in the next five verses:

So the people of Nineveh believed God, and proclaimed a fast, and put on sackcloth, from the greatest of them even to the least of them. For word came unto the king of Nineveh, and he arose from his throne, and he laid his robe from him, and covered him with sackcloth, and sat in ashes. And he caused it to be proclaimed and published through Nineveh by the decree of the king and his nobles, saying, Let neither man nor beast, herd nor flock, taste any thing: let them not feed, nor drink water: but let man and beast be covered with sackcloth, and cry mightily unto God: yea, let them turn every one from his evil way, and from the violence that is in their hands. Who can tell if God will turn and repent, and turn away from his fierce anger, that we perish not? (vv. 5–9 KJV)

There is no other instance in Old Testament history of such profound and universal repentance upon the part of a whole community. All normal activities came to a standstill. The king and the nobles proclaimed a fast, and they themselves set the example. They were followed not merely by all the human inhabitants of Nineveh, but even by the herds and the flocks. The entire city cast itself upon the mercy of God. Words could not paint a more vivid picture. Universal, public fasting became the most complete and appropriate expression of deep inner mourning and self-humbling.

The response of God to Nineveh's fasting is described in the last verse of the chapter: *"And God saw their works, that they turned from their evil way; and God repented of the evil, that he had said that he would do unto them; and he did it not"* (v. 10 KJV). History records that Nineveh, thus spared at the eleventh hour, continued as a more or less stable and prosperous city for about one hundred fifty years and was finally destroyed in 612 B.C., as predicted by the later prophets Nahum and Zephaniah.

PRINCIPLES THAT APPLY TODAY

God's dealings with Nineveh through Jonah illustrate a principle that is more fully unfolded through the prophet Jeremiah. In the book of Jeremiah, the Lord said,

At what instant I shall speak concerning a nation, and concerning a kingdom, to pluck up, and to pull down, and to destroy it; if that nation, against whom I have pronounced, turn from their evil, I will repent of the evil that I thought to do unto them. And at what instant I shall speak concerning a nation, and concerning a kingdom, to build and to plant it; if it do evil in my sight, that it obey not my

*voice, then I will repent of the good, wherewith I said I
would benefit them.*   *(Jer. 18:7–10 KJV)*

In God's dealings with nations, His promises of blessing and
His warnings of judgment are both alike: they are conditional.
Judgment may be averted—even at the eleventh hour—by re-
pentance. Conversely, blessing may be forfeited by disobedience.

By contrasting the destiny of Assyria with that of the
northern kingdom of Israel, we may discern principles of God's
dealings with nations that still apply today.

In the eighth century B.C., the gentile city of Nineveh received one warning of judgment from one prophet—Jonah. The
whole population responded with universal repentance. During
the same period, the northern kingdom of Israel heard the repeated warnings of God not only from Jonah, but from at least
four other prophets: Amos, Hosea, Isaiah, and Micah. Yet they
rejected these prophets and refused to repent.

What was the outcome? The Assyrian empire, of which
Nineveh was the capital, became the instrument of God's judgment upon Israel. In 721 B.C., the kings of Assyria captured and
destroyed Samaria, the capital of Israel, and carried away the
entire northern kingdom into captivity.

The tragic end of the northern kingdom seems to support
the saying, "Familiarity breeds contempt." Israel, with her long
history of special revelation from God, heard many prophets and
rejected them. Nineveh, without any previous revelation from
God, heard one prophet and received him. This lesson from history contains a special warning to those of us who live in lands
with long histories of Christian influence and teaching. Let us
beware that we do not allow our familiarity with the message to
keep us from acknowledging its urgency!

Today, God is speaking once again through His messengers
and by His Spirit to cities and to nations. He is calling to repentance, to fasting, to self-humbling. Those who obey will receive
the visitation of His mercy, as Nineveh did. Those who reject
will receive the visitation of His wrath, as Israel did.

CHAPTER EIGHT

FASTING PREPARES FOR GOD'S LATTER RAIN

All through the Bible, there is a delicate balance between the fulfillment of God's predetermined purposes and the exercise of human free will. On the one hand, the eternal counsels of God, revealed in the prophecies and promises of His Word, are sure of ultimate fulfillment. On the other hand, there are occasions in which God requires the exercise of human faith and human will as an indispensable condition for the fulfillment of His counsels. To understand this balance, and to apply it in prayer, is the essence of true intercession.

THE PATTERN OF DANIEL'S INTERCESSION

An illuminating example of this is found in the intercessory ministry of Daniel. He said,

> *In the first year of his reign* [the reign of Darius] *I Daniel understood by books the number of the years, whereof the word of the LORD came to Jeremiah...that he would accomplish seventy years in the desolations of Jerusalem. And I set my face unto the Lord God, to seek by prayer and supplications, with fasting, and sackcloth, and ashes.*
>
> *(Dan. 9:2–3 KJV)*

Daniel was not only a prophet; he was also a student of prophecy. In the course of studying the prophecies of Jeremiah, he discovered the promise to which he here referred: *"For thus saith the LORD, that after seventy years be accomplished at Baby-lon I will visit you, and perform my good word toward you, in causing you to return to this place* [the land of Israel]" (Jer. 29:10 KJV). Daniel knew that the appointed period of seventy years had almost run its course. He therefore understood that the promised hour of deliverance and restoration was near at hand.

In chapter 4 of this book, we referred to the account of Daniel's prayer given in Daniel 6:10. It is evident from the passage that Daniel already made a practice of regular intercession, three times a day, for the restoration of Israel to their own land. Now the revelation from the prophecy of Jeremiah showed him that the time had come for God to answer his prayers. In studying Daniel's response to this revelation, we gain a vital lesson in the ministry of intercession. A carnally-minded person might have interpreted the promise from Jeremiah as a release from further obligations to pray. If God had promised to restore Israel at that time, what further need was there to pray?

Daniel's response was just the opposite. He did not interpret God's promise as a release from his obligation of intercession, but rather as a challenge to seek God with greater intensity and fervency than ever before. This renewed determination is beautifully expressed in his own words: *"I set my face unto the Lord God."* In the prayer life of each one of us, there comes a time when we have to set our faces. From that moment onward, no discouragement, no distraction, no opposition will be allowed to hold us back, until we have obtained the full assurance of an answer to which God's Word gives us title.

At this point of seeking God with great intensity, Daniel understood that his prayers needed to be undergirded by fasting. He said, *"I set my face...to seek by prayer and supplications, with fasting, and sackcloth, and ashes."* Sackcloth and ashes were the accepted outward evidence of mourning. We see once again how closely fasting is associated with mourning.

As we go on to study the actual prayer of Daniel recorded in the succeeding verses, we see how fasting and mourning were in turn associated with self-humbling. By all human standards, Daniel was one of the most righteous and God-fearing men portrayed in Scripture, yet at no time did he represent himself as more righteous than those for whom he was interceding. He invariably identified himself with his own people in all their re-bellion and backsliding. His cry was, *"We have sinned, and have committed iniquity....O Lord, righteousness belongeth unto thee, but unto us confusion of faces"* (vv. 5, 7 KJV). Always, it was we and us, never they and them. All through to the end of his prayer, Daniel took his place as one of those justly subject to the righteous judgments of God that had come upon his people.

Thus, Daniel's prayer was made effective by his own personal involvement. This is expressed in three ways that are closely related: by fasting, by mourning, and by self-humbling.

In 2 Chronicles, God stated the conditions that His people must fulfill for the healing of their land:

> *If my people, which are called by my name, shall humble themselves, and pray, and seek my face, and turn from their wicked ways; then will I hear from heaven, and will forgive their sin, and will heal their land.*
>
> *(2 Chron. 7:14 KJV)*

God's requirements are fourfold: that His people humble themselves, pray, seek His face, and turn from their wicked ways. Upon meeting these conditions, God promises to hear the prayer of His people and heal their land.

In the example of Daniel now before us, we learn exactly what is meant by each of these requirements. Daniel humbled himself; he prayed; he set himself to seek God's face; and identifying himself with his people's sins, he renounced and turned from those sins. In turn, the outcome proves the faithfulness of God to fulfill His promise whenever His conditions are met, for it was through Daniel's intercession that restoration came to Israel and healing to their land.

Of all the great characters in the Bible, Daniel exemplifies perhaps more clearly than any other the ministry that is the theme of this book: shaping history through prayer and fasting. When Daniel first came to Babylon as a young man, it was his prayers (combined with his gift of revelation) that changed the heart of King Nebuchadnezzar, procuring favor and promotion for the Jews in Babylon. Later, near the end of Daniel's life, when the Babylonian empire had been succeeded by that of

Medo-Persia, it was the prayer and fasting of Daniel that finally opened the way for the restoration of Israel to their own land. Over a period of nearly seventy years, the main successive changes in the destiny of God's people can be traced to the prayers of Daniel.

From this study of Daniel's intercession, there emerges one lesson of special importance for our theme. The prophecies and the promises of God's Word are never an excuse to cease praying. On the contrary, they are intended to provoke us to pray with increased earnestness and understanding. God reveals to us the purposes that He is working out, not that we may be passive spectators on the sidelines of history, but that we may personally identify ourselves with His purposes, and thus become actively involved in their fulfillment. Revelation demands involvement.

JOEL'S THRICE-UTTERED CALL

This lesson applies particularly to the latter-day outpouring of the Holy Spirit that is now making an ever increasing impact in every area of Christendom and in every part of the world. The great prophet of this outpouring is Joel. It is in Joel's prophecy that God reveals His sovereign purpose to send a visitation of His Spirit upon the whole human race:

> And it shall come to pass afterward, that I will pour out my spirit upon all flesh; and your sons and your daughters shall prophesy, your old men shall dream dreams, your young men shall see visions. (Joel 2:28 KJV)

On the Day of Pentecost, when the Holy Spirit was first poured out, this verse of Joel was quoted by Peter:

> But this is that which was spoken by the prophet Joel; And it shall come to pass in the last days, saith God, I will pour out of my Spirit upon all flesh: and your sons and your daughters shall prophesy, and your young men shall see visions, and your old men shall dream dreams.
> (Acts 2:16–17 KJV)

Between the passage in Joel and that in Acts, there is one significant difference. Where Joel said, *"It shall come to pass afterward,"* Peter said, *"It shall come to pass in the last days."* Peter applied these words to events that were then taking place. We may thus infer that the Day of Pentecost marked the beginning of the period defined in Scripture as *"the last days."* This period of the last days still continues, and will do so until the present age closes. Thus, Peter's words give us a scriptural starting point for the last days.

In this connection, it is important also to note that the outpouring of the Holy Spirit predicted by Joel was to be divided into two main phases: *"the former rain"* and *"the latter rain."* This is stated in Joel 2:23: *"He* [God] *will cause to come down for you the rain, the former rain, and the latter rain in the first month"* (KJV). The rain is the type of which the outpoured Holy Spirit is the antitype. In the actual climatic pattern of Israel, the former rain falls at the beginning of winter (about November), and the latter rain falls at the end of winter (about March or April). Thus, the latter rain more or less coincides with the Passover, which, according to the Jewish religious calendar, occurs in the middle of *"the first month"* (Exod. 12:1–12).

By transferring this from type to antitype, we arrive at a logical inference: the former rain of the Holy Spirit marks the beginning of the last days, while the latter rain of the Holy Spirit marks the close of the last days. God both begins and ends His dealings with the church on earth by a universal outpouring of His Holy Spirit. The first rain of the Holy Spirit fell on the early church. The latter rain of the Holy Spirit is now falling on the church worldwide in our days. Such is the implication of Peter's phrase, *"the last days."*

Now let us turn back to the original version of the prophecy, as given in Joel 2:28: *"And it shall come to pass afterward, that I will pour out my spirit upon all flesh."* Where Peter said, *"in the last days,"* Joel said, *"afterward."* In order to understand the total message of Joel, we must rightly interpret this word *"afterward."* What did Joel mean by it? After what? Obviously, he referred to something that he had said earlier in his prophecy.

If we turn back to the beginning of Joel's prophecy, we are confronted with a scene of unrelieved and total desolation.

Every part of the inheritance of God's people is affected. All is blighted; nothing is fruitful. There is no ray of hope, no human solution. What does God tell His people to do? The remedy that God prescribed was united fasting: *"Sanctify ye a fast, call a solemn assembly, gather the elders and all the inhabitants of the land into the house of the LORD your God, and cry unto the LORD"* (Joel 1:14 KJV).

To *"sanctify"* here means "to set apart." God's call to fasting must have absolute preeminence. Every other activity, religious or secular, must take second place. There is particular emphasis upon the elders. The leaders of God's people have a special responsibility in this respect. However, all the inhabitants of the land are included. There must be no exceptions. God's people are required to unite in facing their need. They are called to gather together in fasting, just as they did in the days of Jehoshaphat, of Ezra, and of Esther.

In Joel 2:12, the call is repeated: *"Therefore also now, saith the LORD, turn ye even to me with all your heart, and with fasting, and with weeping, and with mourning"* (KJV). In hours of crisis such as this, prayer alone will not suffice. Prayer must be accompanied by fasting, weeping, and mourning. (We notice again the very close connections between fasting and mourning.)

In Joel 2:15, the call to fasting comes the third time: *"Blow the trumpet in Zion, sanctify a fast, call a solemn assembly"* (KJV). Zion is the assembly of God's people. Blowing the trumpet is the most public form of proclamation that is possible. There is nothing private or secret about a fast that is proclaimed in this way. The Bible makes it plain that there are times when fasting is to be publicly proclaimed for all of God's people.

The passage continues:

> *Gather the people, sanctify the congregation, assemble the elders, gather the children, and those that suck the breasts....Let the priests, the ministers of the LORD, weep between the porch and the altar.* (Joel 2:16–17 KJV)

Once again, although all the people are involved, there is special emphasis upon the leadership: the priests, the ministers, and the elders. In chapter 6 of this book, we saw that the responsibility of leaders to set the example in fasting is carried over into the New Testament church.

Three times in these verses of Joel, God called His people to fasting. Then there follows the promise: *"Afterward...I will pour out my spirit upon all flesh"* (v. 28 KJV). After what? After God's people have obeyed His call to fasting and prayer. Today, God's Spirit is being poured out in a measure. There is ample evidence that the time has come for God's *"latter rain."* But as yet, we see only a small fraction of the total outpouring that the Bible clearly predicts. God is waiting for us to meet His requirements. It will take united prayer and fasting to precipitate the final fullness of the latter rain.

In this respect, our position today is closely parallel to that of Daniel at the beginning of the reign of Darius. He saw God's hand moving in the political situation. He saw from the Scriptures that God's time had come for the restoration of His people. Prompted by this double witness, Daniel gave himself to prayer and fasting. Only in this way could God's promises be brought to their appointed fulfillment.

The central purpose of God in Daniel's day was restoration. God was moving to bring His people back into the inheritance that they had lost through disobedience. The same is true today. The outpouring of the Holy Spirit is God's appointed means of restoration. God declared this in Joel 2:25: *"I will restore to you the years that the locust hath eaten"* (KJV).

Three-and-a-half centuries ago, the church experienced reformation. Today, God is no longer concerned with reformation. His purpose is restoration. God is moving to restore every area of His people's inheritance to its original condition. The *"former rain"* brought into being a church that satisfied the divine standards of purity, power, and order. The *"latter rain"* will restore the church to the same standards. Then—and only then—will the church be able to fulfill its destiny in the world. This is the end toward which God is now working.

ISAIAH'S GREAT FASTING CHAPTER

It is appropriate to close our study of fasting in the Old Testament by turning to Isaiah chapter 58. This is the great fasting chapter of the Old Testament. Isaiah described two different ways of fasting. In verses 3 through 5, Isaiah described the kind of fast that is not acceptable to God. Then in verses 6 to 12, he described the kind of fast that is well pleasing to God.

The fault with the first kind of fasting lies mainly in the motives and the attitudes of those practicing it.

> Behold, in the day of your fast ye find pleasure, and exact all your labours [or things wherewith you grieve others]. Behold, ye fast for strife and debate, and to smite with the fist of wickedness....Is it such a fast that I have chosen? a day for a man...to bow down his head as a bulrush?
> (Isa. 58:3–5 KJV)

For the people here described, fasting was merely an accepted part of religious ritual. This was the kind of fasting practiced by the Pharisees in Jesus' day. There was no real repentance or self-humbling. On the contrary, they continued with all their normal secular affairs and retained all their evil attitudes of greed, selfishness, pride, and oppression. The "bow[ing] down [of the] head as a bulrush" is a very vivid description of certain forms of prayer still practiced by some orthodox Jews, in which they rock to and fro with their torsos, mechanically repeating set prayers of which they scarcely understand the meaning.

On the other hand, the kind of fast that is well pleasing to God springs from motives and attitudes that are totally different. In verse six, Isaiah defined the motives behind this kind of fasting: "To loose the bands of wickedness, to undo the heavy burdens, and to let the oppressed go free, and that ye break every yoke" (KJV). Scripture and experience alike confirm that there are many bands that cannot be loosed, many burdens that cannot be undone, many yokes that cannot be broken, and many oppressed who will never go free until God's people—and especially their leaders—obey God's call to fasting and prayer.

Isaiah continued by describing the attitudes toward other people—and especially toward the needy and the oppressed—that are part of the kind of fasting approved by God: "Is it not to deal thy bread to the hungry, and that thou bring the poor that are cast out to thy house? when thou seest the naked, that thou cover him; and that thou hide not thyself from thine own flesh?" (v. 7 KJV). Fasting of this kind must be united with sincere and practical charity in our dealings with those around us—particularly those who need our help in material and financial matters.

Isaiah once again warned against the wrong attitudes associated with the kind of fasting that is not acceptable to God, and contrasted these attitudes with true, practical charity:

> If thou take away from the midst of thee the yoke, the putting forth of the finger, and speaking vanity; and if thou draw out thy soul to the hungry, and satisfy the afflicted soul.   (vv. 9–10 KJV)

"The yoke, the putting forth of the finger, and speaking vanity" may be summed up in three words: legalism, criticism, and insincerity.

Now let us consider the blessings promised by God through Isaiah to those who practice the kind of fasting acceptable to Him. These blessings are listed in successive stages. First, Isaiah described those of health and righteousness:

> Then shall thy light break forth as the morning, and thine health shall spring forth speedily: and thy righteousness shall go before thee; the glory of the LORD shall be thy re-reward.   (v. 8 KJV)

This is in harmony with the promise of Malachi 4:2: "But unto you that fear my name shall the Sun of righteousness arise with healing in his wings" (KJV). The context in Malachi indicates a special application to the period just prior to the close of the present age.

In verse 9, Isaiah described the blessing of answered prayer: "Then shalt thou call, and the LORD shall answer; thou shalt cry, and he shall say, Here I am" (Isa. 58:9 KJV). Here is God at man's disposal, ready to answer every petition and to supply every need.

Next, Isaiah described the blessings of guidance and fruitfulness:

Then shall thy light rise in obscurity, and thy darkness be as the noon day: and the LORD shall guide thee continually, and satisfy thy soul in drought, and make fat thy bones: and thou shalt be like a watered garden, and like a spring of water, whose waters fail not.   (*vv. 10–11 KJV*)

Finally, Isaiah described the blessings of restoration:

And they that shall be of thee shall build the old waste places: thou shalt raise up the foundations of many generations; and thou shalt be called, The repairer of the breach, The restorer of paths to dwell in.   (*v. 12 KJV*)

Like Joel, Isaiah pointed to a close connection between fasting and the restoration of God's people. Isaiah closed his message on fasting with this theme: "building the old waste places, repairing the breach, restoring paths to dwell in." This work of restoration is the purpose of God for His people at this time. The divinely appointed means to accomplish it is prayer and fasting.

In the light of this clear and consistent message from the Word of God, each one of us is brought to a place of personal decision. In Ezekiel 22:30, God said, *"I sought for a man among them, that should make up the hedge, and stand in the gap before me for the land, that I should not destroy it"* (KJV). Again today, God is looking for a man like that. Will you offer yourself to God for this purpose? Will you give yourself to prayer and fasting? Will you join yourself in fellowship with others of like vision and determination, and with them unite in special periods of prayer and fasting?

Let us sanctify a fast! Let us call a solemn assembly! Let us gather together!

CHAPTER NINE

PRACTICAL GUIDELINES FOR FASTING

For many Christians today—if not for most—the prospect of fasting is unfamiliar and somewhat frightening. Often, after I have preached in a public meeting on fasting, people have come up to me with questions such as: "How do I start fasting?" "Are there any special dangers to guard against?" "Can't you give me some practical hints?"

FASTING IS SIMILAR TO PRAYER

Nearly all those who ask such questions are already familiar in some measure with the practice of prayer. Therefore, it is helpful to begin by pointing out some of the ways in which fasting is similar to prayer.

Every responsible Christian has to cultivate his personal prayer life on a regular basis. Most Christians find it practical to set aside a definite time each day for personal prayer. Quite frequently, this is a period in the early morning before the normal secular activities of the day begin. Others find it better to devote the close of the day to prayer. Some combine both morning and evening. For each believer, this is settled by personal convenience and by the individual leading of the Holy Spirit.

However, in addition to these regular periods of prayer, almost every Christian finds that there are times when the Holy Spirit calls to special seasons of prayer. These may be provoked by some urgent crisis or by some serious problem that has not been resolved by regular daily prayer. These special seasons of prayer are often more intense or more prolonged than the regular prayer period each day.

The same principles apply to fasting. Every Christian who decides to make fasting a part of his personal spiritual discipline would be wise to set aside one or more specific periods each week for this purpose. In this way, fasting becomes a part of regular spiritual discipline in just the same way as prayer. However, in addition to these regular weekly periods of fasting, it is likely that there will also be special occasions when the Holy Spirit calls to fasting that is more intensive and more prolonged.

It is remarkable how quickly the body will adjust itself to a pattern of regular fasting. From 1949 through 1956, I pastored a congregation in London, England. During these years, my wife and I normally observed Thursday as a day of fasting each week. We discovered that our stomachs became set to this day, in much the same way that an alarm clock is set to go off at a certain hour. When Thursday came, even if we happened to forget what day of the week it was, our stomachs would not make their normal demands for food. I remember Lydia saying to me on one occasion, "It must be Thursday. I have no appetite this morning!"

In the early days of the Methodist movement, there was strong emphasis upon regular fasting. John Wesley himself made this a part of his own personal discipline. He taught that the early church practiced fasting on Wednesday and Friday of each week, and he exhorted all Methodists of his day to do the same. In fact, he would not ordain to the Methodist ministry any man who would not undertake to fast until 4 P.M. each Wednesday and Friday.

Of course, in the case of both prayer and fasting, we need to guard against any form of legalistic bondage. In Galatians 5:18, Paul said, *"But if ye be led of the Spirit, ye are not under the law"* (KJV). For the Christian who is led by the Holy Spirit, neither prayer nor fasting should ever become a fixed, legal requirement such as was imposed on Israel under the Law of Moses. A Christian may therefore feel perfectly free at any time to change his patterns of prayer and of fasting, as circumstances may require or as the Holy Spirit may direct. He should never allow this to bring him under any sense of guilt or self-condem-nation.

In chapter 6 of this book, we saw that, in the Sermon on the Mount, Jesus used the same language about fasting that He used about prayer. He gave instructions for individual prayer: *"When thou* [singular] *prayest"* (Matt. 6:5 KJV). He also gave in-structions for collective prayer: *"When ye* [plural] *pray"* (v. 7 KJV). Likewise, He gave instructions for both individual and collective fasting. *"When thou* [singular] *fastest"* (v. 17 KJV) in-dicates the individual. *"When ye* [plural] *fast"* (v. 16 KJV) applies to the group meeting together.

Christians are familiar with the practice of coming together in a group for public prayer. In most churches, the prayer meeting is a part of the normal weekly routine. There is just as much scriptural precedent for coming together in a group for public fasting. In chapters 7 and 8 of this book, we examined a whole series of instances in the Old Testament where God called His people together for collective, public fasting. In chapter 6, we saw from the New Testament that in the early church also collective fasting was practiced by whole congregations, with the leaders setting the example.

People sometimes object that Jesus warned His disciples against fasting in public. They quote Matthew:

> But thou, when thou fastest, anoint thine head, and wash thy face; that thou appear not unto men to fast, but unto thy Father which is in secret: and thy Father, which seeth in se-cret, shall reward thee openly.   (Matt. 6:17–18 KJV)

We have already pointed out that Jesus is speaking here in the singular, to the individual. This is logical. An individual be-liever, who fasts by himself, has no need to make his fasting public.

However, in the preceding verse, Jesus spoke in the plural about collective fasting:

> Moreover when ye fast, be not, as the hypocrites, of a sad countenance: for they disfigure their faces, that they may appear unto men to fast. Verily I say unto you, They have their reward.   (v. 16 KJV)

In this verse, Jesus warned against unnecessary ostentation, but He did not require that fasting be done in secret. This is logical also. Obviously, people cannot come together for collective fasting unless it is arranged by some form of public announcement. This necessarily rules out secrecy.

Without a doubt, the Devil is behind this theory that Christians must only fast in secret. It deprives God's people of the most powerful weapon in their whole armory—that of united, public fasting. Those who speak against public fasting usually emphasize the need for humility. But in this context, so-called humility is really a polite religious name for unbelief or disobedience.

Having established these basic principles that apply both to prayer and to fasting, we may now turn more specifically to fasting. Over the years, on the basis of personal experience, I have arrived at a number of practical guidelines that are designed to produce the maximum benefit from fasting. These are set forth briefly here. For convenience, we will deal first with individual fasting and then with collective fasting.

GUIDELINES FOR INDIVIDUAL FASTING

1. Enter into fasting with positive faith. God requires faith of this kind in all who seek Him. *"But without faith it is impossible to please him: for he that cometh to God must believe that he is, and that he is a rewarder of them that diligently seek him"* (Heb. 11:6 KJV). If you determine to seek God diligently by fasting, you have a scriptural right to expect that God will reward you. In Matthew 6:18, Jesus gave this promise to the believer who fasts with the right motives: *"Thy Father, which seeth in secret, shall reward thee openly"* (KJV).

2. Remember: *"Faith cometh by hearing, and hearing by the word of God"* (Rom. 10:17 KJV). Your fasting should be based upon the conviction that God's Word enjoins this as a part of normal Christian discipline. Hopefully, the preceding three chapters will have helped you to arrive at this conviction.

3. Do not wait for some emergency to drive you to fasting. It is better to begin fasting when you are spiritually up, rather than when you are down. The law of progress in

God's kingdom is *"from strength to strength"* (Ps. 84:7); *"from faith to faith"* (Rom. 1:17); *"from glory to glory"* (2 Cor. 3:18).

4. In the beginning, do not set yourself too long a period of fasting. If you are fasting for the first time, omit one or two meals. Then move on gradually to longer periods, such as a day or two days. It is better to begin by setting a short period as your objective and achieving it. If you set too long a time at the outset and fail to meet it, you may become discouraged and give up.

5. During your fast, give plenty of time to Bible study. Where possible, read a portion of Scripture before each period of prayer. The Psalms are particularly helpful. Read them aloud, identifying yourself with the prayers, the praises, and the confessions contained in them.

6. It is often helpful to set certain specific objectives in your fasting and to make a written list of these. If you keep the lists that you make and turn back to them after an interval of time, your faith will be strengthened when you see how many of your objectives have been achieved.

7. Avoid religious ostentation and boastfulness. Apart from special periods of prayer or other spiritual activity, your life and conduct while fasting should be as normal and unpretentious as possible. This is the essence of the warnings given by Jesus in Matthew 6:16–18. Remember that boasting is excluded by *"the law of faith"* (Rom. 3:27). Fasting does not earn you any merit badges from God. It is part of your duty as a committed Christian. Bear in mind the warning of Jesus in Luke 17:10: *"So likewise ye, when ye shall have done all those things which are commanded you, say, We are unprofitable servants: we have done that which was our duty to do"* (KJV).

8. Each time you fast, keep a watchful check on your motives. Take time to read Isaiah 58:1–12 once again. Note the motives and attitudes that are unpleasing to God. Then study the motives and objectives that are pleasing to God. Your own motives and objectives should line up with these.

PHYSICAL ASPECTS OF FASTING

When practiced with due care and sense, fasting is beneficial to the physical body. Here are some points to observe, if you wish to obtain the physical benefits of fasting.

1. Remember that *"your body is the temple of the Holy* [Spirit]" (1 Cor. 6:19 KJV). It pleases God when you take proper care of your body, seeking to make it a clean and healthy temple for His Spirit. Health is one of the specific benefits promised by fasting when it is properly practiced (Isa. 58:8).

2. If you are on regular medication, or if you suffer from some kind of wasting disease, such as diabetes or tuberculosis, it is wise to obtain medical advice before entering into any fast that extends beyond a meal or two.

3. In the early period of a fast, you may experience unpleasant physical symptoms, such as dizziness, headache, or nausea. Usually these are indications that your fasting is overdue and that you need the purifying physical action of fasting in various areas of your body. Do not allow physical discomfort to deter you. *"Set your face"* (Ezek. 4:3 RSV), and go through with the fast that you planned. After the first day or two, these unpleasant physical reactions usually subside.

4. Remember that hunger is partly a matter of habit. In the early stages of a fast, hunger will probably return at each normal mealtime. But if you hold out, the sensation of hunger will pass away without your having eaten anything. Sometimes you can fool your stomach by drinking a glass of water instead of eating.

5. Guard against constipation. Before and after fasting, choose meals that will help you in this respect, such as fresh fruit or fruit juices; dried figs, prunes, or apricots; oatmeal, etc.

6. During a fast, some people drink only water. Others take various kinds of fluid, such as fruit juices, broth, or skim milk. It is wise to abstain from strong stimulants such as tea or coffee. Do not come under bondage to other people's theories. Work out for yourself the particular pattern of fasting that suits you best as an individual.

7. It is scriptural to abstain at times from fluids as well as from solid food. But do not abstain from fluids for a period exceeding seventy-two hours. This was the limit set by Esther and her maidens (Est. 4:16). To go over seventy-two hours without fluids can have disastrous physical effects. It is true that Moses twice spent forty days without eating or drinking. (See Deuteronomy 9:9–18.) However, Moses was then on a supernatural plane in the immediate presence of God. Unless you are on the same supernatural plane, do not attempt to follow Moses' example.

8. Break your fast gradually. Begin with meals that are light and easy to digest. The longer you have fasted, the more careful you need to be about breaking your fast. At this point, you will need to exercise watchful self-control. Eating too heavily after a fast can produce serious physical discomfort and can nullify the physical benefits of fasting.

9. During any fast that exceeds two days, your stomach will shrink. Do not overexpand it again. If you have been prone to eat too heavily, guard against going back to this habit. If you train yourself to eat more lightly, your stomach will adjust itself accordingly.

Guidelines for Collective Fasting

For periods of collective fasting, all the guidelines given above for individual fasting will normally continue to apply. In addition, here are a few special points to observe in connection with collective fasting.

1. In Matthew 18:19, Jesus emphasized the special power that is released when believers *"agree"* together in prayer. To this end, all those participating in a collective fast should do everything in their power to achieve and to maintain agreement with each other.

2. People participating in a collective fast should make a commitment to pray specifically for each other during the period of the fast.

3. A meeting place should be chosen where those participating in the fast can come together at times mutually agreed upon.

A RECORD OF GOD'S FAITHFULNESS

It is appropriate to bring this chapter to a close with a personal testimony to God's faithfulness. Over the past fifty years or more, I have from time to time devoted myself to periods of special prayer and fasting. For some of these, I set specific objectives in prayer and kept records, which are still available.

As I look back now over these records, I am frequently amazed to see how many times and in how many ways God has answered my prayers. Sometimes there is a long interval between the date on which I recorded a specific prayer request and the date on which it was answered. Quite frequently, I recorded prayer requests and later forgot about them. But looking back through my records, I find that God did not forget. In His way and in His season, God answered even these requests that I myself had forgotten.

As I write, I have before me the record of a special period of prayer and fasting that I undertook in 1951. According to my record, this period began on July 24 and extended through August 16—a total of twenty-four days. At that time, I was engaged in full-time pastoral ministry. I continued to discharge all my normal duties, which included ministering at five services each week and also three street meetings.

I am amused to observe that, for this particular period, I wrote out the complete list of my special prayer objectives in New Testament Greek. The things for which I was praying were so intimate and so sacred to me that I wanted to keep the list known only to God and to myself. For this reason, I made it in a language not understood by most people today!

I divided up this particular list into five main sections:

1. My own spiritual needs
2. Needs of my family
3. Needs of the church
4. Needs of my country (Great Britain)
5. Needs of the world

Many of the things I prayed for are still too personal for me to divulge. However, there are points about which I feel free to write.

As I look through the various requests made on behalf of my family, I can see that every one of them has definitely been answered. The last request in this section was for the salvation of my mother. This took place about fourteen years later.

Among the requests that I made for myself was one for the exercise of four specific spiritual gifts. At that time, I scarcely understood the nature of the gifts that I was seeking. Yet today I can say that all these four gifts are regularly manifested in my ministry.

The requests I made for the church and the world are in a large measure being answered by the worldwide outpouring of the Holy Spirit that is now taking place. However, if God's people will seek Him more earnestly in prayer and fasting on a wider scale, I believe that we will see a move of the Holy Spirit throughout the entire world, such as history has yet to record. Indeed, we will see fulfilled the prophecy of Habakkuk 2:14: *"For the earth shall be filled with the knowledge of the glory of the LORD, as the waters cover the sea"* (KJV).

Of my requests for Britain, only a small fraction have so far been answered. However, in 1953—two years after this particular period of fasting—God awakened me one night and spoke to me audibly. The first promise that He gave me was, "There shall be a great revival in the United States and Great Britain." This revival is already underway in the United States, and there are evidences that it is beginning also in Britain. I have no doubt in my heart that God's promise for Britain will be fulfilled. By His grace, I expect to witness it.

As I meditate on these personal experiences of God's power and faithfulness, I find myself spontaneously echoing Paul's words:

Now unto him that is able to do exceeding abundantly above all that we ask or think, according to the power that worketh in us, unto him be glory in the church by Christ Jesus throughout all ages, world without end. Amen.
(Eph. 3:20–21 KJV)

CHAPTER TEN

LAYING A FOUNDATION BY FASTING

I n 1970 and 1971, the city of Plymouth, Massachusetts, celebrated the 350th anniversary of the landing of the Pilgrims at that point on the coast of America. A special committee was appointed by the city to organize various kinds of celebration that were appropriate to the occasion. This committee paid me the honor of inviting me to give a series of addresses in the Church of the Pilgrimage in the city of Plymouth. During my visit there, two members of the committee were kind enough to show me the main places of historical interest and also to introduce me to some of the original records of the period of the Pilgrims. In this way, I became acquainted for the first time with the history, *Of Plymouth Plantation,* written by William Bradford.

BACKGROUND OF THE PILGRIMS

Having been educated in Britain, I do not recall ever having learned anything at school about the Pilgrims. The phrase, "Pilgrim Fathers," commonly used by Americans, had created in my mind a vague impression of severe old men with long white beards, probably attired in dark formal clothing similar to that associated with ministers of religion. I was surprised to discover that the majority of the Pilgrims at the time of their arrival in America were still young men and women. For example, William Bradford was thirty-one years old in 1621, when he was first appointed governor of the colony. Most of the other Pilgrims were about the same age or younger. As portrayed in wax in the historical tableau on board the replica of the Mayflower in

Plymouth harbor, Bradford and his companions reminded me not a little of the Jesus People who emerged on this continent in the 1960s.

As I studied Bradford's own firsthand account of the founding of Plymouth Colony and of its early struggles, I developed a strong sense of spiritual kinship with him and his fellow Pilgrims. I discovered that their whole way of life was based upon the systematic study and application of the Scriptures. With the main conclusions and convictions to which this study led them, I found myself in complete accord. In fact, they are in close agreement with some of the main themes developed in this book.

Having obtained my own degrees from the University of Cambridge and having held a fellowship at King's College, Cambridge, I was particularly interested to see how many of the Pilgrims' spiritual leaders had received their education at Cambridge. Three of those most closely associated with the Pilgrims' story were Richard Clyfton, John Robinson, and William Brewster. Clyfton was the elder of the original congregation at Scrooby, in England. Robinson was the elder of the Pilgrims' congregation at Leyden, in Holland. Brewster was the elder who actually traveled over on the *Mayflower* and became the chief spiritual leader of the original colony in Plymouth. All three of these men received their education at Cambridge.

During the months that followed my visit to Plymouth, I traveled widely and conducted meetings in various parts of the United States. I began to share with those I met some of my stimulating discoveries from Bradford's book, *Of Plymouth Plantation*. To my surprise, I encountered almost complete and universal ignorance of the whole subject. Many people of at least average education, born and raised in the United States, confessed that they had never heard of the book. A few acknowledged that they had heard of the book, but none, as I recall, had actually read it.

For this reason, I feel that I need offer no apology for quoting from Bradford's book various passages that relate to the theme of our present study. All the quotations that follow are taken from the edition published by Modern Library Books, with an introduction and notes by Samuel E. Morison.

The whole course of Bradford's life was determined by spiritual experiences of his boyhood and early manhood. In Morison's introduction to his edition of Bradford's book, these early experiences are briefly described as follows:

> William Bradford was born at Austerfield, Yorkshire, in the early spring of 1590....At the age of twelve he became a constant reader of the Bible—the Geneva version that he generally quotes—and when still a lad he was so moved by the Word as to join a group of Puritans who met for prayer and discussion at the house of William Brewster in the nearby village of Scrooby. When this group, inspired by the Rev. Richard Clyfton, organized itself as a separate Congregational Church in 1606, Bradford joined it despite "the wrath of his uncles" and the "scoff of his neighbors." From that date until his death half a century later, Bradford's life revolved around that of his church or congregation, first in Scrooby, next in the Low Countries and finally in New England.

RESTORATION, NOT REFORMATION

Although the Pilgrims were initially associated with the Puritans, there were important differences between them. Both saw the need of religious reform, but they differed concerning the means by which reform was to be achieved. The Puritans determined to remain within the established church and to impose reform from within—by compulsion, if necessary. The Pilgrims sought liberty for themselves, but declined to use the machinery of secular government to enforce their views upon others. These differing points of view are expressed in the following passage from Leonard Bacon's *Genesis of the New England Churches*:

> In the Old World on the other side of the ocean, the Puritan was a Nationalist, believing that a Christian nation is a Christian church, and demanding that the Church of England should be thoroughly reformed; while the Pilgrim was a Separatist, not only from the Anglican Prayer Book and Queen Elizabeth's episcopacy, but from all national churches....
>
> The Pilgrim wanted liberty for himself and his wife and little ones, and for his brethren, to walk with God in a

Christian life as the rules and motives of such a life were revealed to him from God's Word. For that he went into exile; for that he crossed the ocean; for that he made his home in a wilderness. The Puritan's idea was not liberty, but right government in church and state—such government as should not only permit him, but also compel other men to walk in the right way.

The difference between Puritans and Pilgrims could be expressed in the two words *reformation* and *restoration*. The Puritans sought to reform the church as it existed in their day. The Pilgrims believed that the ultimate purpose of God was to restore the church to its original condition, as portrayed in the New Testament. This shines forth very clearly in the first paragraph of the first chapter of Bradford's book, where he expressed the Pilgrims' vision of restoration in the following words:

The churches of God revert to their ancient purity and recover their primitive [i.e. original] order, liberty and beauty. (P. 3)

Later in this chapter, Bradford returned to this theme when he declared the Pilgrims' purpose:

[They labored] to have the right worship of God and discipline of Christ established in the church, according to the simplicity of the gospel, without the mixture of men's inventions; and to have and be ruled by the laws of God's Word, dispensed in those offices, and by those officers of Pastors, Teachers and Elders, etc., according to the Scriptures. (P. 6)

With this purpose in view, the original group of believers in Nottinghamshire, Lincolnshire, and Yorkshire

joined themselves (by a covenant of the Lord) into a church estate, in the fellowship of the gospel, to walk in all His ways made known, or to be made known unto them, according to their best endeavors, whatsoever it should cost them, the Lord assisting them. (P. 9)

Later when the congregation moved to Leyden, in Holland, Bradford described their way of life there:

They came as near the primitive [original] pattern of the first churches as any other church[es] of these later times have done. (P. 19)

Again in his fourth chapter, Bradford described the main motive of the Pilgrims in undertaking their journey to America:

Lastly (and which was not least), a great hope and inward zeal they had of laying some good foundation...for the propagating and advancing of the gospel of the kingdom of Christ in those remote parts of the world; yea, though they should be but even as steppingstones unto others for the performing of so great a work. (P. 25)

PUBLIC DAYS OF FASTING PROCLAIMED

One distinctive practice employed by the Pilgrims to achieve their spiritual goals was that of united public prayer and fasting. There are various references to this in Bradford's book. One of the most poignant passages describes the Pilgrims' preparation for their departure from Leyden:

So being ready to depart, they had a day of solemn humiliation, their pastor [John Robinson] taking his text from Ezra 8:21: *"And there at the river, by Ahava, I proclaimed a fast, that we might humble ourselves before our God, and seek of him a right way for us, and for our children, and for all our substance."* Upon which he [Robinson] spent a good part of the day very profitably and suitable to their present occasion; the rest of the time was spent in pouring out prayers to the Lord with great fervency, mixed with abundance of tears. (P. 47)

Bradford's use of the word *humiliation* indicates that the Pilgrims understood the scriptural connection (explained in chapters 6 through 8 of this book) between fasting and self-humbling. Robinson's choice of the text from Ezra is singularly appropriate. Both in motivation and in experience, there is a close parallel between the Pilgrims' embarking on their journey to the New World and Ezra's company of exiles returning from Babylon to Jerusalem to help in the restoration of the temple.

The end of Robinson's address is given by Edward Winslow in Verna M. Hall's *Christian History of the Constitution*:

> We are now ere long to part asunder, and the Lord knoweth whether he [Robinson] should live to see our face again. But whether the Lord had appointed it or not, he charged us before God and His blessed angels, to follow him no further than he followed Christ; and if God should reveal anything to us by any other instrument of His, to be as ready to receive it, as ever we were to receive any truth by his ministry; for he was very confident the Lord had more truth and light yet to break forth out of His holy Word. He took occasion also miserably to bewail the state and condition of the Reformed churches who were come to a period [standstill] in religion, and would go no further than the instruments of their reformation [i.e. those who had been leaders in the Reformation].
>
> As for example, the Lutherans, they could not be drawn to go beyond what Luther saw; for whatever part of God's will He had further imparted and revealed to Calvin, they [the Lutherans] will rather die than embrace it. And so also, saith he, you see the Calvinists, they stick where he [Calvin] left them, a misery much to be lamented; for though they were precious shining lights in their times, yet God had not revealed His whole will to them; and were they now living, saith he, they would be as ready and willing to embrace further light, as that they had received.
>
> Here also he put us in mind of our church covenant, at least that part of it whereby we promise and covenant with God and one another to receive whatsoever light or truth shall be made known to us from His written Word; but withal [he] exhorted us to take heed what we received for truth, and well to examine and compare it and weigh it with other Scriptures of truth before we received it. For saith he, it is not possible [that] the Christian world should come so lately [recently] out of such thick antichristian darkness, and that full perfection of knowledge should break forth at once. (P. 184)

John Robinson's message on this occasion sums up the essence of the Pilgrims' theological position. This is indicated by their very choice of the name *Pilgrims*. They did not claim to have arrived at a final understanding of all truth. They were on a pilgrimage, looking for the further revelation of truth that lay ahead as they walked in obedience to truth already received.

Bradford himself believed firmly that he and his companions were in the same line of spiritual pilgrimage as the saints of the Old and New Testaments, and he habitually resorted to the language of the Bible to express his feelings and reactions. In chapter 9, he described the arrival of the *Mayflower* at Cape Cod, and the many dangers and hardships that the Pilgrims encountered. He concluded the chapter with this:

> What could now sustain them but the Spirit of God and His grace? May not the children of these fathers rightly say: "Our fathers were Englishmen which came over this great ocean, and were ready to perish in this wilderness; but they cried unto the Lord, and He heard their voice and looked on their adversity." [This is Bradford's own paraphrase of Deuteronomy 26:5, 7.]
>
> "Let them therefore praise the Lord, because He is good: and His mercies endure forever. Yea, let them which have been redeemed of the Lord, shew how He hath delivered them from the hand of the oppressor. When they wandered in the desert wilderness out of the way, and found no city to dwell in, both hungry and thirsty, their soul was overwhelmed in them. Let them confess before the Lord His lovingkindness and His wonderful works before the sons of men." [This is Bradford's version of Psalm 107:1–5, 8.]

It is not possible to quote the many instances of answered prayer that Bradford recorded, but there is one further instance of a public fast that must be mentioned. In the summer of 1623, the corn crop that the Pilgrims had so carefully planted was threatened:

> By a great drought which continued from the third week in May, till about the middle of July, without any rain and with great heat for the most part, insomuch as the corn began to wither away....It began to languish sore, and some of the drier grounds were parched like withered hay....Upon which they set apart a solemn day of humiliation to seek the Lord by humble and fervent prayer....And He was pleased to give them a gracious and speedy answer, both to their own and the Indians' admiration [i.e. amazement]....For all the

morning, and greatest part of the day, it was clear weather and very hot, and not a cloud or any sign of rain to be seen; yet toward evening it began to overcast, and shortly after to rain with such sweet and gentle showers as gave them cause of rejoicing and blessing God.

Normally, if rain had fallen at all in such conditions, it would have been in the form of a thunderstorm, which would have beaten down the corn and destroyed the last hope of a harvest. But on this occasion, Bradford went on to relate,

> It came without either wind or thunder or any violence, and by degrees in that abundance as that the earth was thoroughly...soaked therewith. Which did so apparently revive and quicken the decayed corn and other fruits, as was wonderful to see, and made the Indians astonished to behold. And afterwards the Lord sent them such seasonable showers, with interchange of fair warm weather as, through His blessing, caused a fruitful and liberal harvest....For which mercy, in time convenient, they also set apart a day of thanksgiving. (PP. 131–2)

This practice of setting aside special days of prayer and fasting became an accepted part of the life of Plymouth Colony. On November 15, 1636, a law was passed allowing the governor and his assistants "to command solemn days of humiliation by fasting, etc. and also for thanksgiving as occasion shall be offered."

In chapter 8 of this book, we examined the promises given in Isaiah to those who practice the kind of fasting approved by God, and we saw that these come to their climax in this verse:

> *And they that shall be of thee shall build the old waste places: thou shalt raise up the foundations of many generations; and thou shalt be called, The repairer of the breach, The restorer of paths to dwell in.*   (Isa. 58:12 KJV)

History has demonstrated that the results of fasting promised in this verse were achieved by the Pilgrims. Both spiritually and politically, they *"raise[d] up the foundations of many generations."* Three-and-a-half centuries later, the people of the United States are still building on the foundations that the Pilgrims laid.

CHAPTER ELEVEN

FASTS PROCLAIMED IN AMERICAN HISTORY

T he pattern set by the Pilgrims of proclaiming public days of fasting was followed in subsequent generations both by the governing bodies and by the most famous individual leaders of the American people. The following are some documented examples of this practice.

GEORGE WASHINGTON AND THE ASSEMBLY OF VIRGINIA

In May of 1774, news was received in Williamsburg, Virginia, that the British Parliament had ordered an embargo on the port of Boston, Massachusetts, to become effective on June 1. Immediately, the House of Burgesses of Virginia passed a resolution protesting this act and setting aside the day appointed for the commencement of the embargo—June 1—as a day of fasting, humiliation, and prayer.

The following is the main part of the resolution, as recorded in the *Journals Of The House Of Burgesses Of Virginia, 1773–1776*, edited by John Pendleton Kennedy:

Tuesday, the 24th of May, 14 Geo. III. 1774

This House, being deeply impressed with Apprehension of the great Dangers, to be derived to British America, from the hostile Invasion of the City of Boston, in our Sister Colony of Massachusetts Bay, whose Commerce and Harbour are, on the first Day of June next, to be stopped by an armed Force, deem it highly necessary that the said first Day of June be set apart, by the Members of this House, as a Day of Fasting, Humiliation, and Prayer, devoutly to implore the Divine Interposition, for averting the heavy Calamity which threatens Destruction to our civil Rights, and the Evils of civil War; to give us one Heart and one Mind to oppose, by all just and proper Means, every Injury to American Rights....

Ordered, therefore, that the Members of this House do attend in their Places, at the Hour of ten in the Forenoon, on the said first Day of June next, in order to proceed with the Speaker, and the Mace, to the Church in this City, for the Purposes aforesaid; and that the Reverend Mr. Price be appointed to read Prayers, and the Reverend Mr. Gwatkin, to preach a Sermon, suitable to the Occasion.

That this resolution was adhered to is attested by no less a person than George Washington, who wrote in his diary for that first day of June: "Went to Church and fasted all Day." (*The Diaries of George Washington, 1748–1799*, edited by John C. Fitzpatrick.)

The church referred to in the resolution and in Washington's diary was the Parish Church of Bruton in the city of Williamsburg.

Washington not only believed in praying for divine intervention, but he also believed in acknowledging such intervention when prayer was answered. On January 1, 1795, as president of the United States, Washington issued a proclamation setting aside February 19, 1795 for national thanksgiving and prayer. The following is part of the proclamation's text:

When we review the calamities which afflict so many other nations, the present condition of the United States affords much matter of consolation and satisfaction....In such a state of things it is, in an especial manner, our duty as a people, with devout reverence and affectionate gratitude, to acknowledge our many and great obligations to Almighty God, and to implore Him to continue and confirm the blessings we experience.

Deeply penetrated with this sentiment, I, GEORGE WASHINGTON, President of the United States, do recommend to all religious societies and denominations, and to all persons whomsoever within the United States, to set apart and observe Thursday, the nineteenth day of February next, as a day of public Thanksgiving and Prayer; and on that day to meet together, and render their sincere and hearty thanks to the great Ruler of Nations for the manifest and signal mercies which distinguish our lot as a Nation...and at the same time, humbly and fervently to beseech the kind author of these blessings graciously to prolong them to us,—to imprint on our hearts a deep and solemn sense of our obligations to Him for them—to teach us rightly to estimate their immense value—to preserve us from the arrogance of prosperity, and from hazarding the advantages we enjoy by delusive pursuits—to dispose us to merit the continuance of his favors, by not abusing them, by our gratitude for them, and by a correspondent conduct as citizens and as men; to render this country more and more a safe and propitious asylum for the unfortunate of other countries; to extend among us true and useful knowledge; to diffuse and establish habits of sobriety, order, morality, and piety, and finally to impart all the blessings we possess, or ask for ourselves, to the whole family of mankind. (Appendix no. 5, Volume 11, U.S. Statutes At Large.)

FASTS PROCLAIMED BY ADAMS AND MADISON

Under the next president, John Adams, the United States came to the verge of open war with France. On March 23, 1798, Adams proclaimed May 9, 1798 as a day of solemn humiliation, fasting, and prayer. The following is part of his proclamation:

As the safety and prosperity of nations ultimately and essentially depend on the protection and the blessing of Almighty God, and the national acknowledgment of this truth is not only an indispensable duty which the people owe to Him, but a duty whose natural influence is favorable to the promotion of that morality and piety, without which social happiness cannot exist, nor the blessings of free government be enjoyed...and as the United States of America are, at present, placed in a hazardous and afflictive situation, by the unfriendly disposition, conduct, and demands of a Foreign Power (i.e. France)....Under these considerations it has appeared to me that the duty of imploring the mercy and benediction of Heaven on our country, demands, at this time, a special attention from its inhabitants.

I have, therefore, thought fit to recommend and I do hereby recommend that Wednesday, the ninth day of May next, be observed throughout the United States, as a day of Solemn Humiliation, Fasting, and Prayer: That the Citizens of these States, abstaining on that day from their customary worldly occupations, offer their devout addresses to the Father of Mercies, agreeably to those forms or methods which they have severally adopted as the most suitable and becoming: That all Religious Congregations do, with the deepest humility, acknowledge before God the manifold sins and transgressions with which we are justly chargeable as individuals and as a nation, beseeching Him at the same time of His infinite grace through the Redeemer of the World, freely to remit all our offenses, and to incline us, by His Holy Spirit, to that sincere Repentance and Reformation, which may afford us reason to hope for His inestimable favor and Heavenly Benediction: That it be made the subject of particular and earnest supplication, that our country may be protected from all the dangers which threaten it: That our civil and religious privileges may be preserved inviolate, and perpetuated to the latest generations. (Appendix no. 7, Volume 11, U.S. Statutes At Large.)

Under the fourth president, James Madison, the United States found itself at war with Britain. In the face of this situation, the two houses of Congress passed a joint resolution desiring a day of public humiliation, fasting, and prayer. In response, Madison set apart January 12, 1815 for this purpose. His proclamation opened as follows:

The two houses of the National Legislature having, by a joint resolution expressed their desire that, in the present time of public calamity and war, a day may be recommended to be observed by the people of the United States as a day of public humiliation and fasting, and of prayer to Almighty God for the safety and welfare of these States, his blessing on their arms and a speedy restoration of peace: I have deemed it proper, by this proclamation, to recommend that Thursday the twelfth of January next be set apart as a day on which all may have an opportunity of voluntarily offering, at the same time, in their respective religious assemblies, their humble adoration to the great Sovereign of the Universe, of confessing their sins and transgressions, and of strengthening their vows of repentance and amendment. (Appendix no. 14, Volume 11, U.S. Statutes At Large.)

The outcome of this national day of fasting and prayer presents a historical fulfillment of God's promise given in Isaiah 65:24: *"And it shall come to pass, that before they call, I will answer; and while they are yet speaking, I will hear"* (KJV).

Four days before the day set by Madison, the last battle of this war was fought at New Orleans, resulting in a victory for the United States. Peace followed shortly afterwards. As a result, the two houses of Congress requested Madison to proclaim a day of public thanksgiving. The day that he appointed was the second Thursday of April, 1815. The following is part of his proclamation:

> The Senate and House of Representatives of the United States, have, by a joint resolution, signified their desire that a day may be recommended to be observed by the people of the United States with religious solemnity, as a day of thanksgiving, and of devout acknowledgments to Almighty God for His great goodness manifested in restoring to them the blessing of peace.
>
> No people ought to feel greater obligations to celebrate the goodness of the Great Disposer of events, and of the destiny of nations, than the people of the United States. His kind providence originally conducted them to one of the best portions of the dwelling-place allotted for the great family of the human race. He protected and cherished them, under all the difficulties and trials to which they were exposed in their early days. Under His fostering care, their habits, their sentiments, and their pursuits prepared them for a transition, in due time, to a state of independence and self-government. In the arduous struggle by which it was attained, they were distinguished by multiplied tokens of His benign interposition. During the interval which succeeded, He reared them into the strength and endowed them with the resources which have enabled them to assert their national rights, and to enhance their national character, in another arduous conflict, which is now so happily terminated by a peace and reconciliation with those who have been our enemies....
>
> It is for blessings such as these, and especially for the restoration of the blessing of peace, that I now recommend

that the second Thursday in April next, be set apart as a day on which the people of every religious denomination, may, in their solemn assemblies, unite their hearts and their voices in a free will offering to their heavenly Benefactor, of their homage of thanksgiving, and of their songs of praise. (Appendix no. 16, Volume 11, U.S. Statutes At Large.)

Three Fasts Proclaimed by Lincoln

During the presidency of Abraham Lincoln, three separate days of national humiliation, prayer, and fasting were proclaimed. The prime cause for each of these was the Civil War, and the central theme of petition was for the restoration of national peace and unity.

Lincoln's first proclamation was requested by a joint committee of both houses of Congress, and the day set apart was the last Thursday in September, 1861. The following is part of the proclamation:

> Whereas a joint committee of both Houses of Congress has waited on the President of the United States, and requested him to "recommend a day of public Humiliation, Prayer and Fasting, to be observed by the people of the United States with religious solemnities, and the offering of fervent supplications to almighty God for the safety and welfare of these States, His blessing on their arms, and a speedy restoration of peace."
>
> And whereas it is fit and becoming in all people, at all times, to acknowledge and revere the Supreme Government of God; to bow in humble submission to his chastisements; to confess and deplore their sins and transgressions, in the full conviction that the fear of the Lord is the beginning of wisdom, and to pray, with all fervency and contrition, for the pardon of their past offenses, and for a blessing upon their present and prospective action....
>
> Therefore, I, ABRAHAM LINCOLN, President of the United States, do appoint the last Thursday in September next, as a day of Humiliation, Prayer, and Fasting, for all the people of the nation. And I do earnestly recommend to all the people, and especially to all ministers and teachers of religion, of all denominations, and to all heads of families, to observe and keep that day, according to their several creeds and

modes of worship, in all humility, and with all religious solemnity, to the end that the united prayer of the nation may
ascend to the Throne of Grace, and bring down plentiful
blessings upon our Country. (Appendix no. 8, Volume 12,
U.S. Statutes At Large.)

By specifically including "all heads of families" in his proclamation, Lincoln apparently envisaged prayer and fasting being
carried out in the homes of the nation, with parents and children uniting in their worship and petitions. In this, as in other
respects, both the language and the spirit of his proclamation
are in perfect accord with Scripture.

Lincoln's second proclamation is the one reproduced fully at
the beginning of this book.

Lincoln's third proclamation was requested by a concurrent
resolution of both Houses of Congress, and the day set apart was
the first Thursday of August, 1864. In the closing paragraph of
this proclamation, Lincoln made a special plea for the cooperation of all who held positions of authority in every area of national life:

> I do hereby further invite and request the heads of the ex-
> ecutive departments of this government, together with all leg-
> islators, all judges and magistrates, and all other persons
> exercising authority in the land...and all the other law-abiding
> people of the United States, to assemble in their preferred
> places of public worship on that day, and there and then to
> render to the Almighty and Merciful Ruler of the universe such
> homages and such confessions, and to offer to Him such suppli-
> cations as the congress of the United States have...so solemnly,
> so earnestly, and so reverently recommended. (Appendix no.
> 17, Volume 13, U.S. Statutes At Large.)

No claim is here put forward that the above list of public
fasting days is in any sense comprehensive or complete. However, combined with the material in our previous chapter about
the Pilgrims, it suffices to establish one historical fact: from the
beginning of the seventeenth century until at least the second
half of the nineteenth century, public days of prayer and fasting
played a vital and continuing role in shaping the national destiny of the United States.

In the light of these official national records, thoughtful Americans should ask of themselves this question: How many of the blessings and the privileges we now enjoy were obtained for us by the prayers of our leaders and governments in previous generations?

Today, as we look back over more than three hundred and fifty years of American history, we form the impression of an elaborate pattern, woven out of threads of varying colors and textures. Each thread represents a different background and is associated with differing motives and purposes. Clear and strong throughout the length of the pattern, we may distinguish one thread of divine purpose. This purpose was born out of the fellowship of the Pilgrims and their united prayer and fasting. In each succeeding generation, it has been sustained and continued by the faith, prayers, and fasting of like-minded believers. The full and final outworking of this purpose still lies ahead. It is to this that we will devote the final chapter of this book.

CHAPTER TWELVE

CLIMAX: THE GLORIOUS CHURCH

I n the opening chapters of this book, we saw that the church of Jesus Christ, indwelled by the Holy Spirit, is the main representative of God in the earth and the main agent of God's purposes for the world in this age. Later, in chapter 8, we saw that, through the *"latter rain"* (Joel 12:23) of the Holy Spirit, God is now restoring the church to His own ordained standards of purity, power, and order. The church, thus restored, will then be enabled to fulfill its God-appointed destiny in the world and to bring to a triumphant climax God's purposes for the close of this age.

PAUL'S PICTURE OF THE COMPLETED CHURCH

In his letter to the Ephesians, Paul described how the church will be brought to completion and what it will be like when it is complete. In Ephesians 1:22–23, he told us that the church is Christ's body, and that Christ is the sole and sovereign Head over this body. Then in chapter 4, Paul listed the main ministries given by Christ to His church and the purpose for which they were given:

> *And he gave some, apostles; and some, prophets; and some, evangelists; and some, pastors and teachers; for the perfecting of the saints, for the work of the ministry, for the edifying of the body of Christ: till we all come in the unity of the faith, and of the knowledge of the Son of God, unto a perfect man, unto the measure of the stature of the fulness of Christ.*
> *(Eph. 4:11–13 KJV)*

The five main ministries in the church are listed in verse 11: apostles, prophets, evangelists, pastors, and teachers. Verse 12 tells us the purpose of these ministries: the edifying, or building up, of the body of Christ. Verse 13 gives four marks of the completed body. This verse may be more literally rendered: "Until we all come into the unity of the faith, and of the acknowledging of the Son of God, unto a full-grown man, unto the measure of the stature that represents Christ in His fullness."

Too often we think of the church as being in a static condition. This is not correct. The church is in a condition of growth and development. The opening word of verse 13, *"till,"* indicates that we are moving toward a predetermined end. This is confirmed by the expression *"in*[to] *the unity of the faith."* We are not yet in the unity of the faith. One glance at the different groups and denominations around us proves this. But we are moving into this unity. The time is coming when all true Christians will be united in their faith.

The way that leads into this unity is indicated by Paul's next phrase, *"the* [acknowledging] *of the Son of God."* All the doctrines of the New Testament center in the person and work of Christ: the doctrine of salvation centers in the Savior; the doctrine of healing centers in the Healer; the doctrine of sanctification centers in the Sanctifier; the doctrine of deliverance centers in the Deliverer; and so on with all the other great doctrines of Christianity. The true and full expression of each doctrine is in the person and work of Christ. History has demonstrated that Christians do not achieve unity by discussing doctrine in the abstract. But as Christians are willing to acknowledge Christ in His fullness, and to give Christ His rightful position in their lives and in the church, the various doctrines of Christianity all fit together in Him, just like the spokes of a wheel fitting into its hub. Thus, the way *"in*[to] *the unity of the faith"* is through *"the* [acknowledging] *of the Son of God."*

This leads also *"unto a* [full-grown] *man."* The church is growing up into mature manhood. This man, grown to full stature, will be able to represent Christ in all His fullness. He will be, in the truest sense, the embodiment of Christ. He will constitute the consummation of God's purposes for the church as Christ's body: that is, the perfect revelation of Christ. Endowed with every grace, every gift, every ministry, this completed church will present to the world a complete Christ.

In Ephesians chapter 5, Paul filled out his picture of the church at the close of this age. He had already presented the church as Christ's body. In this passage, he presented the church as Christ's bride, comparing Christ's relationship to His church with that of a husband to his wife:

> *Husbands, love your wives, even as Christ also loved the church, and gave himself for it; that he might sanctify and cleanse it with the washing of water by the word.*
>
> *(Eph. 5:25–26 KJV)*

In these verses, Paul presented Christ in two main aspects: first as Redeemer, then as Sanctifier. The means of redemption is the blood of Christ. The means of sanctification is the Word of God. Christ first redeemed the church by His blood, shed on the cross, that He might thereafter sanctify the church by His Word. The sanctifying operation of God's Word is compared to the washing of pure water. It requires both these ministries of Christ to make the church complete.

This agrees with the picture of Christ presented in 1 John 5:6: *"This is he that came by water and blood, even Jesus Christ; not by water only, but by water and blood. And it is the Spirit that beareth witness, because the Spirit is truth"* (KJV).

Through His blood, shed on the cross, Christ is the church's Redeemer. Through the pure water of God's Word, Christ is the church's Sanctifier. It is the Holy Spirit that bears witness to both these aspects of Christ. In the present *"latter rain"* (Joel 2:23) outpouring, the Holy Spirit is once again placing all the emphasis of His divine authority upon these two provisions of God for the church: redemption by Christ's blood, and sanctification by God's Word. Both alike are essential for the completion of the church.

In Ephesians 5:27, Paul went on to describe the results that Christ will accomplish in the church through this double ministry: *"That he might present it to himself a glorious church, not having spot, or wrinkle, or any such thing; but that it should be holy and without blemish."*

The first and most conspicuous feature of the church, as here described, is that it will be *"glorious."* That is to say, it will be permeated by God's glory. The word *glory* denotes the personal presence of God, made manifest to human senses. After the deliverance of Israel from Egypt, this glory took the form of a cloud, which overshadowed the tabernacle in the wilderness, and which also filled and illuminated the Holy of Holies within the tabernacle. In like manner, the completed church will be overshadowed, filled, and illuminated by the manifest glory of God. As a result, the church will also be holy and without blemish.

The church pictured by Paul in Ephesians will be the fulfillment of Christ's prayer to the Father for His disciples in John 17:22: *"And the glory which thou gavest me I have given them; that they may be one, even as we are one"* (KJV). It is the glory that will complete the unity. Conversely, it is the united church that alone can show forth the glory. In the preceding verse, Jesus said, *"That the world may believe"* (KJV), and in the following verse He said, *"That the world may know"* (KJV). The united, glorified church will be Christ's witness to the whole world.

By combining Paul's picture of the church in Ephesians 4:13 with that in Ephesians 5:27, we arrive at seven distinctive marks of the church at the close of this age:

1. The church will be united in its faith.
2. The church will acknowledge Christ as its Head in every aspect of His person and work.
3. The church will be full grown.
4. The completed church will present to the world a complete Christ.
5. The church will be permeated by God's glory.
6. The church will be holy.
7. The church will be without blemish.

Of these seven marks, the first four describe the church as Christ's completed body. The last three describe the church as Christ's completed bride.

ISAIAH'S PORTRAIT OF THE END-TIME CHURCH

This New Testament picture of the church at the close of this age is confirmed by various prophecies of the Old Testament. One of the most striking of these prophecies is found in Isaiah. Against a worldwide background of darkness, distress, and confusion, Isaiah portrayed the end-time church emerging in glory and power:

So shall they fear the name of the LORD from the west, and his glory from the rising of the sun. When the enemy shall come in like a flood, the Spirit of the LORD shall lift up a standard against him. And the Redeemer shall come to Zion, and unto them that turn from transgression in Jacob, saith the LORD. As for me, this is my covenant with them, saith the LORD; My spirit that is upon thee, and my words which I have put in thy mouth, shall not depart out of thy mouth, nor out of the mouth of thy seed, nor out of the mouth of thy seed's seed, saith the LORD, from henceforth and for ever. Arise, shine; for thy light is come, and the glory of the LORD is risen upon thee. For, behold, the darkness shall cover the earth, and gross darkness the people: but the LORD shall arise upon thee, and his glory shall be seen upon thee. And [the nations] shall come to thy light, and kings to the brightness of thy rising. Lift up thine eyes round about, and see: all they gather themselves together, they come to thee: thy sons shall come from far, and thy daughters shall be nursed at thy side. Then thou shalt see, and flow together, and thine heart shall fear, and be enlarged; because the abundance of the sea shall be converted unto thee, the forces [literally, wealth] *of the* [nations] *shall come unto thee.* (Isa. 59:19–60:5 KJV)

In the first part of verse 19 of chapter 59, Isaiah declared the end purpose of God, which is to be achieved through the events that will follow: *"So shall they fear the name of the LORD from the west, and his glory from the rising of the sun."* There is to be a worldwide demonstration of God's glory that will cause awe and wonder among all nations.

The second half of this verse reveals that Satan, *"the enemy,"* coming *"in like a flood,"* will attempt to oppose God's purposes, but that his opposition will be overcome by the Holy Spirit. Historically, it is the darkest hour of man's need that calls forth the mightiest intervention of God. It is *"where sin* abounded" that God's grace "did much more abound" (Rom. 5:20 KJV).

The Holy Spirit is here presented in Isaiah 59:19 as the Standard Bearer of God's army. Just at the moment when God's people are in danger of being totally scattered and defeated, the Holy Spirit lifts up the divine standard. Encouraged by this evidence that God is coming to their help, the people of God from every direction gather around the uplifted standard and regroup for a fresh offensive.

What is the standard that the Holy Spirit uplifts here? In John 16:13–14, Jesus spoke of the Holy Spirit's coming and declared, "He shall glorify me" (KJV). The Holy Spirit has only one standard to uplift. It is not an institution or a denomination or a doctrine. It is a Person: "Jesus Christ the same yesterday, and to day, and for ever" (Heb. 13:8 KJV). For every true believer, loyalty to this standard—Jesus Christ—is primary. Every other commitment—to institution, denomination, or doctrine—is secondary. Wherever such believers see Christ truly uplifted by the Holy Spirit, they will gather.

In the decades since World War II, this prophecy in the latter part of Isaiah 59:19 has been exactly fulfilled. First, "the enemy [has] come in like a flood." There has been an unparalleled inundation of Satan's influence and activity in every area of life—religious, moral, social, political. Second, "the Spirit of the LORD [has] lift[ed] up a standard against him." Every section of Christendom has begun to experience a sovereign, supernatural visitation of the Holy Spirit. This visitation centers around no institution and no human personality, but only around the Lord Jesus Christ. Around the person of Christ, uplifted by the Holy Spirit, the people of God from every background are now regathering. Isaiah 59:19–20 describes various effects of this visitation. God's people are turning back to Him in repentance. Christ is working again in His church, bringing redemption and deliverance. He is renewing His covenant and restoring the fullness of His Holy Spirit. Once again, God's people have become His witnesses. With God's Spirit upon them, His Word is being proclaimed through their lips.

All age groups are included in this visitation. It is for parents, children, and children's children. Indeed, there is special emphasis upon the young people. This is the same outpouring that is predicted in Joel 2:28 and Acts 2:17: *"Your sons and your daughters shall prophesy...your young men shall see visions"* (KJV).

Nor is this a brief or a temporary visitation. It is *"from henceforth and for ever."* The Holy Spirit's fullness, now being restored to God's people, will never again be taken from them.

The first two verses of Isaiah chapter 60 emphasize the increasing contrast between the light and the darkness: *"Darkness shall cover the earth, and gross darkness the people."* But upon God's people, the light and glory of His presence will shine forth all the more brightly in the surrounding darkness. The darkness is growing darker, but the light is growing brighter. This is the hour of decision, the parting of the ways. There can be no more neutrality, no more compromise: *"For what fellowship hath righteousness with unrighteousness? and what communion hath light with darkness?"* (2 Cor. 6:14 KJV).

In verse 3 of Isaiah 60, the prophet described the impact to be produced upon the world by the manifestation of the church in its glory. Nations and their rulers will turn and seek for help. Of this hour, Jesus spoke in Luke 21:25, *"Distress of nations, with perplexity"* (KJV). The multiplying problems of recent decades have brought the rulers of the nations to the point where they no longer claim to have the solutions. Therefore, whole nations will turn to Christ as He reveals His wisdom and His power through the church.

In chapter 60, verse 4, Isaiah challenged the church to look out over the great influx of people that is coming in. Here again, we see particular emphasis upon the young people: *"thy sons"* and *"thy daughters."*

Verse 5 brings this part of the prophecy to its climax: *"Thou shalt see, and flow together."* The vision of what God is doing will bring His people together. From every historical background and from every section of Christendom, the streams of revival will flow, finally uniting themselves into a single irresistible river. *"Thine heart shall fear, and be enlarged."* Holy awe will come over God's people at the revelation of His power and glory. Yet there also will be an enlargement of heart—an enlarged capacity to comprehend and to fulfill the purposes of God.

To God's people thus regathered, united, and empowered, there will be made available vast financial and material resources: *"the abundance of the sea"* and *"the* [wealth] *of the* [nations]*."* God has these resources reserved and set aside for the final task that the church has to fulfill.

THE LAST GREAT TASK

In Matthew 24:3, the disciples asked Jesus a question: *"What will be the sign of your coming and of the close of the age?"* (RSV). Their question was specific. They did not ask for signs in the plural, but for the sign—the one final, definite indication that the close of the age was at hand.

In verses 5 through 13, Jesus gave them various signs— various events or trends that would characterize the closing period. However, it was not until verse 14 that He actually answered their specific question: *"And this gospel of the kingdom shall be preached in all the world for a witness unto all nations; and then shall the end come"* (KJV).

Here is a specific answer to a specific question. When will the end come? When this Gospel of the kingdom will have been preached in all the world and to all nations. This confirms a theme that has been emphasized throughout this book: the initiative in world affairs is with God and His people. The climax of the age will not be brought about by the actions of secular government or military power, nor by the floods of satanic deception and lawlessness. The final decisive activity will be the preaching of the Gospel of the kingdom. This is a task that can be accomplished only by the church of Jesus Christ.

Scripture is very precise about the message that is to be preached. It is to be *"this gospel of the kingdom."* This is the same message that was preached by Christ and the first disciples. It sets forth Christ in His kingly victory and power. *"Where the word of a king is, there is power"* (Eccl. 8:4 KJV). *"For the kingdom of God is not in word, but in power"* (1 Cor. 4:20 KJV). The kingdom Gospel is supernaturally attested *"with signs and wonders, and with divers miracles, and gifts of the Holy* [Spirit]*"* (Heb. 2:4 KJV). It will be a true and effective *"witness unto all nations"* (Matt. 24:14 KJV).

Today, the scene is set for the last great act of the church's drama. For the first time in human history, the task of bringing the kingdom Gospel to all nations can be fulfilled within a single generation. Technology has provided both the means of travel and the media of communication that are needed. The cost of utilizing these resources will be tremendous, but in Isaiah 60:5, God has promised to the end-time church *"the abundance of the sea"* and *"the* [wealth] *of the* [nations]." These are His appointed means of provision. The financial and technological resources of the nations are to be made available to the church for the fulfillment of its final task on earth.

At the same time, the *"latter rain"* of the Holy Spirit is bringing forth, as Joel promised, a dedicated army of young men and women, ready to fulfill the commission of Jesus in Acts 1:8: *"But ye shall receive power, after that the Holy* [Spirit] *is come upon you: and ye shall be witnesses unto me...unto the uttermost part of the earth"* (KJV). This is the generation to which David looked forward in Psalm 22:30: *"A seed shall serve him; it shall be accounted to the Lord for a generation"* (KJV). It is also the period of which Jesus spoke in Matthew 24:34: *"This generation shall not pass, till all these things be fulfilled"* (KJV).

For the final outworking of His purposes, God is thus bringing together the various resources that are needed: the human resources of Spirit-filled young people and the material resources of wealth and technology. In both these respects, the United States has a unique contribution to make. The first mass outpouring of the Holy Spirit upon today's youth has taken place in the United States and is still proceeding across the nation. At the same time, the financial and technological resources of the United States are the greatest in the modern world. The nation that first placed men on the moon is uniquely qualified to place the messengers of the kingdom Gospel in every nation on earth. By the combined offering of its resources—both human and material—for the worldwide proclamation of the kingdom Gospel, the United States will complete the thread of divine destiny that has run through its history for three-and-a-half centuries.

This special purpose of God for the United States was born out of the fellowship of the Pilgrims. The vision God gave them was for the restoration of the church. To this they devoted themselves with labor and sacrifice, with prayer and fasting. Today, those who share the Pilgrims' vision can see its fulfillment approaching. The church of Jesus Christ stands poised to carry the Gospel of the kingdom to all nations on earth. Through the achievement of this final task, the church will itself be brought to completion.

From the study of the Scriptures, the Pilgrims learned two great truths that they have in turn bequeathed to their spiritual descendants in their own and other lands. First, the end-time purpose of God is the restoration and completion of the church. Second, the source of power for the achievement of this purpose is united prayer and fasting.

SPIRITUAL WARFARE

CONTENTS

PART 1:

THE NATURE OF THE WAR

CHAPTER ONE

TWO OPPOSING KINGDOMS

There are many pictures of God's people in the New Testament. In Ephesians, for instance, God's people are presented through the following pictures: a legislative assembly, a family, a temple, and as the bride of Christ. However, the final picture of God's people in Ephesians is that of an army.

This army is committed to fight a war that is global in its proportions, that affects and includes every portion of this globe on which we live. In fact, even the word *global* does not do justice to the scope of this conflict. It embraces not only the earth, but extends beyond the earth into the very heavens. In fact, the adjective that correctly describes this conflict is not *global* but *universal*. It includes the entire created universe.

The Scripture that most clearly introduces this conflict and describes its nature is Ephesians 6:10–12. I will cite first the New International Version, then I will compare some other versions.

> *Finally, be strong in the Lord and in his mighty power. Put on the full armor of God so that you can take your stand against the devil's schemes.*

Paul took it for granted that, as Christians, we are involved in a war for which we need the appropriate armor, and that our adversary is the Devil himself. He then went on in verse 12 to explain more fully the nature of this war:

> *For our struggle is not against flesh and blood, but against the rulers, against the authorities, against the powers of*

*this dark world and against the spiritual forces of evil in
the heavenly realms.* *(NIV)*

In the New American Standard version, this verse reads,

*For our struggle is not against flesh and blood, but against
the rulers, against the powers, against the world forces of
this darkness, against the spiritual forces of wickedness in
the heavenly places.*

The Living Bible, which is not exactly a literal translation
but a paraphrase, reads as follows:

*For we are not fighting against people made of flesh and
blood, but against persons without bodies—the evil rulers
of the unseen world, those mighty satanic beings and great
evil princes of darkness who rule this world; and against
huge numbers of wicked spirits in the spirit world.*

Whichever version you wish to follow, it is clear that as Christians we are engaged in a titanic conflict that staggers the mind
to consider.

I have meditated so often and so long on Ephesians 6:12 in
the original Greek that I have come up with my own paraphrase. You might call this "the Prince version."

For our wrestling match is not against flesh and blood, not
against persons with bodies, but against rulers with various
areas and descending orders of authority, against the world
dominators of this present darkness, against spiritual forces
of wickedness in the heavenlies.

Let me explain why I chose some of those words. I say,
"rulers with various areas and descending orders of authority,"
because that pictures a very highly structured and well-organized
kingdom with descending orders of authority and different rulers
and sub-rulers responsible for different areas of their territories. I
use the word *dominators* in "the world dominators of this present
darkness," because the term *dominate* so vividly describes the
way Satan treats the human race.

Notice that all translations except the Living Bible empha-size that the headquarters of this highly organized kingdom is in the heavenlies.

Here are some points that emerge from Ephesians 6:12. First, the conflict involves all Christians—not some special group like missionaries, pastors, or evangelists—but all of us. Many Christians have not seen it that way.

The King James Version of verse 12 states, *"For we wrestle not against flesh and blood."* I once heard someone comment that most Christians punctuate that verse wrong. They read, "We wrestle not—period." In other words, all we need do is sit in the church pew and sing hymns. However, Paul said, "We're in a wrestling match but it's not against flesh and blood."

Consider also the import of the term *wrestling match*. Wres-tling is the most intense of all forms of conflict between two persons. Every part of the body, every skill, and every trick must be used for success. It is a total conflict.

Satan has a highly organized kingdom. In that kingdom, there are various areas and levels of authority. The headquar-ters of this kingdom are in the heavenly regions. That is a stag-gering fact, but it is quite clear.

The fact that Satan heads a highly organized kingdom as-tonishes some people, yet there are many clear indications of this in the Scriptures. In Matthew 12:22–28, the following inci-dent in the ministry of Jesus is recorded. Jesus had brought healing to a demon-possessed man who was blind and mute by driving out the evil spirit.

> *All the people were astonished and said, "Could this be the Son of David?" But when the Pharisees heard this, they said, "It is only by Beelzebub, the prince of demons, that this fellow drives out demons."*   (vv. 23–24 NIV)

Beelzebub means, literally, "lord of flies." It is the title of Satan particularly as the ruler over demons because the demons are compared to the whole insect domain. Jesus responded to the Pharisees in the following verses:

> *Jesus knew their thoughts and said to them, "Every king-dom divided against itself will be ruined, and every city or*

*household divided against itself will not stand. If Satan
drives out Satan, he is divided against himself. How then
can his kingdom stand?"*   *(vv. 25–26 NIV)*

There is a clear implication that, first, Satan has a kingdom. Second, it is not divided but highly organized. Third, it
stands and has not yet been overthrown. Jesus continued,

*And if I drive out demons by Beelzebub, by whom do your
people drive them out? So then, they will be your judges.
But if I drive out demons by the Spirit of God, then the
kingdom of God has come upon you.*   *(vv. 27–28 NIV)*

Jesus here mentioned another kingdom, the kingdom of
God. In particular, He described one point where the conflict
between these two kingdoms is brought out into the open. He
said, "When I drive out demons by the Spirit of God, then you
know the kingdom of God has come." The implication is that
the ministry of driving out demons brings the forces of Satan's
kingdom out into the open and also demonstrates the superiority of the kingdom of God because the demons are driven out
under the authority of the kingdom of God. In the final analysis,
there are two kingdoms in opposition: the kingdom of God and
the kingdom of Satan.

Again, in Colossians 1:12–14, Paul said the following:

*Giving thanks to the Father, who has qualified you to
share in the inheritance of the saints in the kingdom of
light. For he has rescued us from the dominion of darkness
and brought us into the kingdom of the Son he loves, in
whom we have redemption, the forgiveness of sins.*   *(NIV)*

Notice again, there are two domains or kingdoms. There is
the kingdom of light, in which our inheritance lies, but there is
also the dominion of darkness. The word translated *"dominion"*
is the Greek word *exusia*, which means "authority." In other
words, whether we like it or not, Satan has authority. He is the
ruler of a kingdom that the Bible recognizes. So these two kingdoms are engaged in mortal warfare and the war is coming to its
climax in our day as this age comes to a close.

CHAPTER TWO

SATAN'S HEADQUARTERS

I n Ephesians 6:12, Paul made it very clear that, as Christians, we are involved in a life-and-death struggle with a highly organized kingdom inhabited by evil, rebellious spirit beings and that the headquarters of this kingdom is in the heavenly realm.

The phrase, "the heavenly realm," raises a particular problem in the minds of Christians. If Satan was cast out of heaven long ago, how then can he still occupy a place in the heavenly realm?

Let me answer this question by pointing out some passages that describe events that took place long after the initial rebellion and casting down of Satan by God. These passages indicate that Satan still had access to the presence of God in heaven at that time. Look at Job 1:6–7:

> One day the angels came to present themselves before the LORD, and Satan also came with them. The LORD said to Satan, "Where have you come from?" Satan answered the LORD, "From roaming through the earth and going back and forth in it." (NIV)

Almost exactly the same incident is recorded again in Job 2:1–2:

> On another day the angels came to present themselves before the LORD, and Satan also came with them to present himself before him. And the LORD said to Satan, "Where have you

*come from?" Satan answered the LORD, "From roaming
through the earth and going back and forth in it."*   (NIV)

So, at that time, which was in the days of Job, we see that
Satan still had direct access to the presence of the Lord. When
God's angels came to present themselves and report to the Lord,
Satan was there among them. The passage seems to indicate
that the other angels did not identify Satan. I can understand
this because in 2 Corinthians 11:14, Paul said that Satan is
transformed as *"an angel of light."* The passage creates in my
mind the impression that the only one who could identify Satan
was the Lord. Apparently, he could appear in the presence of
God mingling with the other angels and not be detected.

The Lord said, "Where have you come from, Satan?" In
other words, "What are you doing here?" The Lord did not immediately banish Satan from His presence, but actually had a
conversation with him. Therefore, we know that in the time of
Job, Satan still had access to the presence of God in heaven.

> *Then I heard a loud voice in heaven say: "Now have come
> the salvation and the power and the kingdom of our God,
> and the authority of his Christ. For the accuser of our
> brothers, who accuses them before our God day and night,
> has been hurled down."*   (Rev. 12:10 NIV)

The *"accuser of our brothers"* is Satan. Notice that at this
time, he is still accusing God's people before God day and night.
Revelation 12:11–12 continues with the following:

> *They overcame him* [Satan] *by the blood of the Lamb and by
> the word of their testimony; they did not love their lives so
> much as to shrink from death. Therefore rejoice, you heav-
> ens and you who dwell in them! But woe to the earth and the
> sea, because the devil has gone down to you! He is filled with
> fury, because he knows that his time is short.*   (NIV)

This passage indicates that Satan still has access to the
presence of God, and he uses his access to accuse God's people in
the presence of God. Clearly, all the above passages that I have
quoted refer to periods long after the original rebellion of Satan.

So what is the answer? There is more than one heaven. I believe this is clearly indicated all through Scripture. For instance, in the first verse of the Bible, Genesis 1:1 says, *"In the beginning God created the heavens and the earth"* (NIV). The Hebrew word for heavens is *shamayim*. *"Im"* is the plural ending. The first time heaven is introduced, it is introduced in the plural.

In 2 Chronicles 2:6, we have this utterance of Solomon in his prayer to the Lord at the dedication of the temple: *"But who is able to build a temple for him* [the Lord], *since the heavens, even the highest heavens, cannot contain him?"* (NIV).

Where the translation says, *"the highest heavens,"* the Hebrew says, literally, "the heaven of heavens." Either translation clearly indicates there is more than one heaven. The word *heaven* of the phrase "heaven of heavens" suggests a heaven that is as high above heaven as heaven is above earth.

In 2 Corinthians 12:2–4, Paul was even more specific:

> *I know a man in Christ who fourteen years ago was caught up to the third heaven. Whether it was in the body or out of the body I do not know—God knows. And I know that this man—whether in the body or apart from the body I do not know, but God knows—was caught up to paradise. He heard inexpressible things, things that man is not permitted to tell.*
>
> (NIV)

Before I became a preacher, I was a logician, and sometimes I cannot get away from logic. Logic convinces me that if there is a third heaven, there must be a first and a second. So there are at least three heavens. Apparently, the third heaven is where paradise, the place of rest of the departed righteous, is now located. It is also where God Himself dwells.

Ephesians 4:10 speaks about the death and resurrection of Jesus:

> *He who descended is the very one who ascended higher than all the heavens, in order to fill the whole universe.* (NIV)

Notice that phrase *"all the heavens."* The word *all* can only be correctly used of at least three. When I was teaching English to African students in Kenya, a student once said to me, "All my parents have come to see me." I said, "You can't say 'All my parents,' because no one has more than two parents. If you only have two, you can't say 'All.'" The same applies to the phrase *"all the heavens."* There must be at least three. I think that is clearly indicated by the whole tenor of Scripture. That leads us to the answer of the problem of how Satan's kingdom is still in the heavenly realm.

In colloquial speech, we sometimes use the phrase "seventh heaven" to describe a condition of great happiness. I suggest that is not scriptural. Actually, that phrase is taken from the Koran, the sacred book of Islam, and is probably not appropriate for Christians. Instead, if you are feeling particularly happy, let me suggest that you say you are "on cloud nine." There are plenty of clouds in heaven, and that expression is more in line with Scripture. Jesus is coming in the clouds.

That there are three heavens is my opinion and not an established doctrine. However, I believe it to be a reasonable opinion that fits all the known facts of Scripture and experience. What are the three heavens? The first heaven is the visible and natural heaven with the sun, the moon, and the stars that we see with our eyes. The third heaven, we know from 2 Corinthians 12, is God's dwelling place. It is paradise, the place of rest of the departed righteous. It is the place to which the man was caught up and heard God speaking words that could not be uttered.

So we are left with the second heaven. Clearly, this must be between the first and the third. I understand it to be an intermediate heaven between the heaven of God's dwelling and the visible heaven that we see here on earth. I also believe this intermediate heaven is where Satan's headquarters are located. This would explain why we often find ourselves in an intense wrestling match when we pray. Sometimes, we do not realize how hard it is to break through to God. Sometimes, we pray a prayer that is in the will of God, we believe God hears, and yet the answer tarries. There can be more than one explanation for that, but one major reason for experiences of this kind in the life of sincere, committed believers is that we are involved in a warfare and that the headquarters of Satan's kingdom is located between the visible heaven and the heaven of God's dwelling.

CHAPTER THREE

BATTLE OF ANGELS

The book of Daniel has a specific example of spiritual warfare that casts further light on the location of Satan's kingdom. In fact, it describes a battle of angels. In chapter 10, Daniel describes how he set himself to pray and seek God for a revelation concerning the future of His people Israel. For three weeks, he devoted himself with special intensity to prayer and waiting on God. At the end of the three weeks, an angel from heaven came to Daniel with the answer to his prayer. The angel was so glorious and powerful that all the people with Daniel were scattered and he was the only one who remained to receive the revelation. Daniel 10:2–6 states the following:

In those days I, Daniel, had been mourning for three entire weeks. I did not eat any tasty food, nor did meat or wine enter my mouth, nor did I use any ointment at all, until the entire three weeks were completed. And on the twenty-fourth day of the first month, while I was by the bank of the great river, that is, the Tigris, I lifted my eyes and looked, and behold, there was a certain man dressed in linen, whose waist was girded with a belt of pure gold of Uphaz. His body also was like beryl, his face had the appearance of lightning, his eyes were like flaming torches, his arms and feet like the gleam of polished bronze, and the sound of his words like the sound of a tumult. (NAS)

As I have already mentioned, Daniel's companions could not stand this glorious apparition and just disappeared. Then the angel began to speak to Daniel, and the part on which I want to focus is verses 12–13.

> Then he said to me, "Do not be afraid, Daniel, for from the first day that you set your heart on understanding this and on humbling yourself before your God, your words were heard, and I have come in response to your words."
>
> (v. 12 NAS)

It is important to see that the first day that Daniel started praying, his prayer was heard and the angel was dispatched with the answer. However, the angel did not arrive on earth with Daniel for three entire weeks, or twenty-one days. What kept the angel three weeks on the journey? He was opposed by Satan's angels. Somewhere in the journey from the heaven of God to earth, the angel was required to go through Satan's kingdom in the heavenlies. There he was opposed by evil angels who tried to prevent him from getting through with a message to Daniel. Verse 13 continues with the following:

> But the prince of the kingdom of Persia was withstanding me for twenty-one days [The angel took twenty-one days because he had resistance and opposition in the heavenlies]; then behold, Michael, one of the chief princes [or archangels], came to help me, for I had been left there with the kings of Persia."
>
> (NAS)

All this took place in the heavenly realms. The leader of Satan's angels is called "the prince of the kingdom of Persia," the chief ruler over Persia. Related to him and apparently under him, were various "kings" or lesser angels. Then, on God's side, the angel that came to help the original angel was the archangel Michael.

In Daniel 12:1, we read this about Michael:

> Now at that time Michael, the great prince who stands guard over the sons of your people, will arise. (NAS)

The word "great prince" we can interpret as "archangel." This particular archangel, Michael, stands guard over the sons of Daniel's people, the children of Israel.

Michael, in some special way, is charged by God with watching over the interests of and protecting Israel. Because this whole revelation centered around the future of Israel, it was very much in the interests of Israel that the messenger should get through. So when the first angel was held up, then the archangel Michael came to help him and they battled there with the satanic angels for twenty-one days.

The satanic angels were represented by one who was known as *"the prince of the kingdom of Persia"* (the supreme ruler) and under him various kings or subordinate rulers who had various areas of authority. For instance, there might be one king over each major city of the Persian empire, one over each major ethnic group, perhaps one also over each of the various religious and pagan cults of the Persian empire. We get a picture of a highly organized, structured kingdom with various areas and descending levels of authority with headquarters in the heavenlies that is a kingdom of rebellious, fallen spirit beings.

The angel again spoke about this conflict in Daniel 10:20:

> *Do you understand why I came to you? But I shall now return to fight against the prince of Persia.* (NAS)

In other words, the battle against this evil, satanic angel who dominated the empire of Persia was not yet complete. There would be further war in the heavens. The angel continued with the following:

> *I am going forth, and behold, the prince of Greece is about to come.* (v. 20 NAS)

In other words, once victory was gained over the evil angel who ruled the empire of Persia, the next empire that would arise would be the empire of Greece, and that also would have its own specific evil angel who was the ruler, or prince, of Greece.

In verse 21, the angel who was speaking to Daniel said the following:

> *Yet there is no one who stands firmly with me against these forces except Michael your prince.* (NAS)

So we see again that the archangel Michael is specifically associated with protecting and watching over the interests of God's people, Israel. We also see that it took the united strength of the first angel and Michael to overcome the ruling angels in Satan's kingdom who were opposing the outworking of God's purpose for Israel.

You might wonder at the reference to Persia and Greece. Let me remind you that there were four major gentile empires that successively dominated Israel and the city of Jerusalem from about the fifth century B.C. and onwards. They were Babylon, Persia, Greece, and Rome. Persia and Greece were significant because, at that time, they were the two dominant gentile empires.

We see from these passages in Daniel that the battle centered around God's people and God's purposes. I believe that is still true today. Wherever God's people are and God's purposes are being worked out, that is where the spiritual battle will be most intense. In my opinion, in the days in which we now live, the center of the conflict is once again over Israel and the city of Jerusalem.

The effect of Daniel's prayers is somewhat staggering. When Daniel started to pray on earth, it set all heaven in motion, both the angels of God and the angels of Satan. That gives us a terrific insight into what prayer can do.

I am also impressed by the fact that God's angels apparently needed the help of Daniel's prayers to get them through and accomplish their mission. Again, that gives us a tremendous insight into the effectiveness of prayer.

CHAPTER FOUR

THE WEAPONS AND
THE BATTLEGROUND

We will now look at two related aspects of spiritual warfare. First, the weapons that we must use. Second, the battleground on which the war is fought. Both are revealed in 2 Corinthians 10:3–5. First, the New American Standard version says the following:

> For though we walk in the flesh, we do not war according to the flesh, for the weapons of our warfare are not of the flesh. *(v. 3)*

Notice, Paul said we are living in the flesh, engaged in a war, but our war is not in the fleshly realm. Therefore, the weapons we use must correspond to the nature of the war. If the nature of the war were fleshly or physical, then we could use fleshly or physical weapons, such as tanks, bombs, or bullets. Because the war is spiritual and in a spiritual realm, the weapons also must be spiritual.

> For the weapons of our warfare are not of the flesh, but divinely powerful for the destruction of fortresses. We are destroying speculations and every lofty thing raised up against the knowledge of God, and we are taking every thought captive to the obedience of Christ. *(vv. 4–5 NAS)*

Notice, our weapons are appropriate to the war, and we are dealing with fortresses.

The King James Version reads as follows:

For though we walk in the flesh, we do not war after the flesh: (for the weapons of our warfare are not carnal [fleshly or physical], *but mighty through God to the pulling down of strong holds;) casting down imaginations, and every high thing that exalteth itself against the knowledge of God, and bringing into captivity every thought to the obedience of Christ.* (vv. 3–5)

Where the New American Standard says *"fortresses,"* the King James says *"strong holds."*

The warfare is in the spiritual realm; therefore, the weapons are spiritual and appropriate to the realm of the warfare. These weapons will be my main theme in the two following sections, "Our Defensive Armor" and "Weapons of Attack."

It is tremendously important that we understand where the battle is taking place. Speaking of the battleground and our objectives, Paul used various words. I will choose from different translations the following words: *imaginations, reasonings, speculations, arguments, knowledge,* and *thought.* Notice that every one of those words refers to the same particular realm, the realm of the mind. We absolutely must understand the battleground is in the realm of the mind. Satan is waging an all-out war to captivate the minds of the human race. He is building strongholds and fortresses in their minds, and it is our responsibility, as God's representatives, to use our spiritual weapons to break down these strongholds, to liberate the minds of men and women, and then to bring them into captivity to the obedience of Christ. What a staggering assignment that is!

Satan deliberately and systematically builds strongholds in people's minds. These strongholds and fortresses resist the truth of the Gospel and the Word of God and prevent people from being able to receive the message of the Gospel.

What kind of strongholds does the Bible indicate? I would suggest two fairly common English words that describe the type of strongholds in people's minds. These are *prejudices* and *preconception.*

Maybe you have heard this definition: "Prejudice is being down on what you are not up on." In other words, if you know nothing about it, it is sure to be wrong. If you were not the first to think of it, then it is dangerous. If ever that was true of any group of people, it is true of religious people. Almost anything about which religious people have not heard, they view with intense fear and suspicion.

There is another example of prejudice that is contained in the famous statement, "Don't confuse me with the facts, my mind is made up!" That is prejudice. When a person's mind is already made up in advance, no amount of facts, truth, evidence, or reason can change it. Only spiritual weapons can break down those strongholds. People are driven and dominated by prejudices and preconceptions, often to their own destruction. One example really impressed me, maybe because I am English by background.

In the American Revolutionary War, the English soldiers were fighting the American rebels. The English idea of war was to put on full, highly colored uniforms and march in rank with the drums rolling, into battle. The American sharpshooters just hid in the trees and swamps and simply shot these people down without ever being seen. By our standards today, that would be considered military suicide. In that time, however, people could not conceive of fighting in any other way. It was a stronghold of prejudice and preconception that caused the unnecessary death of thousands of English soldiers. This is just one example of how a mental prejudice can drive people to their own destruction.

There are other examples of prejudices that grip people's minds, such as religious cults, political ideologies, and racial prejudices. These are found, frequently, among professing Christians.

Some little while back, I was preaching in South Africa. I was asked to preach on the theme of principalities and spiritual warfare. As I meditated on it, the Lord seemed to give me the identity of the strong man over South Africa. It is bigotry. I looked up the word *bigot* in the dictionary, and this was the definition: "One who holds, irrespective of reason, and attaches disproportionate weight to some creed or view." That is a bigot.

It is also a stronghold. It is something Satan builds in people's minds.

After I had given this talk, a minister who was born in South Africa and knew the country well, said to me, "You couldn't have described the problems of South Africa any better. South Africa is riddled with bigotry: religious, racial, and denominational. The root problem of this nation is bigotry." South Africans, individually, are a most delightful group of people, but their minds have been captivated and held by this stronghold of bigotry. I am not suggesting that South Africans are different from other people; they just have their own particular kind of stronghold. 2 Corinthians 4:4 states the following:

The god of this age has blinded the minds of unbelievers,
so that they cannot see the light of the gospel of the glory of
Christ, who is the image of God.   *(NIV)*

A stronghold is something that blinds men's minds so that the light of the Gospel cannot shine in. When a person is in that condition, it is worse than useless to argue with him or her. The more you argue, the more they restate their error and the more firmly they are stuck in that error. The only way to deliver such people is to use our spiritual weapons and break down the strongholds in their minds.

CHAPTER FIVE

THE BASIS OF OUR VICTORY

I will now explain the most important single fact that we must know in order to be assured of victory in our spiritual warfare. In Colossians 2:13–15, Paul described what God has done for us, as believers, through the death of Christ on the cross on our behalf.

> *When you were dead in your sins and in the uncircumcision of your sinful nature, God made you alive with Christ. He forgave us all our sins, having canceled the written code, with its regulations, that was against us and that stood opposed to us; he took it away, nailing it to the cross. And having disarmed the powers and authorities, he made a public spectacle of them, triumphing over them by the cross.*
> (NIV)

Let me first warn you that Satan is extremely determined that you will not grasp this fact. He wants to keep all Christians from understanding it, because it is the key to his defeat. The great essential fact is this: Christ has already defeated Satan and all his evil powers and authorities totally and forever.

If you remember nothing else, remember that. Christ has already defeated Satan and all his evil powers and authorities totally and forever. He did that through His death on the cross, through His shed blood, and through His triumphant resurrection.

To understand how this was accomplished, we must recognize Satan's primary weapon against us, and that weapon is guilt. Revelation 12:10 states the following:

Then I heard a loud voice in heaven say: "Now have come the salvation and the power and the kingdom of our God, and the authority of his Christ. For the accuser of our brothers, who accuses them before our God day and night, has been hurled down."   (NIV)

Who is the *"accuser of our brothers"*? We know that is Satan. I have already pointed out that Satan has access to the presence of God, and his chief occupation is to accuse us who believe in Jesus.

Why does Satan accuse us? What is his objective? It can be stated in one simple phrase: to make us feel guilty. So long as Satan can keep us feeling guilty, we cannot defeat him. Guilt is the key to our defeat, and righteousness is the key to our victory.

God, through the cross, has dealt with this problem of guilt, both in the past and in the future. He has made complete provision for both. How did God deal with the past? Colossians 2:13 says, *"He forgave us all our sins"* (NIV).

Through the death of Jesus Christ on our behalf, as our representative, carrying our guilt and paying our penalty, God is now able to forgive us for all our sinful acts. Because His justice has been satisfied by the death of Christ, He can forgive every sin we have ever committed without compromising His own justice. The first thing we must understand is that all our past sinful acts, no matter how many or how serious, have been forgiven when we put our faith in Jesus.

Then God made provision for the future, as shown in verse 14:

Having canceled the written code, with its regulations, that was against us and that stood opposed to us; he took it away, nailing it to the cross.   (NIV)

The *"written code"* is the Law of Moses. Jesus, on the cross, did away with the Law of Moses as a requirement for obtaining righteousness with God. As long as the Law of Moses was the requirement, every time we broke even one of the most minor requirements, we were guilty before God. But when the Law was taken out of the way as a requirement for achieving righteousness, then provision was made for us to live free from guilt because our faith is reckoned to us for righteousness.

There are two related passages. One of these is Romans 10:4:

> For Christ is the end of the law for righteousness to every-
> one who believes. (NAS)

That is an important statement. Jew or Gentile, Catholic or Protestant, it makes no difference. Christ is not the end of the Law as part of God's Word, or as a part of the history of Israel, or in any other aspect. He is the end of the Law as a means to achieve righteousness with God. We are not required to keep the Law in order to be righteous.

The second relevant Scripture is 2 Corinthians 5:21:

> God made him who had no sin [Jesus] to be sin for us, so
> that in him we might become the righteousness of God.
> (NIV)

That is the divine exchange. Jesus was made sin with our sinfulness so that we might be made righteous with His righteousness. Once we grasp the fact that we have been made righteous with the righteousness of Christ, then the Devil cannot make us feel guilty any longer. Satan's main weapon will thus be taken from him. Jesus disarmed the principalities and powers by His death on the cross. He took from them their main weapon against us.

Now I want to show you the outworking of Christ's victory through us. We have already seen the statement of Christ's victory in Colossians 2:15:

> And having disarmed the powers and authorities [Satan's
> whole evil kingdom], he made a public spectacle of them,
> triumphing over them by the cross. (NIV)

A triumph is not actually the winning of a victory; it is the celebration and demonstration of a victory that has already been won. Jesus, through His death on the cross, demonstrated to the whole universe His victory over the entire satanic kingdom. However, Jesus did not win that victory for Himself; He did not need it. He won it for us. It is God's purpose that the victory should be worked out and demonstrated through us. In 2 Corinthians 2:14 (one of my favorite verses), Paul said the following:

> But thanks be to God, who always leads us in His triumph in Christ, and manifests through us the sweet aroma of the knowledge of Him in every place.　　　　　　　　(NAS)

No wonder Paul said, "Thanks be to God." Thanking God could not be helped if you really grasped the message of that verse. God always causes us to share Christ's triumph over Satan's kingdom. There are two adverbial phrases, "always" and "in every place." That means there is no time and no place when we cannot visibly share the triumph of Christ over Satan's kingdom.

In Matthew 28:18–20, Jesus declared the following:

> Then Jesus came to them and said, "All authority in heaven and on earth has been given to me. Therefore go and make disciples of all nations, baptizing them in the name of the Father and of the Son and of the Holy Spirit, and teaching them to obey everything I have commanded you. And surely I am with you always, to the very end of the age."　　　　　　　　(NIV)

Here Jesus said that through His death on the cross, He has wrested the authority from Satan and obtained it for Himself, and that God has vested in Him all authority in heaven and earth. Then He said, "Therefore go and make disciples." What is the implication of the "therefore"? Jesus says, "I have won the authority; you go and exercise it. You go and demonstrate My victory to the whole world by fulfilling My commission."

I would now like to make three simple statements about the victory of Jesus. First, in the wilderness temptation, Jesus defeated Satan on His own behalf. He met Satan, resisted his temptation, and defeated him. Second, on the cross, Jesus defeated Satan on our behalf, not for Himself, but for us. He did not need the victory for Himself because He already had it, but

He won the victory for us and defeated our enemy. He disarmed our enemy, stripped him, and made a show of him openly on our behalf. Third, it is now our responsibility to demonstrate and administer the victory of Jesus.

> *But thanks be to God, who always leads us in His triumph in Christ, and manifests through us the sweet aroma of the knowledge of Him in every place.* (2 Cor. 2:14 NAS)

Remember that *"always"* and *"in every place"* Christ has made victory possible for us.

PART 2:

OUR DEFENSIVE ARMOR

CHAPTER SIX

THE FULL ARMOR OF GOD

I have already explained that as the representatives of God's kingdom here on earth, we find ourselves involved in an all-out war with a highly organized opposing kingdom ruled by Satan. This is a kingdom of evil spirit beings (persons without bodies) whose headquarters are in the heavenly realms.

The battleground on which this war is being fought is the minds of humanity. Satan has built up strongholds of prejudice and unbelief in the minds of the members of the human race to keep them from receiving the truth of the Gospel. Our God-given task is to break down these mental strongholds, thus releasing men and women from Satan's deception, and then bring them into submission and obedience to Christ.

Our ability to achieve this God-given task depends mainly upon two factors. First, that we see clearly from Scripture that on the cross Jesus totally defeated Satan on our behalf and that it is now our responsibility to demonstrate and administer the victory that Jesus has already won. Second, that we make proper use of the necessary spiritual weapons with which God has provided us. These spiritual weapons fall into two main categories: weapons of defense and weapons of attack. In this section, we will deal with the first category, weapons of defense.

Ephesians 6:10–17 is our basis:

Finally, be strong in the Lord, and in the strength of His might. Put on the full armor of God, that you may be able to stand firm against the schemes of the devil. For our struggle is not against flesh and blood, but against the rulers, against the powers, against the world forces of this darkness, against the spiritual forces of wickedness in the heavenly places. Therefore, take up the full armor of God, that you may be able to resist in the evil day, and having done everything, to stand firm. Stand firm therefore, HAVING GIRDED YOUR LOINS WITH TRUTH, and HAVING PUT ON THE BREASTPLATE OF RIGHTEOUSNESS, and having SHOD YOUR FEET WITH THE PREPARATION OF THE GOSPEL OF PEACE; in addition to all, taking up the shield of faith with which you will be able to extinguish all the flaming missiles of the evil one. And take THE HELMET OF SALVATION, and the sword of the Spirit, which is the word of God. (NAS)

Early in that passage, Paul said, *"Therefore, take up the full armor of God."* We are dealing with taking up the full armor of God.

You may have heard me comment before that whenever you find a *therefore* in the Bible, you want to find out what it is "there for." The *"therefore"* in this verse is there because of the preceding verse where Paul said, *"Our struggle is not against flesh and blood, but against the rulers, against the powers, against the world forces of this darkness, against the spiritual forces of wickedness in the heavenly places."* It is because we are involved in this life-and-death struggle with the evil spirit forces of Satan's kingdom that we owe it to ourselves (and God's Word requires it of us) to put on the full armor of God. It is significant that twice in this passage (vv. 11, 13), Paul said, *"Put on [take up, v. 13] the full armor of God."* Surely, we have been clearly warned by Scripture that we must protect ourselves with the full armor of God.

In verse 13, Paul gave a further reason: *"That you may be able to resist in the evil day, and having done everything, to stand firm."* Notice the phrase, *"the evil day."* I do not believe this means the Great Tribulation or some prophetic disaster that is going to come on the world (although I do believe there may be such disasters). I believe in that context, *"the evil day"* refers to something that every Christian will go through. This will be a time when he must confront the forces of evil, when his faith is going to be challenged, and where every kind of opposition and problem will be loosed against him.

Paul does not question our need to face the evil day. It is not an option but a certainty. I always think of the parable Jesus gave concerning the two men who built houses. The foolish man built on sand, and the wise man built on rock. The foolish man's house collapsed, but the wise man's house stood. The difference between those two houses was not the tests to which they were subjected, because each house was subjected to the same test: the wind, the rain, the storm, and the flood. The difference was the foundation on which they were built.

Nothing in the Scripture indicates that we, as Christians, will escape these tests. We will not escape the evil day. We must be prepared to go through it. In the light of this, Paul said, *"Put on the full armor of God."*

Paul takes his picture from a Roman legionary of his day and lists six pieces of equipment that a legionary would normally wear. Let me list them for you:

1. The girdle of truth
2. The breastplate of righteousness
3. The shoes of the preparation of the Gospel
4. The shield of faith
5. The helmet of salvation
6. The sword of the Spirit

You will understand, as you meditate on that, that if you put on all these six pieces of equipment, you will be fully protected from the crown of your head to the soles of your feet with one exception. There is no protection for the back. I will cover that at the end of this section.

CHAPTER SEVEN

THE GIRDLE OF TRUTH

The first item of equipment is the girdle of truth. We must understand why a Roman legionary would need a girdle as part of his equipment. Remember that in those days, men's clothing (as well as women's) was usually a loose garment that came at least to the knees. In the case of the Roman legionary, it was a kind of tunic. When a Roman legionary was required to do something active, such as fight or use his weapons, he would need to take care of that loose garment. If he did not, its flaps and folds would hinder his movements and prevent him from using the rest of his equipment effectively.

The first thing he had to do was to tie his girdle tightly around his waist in such a way that the tunic no longer flapped freely and could not hinder his further movements. This was essential, and it was the basis for everything else. That is why Paul mentioned the girdle of truth before he spoke about anything else.

Quite often, the Bible speaks about a man "girding up his loins." This is what is meant by that phrase.

Paul said the girdle for us is truth. I believe that does not mean abstract, theological truth, but truth in daily living. It means honesty, sincerity, openness, and frankness.

As religious people, we are often encumbered with much sham and hypocrisy. Many things we say and do are not really meant, but we say them only because they sound good. We are full of religious clichés and insincerities. There are things we do, not to please God or because we really want to do them, but to please other people. Almost every religious group has its own particular clichés like, "Jesus will help you, brother." Sometimes that is nothing but a cop-out, because it is not Jesus who needs to help your brother; you need to help your brother.

Religious talk like that is just like a loose, hanging garment. It gets in our way and prevents us from doing the kind of thing that God asks us to do. It prevents us from being active, energetic, effective Christians. It also prevents us from using the other items of equipment.

We are required, first of all, to put on the girdle of truth. We must put away sham, hypocrisy, religious clichés, and saying and doing things we do not mean.

Often truth is quite painful. You must begin to show other people the kind of person you really are. You may have been hiding away or putting on a religious front all this time, and now you are confronted with the need for real truth, openness, and frankness. You must put on the girdle and tie it around so that these religious insincerities and shams no longer hang around you and get in the way of things God is asking you to do.

CHAPTER EIGHT

THE BREASTPLATE OF RIGHTEOUSNESS

The breastplate of the Roman legionary protects, above all else, one absolutely vital organ of the human body: the heart. The Bible indicates that the heart is of supreme importance in our lives as stated by Solomon in Proverbs 4:23:

> *Watch over your heart with all diligence, For from it flow the springs of life.* (NAS)

I was a teacher in Kenya, East Africa, for five years. I became acquainted with a number of the tribes and learned a little of their languages. One day, on the wall of a student's dormitory, I saw Proverbs 4:23 quoted in the Maragoli language. I translated it to myself literally, and I have always remembered the translation: "Guard your heart with all your strength for all the things there are in life come out of it."

What you have in your heart must ultimately determine the course of your life, for good or for evil. It is essential that we protect our hearts from all kinds of evil. Paul spoke about the breastplate of righteousness as a protection of the heart.

We must ask ourselves what is meant by righteousness in this context. Fortunately, Paul returned to this theme of armor in another epistle. In 1 Thessalonians 5:8, he said this:

> *But since we are of the day, let us be sober, having put on the breastplate of faith and love.* (NAS)

Here Paul described the breastplate from another point of view. He called it *"the breastplate of faith and love."* Put these two passages together: *"The breastplate of righteousness"* (Eph. 6:14) is a *"breastplate of faith and love."* This tells us the kind of righteousness that Paul had in mind. It is not the righteousness of works, or religious law, but it is the righteousness that comes only by faith.

Paul spoke about this kind of righteousness again in Philippians 3:9:

> [That I] *may be found in Him* [Christ], *not having a righteousness of my own derived from the Law, but that which is through faith in Christ, the righteousness which comes from God on the basis of faith.*   (NAS)

Paul now put the two kinds of righteousness side by side. First of all, he spoke about a righteousness of his own derived from the Law and said this is not sufficient. As an alternative, he spoke of the righteousness that comes from God on the basis of faith. That is the kind of righteousness that he had in mind when he spoke about the breastplate of righteousness that protects the heart. As long as we are wearing a breastplate that is simply our own righteousness, Satan can find many weak points in that type of righteousness and can often penetrate it with his attacks and damage our heart. We must put on a breastplate that is not our own righteousness but the righteousness of Christ. 2 Corinthians 5:21 says the following:

> [God] *made Him who knew no sin* [Jesus] *to be sin on our behalf, that we might become the righteousness of God in Him* [Christ].   (NAS)

We must be convinced from Scripture and accept by faith that we have become the righteousness of God. That is the only kind of breastplate that can adequately protect our hearts and our lives.

This kind of righteousness, Paul emphasized, comes only through faith. Therefore, it is a breastplate of faith and love. There is no other way to achieve this kind of righteousness.

I am always moved by the prayer of Jesus for Peter on the night before His passion, when Jesus warned Peter that he was going to betray Him the same night. In the context of that warning, Jesus said, "Peter, I have prayed for you." Jesus did not pray that Peter would not betray Him. In those circumstances, under the pressures that would develop and with the known weaknesses in Peter's character, it was inevitable that Peter would betray Jesus. But Jesus prayed a different kind of prayer, the only prayer that could really help Peter. Jesus said in Luke 22:31–32,

> *Simon, Simon, Satan has asked to sift you as wheat. But I have prayed for you, Simon, that your faith may not fail.*
>
> (NIV)

Notice, *"that your faith may not fail."* Even though he was going to deny the Lord and show himself very weak and cowardly, everything could still be retrieved provided his faith did not fail. This is the breastplate of faith and love. Faith is the essential element for this breastplate.

The kind of faith that we are analyzing works only through love. Galatians 5:6 says the following:

> *For in Christ Jesus neither circumcision nor uncircumcision means anything, but faith working through love.* (NAS)

As I understand it, what Paul was really saying was, "No kind of outward ceremony or ritual, in itself, is sufficient. The one essential thing, without which we cannot succeed in the Christian life, is faith, the kind of faith that works through love. It is not a passive or theoretical faith. It is an active faith that works only through love."

The more I meditate upon it, the more I am impressed by the irresistible power of love. I love the passage in Song of Solomon 8:6–7:

> *Place me like a seal over your heart, like a seal on your arm; for love is as strong as death....Many waters cannot quench love; rivers cannot wash it away.* (NIV)

Think of the statement *"love is as strong as death."* Death is the one irresistible thing that we all must encounter. There is not one of us who can resist it. There is no way to avoid it. Scripture says that *"love is as strong as death."*

Think about it. Love is irresistible. It always conquers. There is no way it can be defeated. Love protects us from all negative forces like resentment, unforgiveness, bitterness, discouragement, and despair that can corrupt our hearts and spoil our lives. Remember, all that there is in life comes out of the heart.

Paul described this kind of love in 1 Corinthians 13:4–8:

Love is patient, love is kind. It does not envy, it does not boast, it is not proud. It is not rude, it is not self-seeking, it is not easily angered, it keeps no record of wrongs. Love does not delight in evil but rejoices with the truth. It always protects, always trusts, always hopes, always perseveres. Love never fails. (NIV)

That is the breastplate we need—one that never fails. A breastplate in which there are no weak points that Satan can penetrate. What Paul said there is so appropriate to the picture of the breastplate. Love always protects, always trusts, always hopes, always perseveres. When you have on that breastplate of faith that works by love, it will always protect you. It will keep your heart from every attack and attempt of Satan to penetrate that vital area of your life.

CHAPTER NINE

THE SHOES OF THE PREPARATION OF THE GOSPEL

The shoes Roman legionaries usually wore were strong, heavy sandals with thongs to keep them in place. They usually laced at least halfway up the calf with leather thongs. They were a very important part of the legionary's equipment because they enabled him to march long distances at speed. This gave him mobility. It made him available to his commander at the time and the place where he was needed in the battle. Think of shoes as providing mobility and availability to your commander, the Lord Jesus Christ. This became very real to me in my own personal experience.

For two years during World War II, I served with a hospital unit with the British army in the deserts of North Africa. There were times while we were working with an armored division that we were very close to the enemy lines, sometimes at night. In the desert, it is not easy to know exactly where the enemy lines are because the whole war is very mobile. In such situations, our commanding officer always gave orders that we were not to take our boots off at night. We were to sleep with our boots on. Of course, the reason is obvious. You are usually not at your best when you wake out of sound sleep. If you do not have your boots on and there is confusion all around you, you can spend several valuable minutes groping in the dark for your boots, then trying to put them on and lace them up. If, however, you have your boots on, you are instantly available. The key is availability or mobility.

This is also true of the spiritual counterpart of our equipment about which Paul spoke. The shoes, or the sandals, are called *"THE PREPARATION OF THE GOSPEL"* (Eph. 6:15 NAS). In other words, it means being ready with something. As Christians, we are obligated to have an intelligent understanding of the Gospel. Many Christians claim to be saved and born again, but they cannot give an intelligent account of how they were saved or how someone else can be saved.

I believe *"PREPARATION"* includes study of the Scripture, memorization of Scripture, and the ability to communicate intelligently the gospel message. Notice also that Paul called it *"THE GOSPEL OF PEACE"* (v. 15 NAS). It is a Gospel that produces peace of heart and mind in those who believe it and obey it.

There is one thing very certain about peace. We can only transmit peace to others if we have peace ourselves. We cannot transmit something that we do not experience. We can talk about it, we can theorize, but we cannot transmit it.

There is a very significant passage in Matthew 10:12–13, in which Jesus gave instructions to the first disciples when He sent them out for the first time to preach the Gospel. This is part of His instruction:

> *As you enter the home, give it your greeting. If the home is deserving, let your peace rest on it; if it is not, let your peace return to you.* (NIV)

Notice that significant phrase: if a home is deserving, *"let your peace rest on it."* You are to impart your peace to it. When you go into a home, do you have peace to impart? You cannot impart something that you are not enjoying yourself.

Let me give you a little example of how this might work. Suppose you are a lady doing your grocery shopping in a supermarket. As you wait in the checkout line, there is a lady who is obviously on the verge of a nervous breakdown. She is nervous and jittery, and God directs you to help her. What are you going to do? Are you going to say, "Come to church on Sunday morning"? That will not meet her need. If that were all you could say, you would not have your shoes on.

Having your shoes on means you are ready to do something right then and there when God directs you. First of all, you must have peace. You must let her feel that you have something that she does not have and desperately needs. People can feel peace in other people.

When she reaches out for that peace, you must be able to tell her in simple, non-religious language just how she can find peace. You must be able to communicate the Gospel to her. That is the shoes of *"THE PREPARATION OF THE GOSPEL OF PEACE"* (Eph. 6:15 NAS).

CHAPTER TEN

THE SHIELD OF FAITH

In the Greek of the New Testament, there are two different words for *shield*. One is a small, circular shield, shaped more or less like a large, round, flat wicker basket. The other one is a long rectangular shield and is taken from the word for a door because it is shaped somewhat like a door. This is the kind of shield Paul spoke of when he said *"the shield of faith"* (Eph. 6:16).

A properly trained Roman legionary could use that shield so that no part of his body could be reached by the missiles of the enemy. It protected him completely. This is the kind of faith Paul was speaking about when he referred to it as a shield.

When we go out against Satan, if we begin to cause him any trouble, you can be sure he will counterattack. First, he may counterattack our minds, our hearts, our bodies, or our finances, so we need to have a shield that covers us. He will attack any area he can reach. If he cannot attack us, he will attack those closest to us. If you are a married man, the first thing that Satan will attack is your wife. It is almost to be guaranteed. That is one of the ways he will get back at you. You must have a shield big enough to protect everything for which God has made you responsible, including yourself, your family, and everything God has committed to you. I once learned this lesson in a very vivid way.

I was ministering once to a woman who had a demon of suicide. At a certain point, she received a very definite, dramatic deliverance, and she knew she was free. We both praised God. The next day, she came back to see me and related this remarkable incident. She said that just about the time she received her deliverance, her husband was driving along the highway in his open pick-up truck and their German shepherd dog was standing (as the dog always loved to do) in the back of the truck. For no reason, while the truck was traveling at high speed, the shepherd dog suddenly jumped out and was instantly killed.

The moment she told me that, I understood that the demon of suicide that had left the woman had gone into the dog. Satan attacked the nearest thing he could reach. I learned a lesson I trust I will never need to learn again. Whenever I minister deliverance to people, I always claim the protection of faith in the blood of Jesus over everything that is connected with them. Nothing like that has ever happened to me again. This taught me the importance of the shield of faith as a great, door-shaped shield that protects everything God has committed to us.

Faith is indicated twice in this list of the armor (vv. 14, 16). The breastplate (v. 14) is *"faith and love"* (1 Thess. 5:8 NAS) and the shield is the *"shield of faith"* (Eph. 6:16). Each use of *"faith"* must be understood slightly differently. The breastplate is faith for our own personal righteousness, but the shield is faith for protection and provision for ourselves and all whom God has committed to us. It is that which covers everything.

I learned this in a vivid way at the beginning of my radio ministry. When I got launched into this ministry, it was remarkable how many things simultaneously went wrong in the office and in production. Equipment that should have functioned perfectly suddenly ceased to function. Personnel became sick; messages went astray. Confusion broke loose in our usually well-ordered organization. Then I realized I was required to stretch out the shield of faith. Satan was counterattacking, and he could not reach me, personally, so he attacked something that I depended upon—those who supported my ministry. But I held out the shield of faith, rebuked that power of confusion, and peace and order were restored. Once again, I learned a lesson. We must hold out a shield of faith for full protection and provision.

CHAPTER ELEVEN

THE HELMET OF SALVATION

The fifth item of equipment is the helmet of salvation. I will share some precious truths concerning this that I learned from my own conflicts. When I look back on these conflicts, I am reminded of the words of Paul in Romans 8:37:

No, in all these things we are more than conquerors through him who loved us.   (NIV)

What does it mean to be *"more than conquerors"*? It means we not only win the battle but actually come out of it with more than we had when we went into it. I have proved this many times in my own experience.

In dealing with the breastplate, we saw that the breastplate protects the heart. Now that we are looking at the helmet, we can see that it protects the head and that the head represents the mind. In effect, we are talking about a helmet that protects our minds.

We saw previously that the battlefield on which this entire spiritual war is being fought is the mind of humanity. Because the mind is the battlefield, it is obvious that we need to be particularly careful to protect our own minds.

As a hospital attendant in World War II, I became aware of this from experience. In the natural, a person wounded in the head can no longer make effective use of the rest of his equipment. He may be a very brave and efficient soldier and have excellent equipment, but when he is wounded in the head, it becomes very difficult for him to make effective use of his ability and his equipment.

In the spiritual, this is true of many Christian workers. I have been privileged to be associated in ministry at different times and in different places with many wonderful servants of God, both men and women. I think particularly of missionaries, who are usually under extreme spiritual pressure. Some missionaries that I worked with were dedicated, qualified men and women of God, with great ability and a real calling. Many times, however, they allowed themselves to be wounded in the head. By this I mean that they allowed themselves to become prey to depression or to mistrust other Christian workers. This problem in their minds prevented them from being the kind of effective missionaries and servants of God that they could have been. Being wounded in the head, they could not use the rest of their equipment.

In my own experience, I had a tremendous personal struggle with depression for many years. It was like a dark gray cloud or mist that settled down over me, shut me in, shut me off, and made it difficult for me to communicate with others. It gave me a sense of hopelessness and, although in many ways I am a gifted and qualified servant of the Lord, I got the impression, "Others can, but you can't. You'll never make it. You're going to have to give up."

I struggled with this depression for a good many years. I did everything I could. I prayed, I fasted, I sought God, I read the Bible. Then one day God gave me a revelation that solved my problem. I was reading the following words from Isaiah 61:3:

> *To appoint unto them that mourn in Zion, to give unto them beauty for ashes, the oil of joy for mourning, the garment of praise for the spirit of heaviness.* (KJV)

When I read that phrase, *"the spirit of heaviness,"* something leaped within me. I said, "That's my problem! That's what I need to be delivered from." I read other passages of Scripture on deliverance, I prayed a simple prayer of faith, and God supernaturally delivered me from that spirit of heaviness.

I then saw that I needed some special protection for my mind. I was familiar with the passage in Ephesians 6. I said to myself, "That must be the helmet of salvation."

Then I said, "Does that mean I have the helmet because I'm saved? Is it automatic?" I saw that could not be so because Paul was writing to people who were Christians when he said, "Put on the helmet of salvation." I was directed to a parallel passage in 1 Thessalonians 5:8:

> But let us, who are of the day, be sober, putting on the breastplate of faith and love; and for an helmet, the hope of salvation.　　　　　　　　　　　　　　　　　　　(KJV)

And when I read that phrase, *"the hope of salvation,"* I had an instantaneous revelation from the Holy Spirit. I saw that the protection for the mind is hope, but the protection for the heart is faith. We often get these mixed up. Biblical faith is in the heart: *"With the heart man believeth unto righteousness"* (Rom. 10:10 KJV). Biblical faith is the breastplate that protects the heart. But the protection of the mind is hope.

We need to see the connection between faith and hope. It is stated clearly in Hebrews 11:1:

> Now faith is the substance of things hoped for.
>
> 　　　　　　　　　　　　　　　　　　　(KJV)

Faith is the underlying basic reality on which hope is built. When we have valid faith, then we have valid hope. When we do not have valid faith, we may not have valid hope, either. Hope may be mere wishful thinking. But when we have a real foundation of faith, we can build a valid hope, which is the protection of our minds.

I would like to define hope, very simply, according to Scripture. Hope is a quiet, steady expectation of good based on the promises of God's Word. In a sense, it is continuing optimism. That is the protection of the mind. Hope is an optimistic attitude that always chooses to see the best and will not give way to depression, doubt, and self-pity.

There is one sufficient basis for hope in the Word of God in Romans 8:28:

*And we know that God causes all things to work together
for good to those who love God, to those who are called according to His purpose.* (NAS)

If we really know that everything that happens in our lives
is being worked together by God for our good, then there never
is a reason for pessimism. Every situation is always a reason for
optimism. Optimism is the helmet. While we keep it on, our
minds are protected against all Satan's subtle attacks of doubt,
discouragement, self-pity, mistrust, and so on.

When the Holy Spirit showed me that the helmet to protect
our minds is hope, He preached a kind of sermon to me. I suddenly brought together a number of passages in the New Testament, all dealing with hope. Let me share just a few of them.
The first one I want to share is Romans 8:24:

For we are saved by hope.

(KJV)

What does that mean? No hope, no salvation. Hope is an
essential part of our salvation experience. Contrast the condition of the unsaved in Ephesians 2:12:

[Before you knew Christ] *ye were without Christ, being
aliens from the commonwealth of Israel, and strangers
from the covenants of promise, having no hope, and without God in the world.* (KJV)

Being without Christ, without hope, and without God is the
condition of the lost. It should never be the condition of the
Christian. If we have Christ, then we have hope and we have
God. Colossians 1:27 states the following:

*To whom God willed to make known what is the riches of
the glory of this mystery among the Gentiles, which is
Christ in you, the hope of glory.* (NAS)

The real mystery, the secret of the Gospel, is *"Christ in
you."* If Christ is in you, you have hope. If you do not have hope,
it is just as if Christ is not in you. You are not a lost soul, but I

mean that you are not living in the experience of salvation. Hope in your mind is an essential part of your salvation experience. In Hebrews 6:17–20, there are two beautiful pictures of hope:

> *Because God wanted to make the unchanging nature of his purpose very clear to the heirs of what was promised, he confirmed it with an oath. God did this so that, by two unchangeable things in which it is impossible for God to lie, we who have fled to take hold of the hope offered to us may be greatly encouraged. We have this hope as an anchor for the soul, firm and secure. It enters the inner sanctuary behind the curtain, where Jesus, who went before us, has entered on our behalf.*
>
> (NIV)

The first picture of hope is an altar. Under the old covenant, the altar was a place of protection from the avengers of blood. When you fled to the altar, you were safe. The writer of Hebrews said that when all the pressures are against us, we should flee to the altar, catch hold of the horns of the altar, and let nothing pull us away. The altar is hope.

Second, hope is like an anchor that reaches out of time into eternity, into the very presence of God. In this world, we are like a little vessel on the sea; everything around us is temporary, impermanent, unreliable, changeable. There is nothing to give us security and stability. If we are to have security and stability, we need an anchor that reaches out of time into eternity and fastens in the Rock of Ages. When we have hope, we are anchored.

Finally, in Hebrews 10:23, we read the following:

> *Let us hold unswervingly to the hope we profess.*
>
> (NIV)

Keep on hoping. Do not give up hope; be an optimist. It is the protection of your mind.

CHAPTER TWELVE

THE SWORD OF THE SPIRIT

There is one thing that distinguishes the sword from the other five items that we have examined. The sword is the first item that is not purely defensive. Without it, we have no way to drive off the Devil. If we put on all the other items of equipment, we may be able to prevent the Devil from actually wounding us, but we cannot drive him from our presence. The only thing in that list that can do that is the sword, which is called *"the word of God"* (Eph. 6:17).

The Bible compares God's Word to a sword because God's Word pierces and penetrates. Hebrews 4:12 declares the following:

> *The word of God is living and active. Sharper than any double-edged sword, it penetrates even to dividing soul and spirit, joints and marrow; it judges the thoughts and attitudes of the heart.* (NIV)

God's Word penetrates to every area of human personality. It penetrates to the marrow, the very innermost part of the physical being. It also penetrates and divides between soul and spirit, the innermost area of human personality. It is sharper than any double-edged sword.

In Revelation 1:16, where John had a vision of Jesus in His glory as the Lord of the church, one of the things that he saw was a sword coming out of the mouth of Jesus.

> *In his right hand he held seven stars, and out of his mouth came a sharp double-edged sword.* (NIV)

That sharp double-edged sword is the Word of God coming out of the mouth of Jesus. Since it is indicated in Scripture that Jesus Himself uses the sword of the Word of God, we would do well to study just how Jesus used it in His earthly life. The clearest picture of this is found in Matthew 4:1–11, which describes the temptation of Jesus by Satan in the wilderness. Let me point out that every time Jesus encountered Satan personally, the only weapon He used against him was the sword of the Spirit, or the Word of God.

Then Jesus was led by the Spirit into the desert to be tempted by the devil. After fasting forty days and forty nights, he was hungry. The tempter came to him and said, "If you are the Son of God, tell these stones to become bread." Jesus answered, "It is written: 'Man does not live on bread alone, but on every word that comes from the mouth of God.'" Then the devil took him to the holy city and had him stand on the highest point of the temple. "If you are the Son of God," he said, "throw yourself down. For it is written: "'He will command his angels concerning you, and they will lift you up in their hands, so that you will not strike your foot against a stone.'" Jesus answered him, "It is also written: 'Do not put the Lord your God to the test.'" Again, the devil took him to a very high mountain and showed him all the kingdoms of the world and their splendor. "All this I will give you," he said, "if you will bow down and worship me." Jesus said to him, "Away from me, Satan! For it is written: 'Worship the Lord your God, and serve him only.'" Then the devil left him, and angels came and attended him.
                                                                    (NIV)

I would like to point out some interesting things about that passage. First, neither Jesus nor Satan even questioned the authority of Scripture. Isn't that remarkable? In particular, Jesus quoted each time from the book of Deuteronomy, the one book that has been singled out for attack by modern theologians and critics. Personally, I believe Jesus and Satan were wiser than the modern theologians. They both knew the authority of those words.

Second, the basis of every temptation against Jesus was a temptation to doubt. Every time Satan began with the word *"if,"* he called something into doubt.

Third, as I have already indicated, Jesus did not vary His method of dealing with Satan, but always used the same weapon of the Word of God against him. *"It is written....It is written....It is also written...."*

It is significant that the Devil can quote Scripture, but he misapplies it. He quoted from Psalm 91, but Jesus quoted again from Deuteronomy. The Devil tried to use Scripture against the Son of God. If he did it against Jesus, he might do it against you or me. We must know Scripture thoroughly and we must know how to apply Scripture if we are going to be able to handle the Devil. We must be careful of people who misapply Scripture and try to tempt us to do the wrong thing.

Jesus did not answer the Devil with theology or religious affiliation. He did not tell which synagogue He attended or which rabbi had taught Him. He always went straight to the Scripture. *"It is written....It is written....It is also written...."* After the third thrust of that sharp double-edged sword, Satan backed off; he had had enough. You and I are given the privilege of using the same weapon.

In Ephesians 6:17, where Paul spoke about the sword of the Spirit, the Word of God, the Greek word he uses for *"word"* is *rhema,* which always primarily means a spoken word. It is significant that the sword of the Spirit is not the Bible on the bookshelf or on the nightstand. That does not scare the Devil. But when you take the Scripture in your mouth and quote it directly, then it becomes the sword of the Spirit.

Notice also the significance of the phrase, *"the sword of the Spirit"* (Eph. 6:17). This indicates cooperation between the believer and the Holy Spirit. We must take the sword. The Holy Spirit will not do that for us. But when we take the sword in faith, then the Holy Spirit gives us the power and the wisdom to use it.

CHAPTER THIRTEEN

THE UNPROTECTED AREA

We have now covered all six items of protective armor. They are the girdle of truth, the breastplate of salvation, the shoes of the preparation of the Gospel, the shield of faith, the helmet of salvation, and the sword of the Spirit, which is the Word of God. If we put on and use this entire protective equipment that God has provided, we are totally protected from the crown of our head to the soles of our feet, except for one area.

The one area for which there is no protection is our back. I believe this is very significant and has a twofold application. First, never turn your back on the Devil because if you do, you are giving him an opportunity to wound you in an unprotected area. In other words, never give up. Never turn around and say, "I've had enough. I can't stand this. I can't take anymore." That is turning your unprotected back to the Devil, and you can be sure he will avail himself of the opportunity to wound you.

Second, we are not always able to protect our own back. In the legions of Rome, foot soldiers fought in close ranks. The Greek word for such a close rank was a *phalanx*. They were trained to fight this way and to never break rank. Every soldier knew the soldier on his right and on his left so that if he was being hard-pressed and could not protect his own back, there would be another soldier to do it for him.

I believe the same is true with us, as Christians. We cannot go out as isolated individuals and take on the Devil's kingdom. We must come under discipline, find our place in the body (which is the army of Christ), and know who stands on our right and who stands on our left. We must be able to trust our fellow soldiers. Then, when we are under pressure, we ought to know who will be there to protect our back when we cannot protect it.

I have been in the ministry nearly forty years and have seen a great deal. The real tragedy of our Christian experience is that the very person who protects your back sometimes wounds you. How often we, as Christians, are wounded in the back by our fellow Christians. That is something that never ought to happen. Let us make up our minds to stand together, protect one another's backs, and not wound one another.

PART 3

WEAPONS OF ATTACK

CHAPTER FOURTEEN

TAKING THE OFFENSIVE

We have dealt with the six items of defensive armor listed by Paul in Ephesians 6:14–17: the girdle of truth, the breastplate of righteousness, the shoes of the preparation of the Gospel, the shield of faith, the helmet of salvation, and the sword of the Spirit. I pointed out that, with the exception of the sword, all these items are essentially for protection or self-defense. Even the sword can reach no further than the arm of the person who wields it. In other words, there is nothing in this list of defensive equipment that will enable us to deal with Satan's strongholds as Paul described them in 2 Corinthians 10:4–5, where he spoke about our obligation to cast down Satan's strongholds or fortresses.

Now we want to move from the defensive to the offensive. We want to deal with weapons of attack that will enable us to assail and cast down Satan's strongholds. It is important that we see our obligation to take the offensive, to move out and actively attack Satan's kingdom. It is a fact of history and experience that no army ever won a war on the defensive.

In the early part of this century, someone asked a well-known French general, "In a war, which army wins?" The general replied, "The one that advances."

That is probably an oversimplification, but at least it is true that we will never win a war by retreating or even by merely holding our ground. As long as Satan keeps the church on the defensive, his kingdom will never be overthrown. Therefore, we have an absolute obligation to move out from the defensive and from mere self-protection to an attack position.

When Jesus first unveiled His plan for the church, He envisioned it being on the offensive and attacking Satan's strongholds. The first time the word *church* is used in the New Testament is in Matthew 16:18. Jesus was here speaking to Peter, and He said, *"You are Peter, a stone; and upon this rock I will build my church; and all the powers of hell shall not prevail against it"* (TLB). An alternative reading is "all the gates of hell shall not be too strong for it." The word for hell, in Greek, is the word *hades*. The root meaning of the word *hades* is "invisible, unseen." So *hades,* or hell, is the unseen world of Satan's kingdom.

Jesus pictured His church in the light of two primary activities: building and battling. These must always go together. It is no good doing battle if we do not build. On the other hand, we cannot build if we do not battle. So we must think always in terms of building the church and battling the forces of Satan.

Many people have interpreted these words of Jesus incorrectly. They have somehow assumed that Jesus pictured the church on the defensive, being besieged in a city by Satan's forces. They have taken His promise to mean that Satan would not be able to batter the gate of that city down before Jesus came and caught the church away. That is really a totally defensive concept of the church in the world but it is completely incorrect.

Jesus pictured the church on the offensive, attacking the gates of Satan. Jesus promised that Satan's gates will not hold out against the church and that Satan will not be able to keep the church out. It is not the church trying to keep Satan out; it is Satan failing to keep the church out. Jesus promised us that, if we obey Him as our Commander-in-Chief, we will be able to move out, storm Satan's citadels, break through his gates, release his captives, and carry away his spoil. That is the church's assignment, and it is essentially offensive, not defensive.

The word *gate* has a great deal of meaning in Scripture. First of all, the gate is the place of counsel and rule. For instance, in Proverbs 31:23, it says of the husband of the ideal wife, the faithful wife:

> *Her husband is respected at the city gate, where he takes his seat among the elders of the land.* (NIV)

Notice the city gate was the place where the ruling council of elders sat and ruled and administered the city. So when the Scripture says that the gates of Satan will not prevail against the church, it means that Satan's councils will not prevail against the church but will be frustrated and brought to naught.

In attacking a city, the natural place to attack is the gates, because they are weaker than the walls. Isaiah 28:6 says, *"A strength to those who repel the onslaught at the gate"* (NAS). The picture presented is the church making an onslaught on the gates of Satan's citadel and that the gates of Satan will not be able to keep the church out. So we must stop thinking on the defensive and start thinking on the offensive.

My experience is that most Christians have the attitude, "I wonder where the Devil is going to strike next?" I suggest to you that the boot should be on the other foot. The Devil should be wondering where the church is going to strike him next!

To continue with this theme of the church taking the offensive, I want to explain the scriptural basis for our doing so. It is found mainly in one verse, Colossians 2:15, which describes what God accomplished through the death of Christ on the cross on our behalf: *"When He had disarmed the rulers and authorities"* (NAS). Now, the rulers and authorities are the same spiritual forces of Satan that are referred to in Ephesians 6:12. Through the cross, God disarmed those rulers and authorities. Have you ever thought that Satan has been left without armor? He has been stripped of his weapons. God, through the cross, disarmed the rulers and authorities. Then it says, *"He made a public display of them, having triumphed over them through Him"* (Col. 2:15 NAS).

So God, through the cross, disarmed Satan's kingdom; He made a public display of the representatives of Satan's kingdom, and He triumphed over them in the cross.

A triumph is not so much winning a victory as it is the celebration of a victory that has already been won. It is a public demonstration that complete victory has been won.

On the cross, Jesus did not win the victory for Himself. He always had the victory. As our representative, He won the victory on our behalf. Thus, His victory becomes our victory. Second Corinthians 2:14 declares the following:

> *But thanks be to God, who always leads us in His triumph*
> *in Christ, and manifests through us the sweet aroma of the*
> *knowledge of Him in every place.*   *(NAS)*

"Always" and *"in every place"* we are to represent Christ's victory. God is going to demonstrate, publicly, the victory that Christ has won through us. That is the victory over Satan's rulers and authorities or principalities and powers. The victory is to be worked out through us.

This is the final commission of Jesus, given to His disciples in Matthew 28:18–19:

> *And Jesus came up and spoke to them, saying, "All author-*
> *ity has been given to Me in heaven and on earth.* [If Jesus
> has all authority, that leaves none for anybody else, except
> as He yields it.] *Go therefore and make disciples of all the*
> *nations, baptizing them in the name of the Father and the*
> *Son and the Holy Spirit."*   *(NAS)*

Jesus said, "*'All authority has* [already] *been given to Me.'* You go, therefore...." What does the *"therefore"* mean? I understand it to mean, "You go and exercise, on My behalf, the authority that I have already won." Our assignment is to administer the victory, demonstrate the triumph, and exercise the authority that Jesus has won on our behalf. Authority is only effective when it is exercised. If we do not exercise the authority that He has given to us, it remains ineffective.

The world can only see Christ's victory when we demonstrate it. Christ has won the victory but our assignment is to demonstrate the victory over Satan and his kingdom that Jesus has already won; this we can only do when we move from the defensive to the offensive.

CHAPTER FIFTEEN

THE WEAPON OF PRAYER

In order that we may assail and cast down Satan's strongholds, God has provided us with appropriate spiritual weapons. Second Corinthians 10:4 reads as follows:

For the weapons of our warfare are not of the flesh [they are not carnal, physical, or material; they are not bombs, bullets, tanks, or war planes], *but divinely powerful for the destruction of fortresses.*   (NAS)

Of course, that refers to Satan's fortresses. In other words, God has provided us with spiritual weapons. On the basis of much study and personal experience, I believe Scripture reveals four main spiritual weapons of attack. These are: prayer, praise, preaching, and testimony. We will consider first the weapon of prayer.

I must qualify this by saying that prayer is much more than a weapon. There are many different aspects to prayer, one being that prayer is a weapon of spiritual warfare. I believe it is the most powerful of all the weapons that God has committed to us.

In Ephesians 6:18, after Paul listed the six items of defensive armor, he said, *"And pray in the Spirit on all occasions with all kinds of prayers and requests"* (NIV). At that point, he moved from the defensive to the offensive. It is no accident that this command comes immediately after the list of defensive armor. He mentions there the greatest of all weapons of attack, which is prayer.

Think of prayer as an intercontinental ballistic missile. This is a missile that is launched from one continent, directed by an advanced guidance system to a target in a completely different continent to destroy an assigned target. There is no limitation of time or distance in prayer. Prayer is like that intercontinental ballistic missile. With it, we can assail Satan's strongholds any-where, even in the heavenlies.

An example of a prayer of attack is related in Acts 12:1–6. The church had come under persecution by King Herod. James, one of the leaders, had already been executed by Herod. Now Peter was also arrested and was scheduled for execution shortly. This was the situation:

> *It was about this time that King Herod arrested some who belonged to the church, intending to persecute them. He had James, the brother of John, put to death with the sword. When he saw that this pleased the Jews, he pro-ceeded to seize Peter also. This happened during the Feast of Unleavened Bread. After arresting him, he put him in prison, handing him over to be guarded by four squads of four soldiers each. Herod intended to bring him out for public trial after the Passover* [He would not do it during the Passover because that would have been considered desecrating a holy period in the Jewish calendar]. *So Peter was kept in prison, but the church was earnestly praying to God for him. The night before Herod was to bring him to trial, Peter was sleeping between two soldiers, bound with two chains, and sentries stood guard at the entrance.* (NIV)

Peter was in the maximum security jail. Herod was so de-termined that no one rescue Peter that he actually had four squads of four soldiers each watching him night and day, four hours at a time. It is implied that one soldier was chained either to Peter's hands or feet. In the natural, any kind of rescue was totally impossible. The church, however, was earnestly praying.

A crisis adjusts our priorities. I do not know how earnestly the church had been in prayer, but suddenly James had been snatched from them. Now they saw the danger of Peter, their natural leader, being taken. That was motivation for earnest prayer. They were not only praying in the daytime, but the record indicates they were praying at night, as well. It is important to notice that there are times when merely praying in the day will not be enough. Jesus said in Luke 18 that God would avenge His own elect who cried unto him *"day and night"* (v. 7). There is an intensity in prayer that is sometimes needed to release God's intervention.

Jesus had given a promise to Peter in John 21:18–19:

"I tell you the truth, when you were younger you dressed yourself and went where you wanted; but when you are old you will stretch out your hands, and someone else will dress you and lead you where you do not want to go." Jesus said this to indicate the kind of death by which Peter would glorify God. Then he said to him, "Follow me!" (NIV)

I wonder whether Peter was meditating on that promise in the prison. Jesus said, *"When you are old."* At that time, Peter was not yet an old man. I suppose he must have reasoned something was going to happen to cause the word of Jesus to stand, and stand it did, but it took the prayer of the church to make it effective.

God answered the prayer of the church by sending an angel to deliver Peter. Acts 12:8–11 states,

Then the angel said to him, "Put on your clothes and sandals." And Peter did so. "Wrap your cloak around you and follow me," the angel told him. Peter followed him out of the prison, but he had no idea that what the angel was doing was really happening; he thought he was seeing a vision. They passed the first and second guards and came to the iron gate leading to the city. It opened for them by itself, and they went through it. When they had walked the length of one street, suddenly the angel left him. Then Peter came to himself and said, "Now I know without a doubt that the Lord sent his angel and rescued me from Herod's clutches and from everything the Jewish people were anticipating." (NIV)

God answered the prayers of the church by supernatural intervention through an angel. However, the deliverance was only the first part of the result of their prayer. We must also see the second part, which was a judgment by an angel on the persecutor, King Herod. In Acts 12:19–23, we read,

After Herod had a thorough search made for him and did not find him, he cross-examined the guards and ordered that they be executed. Then Herod went from Judea to Caesarea and stayed there a while. He had been quarreling with the people of Tyre and Sidon; they now joined together and sought an audience with him. Having secured the support of Blastus, a trusted personal servant of the king, they asked for peace, because they depended on the king's country for their food supply. On the appointed day Herod, wearing his royal robes, sat on his throne and delivered a public address to the people. They shouted, "This is the voice of a god, not of a man." [In other words, they flattered Herod by calling him a god. Notice the result.] *Immediately, because Herod did not give praise to God, an angel of the Lord struck him down, and he was eaten by worms and died.* (NIV)

Let us examine how prayer worked in that situation as a weapon of attack. Prayer broke through in the heavenlies and released the intervention of angels. We can compare it to the time in Daniel 10, when Daniel prayed and the angel came from heaven with the answer.

The final comment of Scripture is in Acts 12:24: *"But the word of God continued to increase and spread"* (NIV). This pictures the irresistible progress of God's Word, especially the promise that Jesus had given to Peter that he was to be an old man before he died. But it took prayer to enforce the promises of God's Word. This is what we must understand. The promises of God's Word are not a substitute for our prayers; they provoke our prayers, and it takes our prayers to make the promises of God's Word effective in our spirits. It also takes our prayers to release the intervention of angels on our behalf.

The Scripture says that angels are *"ministering spirits,"* sent forth for our benefit (Heb. 1:14), but they do not come, as a rule, until we pray through. By our prayer, we release that intervention of angels that is God's answer. Bear in mind that prayer breaks through Satan's kingdom in the heavenlies and releases divine angelic intervention.

CHAPTER SIXTEEN

THE WEAPON OF PRAISE

The next great weapon of attack that follows logically after prayer is praise. In a sense, you could consider praise one type of prayer. In the Bible, praise is frequently related to God's awesomeness or fearfulness. Praise calls forth God's supernatural intervention and is also the appropriate response to that intervention. In Exodus 15:10–11 is found the song that Moses and Israel sang after their deliverance from Egypt and after Pharaoh's army had been destroyed by the waters of the Red Sea:

> *Thou didst blow with Thy wind, the sea covered them; They sank like lead in the mighty waters. Who is like Thee among the gods, O LORD? Who is like Thee, majestic in holiness, Awesome in praises, working wonders?* (NAS)

Note the phrase *"awesome in praises."* Praise reveals and calls forth God's awesomeness and His fearfulness, especially against the enemies of God's people.

Psalm 22:23 declares the following:

> *You who fear the LORD, praise Him; All you descendants of Jacob, glorify Him, And stand in awe of Him, all you descendants of Israel.* (NAS)

Praise is the appropriate response by God's people to His awesomeness, to His fearful acts of war and vengeance on their behalf.

Psalm 8:2 says the following:

From the mouth of infants and nursing babes Thou hast established strength, Because of Thine adversaries, To make the enemy and the revengeful cease. (NAS)

We see here that God has provided strength for His people against their enemies. Two words are used for the enemy. First, *"adversaries,"* in the plural. I believe this means Satan's kingdom, in general. These are the principalities and powers, the rulers and authorities that are spoken of in Ephesians 6:12. The second word is *"enemy,"* in the singular. I believe that refers to Satan himself.

God has provided His people strength to deal with this entire kingdom. The nature of the strength that God has provided is more fully revealed in Matthew 21:15–16. Jesus was in the temple performing miracles, and the little children were running to and fro, crying, "Hosannah!" The religious leaders asked Jesus to silence the children.

But when the chief priests and the scribes saw the wonderful things that He had done, and the children who were crying out in the temple and saying, "Hosanna to the Son of David," they became indignant, and said to Him, "Do You hear what these are saying?" And Jesus said to them, "Yes; have you never read, 'OUT OF THE MOUTH OF INFANTS AND NURSING BABES THOU HAST PREPARED PRAISE FOR THYSELF'?" (NAS)

Jesus answered them by quoting Psalm 8:2, but He changed the quotation just a little. He gave us, as it were, His own comment. The psalmist said, *"From the mouth of infants and nursing babes Thou hast established strength"* (Ps. 8:2 NAS). Jesus said, *"THOU HAST PREPARED PRAISE."* So this reveals that the strength of God's people is praise. Praise is our great source of strength.

Notice certain other things about this revelation. First, in each case it says, *"Out of ["From," Ps. 8:2] the mouth."* The mouth is the primary channel for releasing our spiritual weapons against Satan's kingdom. Second, it speaks of *"infants and...babes.*" This means those who have no natural strength of their own, who must rely on God's strength.

> *At that time Jesus answered and said, "I praise Thee, O Father, Lord of heaven and earth, that Thou didst hide these things from the wise and intelligent and didst reveal them to babes."* (Matt. 11:25 NAS)

He was talking about His own disciples. *"Babes"* are not necessarily those who are just newly born in the natural, but they are those who have no natural strength of their own and must depend totally on God's strength.

The purpose of the use of praise as a weapon is to silence Satan. This lines up with Revelation 12:10. This passage is a vision that has yet to be fulfilled, but it tells us a great deal about Satan's activity at this time.

> *And I heard a loud voice in heaven, saying, "Now the salvation, and the power, and the kingdom of our God and the authority of His Christ have come, for the accuser of our brethren has been thrown down, who accuses them before our God day and night."* (NAS)

This tells us that Satan's primary activity and main weapon against us is accusations. He is accusing us continually before God, both day and night. It occurs to me that if Satan is busy day and night, we cannot afford to be busy only in the daytime. We must meet him day and night.

Satan accuses us to make us feel guilty. This is his main weapon against us.

You might say, "Well, why doesn't God silence Satan?" Simply, because God has given us the means to silence Satan, and He is not going to do it for us. The means to do it is praise *"OUT OF THE MOUTH OF INFANTS AND NURSING BABES."* It is praise that ascends through the heavenlies, reaches the throne of God, and silences Satan's accusations against us.

Revelation 16:13–14 is prophetic. I will not attempt to explain how it will be worked out in history, but I want to point out an important principle. John said the following:

515

And I saw coming out of the mouth of the dragon and out of the mouth of the beast and out of the mouth of the false prophet, three unclean spirits like frogs; for they are spirits of demons, performing signs, which go out to the kings of the whole world, to gather them together for the war of the great day of God, the Almighty.　　　　　(NAS)

The point I want to make here is that unclean satanic spirits also operate through the mouth. Praise that silences Satan comes out of the mouths of God's people. Satanic spiritual forces are released through the mouths of those who are on Satan's side. Out of the mouth of the dragon, the beast, and the false prophet came unclean spirits. In a certain sense, this indicates that the side that uses its mouth most effectively will win this spiritual war. If we do not learn to use our mouths, we cannot win the war.

The unclean spirits are also compared to frogs. It is interesting to note that frogs only make a noise at night, and their noise is a ceaseless, repetitive croaking that goes on all through the hours of darkness. I believe that is a very vivid picture of something with which we are familiar in contemporary civilization—propaganda. Propaganda is often a satanic instrument to promote false ideologies, false political purposes, or false and evil rulers. One of the great ways to deal with these forces is praise that comes out of the mouth of God's people.

Another example of the power of praise is from Psalm 149:6–9:

May the praise of God be in their mouths and a double-edged sword in their hands, to inflict vengeance on the nations and punishment on the peoples, to bind their kings with fetters, their nobles with shackles of iron, to carry out the sentence written against them. This is the glory of all his saints.　　　　　(NIV)

This speaks of something that all God's saints can do through praise. However, that praise is accompanied by a two-edged sword, which is God's Word. In other words, God's Word and praise must go together. Combined with God's Word, praise becomes an instrument of judgment on kings and nations. The kings and nobles referred to are Satan's angelic princes and kings of the unseen world. To us, God's believing people, is committed the authority to administer on them the written sentence. In other words, we administer on them God's revealed judgment, and this privilege is granted to all God's saints.

In 1 Corinthians 6:2–3, Paul said the following to Christians:

> *Do you not know that the saints will judge the world?...Do you not know that we will judge angels?* (NIV)

We have the authority committed to us, through God's Word and through the weapon of praise, to administer God's judgment on angels, rulers, kings, peoples, and nations. That implies tremendous power and authority.

CHAPTER SEVENTEEN

THE WEAPON OF PREACHING

T his weapon of attack is related even more directly and specifically to God's Word. It is solely and exclusively the preaching of God's Word. It in no way applies to the preaching of other things, such as human philosophy, political ideologies, or even elaborate theology.

We begin with the solemn charge of Paul to Timothy in 2 Timothy 4:1–4:

> *In the presence of God and of Christ Jesus, who will judge the living and the dead, and in view of his appearing and his kingdom, I give you this charge: Preach the Word; be prepared in season and out of season; correct, rebuke and encourage—with great patience and careful instruction. For the time will come when men will not put up with sound doctrine. Instead, to suit their own desires, they will gather around them a great number of teachers to say what their itching ears want to hear. They will turn their ears away from the truth and turn aside to myths.* (NIV)

I want to point out certain important things. First, the solemnity of the charge. It is given in the presence of God and Christ Jesus, in the light of the fact that Christ will judge the living and the dead and in view of His appearing in His kingdom. It is one of the most solemn charges ever given to a servant of God.

Second, the charge is to preach the Word. It implies the accountability of the preacher for what he preaches. The reference to the fact that Jesus will judge the living and the dead indicates the preacher will answer to the Lord for the messages he preaches.

It is a warning not to accommodate the desires of self-pleasing rebels who do not want to hear the truth and will look for preachers who will preach the kind of thing they want to hear. There is a warning that not all will receive the truth. Nevertheless, in spite of opposition and criticism, the charge is to preach the Word of God.

Scripture has much to say about the effectiveness of God's Word. In Isaiah 55:11, God said,

> *So is my word that goes out from my mouth: It will not return to me empty, but will accomplish what I desire and achieve the purpose for which I sent it.* (NIV)

Again, in Jeremiah 23:29, God said,

> *"Is not my word like fire," declares the LORD, "and like a hammer that breaks a rock in pieces?"* (NIV)

Then, Hebrews 4:12 states,

> *The word of God is living and active. Sharper than any double-edged sword, it penetrates even to dividing soul and spirit, joints and marrow; it judges the thoughts and attitudes of the heart.* (NIV)

There is tremendous power in the preached Word of God. Its results are guaranteed. It will not return empty. It will accomplish God's pleasure. It is a hammer that will break in pieces every rock that opposes the purposes of God. It is like a sharp sword that pierces to the innermost recesses of the human personality and lays bare the secrets of men's hearts and minds.

Acts 19:8–10 is an example of this power of the preached Word of God from the ministry of Paul in Ephesus:

> *Paul entered the synagogue and spoke boldly there for three months, arguing persuasively about the kingdom of God. But some of them became obstinate; they refused to*

believe and publicly maligned the Way. So Paul left them.
He took the disciples with him and had discussions daily
in the lecture hall of Tyrannus. This went on for two years,
so that all the Jews and Greeks who lived in the province
of Asia heard the word of the Lord. (NIV)

There are three adjectives that describe this preaching of
Paul: intense, continuous, and extensive. Daily, for two years, he
taught the Word of God. It was extensive in the sense that his
teaching reached out to the whole of the large province of Asia.
We often fail to realize that Paul spent over two years in the city
of Ephesus, every day preaching the Word of God.

The results were rather like throwing a stone into a pond and
then watching the ripples go out from the place where the stone
fell, extending wider and wider in every direction until they reach
the margin of the pond. The first result was supernatural attestation. The Scripture says that God will confirm His Word. (See
Mark 16:20.) He does not confirm human theories or philosophy,
or even denominational tags. He will, however, confirm His Word.
So He did for Paul. Acts 19:11 says the following:

God did extraordinary miracles through Paul.

(NIV)

I love those words: *"extraordinary miracles."* Do you know what
that implies? That some miracles were ordinary, but the ones
that happened here in Ephesus were extraordinary.

I have asked myself this question: "In how many of our
churches today do we have even ordinary miracles, let alone extraordinary miracles?" These extraordinary miracles are then
described:

Handkerchiefs and aprons that had touched him were
taken to the sick, and their illnesses were cured and the
evil spirits left them. (v. 12 NIV)

I can testify from personal experience that I have seen
miracles like that happen in my time. This practice is not out of
date. The key factor is preaching the Word of God.

The first result of Paul's preaching in Ephesus was supernatural attestation to his message by miracles. The second result was evil spirits being driven out into the open. Acts 19:13–16 says,

> Some Jews who went around driving out evil spirits tried to invoke the name of the Lord Jesus over those who were demon-possessed. They would say, "In the name of Jesus, whom Paul preaches, I command you to come out." Seven sons of Sceva, a Jewish chief priest, were doing this. One day the evil spirit answered them, "Jesus I know, and I know about Paul, but who are you?" Then the man who had the evil spirit jumped on them and overpowered them all. He gave them such a beating that they ran out of the house naked and bleeding. (NIV)

One of the important things in the ministry is to bring Satan's secret agents out into the open. Demons, or evil spirits, are Satan's secret agents. It represents a great stage of progress in the ministry of God's Word when these evil spirits are brought right out into the open. That is what happened here. I am impressed by what the evil spirit said, "Jesus I acknowledge, Paul I know about." To me, it is a kind of backhanded compliment when the representatives of Satan can say about a preacher, "I know about him; he is achieving something."

The third result of Paul's preaching was that the occult domination over an entire city was broken, as described in Acts 19:17–19:

> When this [the incident of the man with the evil spirit] became known to the Jews and Greeks living in Ephesus, they were all seized with fear, and the name of the Lord Jesus was held in high honor. Many of those who believed now came and openly confessed their evil deeds. A number who had practiced sorcery brought their scrolls together and burned them publicly. When they calculated the value of the scrolls, the total came to fifty thousand drachmas. (NIV)

You see, a lot of people were believers but they had been dabbling in the occult; there is a similar situation in the church today. They had one foot in God's kingdom and one foot in Satan's camp. But when they saw this fearful demonstration of the reality of Satan's power, they decided to commit themselves totally to God and turn their backs on Satan. As evidence of this, they brought the books, or the scrolls, which contained the occult knowledge, magic, and sorcery. All these books were publicly burned in the city of Ephesus.

The value of the books was fifty thousand drachmas. A drachma, at that time, was about a day's wages for a working man. If you estimate a day's wages in the United States at about ninety dollars, fifty thousand drachmas corresponds to $4,500,000. That is a large sum of money. The same thing needs to happen in almost every major city of the United States today.

Let us look at the Scripture's explanation of all this in Acts 19:20:

In this way the word of the Lord spread widely and grew in power. (NIV)

The power behind all this was the Word of the Lord. Paul's ministry of the Word for over two years produced dramatic, powerful results. Satan's kingdom in that area was rocked to its foundations; his fortresses were overthrown.

Acts 20:20 and following is Paul's own account of his ministry in Ephesus:

You know that I have not hesitated to preach anything that would be helpful to you....Therefore, I declare to you today that I am innocent of the blood of all men. For I have not hesitated to proclaim to you the whole will of God.
(vv. 20, 26–27 NIV)

Paul summed up his ministry as one having no reservation and no compromise. That is the kind of preaching of the Word of God that accomplishes similar effects. We need that type of preaching today.

CHAPTER EIGHTEEN

THE WEAPON OF TESTIMONY

We need to begin by distinguishing between testimony and preaching. Preaching is presenting the truths of God's Word directly, but testimony is "witnessing" or "being a witness." Testimony is speaking from personal experience about incidents that relate to the Word of God and confirm the truth of God's Word. For instance, if we are preaching a message on healing, we preach the principles on which God heals, and we offer His promises of healing. But if we are testifying about healing, we speak about an incident in which we experienced God healing us. So testimony and preaching are both related to the Word of God but they approach it from different angles.

Testimony is basic to Jesus' strategy of reaching the whole world with the Gospel. He unveiled this strategy in His closing words on earth as He stood on the Mount of Olives with His disciples, about to leave them, as found in Acts 1:8:

> *But you will receive power when the Holy Spirit comes on you; and you will be my witnesses in Jerusalem, and in all Judea and Samaria, and to the ends of the earth.* (NIV)

We notice, first, that to be effective witnesses for Jesus, we need supernatural power. Our testimony is supernatural. It needs to be backed and enforced by supernatural power, the power of the Holy Spirit. Jesus did not permit His disciples to go out and begin testifying until they had been endued with that power on the Day of Pentecost.

Second, Jesus did not say, "You will witness," which is what a lot of religious people say today. He said, *"You will be... witnesses."* In other words, it is not just the words we speak or the tracts that we hand out, but our total lives are to be witnesses to Jesus and the truth of the Gospel.

Third, Jesus envisaged an ever extending circle. He said to start where you are in Jerusalem. Go and tell people. Let them believe, and let them be filled with the Holy Spirit. Then let them go and tell other people. In turn, let them believe, be filled with the Holy Spirit, and go and tell others. He said it would start in Jerusalem, move out to Judea, then to Samaria, and would not cease until it reached the outermost part of the earth.

Those were the last words Jesus spoke on earth. His mind and His heart were in the uttermost part of the earth. He would never be satisfied until that had been reached. His basic strategy for reaching it was for all God's people to become witnesses, witnessing to and winning others. Those, in turn, were to witness and win until, like the expanding ripples from stones cast into a pond, they reached the uttermost part of the earth.

Looking back on history, when God's people applied this strategy, it worked. Within three hundred years, it had conquered the Roman Empire. I believe that great basic spiritual force that overthrew the pagan Roman Empire was the testimony of thousands and thousands of Christian believers from different backgrounds, races, social levels, and religious persuasions. They all said, "Jesus changed my life!" The impact of this ultimately broke down that stern, strong, cruel empire of Rome.

The Bible indicates that the same weapon will ultimately cast down even Satan's kingdom in the heavenlies. This can be seen in prophetic preview in Revelation 12:7–11. These verses describe a great conflict between angels and men that will span both heaven and earth at the close of this age.

And there was war in heaven. [I believe that is still in the future.] *Michael and his angels fought against the dragon, and the dragon and his angels fought back. But he was not strong enough, and they lost their place in heaven. The great dragon was hurled down—that ancient serpent called the devil, or Satan, who leads the whole world astray. He was hurled to the earth, and his angels with him. Then I heard a loud voice in heaven say: "Now have come the salvation and the power and the kingdom of our God, and the authority of his Christ. For the accuser of our brothers, who accuses them before our God day and night, has been hurled down."* (vv. 7–10 NIV)

The *"accuser of* [the] *brothers"* is Satan. This describes how he will be hurled down from his kingdom in the heavenlies. Then it describes how the believers will overcome Satan. Notice it is a direct, person-to-person conflict:

They [the believers] *overcame him* [Satan] *by the blood of the Lamb and by the word of their testimony; they did not love their lives so much as to shrink from death.* (v. 11 NIV)

Their main weapon is in that word *"testimony."* It is their testimony that will ultimately shake down the whole kingdom of Satan. I believe their testimony centers in two things: the Word of God and the blood of Jesus. Their testimony will release the power that is in the Word and the blood.

We can apply this in a simple, practical way to ourselves. We overcome Satan when we testify personally to what the Word of God says the blood of Jesus does for us. You can see the importance of bearing personal testimony to the Word and to the blood.

There are various ways we can do this. One appointed way is the Lord's Supper, or the Eucharist. Sometimes we do not see it in this light, but this is a continuing testimony of our faith in the Word and the blood. Speaking about the Lord's Supper, Paul said in 1 Corinthians 11:26,

For whenever you eat this bread and drink this cup, you proclaim the Lord's death until he comes. (NIV)

We know the cup represents the blood of the Lord, so in taking the Lord's Supper, we are continually testifying, proclaiming the death and resurrection of Jesus Christ.

In order to testify effectively to what the Word of God says about the blood of Jesus, we must be familiar with what the

Word of God actually tells us about the blood of Jesus. There are five extremely important provisions revealed in God's Word that come to us through the blood of Jesus.

First, we find in Ephesians 1:7:

In him [Christ] *we have redemption through his blood, the forgiveness of sins, in accordance with the riches of God's grace.* (NIV)

That tells us two things that are provided for us through the blood of Jesus. The first is redemption (we are redeemed). The second is forgiveness (we are forgiven), as shown in 1 John 1:7:

But if we walk in the light as He himself is in the light, we have fellowship with one another, and the blood of Jesus His Son cleanses us from all sin. (NAS)

Third, the blood cleanses us continually. Through the blood, we have available to us continual spiritual cleansing. Romans 5:9 states,

Much more then, having now been justified by His blood, we shall be saved from the wrath of God through Him.
(NAS)

Fourth, we are justified. That means we are made righteous. The best description I ever heard of what the word *justified* means is—justified: just-as-if-I'd never sinned. I have been made righteous with a righteousness that knows no sin, which is the righteousness of Christ. Hebrews 13:12 declares the following:

Therefore Jesus also, that He might sanctify the people through His own blood, suffered outside the gate. (NAS)

Fifth, the Bible tells us that we can be sanctified through the blood of Jesus. "To sanctify" means to make holy, or to set apart to God.

These are the five great provisions of the blood of Jesus revealed by the Word of God:

1. We are redeemed;
2. We are forgiven;
3. We are cleansed;
4. We are justified (made righteous);
5. We are sanctified (made holy).

These provisions only become fully effective in our lives when we testify to them personally. We must be bold enough to state our convictions. We must say it like this:

> Through the blood of Jesus, I am redeemed out of the hand of Satan. Through the blood of Jesus, all my sins are forgiven. The blood of Jesus cleanses me from all sins. Through the blood of Jesus, I am justified, made righteous, just-as-if-I'd never sinned. Through the blood of Jesus, I am sanctified, made holy, set apart to God. I am no longer in Satan's territory.

Meditate on those five provisions of the blood of Jesus: redemption, forgiveness, cleansing, justification, sanctification. Then grasp the fact that they become effectually yours when you testify to them personally. By testifying to them personally, we overcome Satan *"by the blood of the Lamb and by the word of [our] testimony"* (Rev. 12:11 NIV).

To be effective in spiritual warfare, we must continually take the offensive with the weapons God has provided for us. It is not sufficient to merely defend ourselves and wait for the Lord to deliver us. We are an army of conquerors, and the nations of the world are ripe for a people who will conquer them with the Gospel of the kingdom.